180204/040

WITHDRAWN

# AMERICA

## IN THE AGE OF

# TRUMP

## OPPORTUNITIES AND OPPOSITIONS IN AN UNSETTLED WORLD

DOUGLAS E. SCHOEN

*AND* JESSICA TARLOV

ENCOUNTER BOOKS
New York • London

© 2017 by Douglas E. Schoen and Jessica Tarlov

All rights reserved. No part of this publication may be reproduced,
stored in a retrieval system, or transmitted, in any form or by
any means, electronic, mechanical, photocopying, recording,
or otherwise, without the prior written permission of
Encounter Books, 900 Broadway, Suite 601,
New York, New York, 10003.

First American edition published in 2017 by Encounter Books,
an activity of Encounter for Culture and Education, Inc.,
a nonprofit, tax exempt corporation.
Encounter Books website address: www.encounterbooks.com

Manufactured in the United States and printed on
acid-free paper. The paper used in this publication meets
the minimum requirements of ANSI/NISO Z39.48-1992
(R 1997) (*Permanence of Paper*).

FIRST AMERICAN EDITION

LIBRARY OF CONGRESS CATALOGING-IN-PUBLICATION DATA
Names: Schoen, Douglas E., 1953– author. | Tarlov, Jessica, 1984– author.
Title: America in the age of Trump : opportunities and oppositions
in an unsettled world / by Douglas E. Schoen and Jessica Tarlov.
Description: New York : Encounter Books, [2017] |
Includes bibliographical references and index. |
Identifiers: LCCN 2017001982 (print) | LCCN 2017023756 (ebook) | ISBN
9781594039485 (Ebook) | ISBN 9781594039478 (hardcover : alk. paper)
Subjects: LCSH: Political culture—United States. | Political ethics—United
States. | Trust—United States. | Public opinion—United States. | United
States—Politics and government—Public opinion. | United States—Politics
and government—21st century.
Classification: LCC JK1726 (ebook) | LCC JK1726 .S365 2017 (print) |
DDC 320.60973—dc23
LC record available at https://lccn.loc.gov/2017001982

*Interior page design and composition by BooksByBruce.com*

# CONTENTS

# INTRODUCTION

# "The Atmosphere Is Collapsing"

Look, you want to know what the biggest national security threat is to this country right now? It's the total dysfunction in Washington—the fact that so little can be done by the Congress. They can't even resolve the issue of homeland security. They can't deal with budgets.

—Leon Panetta[1]

The decisions that created today's growth—decisions about education, infrastructure and the like—were made decades ago. What we see today is an American economy that has boomed because of policies and developments of the 1950s and '60s: the interstate-highway system, massive funding for science and technology, a public-education system that was the envy of the world and generous immigration policies. Look at some underlying measures today, and you will wonder about the future.

—Fareed Zakaria[2]

The American Century, 1914–2014. RIP.

—Michael Lind[3]

On September 19, 2014, President Obama had just left the White House residence with his family, on their way to Camp David for a summer weekend.

Moments later, Omar J. Gonzalez, a U.S. Army veteran of the Iraq war suffering from PTSD, jumped the black iron White House fence and raced across the lawn, undetected and unhindered by the Secret Service. Gonzalez approached the North Portico door, the iconic entrance, flanked by white columns, known to all Americans—and in front of which a Secret Service agent is supposed to stand at all times. No agent was in position as Gonzalez approached, however. He turned the handle; the door was unlocked.

Gonzalez went in. He was met by a female agent, whom he

1

overpowered. Armed with a three-and-a-half-inch knife with a serrated blade, Gonzalez walked around inside the White House, supposedly one of the most heavily guarded buildings in the world. He passed through the Entrance Hall and the staircase leading to the White House family quarters, from which the Obamas had departed minutes earlier. He made it into the 80-foot-long East Room, the stately ballroom from which presidents sometimes give important speeches—as when Obama announced to the nation that U.S. forces had killed Osama bin Laden.

Finally, two Secret Service agents caught up with Gonzalez, tackled him, and subdued him. Gonzalez was arrested and later hospitalized. He pled guilty to two charges and will serve a brief prison sentence.

In a post-9/11 era of hyper-security, in which cities large and small had drawn up plans for all kinds of dreadful contingencies, most Americans assumed that if any place was safe from terrorists, it was the White House. Yet here the president's own home had been breached, not by terrorists but by a lone unstable individual, who had simply walked in through the front door.

In the aftermath, politicians and commentators focused their ire on the Secret Service, which had seen one fiasco after another in recent years—including a security breakdown at a 2009 White House dinner that allowed a couple to crash the event and meet the Obamas, alcohol and sex scandals, a 2011 episode in which bullets struck the White House, and other incidents in which individuals had scaled the White House fence.

Gonzalez-like incidents don't just happen; they are not the result of one-day glitches. They are the byproduct of institutional decay. Secret Service director Julia Pierson resigned soon afterward, and subsequent investigations revealed that agents' radios hadn't functioned properly, that some agents weren't trained properly in how to use them, and that an alarm system in the White House had malfunctioned.[4] It's not clear if the agency can ever recapture its lost prestige.

The Gonzalez episode illustrates more than the decline of the Secret Service: it also stands as a fitting symbol of a nation in a tailspin. When Gonzalez was apprehended, he said that he had wanted to warn the president that "the atmosphere is collapsing." He may have been speaking in meteorological terms, but taken broadly, his phrase is fitting. For millions, it is the atmosphere of American life that seems to be collapsing.

By now, most Americans know that the country faces enormous fiscal, economic, social, and national security challenges: out-of-control federal spending, frighteningly large deficits, massive gaps in income and opportunity, family breakdown and cultural division, political dysfunction and paralysis, and a roiling, violent world in which American power seems increasingly incidental. And in the midst of all this—with two wars essentially lost over a decade, an economy recovering by traditional indicators but creating too few decent-paying jobs, and a vacuum of political leadership in Washington, both in the White House and in Congress—few signs suggest that we are about to turn things around.

Indeed, by this time in our history, the United States faces an existential crisis for our survival. It is a crisis with many facets:

- The crisis of values that jeopardizes our culture—the breakdown of the family, the loss of belief in traditional virtues, and the decline of American confidence.
- The crisis of trust in America's governing institutions that threatens our democracy.
- The crisis of governance that stifles the aspirations of millions of Americans.
- The crisis of education—a corrosive, broad-ranging failure in American schooling—that stunts our competitiveness as a society.
- The crisis of national security that endangers our public safety, imperils the cause of democracy overseas, and weakens America internationally.
- The crisis of solvency of our definitive entitlement programs and the need to find alternatives to President Obama's failing health care program.
- The crisis of an American economy that no longer provides upward mobility.
- The crisis of America's ever-expanding prison population, its persistent underclass, and the consistent weakening of our social fabric.

It has become commonplace to read about American decline, both domestically and overseas; to hear that our political deadlock makes solving our major problems all but unachievable; and to wonder if solutions to these problems are possible anymore. The wreckage mounts, even as the failure of our leaders and institutions to solve the problems becomes depressingly familiar. Is America headed for irrevocable decline, or is there some path forward that can take us to a more promising future? The goal of this book is to answer these questions.

## TEN PROPOSITIONS

What follows are ten propositions about the state of the country that we will amplify in some detail in this introduction and at greater length over the course of this book. We don't pretend that they are all-inclusive for what is wrong in the United States; no such list, in a country as big and complex as ours, can hope to account for everything. But we do believe that these themes account for a substantial portion of what we face—and what we must address. We also maintain that the underlying problems in each area are not commonly understood—that often, we react to symptoms instead of causes, which themselves are poorly understood. It follows, then, that the solutions will also be less commonly known.

1. *The American education system is a failure at every level.*
   Our schools are not preparing our kids, especially those of lower income, for a competitive global economy. The flaws of the current system ensure that the United States will continue to fall behind internationally. And these flaws start at the very outset, with early elementary school education, and extend all the way to postsecondary education and beyond. Begin with the simple statistics:

- Only 24 percent of eighth- and twelfth-grade students can write proficiently.[5]
- Two out of three eighth-graders can't read proficiently.[6]
- Nearly two-thirds of eighth-graders scored below proficient in math.[7]
- Only one in four high school students graduates ready for college in all four core subjects (English, reading, math, and science), which is why a third of students entering college have to take remedial courses.[8]

- Only 4 percent of African American students and 11 percent of Hispanic students finish high school ready for college in their core subjects.[9]

There's more. When compared with our international peers, America looks like an also-ran, with embarrassing—and troubling—performance numbers.

- American students rank 27th in math, 20th in science, and 17th in reading among students in 34 industrialized countries.
- By the end of the eighth grade, the students of Massachusetts are two years behind in math compared with their peers in Shanghai, China.
- Only three-quarters of 15-year-olds in the United States reach a baseline mathematics proficiency, a number below the average of industrialized countries and far below the average of 90 percent or more in China, Korea, and Singapore.
- U.S. students are particularly weak in areas dealing with higher cognitive demands, like the translation of mathematics to real-world situations.
- Only 50 percent of U.S. students are even motivated to learn mathematics, compared with the average of 53 percent of other industrialized countries. [10]

And by the time they reach college age, American students have a host of other problems. Many can't afford college tuition. Others are saddled with student loan debt—in aggregate, it exceeds $1 trillion nationally[11]—that forecloses opportunities. The average undergraduate who takes out a loan to pay for college is more than $37,000 in debt by the time he graduates.[12] Loan defaults are running at nearly 12 percent.[13] And yet, without higher education, young Americans face an even more circumscribed future. Getting good-paying jobs requires a college education today: young people with college degrees earn on average 63 percent more than high school graduates, who are also more likely not to be working period.[14]

Given the importance of getting through school, especially for disadvantaged kids, and the difficulties of paying off student loans and other debts, getting a job after graduation is more pressing than ever. Yet classroom curricula and workplace requirements are out of sync. In a 2013 survey of 2,001 students or recent graduates and 1,000 hiring managers, educational-products firm Chegg evaluated the difference between skills that employers demand and what recent graduates are prepared to take on. Less than 40 percent of the hiring managers found recent graduates qualified for work in the areas in which they had studied.[15] Colleges should update curricula to keep up with changing workplace demands.

One solution some have looked to—as President Obama did—is community colleges, but even these institutions, which offer more practical education, send fewer than one-seventh of their graduates on to earn bachelor's degrees.[16] The problem is only worsening, as can be seen by looking at the numbers of graduates in leading fields: in 2007, the number of college graduates studying STEM fields in China passed the United States, and we haven't caught up.[17]

And even the great hallowed ground of American education—four-year liberal arts colleges—aren't delivering. In *Academically Adrift: Limited Learning on College Campuses*, Richard Arum argues that, for all they pay—or borrow—in tuition, few college students see much improvement in fundamental skills like written expression and critical reasoning.[18] One reason is that colleges have lowered their own academic standards. Students study much less, Arum shows—perhaps as much as 50 percent less than college students in the early 1960s.[19] Not only do many students enter college unprepared; they're not pushed once they are there.

"The college experience," concludes former *New York Times* columnist Bob Herbert, "is to have a good time and walk away with a valuable credential after putting in the least effort possible."[20] The climate is only getting worse with the advent of "safe spaces" and an increasingly hostile environment for free expression and academic freedom on campuses.

The failures of our education system ensure that the United States will continue to fall behind internationally. Despite government spending on education more than doubling over the past 40 years, test scores in reading, math, and science have remained stubbornly flat.[21] There is no silver-bullet solution: vouchers, charters, and national standards, among other worthy solutions, all have their virtues, but a total overhaul—even an educational revolution—is needed.

We will explore what such a revolution might entail. Plans to remake the system should include many components, such as an emphasis on school and teacher accountability (including performance-based pay); the importance of high-quality, content-rich curricula; and giving parents a full range of education choices, including vouchers and charter schools. But the overarching principle that should guide these reforms is that of a market-based education system, with parents as the primary decision-makers. Market-based education that puts parents in the driver's seat could not just reform American education but also remake it.

**2. *By traditional indicators, the American economy is recovering— but wages are stagnant, the middle class is hollowing out, and the American dream is on life support.***

To hear the Obama administration tell it during the president's second term, the American economy was headed back to glory days. "Since I have come into office," President Obama stated during an interview with *The Economist* in August 2014, "there's almost no economic metric by which you couldn't say that the U.S. economy is better and that corporate bottom lines are better. None."[22] The administration did have some successes it can point to: economic growth of 2.8 percent in 2013 and 2014, compared with 2.1 percent during the early years of the recovery that began in 2009.[23] In January 2015, the unemployment rate dropped to 5.7 percent, compared with 7.8 percent when Obama took office and a peak of 10 percent in October of his first year.[24] And by the first quarter of 2016, it had fallen below 5 percent—the lowest in eight years.[25] Fewer Americans filed for unemployment benefits.[26] Moreover, jobs reports from late 2014 to early 2016 were generally robust and encouraging, before slowing down again.

Wall Street certainly can't complain about the Obama years. The stock market shattered records during his presidency. The NASDAQ saw a more than 200 percent increase over the Obama years; the Dow Jones Index improved by more than 100 percent.[27] The housing market showed signs of recovery, GDP grew, and industrial production accelerated. Yet beneath these positive indicators is a raft of trouble signs.

The recovery from the Great Recession has been slow and painful. The GDP growth rate that Obama achieved from 2013 onward is positively anemic compared with previous recoveries. And Mohamed

El-Erian—chief economic adviser for Allianz—warns, "If we don't grow out of our debts, the debt is going to discourage economic activity and we're going to have trouble growing at 2 percent a year."[28]

The job growth numbers in Obama's later years looked good, but most of those jobs pay less than the ones that were lost.[29] The new jobs were heavily concentrated in the service sectors, paying 23 percent less than the old jobs.[30] All too many Americans have experienced the change of fortune of 55-year-old Connie Ogletree, who once worked as an executive assistant in Atlanta but now works at McDonald's in Atlanta for $7.25 an hour.[31] Hers is the story that the "job growth" numbers cannot tell: Americans trading their former standard of living for a lower one.

And that's assuming that they even manage to find a new job. Lots of Americans have stopped looking. In February 2015, the number of Americans not participating in the labor force rose to 93 million for the first time in history,[32] and our labor-force participation rate fell to a 38-year low. Currently, just shy of 63 percent Americans of working age are employed.[33]

With these realities, it shouldn't be surprising that inequality has reached levels not seen since the Great Depression. And this gap applies not only to rich and poor but also to the gap between upper-income and middle-income Americans. According to Pew Research Center, the upper-income families' median worth ($639,400) is nearly seven times that of their middle-income counterparts ($96,500).[34] "When middle class people look up, they see the rich getting richer while they spin their wheels," says Lawrence F. Katz, an economist at Harvard University. "The middle has basically stayed the same; it hasn't improved. You've got an iPhone now and a better TV, but your median income hasn't changed."[35]

And yet, beyond inequality lies a more profound and ultimately more significant problem: the American dream of mobility and the chance for a better life seems increasingly out of reach for millions. Many countries now show more robust rates of economic mobility between generations than does the United States. It's important to remember that America *always* had high rates of inequality, as is suggestive of a country devoted to economic free enterprise, where the most talented and hardworking could soar far ahead of the pack. But those earning less didn't see their more modest circumstances in a negative light, because they knew that they could improve their lots steadily over time. For a long period in our history, most did.

That is what has changed: the engine of economic mobility that once powered the American economy, that played such a large part in our economic vitality and social and cultural cohesion, has broken down. Without it, we face a more top-to-bottom-oriented economy, a fraying, class-stratified society, and a strained social safety net.

These issues are significant not only in individual human terms, but also across the broader economy—especially at a time when America's longstanding leadership position in innovation and economic competitiveness shows signs of weakening. The heavy weight of federal and local regulation has choked off business investment and capital formation for years, our stifling corporate tax code encourages firms to relocate overseas, and political deadlock has forestalled reform. Productivity gains have been in part a result of declining workforce participation. In a Harvard Business School survey, 71 percent of respondents predicted a decline in American competitiveness—basing their views on the ability of U.S. companies to compete internationally and to support rising living standards.[36] Without significant reforms to our regulatory, tax, and legal landscape, we could soon find ourselves lagging behind internationally.

What to do? We are stuck in a loop of arguments about redistribution or pure hands-off, laissez-faire economics. We need a broader rethinking of what kind of economy we want to have, and how we can create jobs for the millions who want to work at a decent wage. And we need to do that by gearing economic and tax reform to benefit the fractured American family—the fundamental unit not only of social cohesion but also of economic vitality.

### 3. We are approaching a national emergency of military readiness and preparedness in a world of mounting security threats.

Under President Obama, the United States cut our conventional and nuclear capabilities while our enemies built theirs up. In downsizing the military, Obama has left it less capable to defend the country than at any other point over the past half century.

In a 2011 deal with Congress to reduce the deficit, Obama agreed to a $480 billion cut to the Pentagon's ten-year budget. By 2014, the Pentagon faced another $52 billion in cuts and an additional $500 billion over the next decade[37] because of "sequestration," a program of automatic spending cuts triggered when Congress and the president failed to reach a long-term budget and deficit-reduction deal.[38] The United States, Obama made clear, would stress reliance on coalitions of allies for future large-scale military engagements.

To hear Obama tell it, the leaner military would still have the manpower and resources to ensure that the United States remains the preeminent military power on the planet.[39] "The world must know the United States is going to maintain our military superiority with armed forces that are agile, flexible and ready for the full range of contingencies and threats," Obama said.[40]

That's not how other experts see it. A 2015 study by the Heritage Foundation foresees a point in the near future in which the United States will no longer possess its traditional capacity to fight two wars simultaneously. The Army will shrink from 570,000 soldiers to 440,000, and maybe even lower.[41] Traditionally, 50 brigades are needed to meet the two-wars standard; that capacity might drop to 33 by the Army's own analysis.[42] The Navy needs 346 ships to meet the two-wars standard but currently has only 284.[43]

"If you listen to the Army, they will give testimony they can no longer guarantee," said Republican congressman J. Randy Forbes of Virginia. "You talk about two wars—they testified they can't guarantee that we could win one war. The Navy will tell you if we get to 260 ships, we cease to be a superpower; we become a regional power."[44]

This crisis was compounded by President Obama's passive leadership. Under Obama's watch, the Middle East, always dangerous, became a five-alarm fire. Iran may very well be on its way to nuclear capability, thanks to the Obama administration's formalizing of an agreement with Tehran that would allow the Islamic regime to keep its nuclear facilities open while providing weak checks on its ability to develop weapons. The agreement was reached through the administration's disregard of stubborn facts about the Tehran regime's behavior and intentions. Iraq, reasonably stable when George W. Bush left office and as late as 2011—before the United States, at Obama's insistence, withdrew its troops—collapsed into a medieval nightmare of slaughter at the hands of the brutal forces of the Islamic State, or ISIS. And during yet another Israel-Palestine war, Israel stood isolated again in international opinion—this time, with the most minimal support from its American ally—even as it took commonsense measures to defend itself from Hamas rocket attacks. Bloodletting in Syria continued after Obama infamously backed off from his "red line." Libya and Yemen descended, too, into primeval nightmares of terrorism and killing—despite Obama's earlier insistence that both countries represented triumphs for his foreign policy vision.

Further, Obama showed weakness in traditional great power dealings. On Obama's watch, Vladimir Putin illegally seized Crimea and massed 20,000 Russian troops on the border of Ukraine, ready to invade at a moment's notice, all while destabilizing the Ukrainian government from within—and flouting Obama's ineffective sanctions regime. On most substantive issues in U.S.-China relations, Xi Jinping ran circles around Obama in the same way that Putin has done—on everything from Pacific trade to cyber warfare to Chinese aggression in the East China Sea against American allies. Obama offered no credible countermeasure to prevent the development of nuclear weapons in North Korea. China continued to support the murderous Pyongyang regime, which threatens to provoke a nuclear arms race in East Asia.

Obama often seemed either unconcerned or caught unawares. He dismissed ISIS as a "JV team" months before its fighters conquered large swaths of Iraq.[45] He seemed disinterested or timid when it came to Putin's provocations—and oblivious to any connection Putin's aggression may have had to the U.S. decision to remove the missile-defense shield from Eastern Europe.

Backing off and letting problem spots fester, Obama has also frittered away American power and prestige. Where the United States has been, for 70 years, the world's lead actor in protecting democratic governments, adjudicating disputes, and putting teeth into U.N. resolutions, Obama adopted a narrower definition of American capabilities, interests, and options. He offers nothing that will dissuade our allies from their growing conviction that they cannot count on a paralyzed United States. "If not letting America have its own way is Mr. Obama's objective, he is an unparalleled foreign-policy success," wrote John Bolton.[46]

The crippling effects of this vision and these policies, along with the degradation of our defenses, made the 2016 presidential election a monumental one—especially given the primary role of the president in setting national security policy.

*4. The American criminal justice system properly punishes those who commit serious crimes, but it is also sentencing generations of young men guilty of less serious offenses to doomed futures—exacerbating the deepening problems of the underclass.*

Increasingly, critics on both the left and right agree that something is seriously out of whack in the American criminal justice system, particularly as regards incarceration. On broad terms, many liberals and conservatives have come to agree that reform is needed. This is not to say, however, that the most adamant left-wing critics are correct. When they argue, as some do, that black Americans are wrongfully or excessively incarcerated, they often simply deny the empirical reality of crime statistics, which show stark racial imbalances in crime rates.

Still, the numbers should give us pause: though Americans compose less than 5 percent of the world's population, American prisons contain nearly 25 percent of the world's incarcerated people.[47] The U.S. prison population is currently estimated at about 2.2 million people and counting.[48]

Many factors go into the high prison population, including the war on drugs. Today, almost half of the inmates in federal prison are sentenced for drug offenses[49] (though the majority of inmates in the country are housed in state facilities). In the 1990s, many states (plus the federal government) passed laws that lengthened sentences for certain crimes, especially drug crimes.[50] Other states passed "three strikes and you're out" laws that stated anyone who was convicted of a third felony would receive a long prison term.[51] These long sentences are not only expensive but also socioeconomically destructive, both for inmates and taxpayers. Generations of young men guilty of less serious offenses are effectively blacklisted from respectable work.

The answer is not to stop policing or incarcerating genuine criminals, but to fundamentally transform the way our criminal justice system interacts with offenders. In this book, we'll explore a number of promising, groundbreaking alternatives for doing just that—many coming from the conservative side of the political spectrum, not associated, until recently, with advocacy on this issue. Ideas include reducing the number of laws—especially federal laws—that lead to prison and removing prison sentences for technical violations. The number of federal crimes has risen from 3,000 in the early 1980s to more than 4,450 by 2008; violators are often locked up not because they're a threat to the public but for transgressions they didn't even know existed.[52] Congress should play a more active role in vetting new criminal laws and taking a skeptical view of new criminal offenses or penalties, at the same time repealing unjust laws. Meanwhile, between 2000 and 2010, 17 states—led by conservative Texas—have reduced their number of prisoners while also reducing crime.[53] These approaches should be adopted more broadly, in addition to emphasizing rehabilitation and vocational training.

But to repeat, the answer to mass incarceration is *not* decriminalization of legitimate crime. Once we have removed the excesses from the system, we will still face the fundamental problems of the underclass: broken families, failing schools, poor work skills and habits, and destructive social environments. Addressing these issues—some of which are in the purview of other chapters—is fundamental to lessening the role the penal system plays in American life.

### 5. We have a health care and entitlement crisis that will only get worse with the aging of the population.

In 2014, former Democratic senator Bob Kerrey and former Republican senator John Danforth updated their 1994 report on America's entitlement crisis—and 20 years later, the numbers were only starker, the implications more daunting. Without changes, they warned, the entirety of federal revenues would soon be consumed by just five programs: Social Security, Medicare, Medicaid, interest on the national debt, and federal employee retirements. There would be no money remaining for defense, education, environmental protections, federal law enforcement, and so on. These and all other functions would have to be financed through deficit spending—and if there is something that the United States cannot have more of, it is deficit spending. In 2014, our national debt exceeded our GDP—meaning we owe more than the entire value of our economy—for the first since World War II. How can we sustain future generations without dramatic reforms, and what prospects exist for bringing those reforms into effect?

In this book, we'll take a look at some serious proposals for saving the safety net as well as long-term plans for putting our entitlement house in order. In a poll Schoen Consulting conducted for the Campaign to Fix the Debt, an overwhelming proportion of respondents supported—80 percent compared to 8 percent opposing—the Simpson-Bowles plan, which would have cut wasteful spending, reformed our outdated tax code, and made changes to entitlements such as Medicare and Social Security to protect them for future generations. Simpson-Bowles, which died in Congress, would have reduced our debt by $2.4 trillion.

Perhaps one reason why the entitlement crisis has proved so intractable, besides the politics, is the frightening nature of its particulars: consider that Social Security is looking at a long-term deficit of $7.7 trillion.[54] People would rather avoid these realities—yet if we face them honestly, real solutions are achievable.

Our health care system's costs have skyrocketed from $256 billion in 1980 to $2.6 trillion in 2010.[55] Up to 60 percent of American bankruptcies now stem from medical costs.[56] How do we ensure that Americans can get health care in ways that do not lead to federal bankruptcy? How do we protect safety nets for a growing population of seniors when the tax dollars will have to come from a generation having fewer children?

For many on the left, the solution is (or was) Obamacare, which would reduce the number of uninsured and fix flaws within existing insurance programs. Yet Obamacare's problems are increasingly self-evident: not only its enormous price tag but also its ineffectiveness. The Affordable Care Act, while insuring over 9 million Americans, has left 32 million uninsured.[57] Meanwhile, some on the right still pursue congressional repeal. Other Republicans are more focused on pursuing changes to the law.

We're more in line with this latter group. Polls show that pluralities of Americans want Obamacare fixed, not repealed. Contrary to their media-painted image as obstructionists with no health care ideas, Republicans have some sensible reform proposals. We're interested most in those that are patient-centered, that put individuals in charge of their health care choices, and that open up markets and drive down costs. These options include repealing the individual mandate for individuals and employers; letting seniors opt out of Medicare; and expanding the availability of health savings accounts. Obamacare sent Medicaid costs skyrocketing; Republican proposals to move able-bodied Medicaid recipients into private insurance and perhaps require work in exchange for benefits make good sense. Medical malpractice reform would also help hold down costs—as would legalizing interstate purchasing of health care plans.

We will explore the options that exist between a doubling down on Obama's statist model and an all-out repeal—in short, a restructuring of our system that emphasizes affordability, choice, and market competition.

### 6. *Never in American history has the public had such little faith in our institutions.*

Trust in institutions across the board is at all-time lows, but the public regards the institutions of government with particular contempt.

According to a June 2014 Gallup survey, no institution is regarded with less trust by Americans today than Congress, which in a recent Gallup poll earned a 7 percent approval rating—the lowest since the statistic began being measured.[58] Its slide has been generational, slipping below 40 percent first in the 1980s and then skidding downward, though with some upticks, until 2004, when it last cleared 30 percent. Since then, the decline has been steady and corrosive. The drop seems bound only by the simple fact that it can't get much lower than it already is. And the 2016 election did nothing to restore faith in government.

The institution that Trump heads isn't doing much better. Gallup found just 29 percent expressing a great deal/quite a lot of confidence in the presidency, the lowest point it reached during Obama's tenure. As for the third branch of government, Americans regard the Supreme Court as about on par with the White House: 30 percent have confidence in it, an all-time low for the high court, which had confidence ratings around 50 percent at the turn of the millennium.

At the higher end, the institution that the American public respects most remains the United States military (74 percent). The military has always ranked near the top in Gallup surveys of public institutions. Next up are small businesses, at 62 percent.

Given the high-profile police controversies of recent years, and the protest movement against police brutality that rose up in response, it is perhaps surprising to see that the public retains a 53 percent confidence level in the police. A closer look, however, shows a grimmer picture. In 2013, the violent-crime level in the United States dropped to its lowest since the 1970s[59]—yet public confidence in the police was not commensurate, resembling the ratings from 1993 and 1994, when crime was much higher.[60] This reflects the fact that while crime has been reduced, the reduction has come at too high a price, at least in the view of many

Americans—especially blacks. Consider the racial disparity in responses that Gallup tabulated: the polling organization found that, on average between 2011 and 2014, 59 percent of white Americans had a "great deal" of trust in the police, while only 37 percent of black Americans said the same.[61]

Lagging further behind is the church and organized religion generally, at just 45 percent, which reflects the steady deterioration in public confidence in this area since the 1970s.[62] Americans would once have given high marks to institutional churches, but today religion is regarded negatively across our popular culture, and statistics show steady drops in church attendance. We'll address these issues in chapter 3.

"When people trust their institutions, they're better able to solve common problems," says Ron Fournier, editorial director of the *National Journal*. "Communities bonded by friendships formed at church are more likely to vote, volunteer, and perform everyday good deeds like helping someone find a job. And governments find it easier to persuade the public to make sacrifices for the common good when people trust that their political leaders have the community's best interests at heart."[63]

Fournier describes what's missing today in America across a broad range of institutions, but especially within our political system. It can't continue this way indefinitely without materially degrading the primacy of the United States as the world's leading democracy. We should remember that most American gains of the past came in the context of a reasonably robust public confidence in our governing institutions. Seeing themselves as self-governing, Americans nonetheless believed in the *legitimacy* of their governing institutions. Not anymore.

Could such a continued decline in public confidence lead to the kinds of extremist movements that have emerged in Europe? That possibility can't be dismissed. More likely, Americans will continue to withdraw from a system that they see as too corrupt to participate in.

### 7. *The United States faces a crisis of values.*

Though we are a secular republic with no state religion, we are also a nation whose social and economic cohesion was grounded in and enhanced by Judeo-Christian tradition. Now we are seeing a wholesale retreat from and denigration of these values, in our schools, institutions, and popular culture—at precisely the time that, at home, our social fabric is fraying and, overseas, we face an existential threat from an enemy professing the very antithesis of these values. A sense persists that we're losing our moral bearings as a society. Any cursory look at our pop culture, our social statistics, our political dysfunction, or the mood of the electorate generally will confirm that impression.

We desperately need to reclaim our traditional heritage before it's too late. It is our belief that strong values-based pitches, in the public realm, should appeal to traditional American virtues not often discussed anymore. Moreover, such appeals should embrace an institution often degraded in our new demoralized landscape: religion. We should make clear that there are positive benefits for people when they embrace religion and other traditional values. We'll explore these and other ideas for triggering a values revival in the American public debate.

### 8. The structure of the American family is in collapse—across racial groups.

When Baltimore went up in flames in April 2015 after the death of a young black man at the hands of the police, conservative commentators were quick to argue that there was no excuse for the lawlessness in the streets, including looting and torching businesses. And, they often argued, whatever the grievances of the city's black community against the cops, the real culprit was closer to home: the breakdown of the black family. President Obama alluded to this problem, condemning the rioters and lamenting the fact that so many black boys have never known their fathers. Yet family breakdown extends to whites, too: 25 percent of whites now grow up in single-parent homes.[64] The American family as a whole has deteriorated dramatically.

Marriage in America is at an all-time low—6.8 marriages per every 1,000 people (it was greater than 10 per 1,000 in 1970).[65] Meanwhile, our divorce rate, though not as bad as many European countries', remains a depressing 53 percent.[66] Just over 50 percent of American adults are married today; in 1960, it was 72 percent.[67] The decline in marriages has also led to smaller family sizes: today's average American household consists of just 2.59 people.[68]

Nearly one-third of all American children are living in homes without fathers.[69] More than half of all babies born to women under 30 in the United States are born out of wedlock,[70] and the United States' teen pregnancy rate is the world's highest.[71] With such a high number of single mothers, especially young ones, it's not surprising that so many wind up on public assistance: over 40 percent of U.S. single mothers are on food stamps,[72] and some projections say that half of *all* American children will have been on food stamps at one point or another by the time they reach 18.[73] Yet at the same time, the birth rates for women in their traditionally most fertile years are falling: from 69.3 live births per 1,000 women in 2007 to 63.2 in 2012.[74]

The result is an erosion of social cohesion. In addition to its human costs—especially on children—family decline has a direct impact on economic growth and our future competitiveness. The literature on family structure unambiguously describes how strong family structures lead to the most economic growth and are the healthiest indicators in a host of other areas. And social health is directly linked with economic health.

We'll discuss the collapse of the family in detail and with candor, as well as proposing serious, substantive policies and public initiatives that might yet turn things around. One thing is certain: for all the challenges that America faces, nothing else we do will amount to much unless we strengthen—rescue, really—the American family.

### 9. *The country faces the most troubling vacuum of political leadership in its history.*

"You want to know what the biggest national security threat is to this country right now?" asked Leon Panetta. "It's the total dysfunction in Washington—the fact that so little can be done by the Congress. They can't even resolve the issue of homeland security. They can't deal with budgets," he said. "They can't deal with immigration reform. They can't deal with infrastructure. They can't deal with other issues."[75]

Indeed, the American political system, once the envy of the world, has become dysfunctional and even sclerotic. We don't have leadership on our entitlement or health care crises; we don't have leadership to take America into a new economic era and get our people the job skills they need; we don't have leadership on education or innovation; and we don't have leadership for protecting our national security and forging a strategically sound foreign policy. Consider what the last 19 years have brought: a presidential impeachment, a disputed presidential election, fiscal and banking crises, government shutdowns, an Ebola panic, a border-control crisis, the failure of the Veterans Administration (VA) to care for our wounded soldiers—and a 2016 election between the most disliked, distrusted presidential candidates in American history.

Partisanship and polarization have rendered the U.S. government the most spectacular example of "too big to fail" in the world: we can barely pay our bills, but we keep chugging along on borrowed money.

We continue to believe that various proposed areas for reform—to lobbying practices, to campaign finance, and to redistricting policies—hold promise. We cannot pretend, though, after years of writing about the dysfunction in Washington, to be as optimistic as we once were that the tectonic plates governing our politics can be readily changed—at least, not in the absence of some national emergency that none of us want to see come to pass. We can only warn that, absent major change, the long-term future of the American democratic system is at stake. Ultimately, it may be that our systemic problems can only be solved through a fundamental rethinking about ideas of service, patriotism, and what true leadership entails and requires. And that, in turn, may depend on how we think about ourselves—which leads to our final proposition.

### 10. *The future of the American idea is very much in question.*

The promise that the United States represents a fresh chance for individuals to start over, assuming that they accept the creed of individual freedom, personal responsibility, and dedication to democratic ideals, has never seemed so endangered. Our very belief in ourselves has been undermined by an elite culture that seems continually focused on America's past evils; we no longer ask newcomers to accept our values (or, often, even to speak the English language). A recent study showed a steep drop in the last few decades in the percentage of countries using the U.S. Constitution to write their own governing charters, and at least one Supreme Court justice, Ruth Bader Ginsburg, has said that our governing document isn't a good model for countries today. Ginsburg's comments perfectly illustrate the endangered American idea: voiced by someone at the highest echelons of the U.S. democratic system, her words reflect a loss of confidence, a loss of faith, and a sense of confusion about the virtues of the United States and our role in the world and in history.

Surveys in recent years reveal that Americans have lost their faith in the American dream—once a defining national idea. In a CNN/

ORC poll, 59 percent of respondents said that the American dream is now unattainable for most Americans.[76] This disillusionment has many roots: institutional failure, we would argue, is perhaps the primary driver. The American economy's failure to support a robust middle class as it once did is also a big part of the loss of conviction. It's hard to believe in "America" when your fortunes are turning downward.

Another daunting challenge is the loss of national cohesion—the ebbing away of a common sense of American identity. We're so tangled by now in identity politics and recriminations on issues like race, religion, sexuality, the teaching of history, and the meaning of America itself that it's no wonder the country feels so divided—not just politically but also along lines of self-definition, loyalties, and first principles. Part of this is class-oriented: the division between the haves and have-nots in America continues to grow. But it's not all about class; it's also about how we understand what it means to be Americans—our rights, yes, but also our responsibilities as citizens and our duty to uphold and carry on the democratic traditions that have brought unparalleled prosperity and inspiration to millions. Even today, looking at a world in tumult, it should be easy to conclude that being American remains the most fortunate of fates.

But do we, as a people writ large, still believe this? Perhaps we're about to find out. The challenges we now face will be difficult to meet without some rebirth of national conviction.

## WHAT THIS BOOK IS ABOUT

In the chapters that follow—each focusing on a foundational area of American life—we will explore, first, what the underlying, under-reported, under-analyzed problems really are in these key areas, and how to understand them; and second, what are the freshest, boldest ideas and proposals by which we can turn things around.

What emerges is a clear and definitive look at a nation in turmoil, facing an unprecedented array of fiscal, economic, social, and national security challenges—and running out of time in which to address them. Yet we believe we can still salvage our present and build a constructive future, if we begin to act.

This book appears just as we've inaugurated a new president. What better time to consider where we have been and where we need to go? We hope this book serves as a manifesto for how we can overcome national self-doubt to reclaim our traditional optimism, reassert our place in the world, rally Americans to the cause of national self-renewal, and secure a prosperous future for our citizens.

# CHAPTER 1

# The Loss of Trust and Optimism

The American public has lost faith in every single institution in this country. They have lost faith in sporting institutions in this country because of many different scandals. They've lost faith in the government. They've lost faith in both political parties.... They've lost faith in corporate institutions. They've lost faith in the media.

—MATTHEW DOWD[1]

The working class feels a very strong sense of betrayal. Betrayed by the institutions that should help them get ahead. They feel betrayed by school because they think it should have helped, and they were told it would, and they feel betrayed by work.

—JENNIFER SILVA, BUCKNELL UNIVERSITY[2]

The fact that trust in government is both historically low and more polarized by party than ever before explains why Washington does not work in the early twenty-first century.

—MARC J. HETHERINGTON AND THOMAS J. RUDOLPH, *WHY WASHINGTON WON'T WORK*[3]

Beginning in the fall of 2015, two of the most unusual presidential candidates in American history surged in the polls, attracting intense support, troubling the establishment of the Democratic and Republican Parties, and puzzling the mainstream media—but thrilling their loyal supporters. Senator Bernie Sanders was a 73-year-old lifelong socialist from Vermont who had only joined the Democratic Party grudgingly; written off as a protest candidate, minimized for his age and his Vermont career—after all, he could think whatever he liked up there, no one was paying any attention—Sanders was given no chance to threaten the expected coronation of Hillary Clinton as the party's presidential nominee. But in early February 2016, he ran to a virtual tie with her in Iowa before trouncing her in New Hampshire. Clinton would prevail in the end, but only after a grueling contest that went on far longer than anyone expected.

On the other side was real estate mogul, reality television star, and tabloid fixture Donald Trump, known to Americans before 2015 mostly for his shameless self-love and masterful playing of the media for maximum exposure. Sensible analysts wrote him off: he had no political experience, his policy proposals were ridiculously unrealistic—he'd build a giant wall to separate us from Mexico, he'd stop taking Muslim immigrants, he'd magically bring American manufacturing jobs back—but Trump, wearing a red baseball hat emblazoned with the old Reagan slogan "Make America Great Again," vaulted to the top of the GOP polls. Along the way he revolutionized our political dialogue, consistently stepping onto third rails of political expression and getting away with it. Pundits struggled to understand the Trump phenomenon.

Yet the appeal of the Sanders and Trump campaigns shouldn't have been surprising to students of the American electorate and observers of the national mood. For what both candidates represented, in admittedly different ways, was a total rejection of the status quo by a quasi-majority of American voters. What both Sanders and Trump supporters were saying, loud and clear, was, *I can't trust the government anymore to look out for me, let alone to tell me the truth, so I refuse to vote for candidates promising more of the same. I want change so badly that I'm willing to take some risks. Sure, Sanders is a bit far left and Trump a bit far gone, but I'd rather trust them with the next four years than elect another professional politician.*

Trust: that's what the Trump and Sanders campaigns were really all about. Their appeal was less about how much their own supporters trusted them—though some surely did—and more about how much they distrusted the "establishment" alternatives. An angry electorate that believes its governing institutions have broken faith with the American people flocked to two unlikely protest candidates in what looked, at times, like a mass cry for help.

According to Gallup, only American confidence in the military (72 percent) and small business (67 percent) approximate past historical averages. Most others have been well below those benchmarks since 2004 or so—which happens to be the last year in which Americans' satisfaction with the current status of the United States averaged better than 40 percent.[4] A Real Clear Politics average in December 2015 showed that just 28 percent of Americans thought the country was headed in the right direction; 63 percent said it's on the wrong track.[5] The *Huffington Post* found similar numbers.

Gallup points to widespread frustration with poor government performance as the chief reason for this erosion of trust in political institutions and to the bursting of the housing bubble (and subsequent financial crisis) for the loss of faith in our financial institutions. Only 4 percent of Americans trust government "a great deal" to handle our domestic problems. Just 8 percent trust the government "a great deal" to handle our international problems. Things have gotten so bad that trust in *other people* has eroded, too, reaching historic lows in 2008 and in 2012.

"The American dream is dead, because we don't have any values anymore," Karen, a woman from Tallulah, Louisiana, told Chris Arnade of the *Atlantic*. "People only care about possessions, about things, about money, not happiness."[6]

No wonder, then, that the overall national mood, according to the 2015 American Values Survey, is "anxiety, nostalgia and mistrust."[7] A majority of respondents—53 percent—believe that "the nation's culture and way of life have changed for the worse since the 1950s," while 49 percent say that America's best days are past.[8] Despite the economic recovery, three out of four respondents believed that the country was still in recession, and 80 percent said the economic system favors the wealthy.[9] American optimism, especially as regards the economic picture, has been gloomy for years. A central issue in the 2016 campaign has been economic inequality and the premise that the economy doesn't serve the interests of average Americans.

Trump and Sanders have sounded this note, too. "This is an economy which is rigged, designed to benefit the people at the top," Sanders said at a Los Angeles rally. "We have a message for the billionaire class, and that message is you can't have it all."[10] Trump: "I watch the speeches of these people, and they say the sun will rise, the moon will set, all sorts of wonderful things will happen, and people are saying, 'What is going on? I just want a job!'"[11]

At the root of it all are two related factors: the loss of faith in the

American dream and the loss of confidence in our institutions, especially those of government.

## GOODBYE, AMERICAN DREAM

"The only people talking about the American dream are politicians," an American told the *Atlantic*'s Chris Arnade. "The rest of us are busting our asses, dealing with shrinking paychecks and rising costs."[12]

Going back generations, the American dream—the idea that no matter how modest our circumstances to start from, we can better our lot by working hard and that we can create a better life for our children—has been a bedrock of aspiration for citizens in the United States. In recent years, however, poll after poll has shown that the majority of Americans no longer believe in the dream—specifically, they don't believe that it applies to them.

For instance, an astounding 76 percent of respondents in an NBC/ *Wall Street Journal* (*WSJ*) poll said that life *wouldn't* be better for the next generation.[13] A CNN poll found that nearly 60 percent think the American dream is unachievable.[14] Indeed, as presidential candidate Senator Ted Cruz put it, "Today, for the first time in history, a majority of Americans believe that our kids will have a worse life than we do. That has never been true in the history of America until this instant, right now—maybe the most un-American idea you can imagine." But the feeling isn't as new as Cruz suggests. Confidence in the American dream has been eroding for years—not always in a straight line, as sometimes confidence rebounds temporarily. But over the long term, many Americans continued to lose confidence in this defining national idea.

In the 2014 American Values Survey, for instance, when asked if they still believed that the American dream holds true, only 42 percent of respondents, among all groups, said yes, while 48 percent said that it "once held true, but not anymore."[15] Only the "white college-educated" cohort expressed majority support for the notion that the dream "still holds true," while among blacks, only 31 percent believed that it did.[16]

The erosion of faith in the American dream can also be seen in a Penn Schoen Berland poll, which found even bleaker numbers across the board, but again with differences among groups. The poll is striking not only for its majority view, across racial groups, that the American dream is "suffering," but also for the extreme skepticism among whites—81 percent of whom expressed that view—compared with the others. In this poll, whites' skepticism far outpaced that of blacks.[17]

Why do minorities, at least in this survey, have more faith in the American dream? Mark Penn, who ran the survey, says, "The election of President Obama and the policies he's enacted have changed a lot of attitudes in the African-American community about their future and the country's. There's no question this is a fundamental change from what we saw in the country five to 10 years ago."[18] Other polls have found similar leanings, with as high as 80 percent of blacks believing that they are living the American dream, compared with less than 70 percent of whites.[19] Blacks' more optimistic take is heartening, especially since, economically, the Obama years haven't been great ones for blacks. Many Hispanics, too, are children or grandchildren of people who came to the United States for a better life and have seen their fortunes rise.[20]

Indeed, the Obama years have seen some legitimate gains—the economy *has* improved and the jobs picture *has* brightened. But key elements of the American dream are simply not reachable anymore for average Americans. Millions feel they are struggling just to make ends meet, not advancing themselves slowly but surely, as Americans once did. Countless Americans are saddled with crippling debts, whether student loans or consumer credit cards or underwater mortgages. Obamacare has not solved the economic problems of health care; on the contrary, many still struggle under crippling health care costs. Few Americans have serious money put away for retirement.[21] And after the Great Recession, the median American family in 2010 had no more wealth than it had in the early 1990s.[22]

"For more and more families, achieving the traditional American dream has become just that—a dream," writes Marianne Cooper, author of *Cut Adrift: Families in Insecure Times.* "Instead, what surveys indicate is that people are downsizing their definition of the American dream. Today, the desire to own a home or to move up economically is often replaced by a desire to be debt free and to have financial stability."[23] No wonder, then, that a 2014 Brookings Institution poll found that just 48 percent of American men and only 37 percent of American women, of all races, agreed that the American dream "still holds true."[24]

The impact of these more constrained economic times has been particularly harsh on the young, who don't have better economic memories
to look back on. Heading into the workforce for the first time, often car-
rying substantial college debt and struggling to find full-time work, they
don't see the American dream that their parents and grandparents did.
We did our own polling, fielded by YouGov, focusing just on millennials'
attitudes. The results were sobering: 63 percent of those polled said that
it is too hard to get a good-paying job. More than half—57 percent—said
that young people can't get ahead without help from family and friends,
and 81 percent reported that society isn't open and fair to everyone.

Crushing student debt is another factor. Parents and children are
told, even now, that getting a college education is the ticket to a good-
paying job. A bachelor's degree has become practically a prerequisite to
economic advancement—but it's far from a guarantor, and it costs more
than ever. Student debt now totals $1.2 trillion. "We've never had a his-
torical era where so much debt was taken out at an early age," said Diana
Elliott, research manager for financial security and mobility at Pew.[25] An
incredible 40 million Americans average $27,000 in debt.[26]

But as the poll figures above demonstrate, the sense of economic
despair isn't confined to the young. Perhaps the bluntest expression
of how millions of Americans feel comes from Johnny Whitmore, an
Indiana homeowner trying to buy his house back from the local bank.
His words speak for millions of Americans: "You can't trust anybody or
anything anymore."[27] About no institution is that sentiment more widely
held than the government in Washington.

## THE CRUX OF THE MATTER: DISTRUST
## IN GOVERNMENT

No statistic makes the trust crisis clearer than this one: the confidence
rate in Congress stands at 8 percent—a one-point *improvement* from
its 2014 rating of 7 percent. Congress has been the lowest-ranked
American institution every year since 2010.[28] As John McCain likes to
say, if it falls any lower, their support will be down to family members
and paid staffers.

The loss of trust has been a generational story. The Vietnam War and
Watergate were the twin events of the 1960s and early 1970s that shattered

the postwar faith in American governing institutions. A decade earlier, in the 1950s, four out of five Americans trusted the government.[29] And from today's perspective, even the diminished trust numbers from the Vietnam/Watergate era look like a comparative golden age. For more than 30 years—from 1972 to 2004—on average, 69 percent of Americans expressed trust in the government on foreign affairs; on average, 62 percent said the same about the government's capacity to deal with domestic issues. Those are remarkable average numbers, considering the problems of the 1970s in particular.[30]

Even in April 1974, just four months before Richard Nixon resigned the presidency due to the Watergate scandal, a slim majority (51 percent) of Americans still trusted the government to handle domestic problems, while 73 percent expressed confidence in the government's ability to deal with overseas matters—remarkable figures, again, especially in a political climate rife with talk of impeachment and constitutional crisis. Compare that with 2015, when only 38 percent expressed confidence in the government to deal with domestic issues.[31]

Today's lack of trust stems from the government's failure to solve problems amid a hyper-partisan environment. The last two presidents, George W. Bush and Barack Obama, both enjoyed periods of unified party control, in which the president's party held both houses of Congress. Yet they used that strong hand to pursue goals—the Iraq war and universal health care—that were not clearly in the national interest and that exacerbated partisan conflict. As a freshman senator from Nebraska, Ben Sasse, said in his first address to Congress this year, "The people despise us all . . . because we're not doing the job we were sent here to do."[32]

One job that government is always sent to do is foreign policy, a subject once capable of uniting party members from both sides of the aisle. But foreign policy has become just another staging area for partisan division—and, partly as a result, Americans have lost faith that either party can handle it. Bush's foreign policy, of course, fostered extraordinary political divisions. While Obama's record didn't provoke the same level of discord, majorities eventually disapproved of the president's handling of terrorism. A December 2015 CNN poll was typical, showing 60 percent disapproval of Obama's counterterrorism approach, with 68 percent of respondents saying that America needed to get tougher against ISIS.[33] An

April 2016 IBD/TIPP Poll showed that 67 percent believed that Obama didn't have a clear plan to fight ISIS, and 83 percent were "not confident" that the president would defeat ISIS before he left office. Moreover, respondents indicated that they had been parsing the contradictions in Obama's public words. The president had said, for example, that defeating ISIS was his top priority, while also insisting that the group didn't represent an "existential threat" to the United States. Respondents believed neither statement: 77 percent regarded ISIS as a "serious threat to the existence or survival of the U.S.," and 59 percent didn't believe Obama when he said ISIS was his top priority.[34]

The issue of trust is heavily influenced along partisan lines—that is, while both Democrats and Republicans express less trust in government than they once did, the party out of the White House tends to feel this way more acutely. "Without trust in government, Democrats today (and Republicans during the late Bush years) could not get people from the opposite party to give their ideas a shot," writes Marc Hetherington. "As a result there is no pressure on members of Congress to do anything other than follow their party leaders. Gridlock ensues. Nothing gets done."[35] Indeed, partisanship and gridlock dominate discussions about lost trust in government. Consider what some respondents told CBS:

- "They can't make a mutually agreeable decision together."
- "They cannot be trusted to work together. . . . The fact that they fight all the time."
- "[Politicians] . . . are set for . . . years, so they don't think about us anymore."
- "Politicians 'can't relate' and 'don't know what's going on with the common man.'"
- "What's good for the country isn't good for Congress."[36]

Over the course of a six-month national research project, pollster Patrick Caddell, along with RNC veteran Bob Perkins and communications consultant Scott Miller, found that

- 86 percent of all voters believe "political leaders are more interested in protecting their power than in doing what's right for the American people."

- 83 percent believe "the country is run by an alliance of incumbent politicians, media pundits, lobbyists, and other interests for their own gain."
- 79 percent believe that "powerful interests from Wall Street banks to corporations, unions, and PACs use campaign and lobbying money to rig the system to serve themselves and . . . loot the national treasury at the expense of every American."[37]

When the pollsters asked what these voters wanted done, they found that 74 percent felt that it was "necessary to fix our broken political system first. . . . Ninety-two percent say we must recruit and support for public office more ordinary citizens and fewer professional politicians. . . . The voters understand that what needs fixing is the political class."[38]

The conclusions of their study bear repeating:

> The disaffection of American voters with the status quo in Washington is not ideological, but structural. Clearly, the public is not looking to merely tinker with the political process, or to simply to swing from the current crop of Democrats to the current crop of Republicans. The difference between today's political structure and the aspirations of Americans is a vision of alternate universes. One is the status quo of the political, media, and establishment elite. The other universe is that of the American people, who demand transformation of the nation's political life.[39]

This need for a "transformation of the nation's political life" underpins the rise of outsider politicians like Trump and Sanders.

## COLLAPSING TRUST ACROSS OTHER INSTITUTIONS

The lost trust in government coexists with an erosion of faith in most other institutions, expanding the scope of the crisis beyond government to nearly every facet of American life.

### *Business*
"It has typically fallen to government to create the context for change, but it is either incapable or unwilling to do it," writes Richard Edelman.

"People trust business to innovate, unite and deliver across borders in a way that government can't. That trust comes with the expectation and responsibility to maintain it."[40] Alas, Americans have a deeply skeptical view of business and, more broadly, of the system of free enterprise that has served as the linchpin of American prosperity. According to the Chicago Booth/Kellogg School financial trust index, 49 percent believe the financial system hurts the economy.[41]

Just 21 percent express confidence in "big business."[42] Poll respondents considered greed and money (54 percent) to be the primary motivations for business.[43] One bright spot was the view of small business, in which 67 percent of U.S. adults reported having "a great deal" or "quite a lot" of confidence.[44]

Considering the impact of the 2008 financial crisis, perhaps it is not surprising that distrust in banks is so widespread. Still, the mere 12 percent expressing "a great deal" of trust in banks is remarkable.[45] A troubling percentage (43 percent) of Americans say they don't plan to save money with a bank account.[46] Financial institutions, especially banks, must respond to these widespread fears—but all private businesses will have to take steps to address the crippling lack of trust and to improve accountability and transparency. These steps could include, for example, using technology to improve communication with shareholders and consumers, providing better explanations for high-level bonuses, and moving to a system of CEO "term limits." Millions of Americans now regard the private sector with deep suspicion; to change that, businesses will have to take some risks and shake up how they do things.

### The Media

Only four in ten Americans say they have "a great deal" or "a fair amount" of trust in the mass media to report the news accurately, according to Gallup's September 2015 survey.[47] The media might be doing well to get 40 percent support, considering how often it has been caught either making egregious errors or manipulating facts. Without question, the 24-hour news cycle and social media have fundamentally changed the way we consume—and report—news. Reporters have changed from "silent skeptics" to "vocal cynics," as one writer put it.[48] For many Americans, the media doesn't so much report the news as shape it. On both sides of the political divide, allegations of bias run rampant.

Perhaps no media event illustrated the public loss of trust in media more vividly than the downfall of Brian Williams at NBC News. Williams, the network's evening news anchor and flagship news personality, was forced out when it came to light that he had been exaggerating, among other things, the peril he faced as he rode in a helicopter with U.S. troops during the Iraq war. Williams was suspended for six months, and he and NBC eventually agreed to part ways.

The Williams scandal showed the impact of social media. Joe Summerlin and other soldiers involved in the Iraq helicopter incident used Facebook and Twitter to undercut the anchor's changing stories and eventually shatter his credibility.[49] "It is just harder to get away with dissembling now," wrote Mitchell Stephens, a journalism professor who studies the history of broadcast news. Social media, he said, "is a great device for catching this stuff."[50]

Republicans and conservatives have long accused the "mainstream media" of bias. These accusations got fresh fuel in late 2015, during one of the early debates of the Republican primary cycle, carried on CNBC. "This is not a cage match," GOP presidential candidate Ted Cruz said. "The questions that are being asked shouldn't be getting people to tear into each other. It should be, 'What are your substantive solutions?'" Cruz was responding to the moderators' intensely adversarial questioning, which struck many as politically motivated. Focus group pollster Frank Luntz found that Cruz's comment earned the highest positive score he'd ever measured.[51]

"When reporting and news analysis become indistinguishable from the output of political operatives. . . . nobody should be surprised if those on the other side come to doubt the media's honesty more generally," writes James Taranto.[52] Given the role of a free press in a democracy, the levels of distrust in the media are troubling and corrosive—yet with our highly partisan, polarized political environment, it seems unlikely that confidence in mainstream media will improve dramatically. We're in a different era.

Not all institutions are doing so badly. Police and organized religion remain among the most trusted institutions in American life, with only the military and small business outranking them.[53] Still, as the following numbers reflect, even these mighty have fallen.

## Organized Religion

In 2015, Gallup recorded the lowest score yet for American confidence in organized religion: 42 percent.[54] In 2013, Gallup found that 77 percent of Americans say religion is losing its influence, yet 75 percent say the country would be better off if we were more religious.[55] The continued decline of religious trust is in line with trends over the last 40 years. Over that period, confidence in organized religion has dropped, in part from a waning of religiosity but also because of scandals, especially involving the Catholic Church. The church's sexual-abuse scandal created a more negative image of organized religion and Christianity generally—not just among Protestants and Catholics but also among non-Christians.[56] Confidence in organized religion among U.S. Protestants and Catholics today stands at 51 percent. This is the lowest mark yet for Protestants— their confidence has been on the wane since 2009—but a slight boost for Catholics after more than a decade, during which their confidence fell as low as 39 percent.

But overall, the trend is downward for organized religion and main-line churches. Some believe the decline is solely due to institutional failures. "Churches are still stuck in the mentality that we just have to fling our doors open, and people will come," says N. Dale Mendenhall, a pastor in Muncie, Indiana, whose congregation has dwindled dramatically over the last 30 years. "That's not the case anymore. Just look around."[57] Yet it is also clear that the decline of religious faith and the rise of Americans who say "none" when asked about their religion is a crucial factor. As with media, though religious institutions have made many missteps, even their best efforts to correct them are unlikely to alter dramatically the trust they enjoy—or let them recapture the trust levels of what now looks like a bygone era in American life.

## Law Enforcement/Police

In 2015, a Gallup poll recorded the lowest confidence levels in police—52 percent—since it started being measured in 1993. In 2016, confidence rallied somewhat, to 56 percent.[58] No doubt, high-profile incidents involving white police officers and the shooting deaths of young black men, which have provoked widespread protests as well as a fervent movement, Black Lives Matter, have had much to do with the shaky confidence.[59] In many of these cases, police have had justification for their actions, or the circumstances have been murky; in others, such as the shooting of Walter Scott in South Carolina or Laquan McDonald in Chicago, the police acted recklessly and lethally.

A September 2015 National Bar Association poll found that 88 percent of blacks think they are treated unfairly by the police; only 59 percent of whites agree that blacks are treated unfairly.[60] The perception gap is dramatic in the South, where 90 percent of blacks feel mistreated by police, while just 55 percent of whites concur with that judgment. In the Northeast, the views of whites and blacks are more closely matched—74 percent of blacks say police treat blacks unfairly compared with 63 percent of whites who share that perception.[61] The story isn't that clear-cut, though. Some two-thirds of whites believe that blacks misunderstand the police, and more than 50 percent of blacks agree.[62]

The growth of the Black Lives Matter movement has certainly contributed to distrust of police. Yet despite the recent incidents and political energy directed against law enforcement, trust in police overall remains above 50 percent. Government and many other institutions would be thrilled to have those numbers.

### Health Care System

"If you like your doctor, you can keep your doctor": surely these words will go down in history (along with "Read my lips, no new taxes") as one of the great broken presidential promises. President Obama relied heavily on this pledge to sell Americans on his signature health care law, the Affordable Care Act—and it turned out to be completely false. Backtracking in 2014, Obama tried to explain why some people would *not* be able to keep their doctors:

> If you're in the middle of life-saving treatment with a particular doctor, then we will work to make sure that you can keep that treatment and not shift. But for the average person, for many folks who don't have health insurance initially, they're going to have to make some choices. They might have to end up switching doctors in part because they're saving money. But that's true if your employer suddenly decides this network is going to give you a better deal. "We think this is going to help keep premiums lower. You gotta use this doctor as opposed to this one."[63]

Obama's "keep your doctor" promise earned him PolitiFact's lie of the year; the ensuing controversy prompted the administration to exempt people with canceled policies from the individual mandate for three years. According to Gallup, just 37 percent of Americans trusted the medical system either "a great deal" or "quite a lot" in 2015. This is down from 41 percent in 2010, but these low numbers didn't start with Obamacare. Trust in the health care system hasn't been higher than 44 percent in more than ten years.[64] In other words, a minority of respondents in the world's most powerful nation express confidence in one of the fundamental institutions of a modern society. The way Americans feel about the health care system is an unfortunate microcosm of what has happened to trust across institutions in American life: they don't know what they can count on anymore.

## LOOKING AHEAD

We believe that the trust crisis, which has been unfolding for years, if not decades, has its roots in the failure of institutions to respond to the needs of constituents, consumers, patients, students, and whomever else they serve. In the chapters ahead, we will look at a broad cross-section of areas in American life in which institutions and practices have failed—education, the economy, the health care system, political leadership—as well as spiraling social problems, like poverty, family breakdown, crime, race relations, and national security, in which similar failures of leadership have allowed problems to deepen and metastasize. We'll offer proposals and innovative solutions that could make a real difference.

When it comes to trust, however, the solutions are less programmatic and more philosophical. After all, the best way to win (or regain) trust is to conduct oneself in a trustworthy fashion. The best way to win the confidence of others in an institutional sense is to *perform*. Thus, the proposals we offer in the subject-specific chapters should boost Americans' trust in, for example, their schools, their health care, their local police, and—crucially—their government.

That said, we offer a few general observations. It is worth noting that for years polls have shown majority public support for goals that the federal government has continually failed to deliver: a higher minimum wage, more robust unemployment support, more effective education spending, student debt relief, affordable health care, and a strong but sensible foreign policy, among others. The failure of leaders on both sides of the aisle to respond to these and other desires is one reason why pluralities of Americans express support for a viable third party—and it's why we believe that, had he entered the 2016 presidential race, former New York mayor Michael Bloomberg could have won.

It's important to note, too, that a majority of the public *doesn't* oppose having a political authority that solves large-scale problems. Our own surveys have found that Americans would welcome a government energetically taking steps that would reempower ordinary people politically and economically. But what citizens see instead is a rigged system that works against them. Further, millions of Americans are troubled by a sense that not only are their material prospects dwindling, but also the country itself—its unity, its principles, its values—is vanishing before their eyes. Such fears are only exacerbated by a sense that a ruling or political class is both corrupt and disconnected from ordinary people's concerns. That sense is widespread among Americans on the right and the left.

It is this failure of politics, as we describe it, that has helped create the trust crisis. But by now, the trust crisis itself reinforces the failure of politics, since leadership and bipartisan cooperation becoming increasingly challenging in an environment of such recrimination and suspicion. America's political leaders don't trust one another, and Americans don't trust their political leaders—or most other fundamental institutions. If we're going to reinvigorate our democracy and civic culture, these dynamics must change. The way to do it is not with speeches and promises but with better performance, based on fresh ideas and effective policies.

## CHAPTER 2

# The Failure of Politics

Neither party is offering real solutions.... The Democrats just keep looking for new funds to pour into the sinkhole; Republicans hope to starve
the beast to force a crisis.... Democrats' proposals stave off present pain
at the cost of making the inevitable day of reckoning that much worse.
Republicans bring on Armageddon now without any idea of what comes
after. Voters are right to hold both approaches in disdain.... Until one or
both parties develops workable approaches to the serious problems the
country faces, politics is going to remain open to demagogues and con
artists.

—WALTER RUSSELL MEAD[1]


The era of a national legislature boldly tackling major problems is over.
The era of the grand bargain is over. Even the era of hold-your-nose-and-
cooperate-for-the-good-of-the-country is over.... It's an every-man-for-
himself atmosphere.

—HOWARD KURTZ[2]


For years, Americans have endured horrific mass shootings, from
Aurora, Colorado, to Newtown, Connecticut. For years, they have
watched as the domestic tide of Islamic terror attacks—from Chattanooga
to San Bernardino—has mounted. On June 12, 2016, in Orlando, the two
forces came together when Omar Mateen, an American-born Muslim,
murdered 49 people and wounded 53 more at the gay nightclub Pulse,
using semiautomatic weapons. It was the deadliest mass shooting in
American history.

For the average non-politicized American observer, the Orlando
horror dramatized two serious problems in the country today: the easy
access to deadly firearms and the growing presence of radicalized, "homegrown" Islamist terrorists, often inspired by—if not in open coordination

with—ISIS. Orlando, then, was about radical Islamic terrorism *and* it was about guns.

Unfortunately, in the immediate aftermath of the attack, politics took over. In the national conversation, the two issues were mostly addressed separately. Either Orlando was an alarm bell about the terrorist threat, as conservatives said, or it was another instance of the need for gun control, as liberals maintained. Somehow, it could not be both. This strange disconnect was foreshadowed in December 2015, when the San Bernardino terror attack (every bit as shocking but fortunately not as deadly) took place. Again, conservatives focused on terror and minimized the problem of guns, while liberals downplayed terrorism and jumped on their gun control soapbox. As a result, the American public—which overwhelmingly supports stricter gun control laws, including universal background checks, while also feeling more fearful about terrorist attacks than at any point since 9/11[3]—was once again denied an opportunity to unify behind common purposes. Americans have good reason to feel the way they do on both issues: between 2004 and 2014, terror suspects successfully purchased guns in the United States more than 2,000 times.[4] The intersection of the two problems should be obvious.

Not to our political class, however. The Orlando aftermath—in which both sides rehearsed the same old themes, interchangeable with those from previous years—offers a stark illustration of the degradation of our politics. The decay has many facets, but its fundamental features are abysmal political leadership on both sides of the aisle, endemic gridlock, refusal to solve or even acknowledge major problems, and the now familiar experience of seeing what should be nationally unifying moments—such as Orlando—devolve into just another ideological war, the latest chapter in the red/blue divide.

Against this backdrop, it's no surprise that Americans are angry. But that word doesn't go deep enough to describe the severity of the situation. Americans are profoundly frustrated with a failed political system and especially with the failure of the parties. The discontent is more fundamental than mere anger: it is a sense that our institutions don't work, our parties don't work, and a representative and responsive government that we all grew up believing in is *gone*—probably forever.

As we detailed in the previous chapter, these failures have led to a breakdown in trust in every important institution in American life—but none more severely than in the institutions of government. This is not just a onetime reaction to episodic conditions; it is, rather, a deep-seated loss of confidence in our political leadership, political institutions, and the political class. Americans have no illusion anymore that their government represents them; they do not believe it works in their interests. They do not believe that it produces positive outcomes. We have the highest percentage of Americans out of the workforce in the nation's history.

Americans have made clear to pollsters how they feel about their government.

In Gallup's June 2016 polling, only 9 percent of Americans said that they trusted Congress either "a great deal" or "quite a lot."[5] In 2015, Pew recorded slightly better numbers, finding that 19 percent of Americans trusted Washington "always or most of the time" in November 2015.[6] And a September 2015 *Washington Post*–ABC News poll found that 72 percent of Americans believed that politicians can't be trusted and two-thirds thought that the country's political system was dysfunctional. In this climate, political radicalism has grown in appeal: 21 percent of those polled would rather see the next president "tear down" the political system and "start over" than try to "fix it."[7] It's no wonder: our political institutions have stopped dealing with real-world problems like terrorism, revitalizing the economy, and reforming entitlement programs.

What we're seeing is a complete collapse of all credibility. Evidence of a dysfunctional political system is all around us, in every area of American life. Even in a country as large and powerful as the United States, the cascade of failures cannot continue indefinitely without the system shutting down. We're as close to that point as we have ever been— at least since the founding of the modern American state in the aftermath of the Civil War. Yes, it's that serious.

## FAILURE TO PERFORM

If there is one line, one theme, that helped propel Donald Trump more than any other, it was this: "America doesn't win anymore." How many hundreds of times did he say those words over the course of the presidential campaign? Yes, they were vague; they offered an overly broad diagnosis of the country's problems. But as a theme, the words were potent. They connected to Americans' pervasive sense that their country seemed to have forgotten how to get things right, how to move forward, in the ways that once made the nation the envy of the world.

Trump's words were an acknowledgment of American failure.

The failures are everywhere you look—and we devote several chapters of this book to specific areas. Our education system in the lower grades has stopped preparing kids, especially those from disadvantaged backgrounds, for future success; at the high school level, it has stopped inspiring kids to pursue careers and higher skills; and at the college level, it combines suffocating political correctness with exorbitant tuitions. Our economic system generates positive-looking macro results but few good-paying jobs; the gap between the rich and poor continues to grow. Our federal government faces generational fiscal challenges involving entitlements, social welfare, and health care, and it makes no serious attempt to address them. Our physical infrastructure is crumbling and in some places is hardly better than that found in third world countries. Our political parties are fraying to their ideological poles and, in Washington, resemble enemy camps, unable to make deals on anything. We face a continuing epidemic of gun violence and mass shootings that make us unique in the developed world, yet even as the carnage mounts, we make no attempt to address it, to change the dynamics that underlie it. We can neither arrive at a definitive approach to securing our national borders nor formulate fair, effective, and productive immigration reform. Our unity as a national polity, electorate, and popular culture has been shattered into fragments; we are increasingly becoming many different political cultures. We cannot even agree on how to defend the country from enemies that ought to unite us all.

One of the paradoxes of Washington failure—well, maybe it isn't much of a paradox—is that the cascade of failures takes place as the government grows ever larger. The federal government, as Jim Geraghty wrote, is "plagued by a culture of complacency in key agencies with no sign of serious accountability for consequential mistakes."[8] Geraghty cataloged a litany of federal government failures: the VA crisis, in which two consecutive administrations have utterly failed to provide adequate care for tens of thousands of Americans veterans; the Obama administration's disastrous launching of the Obamacare website, which didn't work, confused millions who tried to use it, and cost taxpayers at least

$1 billion to fix;[9] and the humanitarian and national security disaster at the Mexican border.

To these can also be added the collapse of the Secret Service, once a revered organization of security and professionalism, now just another federal agency overrun by cronyism, incompetence, and personal abuses—and one that might yet cost a future president his or her life. How about Operation Fast and Furious, a Justice Department program designed to follow illegal firearms as they "walked" across the border to the top of the Mexican drug cartels? But government agents lost track of many of the firearms, and they found their way into criminal hands. One of these guns may have been used in the murder of a U.S. Customs and Border Protection agent.[10] How about the IRS scandal, in which a unit with the bureau specially targeted conservative groups claiming tax-exempt status, telling employees to be on the lookout especially for organizations with the words "Tea Party" or "Patriot" in their names? Or the deadly fertilizer-plant explosion in West, Texas, that killed 12 firefighters—and could have been prevented, the Chemical Safety Board said, if officials at *any* level of government had identified the hazards?

Indeed, as the Texas tragedy made clear, dysfunctional government is a problem at all levels of government—federal, state, and local. We can't even ensure anymore that the drinking water is clean and won't poison our children. If you want a truly vivid example of the collapse of American political and governmental know-how, look no further than Flint, Michigan.

"I can't afford to go buy 20 gallons of water just to bathe him one time," said Ariana Hawk, a 25-year-old single mother, of one of her three children. "We get treated like…we don't matter. That's how it's been feeling."[11] In Flint, nearly 5 percent of children have now tested positive for elevated levels of lead. Some health experts call what's happened in Flint "state-sponsored child abuse."[12]

One might dismiss Flint as a story about local government failure in a depressed community, but it's emblematic of the government's inability to do its job across all levels. In Flint, the blame game ran fast and furious between Democrats and Republicans. Democrats pointed the finger at Michigan's Republican governor, Rick Snyder. Republicans countered that Flint had been a Democratic Party fiefdom for decades. The squabbling and buck-passing epitomize a much larger national problem: the polarization of the two parties in Washington to a point of complete dysfunction.

## POLARIZATION, GRIDLOCK, AND SELF-DESTRUCTION

Congress's job approval rating hovers around 10 percent—getting close to John McCain's oft-repeated quip that soon they'll be "down to family members and paid staffers" in terms of support. It's clear that lawmakers have lost the respect of the public.[13] Polling shows that 86 percent of voters believe "political leaders are more interested in protecting their power than in doing what's right for the American people," 83 percent believe "the country is run by an alliance of incumbent politicians, media pundits, lobbyists, and other interests for their own gain," and 79 percent believe that "powerful interests from Wall Street banks to corporations, unions, and PACs use campaign and lobbying money to rig the system to serve themselves and that they loot the national treasury at the expense of every American."[14]

On both sides, leaders are so flawed or tainted by partisan energies that they cannot hope to provide the stewardship we need at a critical time. "The era of a national legislature boldly tackling major problems is over," as Howard Kurtz writes. "The era of the grand bargain is over. Even the era of hold-your-nose-and-cooperate-for-the-good-of-the-country is over.... It's an every-man-for-himself atmosphere."[15]

One reason for this is the way the parties' ideological lines have hardened and—with a big assist from legislative gerrymandering—created polarized congressional districts, with hard-left or hard-right constituencies pushing their representatives to take uncompromising stands. American politics has never been a game for saints, but bipartisanship was possible in the past with diverse constituencies and the threat of broad public disapproval for those who don't perform. Now, with legislators representing increasingly homogeneous constituencies, politicians focus on shoring up their partisan credentials—not finding common ground. "Deal-making has become a bad word in our (political) culture," says Chris Cillizza.[16]

The result: governing paralysis. Today, "75 percent of the salient issues on Washington's agenda are subject to legislative gridlock—the kind of agree-on-nothing gridlock that's crushed virtually every major piece of legislation heading through Congress today," the Brookings Institute's Sarah Binder says. "So long as some degree of polarization is driven by sheer partisan team play—in which the opposition party is more likely to object to proposals endorsed by the president—then extreme levels of polarization will continue to lead to unprecedented levels of deadlock."[17] Indeed, recordkeeping shows that the number of hours that the Senate and House spend in session is on par with historical averages over the last 70 years—but the number of bills clearing each chamber and getting signed into law is well below those averages.[18]

It would be hard to find a more dramatic example of legislative paralysis than the 2011 debt ceiling fiasco, in which Republicans blocked, until the last conceivable moment, an extension of the nation's credit limit—a customary exercise, if a sobering one, since it serves as a reminder of our national arrears. Since the 1960s, the government in Washington had raised the debt ceiling more than 80 times, with no hint of crisis. But in 2011, for the first time, "the debt limit was consciously held hostage to a set of very strong and nonnegotiable demands," Norman Ornstein said. "It wasn't a spontaneous thing, it was a strategy developed well in advance, and the way it played out led to the first downgrade in credit in the United States in history."[19]

Yet by now, the problem is not entirely rooted in Washington, though one can get that impression from reading polls. For example, a *WSJ/NBC News* poll in the wake of the 2014 midterm elections found that 63 percent of Americans want candidates in elected office who will "bend enough to broker deals," as compared with just 30 percent more concerned with lawmakers keeping their campaign promises.[20] But Americans don't agree on *how* to handle gridlock in Washington and return to a more functional system.

After eight years of Obama, Republicans, at least in surveys, tend to resist the idea of compromise.[21] A 2014 Pew poll found that two-thirds of Republicans would rather the GOP leadership "stand up" to Obama "even if less gets done." A Pew poll found that, by a margin of 57–39, Republicans wanted their leaders to move in a *more* conservative direction, not a more moderate one.

Indeed, Republicans take the brunt of the blame for the gridlock in Washington. A CNN/ORC poll found that 68 percent of Americans believe the GOP wasn't cooperating with Obama enough.[22] As Brookings's Thomas Mann argues, "Republicans have become a radical insurgency— ideologically extreme, contemptuous of the inherited policy regime, scornful of compromise, unpersuaded by the conventional understanding of facts, evidence and science, and dismissive of the legitimacy of its political opposition. The evidence of this asymmetry is overwhelming." The Republican Party is responding mostly to its activist base, Mann continues, making compromise all but impossible.[23]

On the Democratic side, the picture is more mixed. By contrast, in the same Pew poll, Democrats, by a margin of 52–41, said that their leaders should move in a more moderate—not a more liberal—direction.[24] In practice, though, the Democrats haven't exactly led the way on compromise. When they were in the majority in Congress, they decried the 60-vote threshold needed to overcome filibusters; now they embrace it.[25]

In the end, what we see is a zero-sum political system, where one side must win and the other must lose; where policy victories are entirely achieved along partisan lines, with no hope of benefit for the party in the minority; and where suspicion, recrimination, and demonization continue to corrode not only the public dialogue but the very fabric of governance itself. We should not be surprised that the performance failure of our government, at every level, in recent years so closely tracks the degradation of our political dialogue and basic civic functioning of our institutions. They are intimately related: the ever-increasing polarization leads to an ever-declining standard of dialogue and erosion of political functioning, and this loss of deal-making capacity leads directly to the atrocious results from our political leaders that Americans are so furious about. We are crippling ourselves with ideology, partisanship, and the politics of revenge.

## PROBLEMS LEFT TO FESTER AND WORSEN

Incompetence combined with polarization and gridlock equals failure to solve problems. Consider just a few examples of how a nonfunctioning political class leaves problems that threaten our nation's future.

How is it possible, for instance, that the United States could suffer the carnage of one mass shooting after another—events nearly unique to our country, by the way—and a governing system once the envy of the world does nothing whatsoever to try to solve the problem? Washington's failure to enact sensible, limited gun control measures represents an appalling failure to serve the American people.

Obama often said that the worst day of his presidency was December 14, 2012, when 20-year-old Adam Lanza, a mentally disturbed resident of Newtown, Connecticut, killed his mother at home and then took her guns—including a Bushmaster XM-15 rifle and a .22-caliber Savage Mark II rifle—and murdered 26 people, 20 of whom were children aged 6 and 7, at Sandy Hook Elementary School. Lanza had struggled with untreated mental illness his whole life. A state report showed that Lanza had anxiety and obsessive-compulsive disorder.

If ever, in the years of one senseless gun slaughter after another, in all parts of the United States, there was a time when the momentum for sensible gun safety measures had finally reached critical mass, this was it. In the months after Sandy Hook, a determined Obama set out to get a bill passed that would make a real difference.

But he failed. Once again, resistance to sensible limits on gun purchase and ownership killed a commonsense effort to control a deadly problem. Once again, the NRA used its enormous clout within the Republican Party to convince legislators to vote down measures that would have banned some assault rifles, limited the size of ammunition magazines, and imposed more stringent background checks for gun purchases—the latter a measure supported by *nine out of ten Americans.*[26]

"All in all, this was a pretty shameful day for Washington," Obama said. He was right—and regarding guns, the blame lies squarely with Republicans. Only four Democrats voted against the bill; nine out of ten Republicans voted against it. Throughout this book, we will lay blame where it belongs, issue by issue; on some issues, Democrats deserve much more blame than Republicans. Not on guns. Until the Republican Party pushes back against NRA money and lobbying, we won't see sensible gun policy.

Some numbers from a 2015 Harvard study tell the story:

- 40 percent of guns in this country pass hands without a background check.
- Only ten states require background checks for all gun purchases.

- Roughly 30 percent of gun owners didn't purchase their most recent gun, instead obtaining it through a transfer—a gift, an inheritance, or a swap between friends.
- Among gun owners who got their firearms through a transfer, roughly two-thirds did not go through a background check.[27]

Since the massacre at Sandy Hook, over 85 percent of Americans have supported strengthening our background-check system—a figure that has not wavered.[28] By a margin of 55 to 33 percent, Americans say laws on gun sales should be stricter. And yet, it's important to understand that, as a whole, Americans have sensible—and limited—views of gun control, with 72 percent opposing a ban on handguns.[29] Americans—even those in blue states—are not and never will be gun abolitionists. It's not about doing away with guns. It's about taking rational measures to address a problem that no other first world nation suffers from. America's ongoing futility over guns vividly illustrates the collapse of political leadership.

So does the long-running failure to solve another problem overwhelming majorities want solved: our looming fiscal insolvency.

> He [Obama] created a bipartisan debt commission. They came back with an urgent report. He thanked them, sent them on their way, and then did exactly nothing. Republicans stepped up with good-faith reforms and solutions equal to the problems. How did the president respond? By doing nothing...except to dodge and demagogue the issue.[30]

So said Paul Ryan, the GOP's 2012 vice presidential nominee, on the campaign trail, explaining how the United States' debt grew so far out of control. What Ryan didn't say was that, as chairman of the House Budget Committee, he voted against the same "urgent report"—the Simpson-Bowles plan.

Never let inconvenient facts get in the way of a good political line.

Both parties' failure to enact the Simpson-Bowles plan to reduce our debt and deficit represents another glaring failure of a Washington political culture devoted almost solely to self-preservation and political gain, and not at all to the public interest. The commission, led by former senator Alan Simpson and former Clinton White House chief of staff

Erskine Bowles, did everything that was asked of it. It came up with a comprehensive plan to cut wasteful spending, reform the tax code, and make necessary changes to entitlements such as Medicare and Social Security in order to protect them for future generations of Americans—all while reducing our crippling debt by $2.4 trillion.[31]

It's a disgrace that such a measured, centrist, bipartisan plan could not be enacted—even with massive support among the American people.

By a ratio of 80 percent to 8, Americans supported the plan. Once again, on a fundamental issue with high stakes for our national future, the American people showed themselves capable of accepting shared sacrifice to address our fiscal woes—sacrifice that would include possibly higher taxes and a reduction in their Medicare and Social Security benefits. They were willing to make these sacrifices, they made clear, if those conditions were instituted across the board, as part of a comprehensive plan to reduce the national debt, narrow our federal budget deficit, and move toward a balanced budget. Above all, what the American people wanted—on this issue as on other vital issues—was to see some compromise in Washington among the Republicans and Democrats, some give in both parties in favor of a goal transcending party lines and partisan ideology.[32]

They didn't get it. Simpson-Bowles needed the votes of 14 of the 18 congressmen on the bipartisan panel considering it, and only 11 stepped up. Opposition to the plan came from both sides of the aisle, whether based in objections to higher taxes (Republicans) or cuts to Social Security benefits (Democrats). Once again, both parties showed their unwillingness to break out of their ideological boxes, keep their lobbyists and activists at arm's length, and take a stand for the national interest.

The federal government's failure to secure the nation's southern border with Mexico and legislate comprehensive immigration reform reflects again how party divisions prevent good-faith efforts to solve pressing problems. To be sure, under the Obama administration some improvements were made. A decade ago, more than eight in ten individuals evaded Border Patrol—totaling more than 900,000 illegal immigrants. Today, that ratio is down to four in ten, a substantial improvement. For all the criticism it received, the Obama administration deported more people than the George W. Bush administration. Still, when you're touting the fact that "only" four in ten people are slipping into the country illegally, you know you have a problem. As House Homeland Security

Committee Chairman Michael McCaul concedes, the "bottom line is we are far from having operational control of our borders," and "there still are no metrics to quantify progress."[33] Moreover, a January 2015 oversight report from retired Oklahoma senator Tom Coburn found that less than 3 percent of illegal immigrants are ever deported and *more than 700 miles of the border*—more than one-third its total length—were deemed porous because there was "little to no deployment density or aviation surveillance coverage" to detect illegal immigrants, smugglers, or others.[34]

And how about the healthcare debacle that pitted Republicans against Republicans in a grudge match that humiliated President Trump just weeks into his term? Republicans campaigned for three elections on repealing and replacing Obamacare. It was one of the main tenants of their platform and a rallying cry that seemed to unify disparate caucuses. Until it didn't. The fight between moderate Republicans, President Trump, and the Freedom Caucus can't be called anything but a total meltdown. "Republicans land a punch on health care, to their own face," read a *New York Times* headline.[35] *Vox* offered, "The failure of the Republican health care bill reveals a party unready to govern."[36] And from Reuters: "Trump tastes failure as US healthcare bill collapses."[37] Indeed, Trump's comment just a month earlier that "nobody knew health care could be so complicated" meant more than it seemed at the time: Republicans weren't up to the challenge.[38] With seven years to address very real problems with Obamacare, they opted for fiery rhetoric and little substance. The result was a masterclass in political dysfunction.

The costs of these conditions to American society, in government outlays, crime and security issues, and human suffering, are immense. Polls have shown for years that Americans support strong border protections but that majorities would also be amenable—*after* this first condition is ensured—to a path to citizenship for those here illegally. The consistent point is that Americans want the problem solved, and they understand that securing the border systematically will create the conditions that could make a path to citizenship possible. In Washington, however, this perspective just isn't ideological enough for hard-line conservatives, many of whom are unwilling to support a path to citizenship even if the border is secured; or for Democrats, whose emphasis skews entirely the other way, prioritizing legal protections and welfare benefits for illegal immigrants—they won't even call them illegals, insisting on the term "undocumented," as if the Census somehow forgot to count them—before agreeing to the security measures that will ensure the integrity of our borders. The result is a broken immigration system, a still-porous border, deepening divisions among the American people about newcomers to our shores, legitimate concerns about crime and terrorism, and the perpetuation of a national cancer that is eroding our civic health—but serving well the needs of our political class.

## THE LOSS OF UNITY AND THE VACUUM OF LEADERSHIP

"Today, our nation saw evil, the very worst of human nature, and we responded with the best of America, with the daring of our rescue workers, with the caring for strangers and neighbors who came to give blood and help in any way they could."[39]

Everyone remembers these words from George Bush on September 11, 2001, when he addressed the nation after the attacks on the World Trade Center in New York City. On 9/11 and briefly afterward, Bush appealed to what he called "the warm glow of national unity" as Americans rallied around their leaders and one another, seeing themselves as part of a common culture, nation, and cause. Such unifying moments once were more common in our history, whether during the Second World War, when Franklin Roosevelt led the nation through a grueling and terrifying conflict, or during the early years of the Cold War, when Harry Truman, a Democratic hawk, brought the country together behind the policy of containment, which would guide the foreign policy efforts of his successors in both parties. Such unity was blown asunder by Vietnam and has only briefly returned since—during the Persian Gulf War, for example, and after 9/11.

Today, however, that spirit of unity is long since lost, regardless of whether the issue in question is a matter of foreign or domestic policy. Even in the aftermath of the ISIS attacks in Paris in November 2015, and then the San Bernardino terror attacks that followed soon after, our political leaders could rarely find common ground. Despite globally troubling developments that pose existential challenges, we're not unified. If anything, we're more divided than ever—and we can thank our political leaders for that.

At the outset of this chapter, we talked about the polarization in Washington. But by now, polarization is not confined to the political parties—it has extended to the American people themselves. In fact, some political scientists believe that public polarization comes before that of the political class; in other words, our political leaders are responding to a cleavage that already exists in the populace, as opposed to causing it. Whether you see it as chicken or egg, polarization among American voters threatens our prospects of finding good, unifying leaders in the future.

For years now, we have read about how voters in heavily "blue" or "red" areas see voters of the opposite tendency as something like alien beings—*evil* alien beings. They see their own view of the world as morally superior, empirically irrefutable, historically self-justifying. A 2014 Pew survey found that 27 percent of Democrats and 36 percent of Republicans view the other party as "a threat to the nation's well-being."[40] With that kind of thinking, it's not surprising that more Americans are undertaking "ideological migration"—moving to states or localities where most residents share their political and social views. Such trends tend to be self-reinforcing, of course; they segregate like-minded people in the same places and encourage the election of local representatives who tend to veer sharply in one ideological direction or another. Bill Bishop discussed the ramifications of such actions in his important 2008 book *The Big Sort*.

Readers who remember the 2000 presidential election will recall how the networks inadvertently created the imagery for red and blue America during that election night, coloring Republican and Democratic states in those respective colors. When the election became contested, setting off a furious battle over a recount that culminated in a Supreme Court ruling, the red/blue template became fixed in the American mind. In the years since, the media and the political class have often decried the red/blue divide while mostly exacerbating it themselves—whether through journalistic malpractice or political self-dealing.

What it adds up to, in the end, is a loss of American consensus. Critics will say that we're romanticizing the past, but any honest observer of the period from the Great Depression through the 1950s would have to acknowledge that the American electorate had a strong unity around broad national directions. Today, polarization, both in Washington and on Main Street, makes such unity difficult if not impossible.

We simply don't have consensus as a nation—there is no unity, no common sense of purpose. America used to face challenges as Americans, not as Republicans or Democrats. "When the terrorists come for us, they aren't going to ask how you vote," as coauthor Schoen put it on Fox News. But that isn't the prevailing view in what must look, to outsiders, like a nation in love with political squabbles, determined to maintain a sense of Us v. Them, even when events should make clear that there is only Us.

What are the costs of this lost cohesion? In an important essay in *The American Interest*, David Blankenhorn delineates the damage that polarization causes:

- It creates gridlock.
- It coarsens and dumbs-down the public discussion.
- It segregates Americans holding certain views from those holding opposing views, making it less likely that they will know others who think differently.
- It corrodes trust, at both the political and personal levels.
- It lessens empathy and distorts our thinking.
- It makes us poorer citizens.[41]

By now, it is entirely possible that the American people are so far down the road of this "affective polarization" that they wouldn't respond even to the most gifted, unifying political leader. The only way to know for sure is for such a leader to emerge. Alas, there is no sign that such an arrival is imminent. In April 2016, John Podhoretz captured the sense of disgust that millions of Americans have with their leadership choices. On the cover of the *New York Post*, in a headline over photos—none flattering—of Hillary Clinton, Bernie Sanders, Ted Cruz, and Donald Trump, Podhoretz asked, "These are the people who would lead this great nation?"[42]

It's a question that millions of Americans were asking in 2016. In April, an NBC News/*WSJ* survey found that 68 percent of registered voters couldn't imagine supporting Donald Trump for president, while 61 percent said the same for Ted Cruz, Trump's closest competitor for the nomination. The Democrats' presumptive nominee, Hillary Clinton, didn't fare much better—58 percent said the same about her.[43]

It is not merely ideological polarization that leads to such pervasive lack of confidence in our political leaders. It is also the widespread sense that, in crucial ways, our leaders are not very good at leadership. And who can blame the American people for thinking so? What evidence have they seen of effective leadership in recent years?

Leadership means "bringing people together in pursuit of a common cause, developing a plan to achieve it, and staying with it until the goal is achieved," Bill Clinton said in an interview with *Fortune*. Few politicians in the postwar era have enjoyed Clinton's success in appealing to the political center and brokering deals with the opposition. His legacy as a conciliator and deal-maker is ironic, considering how much political opposition he kicked up, culminating in an impeachment trial. Yet Clinton knew that the core American voter is moderate, practical, and often not terribly interested in politics. He or she looks to *leaders* to articulate major policies in a language of fairness, common sense, and inclusion. "I believe lasting positive results are more likely to occur when leaders practice inclusion and cooperation rather than authoritarian unilateralism," Clinton said. "Even those who lead don't have all the answers."[44]

That's not the prevailing view Americans have heard from today's political class.

Americans don't just detest their leadership choices because of issues of personal character (say, with Donald Trump and Hillary Clinton), or because of candidates who are too ideological (say, Ted Cruz and Bernie Sanders), or because they object to what they see as a weak national security emphasis (Obama). They have also lost faith in the leadership class because of its absence of *ideas*. As we said in the introduction to this book, the political class is offering nothing in the way of fresh vision, bold strategies, or new approaches. Instead, both parties cling for dear life to partisan positions that align them with their voting bases—and the circle of futility just keeps spinning.

This is one of the reasons we wrote this book—to offer ideas for a new future. It isn't simply about the challenges America faces in the here and now, though these are substantial. It is also about the fact that, absent new ideas and new policies, America is bound to diminish in its ability to play a constructive role in the world. After all, would you listen to the counsel of a stumbling superpower with a failing education system, $19 trillion in debt, a gun violence epidemic, and an ongoing failure to control its borders and devise a sensible immigration system? "A nation as poorly governed as the United States now is cannot long serve as the cornerstone of world order," Walter Russell Mead writes. "The combination of budget pressures and political dysfunction at home is already sapping the nation's will and capacity to lead abroad, and this is likely to get worse rather than better without a course change."[45]

The question is how to achieve that course change and at what cost?

## CONCLUSION

The subject of political polarization and dysfunction is one we have written about for years. In 2012, coauthor Schoen published *Hopelessly Divided*, an analysis of the forces driving the parties apart and how a range of other forces—not just ideological rigidity but also political money, lobbying, gerrymandering, and the new media—have contributed to a breakdown in American governance. Schoen has proposed reforms—to lobbying practices, to campaign finance, and to redistricting policies—that we continue to believe could help remedy the problem of America's broken politics.

There is no shortage of worthwhile reforms.

Gerrymandering has played an enormous role in the polarization that has paralyzed our system. We must take aggressive steps to eliminate it, state by state. This can be done through creating independent commissions within each state that will design districts based on socioeconomic commonalities and geographic proximity, rather than partisan affiliation. Removing partisanship from the criteria for drawing districts would lead to more competitive elections and greater opportunity for independents and moderates to become involved. In addition, competitive elections would also require representatives to be more accountable to their constituents and run on accomplishments in Congress instead of partisan bluster.

On campaign finance reform, we should institute a new system of publicly financing elections, wherein we match small-donor donations. We should press for a new Securities and Exchange Commission (SEC) rule that requires all publicly traded companies to disclose their political spending; the IRS should issue a rule to crack down on secret political campaign spending by "social welfare" 501(c)(4) nonprofits. We should lower contribution limits—thus bringing more small donors into the process—and ban soft money and issue ads.

Congress should also tighten anticoordination laws surrounding Super PACs and candidates' campaigns. Instead of waiting on the Federal Election Commission to act, the Justice Department should more proactively prosecute clear violations of the coordination bans, especially when Super PAC leaders are seen in highly visible settings alongside candidates and in communication with their campaigns. Ultimately—however unlikely it may seem—we should strive for a constitutional amendment to repeal *Citizens United.*

More than ever, we need competitive third parties in American elections. These candidates would not only serve to offer an outsider perspective but would also minimize the power of political parties—both of which have become, it is painfully clear, key drivers of polarization and partisanship. Over 40 percent of Americans identify as Independents today. We need more enterprises like Americans Elect to jumpstart the third-party movement. And we should reform the presidential debate system to allow outsiders to participate: the current rules demand that candidates have at least 15 percent support to enter. That might sound like a low threshold, but in reality it is a mechanism to shut out alternative candidates and protects the two major party candidates, who already have all the advantages in money and visibility.

We need term limits, across the board. We might also consider doing away with the primary system, which creates a hyper-partisan environment for over a year before the presidential election. We could replace it with a top-two/runoff primary, which would allow the two highest vote-getters, regardless of party, to mount general election campaigns. Allowing voters to select candidates for the general election regardless of party would create more judicious general elections and remove a great deal of partisanship from the primary and election process.

What about the specific policy areas that have proved so intractable in our current political environment? Admittedly, finding solutions in these areas won't be easy without a change in the political culture. But how about this for a straightforward policy recommendation that the vast majority of Americans could support: *Implement Simpson-Bowles now.* Simpson-Bowles offers us ten years of genuine bipartisan compromise, where both sides will have won and lost on certain issues. We should also consider a constitutional amendment requiring a balanced budget.

The same blunt approach applies to commonsense gun safety legislation. Americans overwhelmingly support it. But it's not just Republicans who will have to let go of their intransigence. Democrats will have to accept, for instance, that they're not going to get an assault weapons ban. But we can close the gun-show loophole and mandate background checks in every state when a gun exchanges hands, whether by private seller or over the Internet (in addition to licensed gun dealers). We can also better regulate ammunition sales and speed up the terror watch list appeals process to ensure that no one on the watch list can buy a firearm. Isn't that much worth doing?

On the border crisis and immigration, we must again appeal to the center of the American electorate and grasp the solution that has been there all along: comprehensive border security and an end to the constant flow of illegal immigrants, coupled with a path to citizenship for those already here, on one crucial condition—if you slip up, you're out.

As we have seen, however, on these and other issues, even when the American people express a broad consensus, it is as if the Washington leadership class exists in an entirely different orbit, one governed by the laws of ideology and partisan warfare, not the national interest. This fundamental failure of leadership undergirds the failure of our politics. "I'd like to see members of Congress try and transcend these tribal differences," says Norman Ornstein. "Partisanship is a healthy part of a democracy and it can get plenty rough. But there are times and places where you have to find common ground and find compromise because the future of the country is at stake."[46]

Optimism about such a prospect doesn't come easily in our present circumstances—at least, not in the absence of some national emergency that none of us want to see come to pass. But there is no question that the long-term future of the American democratic system is at stake. Ultimately, it may be that our systemic problems cannot be solved through campaign finance reform, term limits, or Supreme Court decisions but only through a fundamental rethinking about ideas of community, family, service, patriotism, and what true leadership entails and requires. Making our politics functional again will almost certainly depend on reaffirming our values—assuming, of course, that we can agree on what those values are.

# CHAPTER 3

# The Crisis of Values

Of all the dispositions and habits which lead to political prosperity, Religion and morality are indispensable supports.

—George Washington[1]

A people's religion, their faith, creates their culture, and their culture creates their civilization. And when faith dies, the culture dies, the civilization dies, and the people begin to die. Is this not the recent history of the West?

—Pat Buchanan[2]

Family structure has come apart all over the North Atlantic world....Something that was not imaginable 40 years ago has happened.

—Daniel Patrick Moynihan[3]

If the family unit is allowed to fade into eclipse, it may well prove fatal to our civilization.

—Michael Novak[4]

With few exceptions, every aspect of American life is in decline. "Decay" is the word.

—Dennis Prager[5]

Joseph Backholm, director of the Family Policy Institute of Washington, is, by his own description, "a five foot nine white guy." One day in 2016, he decided to conduct an experiment on the campus of the University of Washington, in Seattle. With a videographer, he asked random students a series of questions. He found unanimity among them on the obscure question that has been made into a national obsession: Should transgender people have access to bathrooms of their choice? Of course they should, the students agreed. Backholm moved on to other topics for consideration.

"If I told you I was a woman," he asked, "what would your response be?"

One woman replied, "Good for you, okay. Like…yeah."

A male student: "Nice to meet you."

Another: "I don't have a problem with it."

Then Backholm asked how they would react if he told them he was Chinese.

"I mean, I might be a little surprised," one said, "but I would say, good for you! Like, yeah, be who you are."

"I would have a lot of questions, just because, on the outside, I would assume that you're a white man," one student allowed.

What if, Backholm asked, he told them that he was seven years old?

"I wouldn't believe that immediately," one said.

"If you feel seven at heart, then so be it, good for you," another responded.

Should he then be allowed to enroll in a first-grade class?

"If that's where you feel like, mentally, you should be, then I feel like, there are communities that would accept you for that."

"I would say so long as you're not hindering society, and you're not causing harms to other people, I feel like that should be an okay thing."

How about if he told them that he was six foot five?

"That I would question," one student allowed, laughing. "Why?" Backholm asked. "Because you're not!" she said. But this level of skepticism was rare.

"If you truly believe you're six foot five, I don't think that's harmful, I think that's fine if you believe that," one said. Another: "I feel like that's not my place, as, like, another human, to say someone is wrong or to draw lines or boundaries."

Could he then be a Chinese woman? Backholm asked.

"Sure."

But not a six-foot-five Chinese woman?

"Yes."

Backholm's video, which was popular on the Internet in 2016, was certainly funny—a bit like those man-on-the-street interviews Jay Leno used to do, in which he would ask passersby rudimentary questions about news events or American history and get the most astounding replies. But the video was also deeply disturbing.

As Backholm put it, "It shouldn't be hard to tell a five foot nine white guy that he's not a six foot five Chinese woman. But clearly, it is. Why? What does that say about our culture? And what does that say about our ability to answer the questions that actually are difficult?"[6]

The answers aren't encouraging. What the Backholm video illustrates is how deep-seated a culture of moral relativism—extending even to basic questions of objective reality—has become among millions of Americans, especially among the younger generation. At its root, what the video reveals is a crisis of meaning and judgment and, above all, a crisis of values. If such thinking and behavior were confined to college campuses and millennials, it would be troubling enough—but it isn't.

On the contrary, the crisis of values is a national issue. And don't take it from us: Americans broadly believe this themselves. Survey after survey shows that Americans feel the country is in trouble in terms of morals and ethics, and they worry the future will be worse. A 2016 Gallup poll examining Americans' views of the nation's moral well-being found that most (73 percent) felt that moral values were "getting worse," while only 20 percent felt that they were "getting better."[7] Since Gallup began tracking this question in 2002, large majorities have answered this way.[8]

What many of these Americans sense, even if only vaguely, is that the country is retreating from its long-held moral foundations that helped forge the country. Though we are a secular republic with no state religion, we are also a nation whose social and economic cohesion was grounded in and enhanced by twin bedrocks: the ethical teachings of the Judeo-Christian tradition and the social norms imposed and reinforced by the bourgeois, two-parent family. Now we are seeing a wholesale retreat from and denigration of both of these bedrocks, in our schools, institutions, and popular culture—at precisely the time that, at home, our social fabric is fraying and, overseas, we face an existential threat from an enemy professing the very antithesis of these values.

It might be easier for skeptics to dismiss these concerns if the social indicators weren't so dire. How bad is it? Today, 40 percent of *all* births in the United States are out of wedlock. Among certain demographic groups, it's much higher: 50 percent for Hispanics, 70 percent for blacks. The consequences for the children of out-of-wedlock, non-intact families are grim. Their educational attainment lags behind kids from intact families; they are far less likely to go beyond high school; their job prospects are much narrower, their earnings much less; and they are far more likely to become involved with the criminal justice system. Decades of social science research confirms these outcomes—and liberals and conservatives no longer argue about this point.

And yet, in an increasingly post-religious country, one that has for several decades retreated from training the young with the philosophical, theological, and ethical underpinnings of making moral judgments, we have no anchor to root us. As Pat Buchanan puts it, "Secularism seems to have no answer to the question, 'Why not?'"[9]

Our complete abandonment of moral instruction for the young has produced two generations of people, like those who spoke to Backholm, so uncomfortable with making judgments that they won't even tell someone that up is not down, that short is not tall. In a 2015 *New York Times* op-ed, Justin P. McBrayer, a philosophy professor at Fort Lewis College in Colorado, wrote with dismay, "Our public schools teach students that all claims are either facts or opinions and that all value and moral claims fall into the latter camp. The punchline: there are no moral facts. And if there are no moral facts, then there are no moral truths."[10] How will young people so disabled morally be able to make the fundamental distinctions required for leadership and moral judgment? Would they be comfortable telling Adolf Hitler—as they were not comfortable telling Joseph Backholm—that he was wrong about what he believed? Indeed, Dennis Prager suggests, the answer to that question is no. "Since the Nazis thought killing Jews was right, there is no way to know for sure whether it was wrong; it's the Nazis' opinion against that of the Jews and anyone else who objects," he writes. "I have heard this sentiment from American high-school students—including many Jewish ones—for 30 years."[11]

A people uncomfortable with making ethical judgments is a people ill-equipped to tackle the fundamental values issues facing the United States: family breakdown, the proper education and training of children, the duties we hold to our neighbors and country, the nature of our country's commitments in the world. In the political season just past, we saw and heard furious arguments about the major policy issues of the day— about the border with Mexico, about immigration policy, about jobs and the economy, about foreign policy and terrorism, about race relations.

But as those Gallup surveys show, Americans, as troubled as they are by these questions, are also haunted by a deeper, more nagging sense that we won't solve *any* of our most pressing public policy challenges until we first begin to reclaim our moral and ethical bearings. And to do that, we must first grapple with the undeniable decline of religious faith.

## AMERICA UNCHURCHED: THE DRAMATIC DECLINE OF RELIGION

The numbers in recent years suggest an unambiguous decline of religious faith and practice in the United States, across all regions and demographic groups. A 2015 Pew survey reported an eight-point drop in the percentage of adult Americans describing themselves as Christians—from 79 percent to 71 percent in just seven years. The same trends are seen among whites, blacks, and Latinos as well as college grads, those with only a high school education, and across gender lines.[12] Meantime, over the same period, the percentage of Americans who describe themselves as religiously unaffiliated (atheist, agnostic, or "nothing in particular") went up six points, from 16 percent to nearly 23 percent.[13] White Americans reporting themselves as having no religion reached 24 percent; for Hispanic Americans, that figure reached 20 percent; for blacks, 18 percent.[14]

The most dramatic disparity is found along generational lines. More than one-third of both 18- to 24-year-olds and 25- to 33-year-olds describe themselves as religiously unaffiliated—and fewer than 60 percent of millennials identify with *any* branch of Christianity, compared with more than 70 percent among older generations.[15]

It's true that more Christians live in the United States than anywhere else in the world and that 70 percent of Americans still identify with some branch of Christianity. But *the share* of Americans who identify with Christianity is dropping rapidly—mostly owing to declines among mainline Protestants and Catholics. The percentage of Americans affiliating themselves with non-Christian faiths has risen from 4.7 percent in 2007 to 5.9 percent in 2014.[16] And the share of American adults saying that they believe in God is down, from 92 percent to 89 percent.[17]

The decline in religious faith and practice has surely had something to do with what people of faith tend to call a "war on religion"—the increasingly hostile attitude toward *any* exercise of religion in the public sphere. "More and more Christians feel estranged from mainstream culture," David Brooks wrote in 2015. "They fear they will soon be treated as social pariahs, the moral equivalent of segregationists because of their adherence to scriptural teaching on gay marriage. They fear their colleges will be decertified, their religious institutions will lose their tax-exempt status, their religious liberty will come under greater assault."[18]

They have reason to fear. For many, the war on religion was best dramatized by the fate of Mozilla CEO Brendan Eich, who opposed gay marriage and privately supported political efforts to preserve traditional marriage. When these efforts were discovered, the Mozilla board, under heavy pressure from gay advocates, ousted him.

For decades now, American public schools have blanched at any overt mention of Christianity, even if only in textbook format, while increasingly seeking to accommodate Muslim students. One textbook for elementary school children read, "When the Pilgrims reached America, they said, 'Thank goodness!'"[19]

Most Americans are familiar with some of these stories by now. A good example was the striking from the school calendar of Christmas and Easter (along with Yom Kippur and Rosh Hashanah) holidays in Montgomery County, Virginia, public schools. The school board's decision came in response to the Muslim community's request to give equal treatment to Eid al-Adha, an Islamic holy day. Though the students would still get the Christian and Jewish days off, they wouldn't be referred to as such.[20]

"The disapproval and hostility that Christian students have come to experience in our nation's public schools has become epidemic," says Robert Tyler, general counsel for Advocates for Faith and Freedom, which reports increased incidents of bullying of Christian students by school teachers and officials.[21]

And it isn't just Christian students being bullied. In the Seattle area, Bremerton High School assistant football coach Joe Kennedy was suspended by the school district for praying after games at midfield with players—that is, with players who wished to join. No one was forced. The district warned him that he couldn't resume working, and could lose his job, unless he agreed to stop the practice.

Kennedy's lawyers put their case succinctly and eloquently, with a commonsense view that millions of Americans share: the First

Amendment "protects religious activity that is initiated by individuals acting privately, as is the case with Coach Kennedy. No reasonable observer could conclude that a football coach who waits until the game is over and the players have left the field and then walks to midfield to say a short, private, personal prayer is speaking on behalf of the state."[22]

Examples abound across all sectors of American society. During the 2013 government shutdown, Catholic priests were warned that they could be arrested for celebrating Mass at some military bases. While the military looked for alternative funding for other events—like sporting events—no effort was made to find a solution to ensure Sunday Mass could be held.[23] In June 2010, police in Dearborn, Michigan, arrested three Christian missionaries and charged them with disturbing the peace for discussing their religion on a public sidewalk outside the annual Arab festival.[24]

The school superintendent in Marlboro, New Hampshire, ordered the local American Legion Post not to advertise the town's Christmas tree lighting as such—instead, it had to be billed as the "holiday tree lighting." The head of the Legion, John Fletcher, wrote the following in a letter to the *Sentinel Source*, the paper of record there: "As commander of the American Legion it offends me. I respect all rights; always have. But do not take away our rights because you may offend someone else." Fletcher continued, "In this case, this political correctness has gone too far."[25]

Perhaps the single most disturbing example in recent years concerns Kelvin Cochran, who became Shreveport, Louisiana's first black fire chief in 1999, the fire chief of Atlanta in 2008, and, in 2009, President Obama's U.S. fire administrator—the nation's top firefighter. In 2010, Cochran returned to his position in Atlanta. Four years later, though, Cochran was suspended for 30 days without pay, pending an investigation into his behavior. Upon completing his suspension on January 6, 2014, Atlanta's mayor, Kasim Reed, fired Cochran. The city alleged that it had fired Cochran because he had not gotten the mayor's permission to publish a book, as the city's ethics code dictates.

Cochran's book concerned the lessons that he had learned in Bible classes and "explains how the teachings of Christ can help men fulfill their purpose as responsible husbands and fathers." Cochran serves as a deacon and leads a men's Bible study at Atlanta's Elizabeth Baptist Church. He wrote about the work he had done helping black men lead principled lives and avoid the criminal justice system. He also included reflections on his traditional views of marriage; he argued against same-sex marriage rights and described homosexuality as "a perversion."

Mayor Kasim Reed's statements seem to suggest that the city's claim that it fired Cochran over a protocol violation is a cover story: "I want to be clear that the material in Chief Cochran's book is not representative of my personal beliefs, and is inconsistent with the administration's work to make Atlanta a more welcoming city for all of her citizens—regardless of their sexual orientation, gender, race and religious beliefs," the mayor said. He was echoed by city council member Alex Wan, who is openly gay. "I respect each individual's right to have their own thoughts, beliefs and opinions," Wan said. But then he said, "When you're a city employee, and those thoughts, beliefs and opinions are different from the city's, you have to check them at the door." If Cochran was indeed fired for holding views with which the mayor disagrees, then, as Jason Riley wrote in the *Wall Street Journal*, "the Constitution's protections of free speech and freedom of religion are meaningless in practice."[26]

Thus, in the United States today, we have twin forces reinforcing one another: the decline of religious belief and practice and the growing momentum (and success) among public officials in shutting down public expressions of religious belief or worship.

No single factor is responsible for American society reaching this position regarding religion, especially in regard to Christianity—indeed, one might argue that the real decline in religion in the United States is specifically a decline of Christianity. The decline in religiosity is almost entirely a Christian phenomenon, and the public hostility to religious expressions is also almost entirely directed against acts of Christian worship. By contrast, efforts by Muslims to get greater acknowledgment of their faith in public settings have proved quite successful—likely because opposition to such efforts usually result in accusations of bigotry, whereas opposing Christian faith runs no such risks. Indeed, many Christian Americans felt that this double standard extended to the White House, where President Obama was always quick to sing Islam's praises and warn about anti-Islamic bigotry while saying little in defense of his own professed Christian faith.

Certainly one can point to multiple factors. American society has always had a strong individualistic component, but we live now in age in which individualism has extended into areas—witness the recent phenomenon of the concept of gender *identity*—never dreamed of by previous generations. America has always been a society that looked forward and that questioned established social hierarchies; we were founded in a rebellion against a king, and as early as the 1830s, the sharpest early observer of American society, Alexis de Tocqueville, remarked on how essentially classless American society was. Americans have always had a contested relationship with institutions—skepticism about government is a national tendency—but we've never been this skeptical, even cynical, about institutions, very much including organized religion. And America has always been a technological, consumer-oriented, secular, and futuristic society—but we've never had such capacity to shape our personal realities and carve out our own personal identities that technological tools now provide.

These trends aren't likely to reverse themselves—especially when one considers that the young are leading the charge away from the church door. A full one-third of 18- to 24-year olds prefer "no religion," according to the General Social Survey. Just 17 percent of American Catholics today are under the age of 30.[27] The millennials and the generation behind them are coming of age in a culture where unprecedented secularism and valorization of personal "choice"—regardless of merit—are the ultimate values.

This is not to imply, though, that Americans are wholly serene about this state of affairs. Surveys in recent years make clear that older Americans especially, but also those younger, are deeply concerned. According to Pew, in 2002, 52 percent of Americans believed that religion was losing influence in American life; by 2014, that figure had reached 72 percent.[28] And 56 percent said that this was a negative development, while just 12 percent saw it as a positive.[29] In a 2014 Gallup poll, 75 percent of respondents said that America would be better off if more people were religious.[30] And as recently as last year, 53 percent of Americans said religion was very important to their lives.[31]

Moreover, most Americans continue to support prayer in schools—*Republicans and Democrats.* A 2014 Gallup survey found that 61 percent of Americans supported "allowing daily prayer to be spoken in the classroom" (granted, that figure has been dropping). And 77 percent said that public schools should make facilities available for student religious groups to use after school.[32] Not surprisingly, Republicans favor these things more than Democrats—by 80 percent to 64 percent.[33] But how many readers of this book would have guessed that nearly two-thirds of Democrats support school prayer?

More vitally, why do so many Americans, even if they lack religious faith themselves, rue the loss of religiosity, or at least the influence of religion, in American life? Why is religion important—and what are we losing by giving it up?

## THE CASE FOR RELIGION, MORAL AND PRACTICAL

"Of all the dispositions and habits which lead to political prosperity, Religion and morality are indispensable supports," George Washington reminded his countrymen in his Farewell Address.[34] How vital religion remains to our society can be seen in both a practical and moral sense. Extensive empirical evidence makes clear that religion brings positive, measurable benefits to people's lives—from improved health and longevity to lower rates of divorce, substance abuse, and suicide. The marriage rates and marriage happiness of couples who attend church are higher than those who don't; children who grow up in churchgoing families are less likely to divorce. Church attendance has even been linked to higher levels of educational attainment for low-income children.[35]

Regular church attendance reduces the likelihood that a woman will suffer domestic violence by half.[36] Nearly three-quarters of prison chaplains said that they considered religious counseling and related programs to be "absolutely critical" to successful rehabilitation of inmates—both before release and afterward.[37]

In fathers, religiosity has been closely tied to better relationships with children, greater commitment to stay involved in their children's lives, and a higher likelihood of providing nonfinancial support to children and grandchildren. Religious mothers reported stronger relationships with their children as well.[38]

Young people who consider religion important in their lives and attend church regularly were less likely to cohabitate with a sexual partner.[39] Not cohabitating reduces the chances that these people will have children outside of marriage, or become divorced, for that matter, if they do marry, since studies show that the divorce rate for couples who cohabited before marriage is 33 percent higher than for couples who waited until after marriage to live together.[40]

A 2010 study in the medical journal *Liver Transplantation* found that having faith in God helped patients live longer. Patients with "high religious coping" who actively sought "God's help" and trusted their beliefs had a "more prolonged post-transplant survival than patients with low religiosity," Dr. Franco Bonaguidi said. "We found that an active search for God, (where) the patient's faith in a higher power rather than a generic destiny, had a positive impact on patient survival," he said.[41]

Studies have also found that religious people are more charitable. A 2013 study of over 4,000 American households finds that among Americans who say they are religiously affiliated, 65 percent give to charity, as compared with 56 percent of those who do not identify with a religion and make charitable gifts. Less than half of those who don't attend religious services report that they support any charity.[42]

These are all encouraging indicators and help to make a utilitarian case for religious faith—but the case for religious revival has moral considerations as well. Two scholars who have pointed the way eloquently are Michael Novak and Irving Kristol.

Novak has long argued that the Judeo-Christian tradition has provided the moral and ethical foundations for modern democracy, particularly through three key premises: that each person, as an image of God, has inherent dignity; that all human beings are equal in the sight of God; and that human freedom and liberty are central to God's purposes in creating human life.[43]

"Judaism and Christianity correct and strengthen morals and manners," Novak writes. "While the laws of a free society allow a person to do almost anything, there are many things which religion prevents him from imagining or doing."[44] It is precisely this normative guide to behavior, so integral to religion, that we are losing.

Christianity, Novak writes, also forms the bedrock of our secular success—namely, in undergirding capitalism, which, contrary to its popular image as being antithetical to Christianity, has relied upon it. No institution did more than the church, Novak argues, to put into place the fundamental prerequisites for capitalism: "the rule of law and a bureaucracy for resolving disputes rationally; a specialized and mobile labor force; the institutional permanence that allows for transgenerational investment and sustained intellectual and physical efforts, together with the accumulation of long-term capital; and a zest for discovery, enterprise, wealth creation, and new undertakings."[45]

Moreover, Novak argues, religious faith—specifically, the belief in the immortality of the soul—"prods men to aspire upwards, and to aim for further moral progress along the line of their own dignity and self-government."[46] Can anyone looking at American popular culture today see a society determined to "aspire upwards"?

For Irving Kristol, the argument is more practical but no less essential. Unlike Novak, who studied for the Catholic priesthood, Kristol, raised Jewish, wrote powerfully about the necessity of religion less as a believer himself than as a thinker who saw that purely secular liberalism was not substantive enough to ground a culture and civilization. "There was something in me that made it impossible to become anti-religious, or even non-religious," Kristol wrote in his memoirs.[47] He came to see religion as the foundation of moral knowledge, as well as a safeguard against the most destructive utopian and ideological impulses.[48] Without the anchoring of religion, Kristol believed, people would be drawn deeper and deeper into individualism—and inevitably into discontent, since unbridled individualism without a transcendent moral basis can only lead to nihilism and despair. With nowhere else to look for satisfaction, people would look more and more to the state to satisfy their demands— for recognition, for restitution, for subsistence.[49]

"All human societies," Kristol wrote in 1968, "have to respond to two fundamental questions. The first is: 'Why?' The second is: 'Why not?' . . . It is religion that, traditionally, has supplied the answers to these questions. In our ever more secularized society, it is still religion that has supplied the answer to the second." But "on an ever-larger scale, 'why not' is ceasing to be a question. . . . It is becoming a kind of answer."[50]

Finally, and more recently, consider the reflections of University of Massachusetts professor Guenter Lewy, a nonbeliever who has concluded that the maintenance of a moral order in America depends on the survival of traditional religion. Lewy defined himself as a secular humanist before writing *Why America Needs Religion* and now says he's a non-theist. In his examination of social science research, Lewy finds that negative social indicators ranging from juvenile delinquency and adult crime to prejudice, divorce, and single parenting are lower among those Christians who take religion seriously. Lewy concludes that "it may be that worship and the feeling of being loved by God indeed produce definite changes in a person's behavior."[51] But by now, a culture deeply devoted to individualism has weakened our commitments to more traditional virtues such as civic responsibility, community involvement, and family.[52]

The loss of religion has broader impacts, too—broader even than personal well-being and cultural vigor. What about the survival of our civilization itself? In most Western countries, birth rates have been declining for decades, and in most European countries, births are below replacement rates. Europe as we know it is essentially dying out. With its near open-borders policy and the influx of migrants from the Middle East, Africa, and Asia—a portion of them radical Islamists determined to perpetrate attacks or pursue Sharia law, or both—Europe by now faces a crisis of cultural survival.

The situation is not as dire in the United States, but our birth rates are dropping, too: the fertility rate in the United States fell to a record-low 62.5 births per 1,000 women in 2015.[53] In a growing number of states, deaths outnumber births—an incredible statistic.[54] Many factors have gone into this, but one of them is certainly the loss of religion. "A people's religion, their faith, creates their culture, and their culture creates their civilization," Pat Buchanan has written. "And when faith dies, the culture dies, the civilization dies, and the people begin to die. Is this not the recent history of the West?"[55] By death, Buchanan is referring not just to the loss of cultural cohesion but also to the declining birth rates in most Western democratic countries.

Some argue that we can replace traditional religious values with more modern, secular morality. But the returns on secularism and nonreligious, "spiritual" practices haven't proved satisfying. Why not? Perhaps because they don't provide any answers for what remain the central questions of life. What is the best way to live? Why are we here? What is the meaning of suffering? What is right and what is wrong? Somehow, recycling just doesn't cut it. Nor does "tolerance," often advanced as a transcendent value system that can substitute for theism. Not only is it maddeningly unspecific and undirected—Tolerate everything? Everyone? Under what conditions?—but also, at its best, it is merely one virtue. It would be like asking someone what the meaning life is and having them answer, "temperance," or "patience," or "humility"—to name some of the old-fashioned cardinal virtues. These are important virtues, but they are merely pieces of a much larger puzzle. And "self-esteem" is similar. Should we all feel self-esteem? Doesn't self-esteem have to be earned? And for what behaviors, what virtues, would it be justified?

The soft-headedness of virtues like "tolerance" become clear when we consider things like the YouTube video described at the outset of this chapter. It stands as a comical but also chilling example of how a moral relativism leads to moral paralysis, a complete inability to make even the most rudimentary judgments. Dostoevsky once said, "If there is no God, everything is permitted." Looking around the United States today, one senses what he meant.

## THE BREAKDOWN OF THE FAMILY

Citing Census Bureau figures, the *New York Times* reported on a startling new social reality in 2011: for the first time, married couples had dropped below half of the percentage of all American households. The trend represented "a milestone in the evolution of the American family toward less traditional forms," the *Times* opined.[56]

Here's a blunter way of describing it: the American family is falling apart.

Almost half of *all* American children are now born to unmarried mothers. More than 40 percent of kids live without fathers in the home. Barely 50 percent of adult Americans are married today; in 1960, that figure stood at 72 percent.[57]

As the figures make clear, the structure of the American family has dramatically eroded—and the erosion runs across racial groups. This is a problem most often associated with the underclass, especially in the black community, with its high out-of-wedlock rates and endemic fatherlessness. Yet the problem extends to whites, too: 25 percent of whites now grow up in single-parent homes.[58] The result is an erosion of social cohesion, spiraling criminal and drug subcultures, and a bleak forecast for the future.

At the root of the collapse is the decline of marriage. According to "When Marriage Disappears," an important 2010 report from the National Marriage Project, the annual number of marriages per 1,000 unmarried adult women has declined by more than 50 percent from 1970 to 2009.[59] Several factors account for this massive drop, from delaying first marriages to a major increase in unmarried cohabitation and declining frequency of divorced people remarrying. Moreover, in every generation for which records exist—back to the mid-1800s—more than 90 percent of women eventually marry. In 1960, 94 percent of women had been married at least once by age 45, and this was probably a historical high point. Relying on data from 1990, and assuming a continuation of then-current marriage rates, several demographers projected that only 88 percent of women and 82 percent of men would marry. If and when these figures are recalculated for the early twenty-first century, the percentages will almost certainly be lower.[60]

These declines correspond with an increase in unmarried cohabitation. "Most people now live together before they marry," the report says, and more and more adults live together with no plans *ever* to marry. Furthermore, while some have argued that fewer marriages might lead to better ones—on the suggestion that those who really want to be married will be happier—the data show no measurable uptick in happy marriages.

Declines in marriage correspond with increases in nonmarital childbearing, rising divorce, single-parent households, and cohabitation. And these trends are more exacerbated along class lines: in fact, today, "highly educated America is now both more marriage-minded and religious than is moderately educated America."[61] This marriage gap correlates with a clear, expanding social and economic divide. Among middle Americans—whom the report defines as those with high school diplomas but not four-year college degrees, a demographic constituting 58 percent of the U.S. population—both nonmarital childbearing and divorce are rising, and marital happiness is falling. Marriage, long a stabilizing institution that glued the middle class together and provided a crucial stepping stone into the middle class for those from more modest backgrounds, has lost its appeal among people who need its mediating, foundational influence most.

The remarkable thing, in the context of all these numbers, is that the benefits of marriage have been tested and confirmed again and again. Try out this statistic: children growing up in married homes see their odds of falling into poverty drop by 82 percent. And yet, even as the past two decades have seen greatly encouraging declines in teen pregnancy—once the focus of the out-of-wedlock issue—unmarried births among twentysomethings are on the rise. "If 30 is the new 20, today's unmarried 20-somethings are the new teen moms," declared a 2013 op-ed in the *Wall Street Journal*. "And the tragic consequences are much the same: children raised in homes that often put them at an enormous disadvantage from the very start of life."[62]

Indeed, no group is more affected by this decline than children. In 1960, just 5 percent of American children were born outside of marriage; today, 41 percent of all American children are born to unmarried mothers.[63] The impact of marriage breakdown on children has been blunt and unambiguous. Elementary school children from non-intact families score lower on math and reading comprehension skills; they get lower grades overall. Teenagers from broken homes cut classes, are late for school, or simply don't show up for school more often than students from two-parent families.[64] Children of divorce are twice as likely to drop out of high school.[65]

Beyond high school, it doesn't get better. Single-parented kids are more likely to be unemployed than children from intact families[66]—and to wind up in the welfare system, almost all of which is devoted to the care of children from non-intact families. In 2011, when federal and state governments spent over $450 billion on means-tested welfare benefits for low-income families with children, about three-quarters of this assistance went to single-parent families.[67] More than 75 percent of women in the United States who give birth to children out of wedlock will go on welfare within five years—and the daughters of these women are three times more likely to go on the rolls themselves within three years of giving birth themselves.[68] Children from single-parent homes are 50 percent more likely to live in poverty than children from intact homes.[69] Finally, children from broken homes are more likely to wind up in jail by the age of 30.[70]

University of Virginia professor Brad Wilcox, director of the National Marriage Project, sketches a bleak future if these trends continue:

> It could be the case that we're going to just see the inexorable decline of the two-parent marriage families as the central feature of American family life. And that may happen. And if it does happen, I can guarantee

you more inequality; I can guarantee you a society where demagogues are more likely to pray [*sic*] on the American public, where people are more likely to depend upon support from federal, state and local governments when the going gets tough, and any number of other things. So that may be the future that faces us.[71]

*May be*, he allows. But that's an unacceptable future, one that we must resist with all of our energies. Can anyone seriously question that America needs a moral revival?

## IS THERE ANY WAY TO TURN THIS AROUND?

It's easy enough to believe that massive social changes like this are intractable, that they cannot be reversed. And it's true that many great changes in history, like the advent of the industrial age or mass urbanization, never reversed themselves. We didn't go back to a premodern world; we didn't retreat from technological progress. On the social front, however, things don't tend to be as cut-and-dried. Only a few decades ago, for example, many observers felt the same sense of futility about reversing trends in teen pregnancy; that negative social indicator has been cut in half over the last 20 years or so, in part through a broad-based, ongoing campaign to discourage it. Something similar could be done—with the participation of government, civic and cultural institutions, and schools— to address some of today's crisis of values. We could, for instance, work to reconnect marriage with parenthood in the public mind. We could take other steps to support family formation, including embracing principles and values often rooted in religion. But to do so, we must overcome our squeamishness in talking about values.

When coauthor Schoen worked in the Clinton White House, he found consistently that when the administration campaigned on values, people responded. Though President Clinton was often mocked for some of these initiatives—like his advocacy of the V-chip for televisions to allow parents to block objectionable content—his appeals got through to people who worried that American culture had gone off the rails. It's striking how rarely today politicians make overt pitches to values—with the exception of the value of tolerance. We believe that such appeals would be much more popular than is commonly assumed. They should appeal to traditional American virtues that our popular culture often degrades or ignores, such as loyalty, honor, honesty, philanthropy—as well as more contentious ones, like sexual restraint, delayed childbearing until marriage, and delayed gratification generally as part of a broader emphasis on personal responsibility.

And these appeals should willingly embrace religion. We should be unafraid to acknowledge that religion and other traditional values bring positive benefits to people's lives and to communities. We need a re-moralization of our national dialogue, one that emphasizes traditional virtues and reconnects with a heritage of robust moral and ethical principles—a heritage inseparable from religious faith.

Such proposals might prove less controversial than many think. Surprisingly, 57 percent of Americans say that religion can solve today's problems, which suggests an opening for religious institutions to play a greater role.[72] And religious leaders remain confident that they can combat generational trends that are moving against religion, given that 67 percent of Americans consider themselves moderately (27 percent) or very (40 percent) religious.[73] Indeed, Pew finds that "among the roughly three-quarters of U.S. adults who do claim a religion, there has been no discernible drop in most measures of religious commitment. Indeed, by some conventional measures, religiously affiliated Americans are, on average, even more devout than they were a few years ago."[74]

The main cause of the religious decline, in numerical terms, is the drop-off in faith among millennials. It follows that religious institutions need to rebuild credibility with the young, but even in light of this, there remains an enormous segment receptive to religious leadership on modern issues. But churches must modernize: take to social media and technology, put young people in leadership roles, and make religion more accessible.

Our campuses and universities could certainly do more to foster more spiritually uplifting environments. No doubt, in today's ultra-competitive world, they will remain heavily focused on careerism and professional attainments, but we should also insist that they reintroduce moral and spiritual education. At a minimum, colleges and universities should be called out for their betrayal of their mission to educate students, instead focusing overwhelmingly on politically correct, specious disciplines—to say nothing of their appalling violation of free speech and interchange on campus, in the name of creating "safe" environments. Between the political correctness and the soulless careerism, college life can be terribly demoralizing for the young, who should be working, as David Brooks writes, toward "developing criteria to determine which vocation would lead to the fullest life."[75]

Campus groups will have even more to build on in coming years if our public schools would develop morality-focused components to their curriculum. While respecting the barriers between church and state, morals- and values-based teaching in the public schools could add great value and include religious content, not in a doctrinal sense but as a primary component of ethics. We should also fund further exploration of the effect of religion on educational outcomes in the lives of "at-risk" students and their families. Chances are the outcome will verify what Guenter Lewy found: the most successful students tend to be raised in environments where traditional religion maintains a strong influence.[76]

Religion also has a crucial role to play in encouraging marriage and bolstering families. Traditionally, churches and synagogues have always been critical in providing a spiritual foundation and community support for couples and families. The decline of organized religious practice in the United States obviously presents challenges to that role. But if religion is to revive itself among the coming generation of Americans, its role in consecrating and supporting marriage will be central.

Thinking about the family more broadly, it's clear to us that we need to get back to making normative arguments and to lose the pervasive cultural reluctance to be seen as "judgmental." When it comes to the intact, two-parent family, the benefits of which are unambiguously confirmed by mountains of social science data, we need to advocate for it, in public, without ambivalence. We agree strongly here with Brad Wilcox and his coauthors from the American Enterprise Institute and the Institute for Family Studies, who, in a 2015 report, argued for ongoing public-service ad campaigns to educate and persuade young adults—especially from lower-middle-class and working-class homes—to delay childbearing until marriage. "Marriage first, childbearing second" should be the message. These ads could also stress "the success sequence"—a phrase originated by Brookings Institution scholars Ron Haskins and Isabel Sawhill—that urges young people to pursue "education, work, marriage, and parenthood in that order."[77]

On a more specific level, as Wilcox suggests, more supportive family policies should be adopted, such as eliminating the marriage penalty that currently exists in many social programs targeted to lower-income people. In addition, we should expand the Earned Income Tax Credit, increase the Child Tax Credit, and support proven vocational education and apprenticeship programs, especially for lower- and middle-income men, to encourage them to become steady wage earners and providers.[78]

Michael Novak has been eloquent for decades on subjects including the family and faith. He has written more recently about the essential "human capital" that families cultivate. Whether it's sons and daughters learning a family business from their parents or children getting exposed to classical music because their parents take them to performances, the family stands as the essential social institution. Looking at the more traditional notion of capital—that is, financial—Novak argues for a new reform that he calls "universal family capital," which would consist of "accumulating capital packages for every single family in the nation (and eventually universally)."[79]

The twentieth century focused on the idea of redistributing income through the government to individuals; in the twenty-first century, he suggests, we should "aim at shaping a regime of universal family *capital*." The government could do this by requiring citizens to invest a certain portion of their income in personal savings accounts devoted to retirement and health care expenses. The reform, as Novak envisions it, would eventually replace much of Social Security and Medicare, or at least greatly reduce their bureaucracies, since this family capital would be privately owned and invested. "If it is correct that a major reason for the weakening of the family in recent generations is the expropriation of many of its key functions by the state," Novak concludes, "then a regime of universal family capital would be a major step in the direction of the reappropriation by the family of its own proper powers and responsibilities."[80]

These and other worthy ideas for family support and reformation should be seriously considered, adjusted and refined where necessary, and then aggressively and wholeheartedly adopted. But we also agree with Peter Wehner that, in the end, before good policies can make a difference in what will probably be a generational social struggle, we must first have a change of heart and a reorientation of values. Wehner writes,

A marriage culture will be rebuilt one person at a time, through finding greater fulfillment in self-giving, elevating our affections and desires, and loving others as we love ourselves. None of us does this very well, and all of us could do it much better than we do. Yet for all the moral failures that can be laid at the feet of religion and those acting on its behalf, there is nothing in human history that has helped people improve their character and refine their loves more than faith.[81]

At any rate, the stakes are clear. The loss of a common value system, one crucially guided by religious principles and most tangibly reflected in the institutions of family life, has set American culture into a dangerous and unmoored wilderness, with social costs already apparent. No social cost is graver than the price enacted on the American family, and especially on children. The protection and strengthening of the family unit remains central to our survival. "If the family unit is allowed to fade into eclipse," Novak writes, "it may well prove fatal to our civilization."[82]

# CHAPTER 4

# Poverty and the Underclass

Our aim is not only to relieve the symptoms of poverty, but to cure it and, above all, to prevent it.

—Lyndon B. Johnson[1]

Today, I fear we're facing a crisis in which a chunk of working-class America risks being calcified into an underclass, marked by drugs, despair, family decline, high incarceration rates and a diminishing role of jobs and education as escalators of upward mobility....I fear that liberals are too quick to think of inequality as basically about taxes...but poverty is so much deeper and more complex than that.

—Nicholas Kristof[2]

Our children don't need us to be superheroes, they don't need us to be perfect, they need us to be present. I think it's time for a new conversation about fatherhood in this country.

—President Barack Obama[3]

By 9 pm on April 27, 2015, the pitch-black sky over Baltimore was filled with smoke. Helicopters circled the city, projecting beams of light onto what looked like a movie scene. Police hid behind riot shields, threw tear gas canisters, and fired pepper balls at hundreds of black Baltimoreans. Parked cars were set ablaze. Dozens of storefronts were smashed. A CVS pharmacy was set on fire and the firefighters' hoses were cut. Violence and looting consumed the city.

"They aren't protesting. They aren't making a statement. They're stealing," President Obama said.[4] "They wreaked havoc," former Baltimore police commissioner Anthony Batts commented.[5] "When I was watching the TV reports, Baltimore looked more like East Jerusalem than an American city with a proud patriotic heritage," Allen West wrote.[6] By the next night, Baltimore had a 10 pm curfew. Thousands of police officers and the National Guard had arrived, marking the first time since the assassination of Martin Luther King Jr. that the Guard were called out to quell unrest. Baltimore was under siege.

The trouble began on April 18, when citizens gathered outside the police station to protest the death of Freddie Gray, a young black man who died in police custody and whose name joined others in a gallery of tragic encounters between American blacks and the police. By the time Baltimore mayor Stephanie Rawlings-Blake uttered her infamous instruction to police to give space to "those who wished to destroy," the damage to the city had already been done.[7]

Freddie Gray sustained fatal injuries to his neck and spine while being transported in a police vehicle. Though his death was the spark for awful unrest, the question of who should bear responsibility for his fate remains contested. Baltimore's prosecutor, Marilyn Mosby, brought highly criticized indictments against the six police officers involved in the incident—but three were acquitted, one case ended in a mistrial, and charges against the other two were dropped. No matter what happened inside the police van, the Gray episode became another flashpoint episode of recent years involving blacks, police, and cities.

Yet more than anything, the Baltimore riots are a story about the underclass in America. Robert Stokes, a 36-year-old Baltimore resident, told reporters as he held a dustpan on a street corner during the cleanup after the riots, "It's so much bigger than the police department. This place is a powder keg waiting to explode."[8] Baltimore was just the latest illustration of a problem that has plagued us for generations now: the problem of the underclass and poverty, especially in cities and especially among blacks.

More than half a century ago, in 1965, Daniel Patrick Moynihan sounded the warning. In an effort to understand what was happening in poor communities, especially black communities, he wrote *The Negro Family: The Case for National Action*. Moynihan examined poverty in the black community, expecting to find the problem to be mainly an economic one—as unemployment declined, he assumed, poverty would decline with it. What he found instead surprised him: in the early 1960s, while unemployment was dropping, poverty among blacks was on the rise.[9] One crucial fact jumped out: nearly 20 percent of black children were born to unmarried mothers in the early 1960s, compared with 2 to 3 percent of white children in that period.[10] Moynihan urged a new focus on the family. His warnings proved prescient; by 2009, nearly three-quarters of black births and three-tenths of white births took place outside marriage.[11]

Across the aisle from Moynihan, Republican congressman Jack Kemp, former football star and later secretary of Housing and Urban Development, had his own ideas for transforming underclass life, inspired by Abraham Lincoln's notion of entrepreneurial capitalism: "allow the humblest man an equal chance to get rich with everybody else."[12] Kemp's vision involved empowering the underclass through greater economic opportunity. His "enterprise zones," wherein tax incentives would be targeted toward impoverished areas, were a cutting-edge idea in the 1980s; more recently, President Obama borrowed the concept with his "freedom zones," which combine federal support with state and local initiatives to jumpstart growth and employment. Kemp worked tirelessly to develop fresh approaches for those isolated in struggling inner cities.

Moynihan and Kemp's ideas remain important today because they highlight, respectively, two key insights: first, the role of family breakdown in causing and perpetuating poverty; and second, the need for innovation, opportunity, and vision in uplifting the poor. What both men saw was that the solutions Washington had devised had failed. Unfortunately, a generation later, we haven't come much farther. In fact, at present, the United States has no vision and no strategy for dealing with our underclass, a problem that threatens the fabric of our society while also sentencing millions of innocent people to lives of deprivation.

As of 2013, more than 13.9 million Americans lived in neighborhoods of concentrated poverty—where the poverty rate meets or exceeds 30 percent and residents lack essential services and remain exposed to high crime.[13] The concentrated poverty rate remains highest in big cities, where Democratic policies have arguably kept many residents dependent on government assistance. In those big cities, the underclass is heavily and disproportionately minority (black and Hispanic), giving the problem a racial dimension that itself is freighted with history, most of it unhappy.[14]

In Baltimore, one-quarter of residents live below the poverty line, and

24 percent of adults and 42 percent of children receive food stamps. In Freddie Gray's neighborhood, 52 percent were unemployed between 2008 and 2012.[15] In Louisville, Kentucky, 29 percent of the population makes under $25,000 per year; that figure stands at 35 percent in Memphis, Tennessee, and approaches 50 percent in Detroit.[16]

In these troubled places and elsewhere in America where poverty is widespread, family breakdown tends to be endemic, and intergenerational cycles of underclass living are commonplace. Girls who haven't finished high school get pregnant by young men who have no intention and no ability to be fathers; the girls wind up having multiple children by different men. Their own mothers, now grandmothers, are often as young as 35 or 40 and themselves lack stable relationships. The children grow up in unstable, often violent environments, with constantly shifting adult presence, little to no educational emphasis, and poor nutrition. They come of age in violent neighborhoods.

The solutions for these complex, generational socioeconomic problems are twofold: address family breakdown among the poor and formulate policies that will spark economic opportunity and mobility. In short, we have a values crisis and a policy crisis. Without the values piece—family reformation and a new commitment to fatherhood, education, and aspirational virtues like hard work, thrift, and delayed gratification—even the best-intentioned policy won't have much effect. Yet without such policies (ideas that build on what Kemp proposed), even the most determined people will struggle in a globalized economy that makes it very difficult for low-wage workers.

Problems aren't solved with the same thinking that created them, an old adage goes. That principle is apt when it comes to the American underclass—which, in some ways, is more entrenched and more isolated than it was even in Lyndon Johnson's day.

## POVERTY: A WAR NOT WON

On the whole, Lyndon B. Johnson's War on Poverty has to be judged a failure, but that doesn't mean it didn't have some successes. Many of its original programs—namely Medicaid, Medicare, food stamps, and the Job Corps—have brought some modest improvement. A Columbia University study found that government intervention from 1967 to 2012 brought poverty down from 26 percent to 16 percent.[17] Yet even this success brings with it a troubling byproduct—increased dependency on government assistance. In 2013, the Census Bureau found that more than 100 million Americans received some sort of benefit from a means-tested federal welfare program.[18] As Michael Tanner and Charles Hughes argued in a Cato Institute report, "We may have made the lives of the poor less uncomfortable, but we have failed to truly lift people out of poverty."[19]

Indeed, much of federal poverty policy for the last half century has sought merely to manage the problem. Instead of providing people with the skills and opportunity to pull themselves out of poverty, we have developed a massive welfare system that regards a sizable portion of the American population as wards of the state.

"America is divided into two separate and unequal economies, one that works well and one that is fatally flawed and must be fixed so as to combat poverty," Jack Kemp wrote.[20] The poverty economy "denies people an entry into the mainstream due to the barriers to economic activities along with a virtual absence of any link between human effort and reward. It perpetuates poverty, dependency and welfare while discouraging employment, and it prevents access to capital, ownership of assets and quality education."[21] Without question, the incentive structure of government social programs has played a key role in the persistence of poverty—especially in an economy that struggles to provide opportunity and mobility for lower-income, low-skill workers.

But the government's role is only one piece of the poverty story. Family breakdown and cultural malaise make the picture grimmer still.

### Family Breakdown and Poverty

"At the heart of the deterioration of the Negro society is the deterioration of the Negro family," Moynihan wrote in 1965. "It is the fundamental source of weakness in the Negro community at present time."[22] It turns out that Moynihan not only had it right for the black community, he was also speaking to what would become a national phenomenon that cuts across racial groups. And while the case may be more acute for African Americans, Moynihan was correct that "the single most important determinant of poverty is family structure."[23] Fifty years on, he would be dismayed by these figures:

- In 1960, only 6 percent of white children lived in single-mother households; 20 percent of black children lived in single-mother households.[24]
- By 2013, nearly 18 percent of white children lived in single-mother households;[25] among black children, that number had climbed to 50 percent.[26]
- By 2013, 30 percent of white children were born out of wedlock;[27] approximately 72 percent of black births occurred to unwed mothers.[28]
- In 2014, some 33 percent of Hispanic children lived in single-parent households.[29]
- In 2013, 35 percent of all children—of any race—were being raised without fathers, and nearly half of them lived below the poverty line.[30]

That the family breakdown problem transcends race is evident not only in the rising number of out-of-wedlock births among whites, but also in the stories of the white underclass, which don't differ dramatically from those of the black underclass. Consider 24-year-old mother of three Desiree Metcalf, who has lived in poverty for most of her life. The woman from Bath, New York, "did not just become poor," a 2014 NPR profile asserted. "A series of misfortunes and misdirections, like so many other Americans, brought her there."[31] As a young girl, Metcalf argued so much with her mother—who threatened to kill her—that she threatened suicide and was admitted to a psychiatric ward. She eventually graduated high school and applied to college. Metcalf earned a scholarship to a Florida university but became pregnant with her first daughter and gave up the scholarship, remaining in New York to raise her daughter.

Over the next five years, Metcalf became pregnant with two more daughters—each fathered by a different man—and married still another man, who soon left her. Metcalf aspires to be a nursing assistant, for which she received government-funded training, but her circumstances—familial, financial, social—make it difficult for her to get a job. She has earned scant income from periodic odd jobs. She is reluctant to get a steady job because "they take you off public assistance, then they don't pay for day care."[32] Her day-care expenses alone would likely eat up most of her earnings.

Metcalf is a sympathetic person, and one hopes that she and millions like her can find a way to improve their circumstances. But the NPR profile made no mention of how her family upbringing—her violent and unstable mother, especially—shaped the rest of her life, especially the choices that led her to become, three times over, the mother of out-of-wedlock children, each of whom has a different absentee father. Family dynamics have shaped her life, as they do for all of us.

"The inequalities that stem from the workplace are now trivial in comparison to those stemming from family structure," wrote political scientist Lawrence Mead in the early 1990s. "What matters for success is less whether your father was rich or poor than whether you knew your father at all."[33] President Obama acknowledged this reality a number of times during his presidency, though his critics believed that he should have done so far more regularly. Still, in launching his fatherhood initiative in 2010—a fund that supports a transitional jobs program for parents having trouble finding work—Obama said, "There are too many fathers missing from too many homes, missing from too many lives. There is harm done to those kids. Our children don't need us to be superheroes, they don't need us to be perfect, they need us to be present. I think it's time for a new conversation about fatherhood in this country."[34] And in his 2015 Father's Day address Obama said, "But no matter how advanced we get, there will never be a substitute for the love and support and, most importantly, the presence of a parent in a child's life. And in many ways, that's uniquely true for fathers."[35]

Many on the left are reluctant to acknowledge this fundamental truth, in part because, among liberals, it has become taboo to pass judgment on anyone's life choices. Gay, straight, bi, transgender, single, cohabitating, living apart but raising children together, or married—it's all equal in the progressive worldview. Maybe that's true among adults—but it certainly isn't true when it comes to children. A 2015 paper by Raj Chetty and Nathaniel Hedren, both Harvard professors, found that single parenthood is one of five major factors that determines economic success in low-income areas.[36]

"Liberals, out of compassion, have gone too far in destigmatizing single motherhood.... A little bit of stigma can have broad societal benefits,"[37] *Bloomberg* columnist Francis Barry writes. Barry cites the ad campaign New York mayor Michael Bloomberg launched in the subways in 2013 that raised awareness about the link between teen poverty and youth pregnancy. One poster read, "If you finish high school, get a job, and get married before having children, you have a 98 percent chance of not being in poverty."[38] These points are as statistically solid as anything that exists in social science, yet many reacted badly to the campaign, calling it "shaming." The resistance to speaking such obvious truths illustrates the corrosive impact of political correctness.

Fortunately, not everyone is shying away from these realities. Michael Barone points out how children raised in single-parent households "do worse in school, have more trouble with the law and make less money and gain less satisfaction in life than those from the stable families of the upper third."[39] And Nick Schulz writes, "While children are born with certain innate capacities, those capacities can be broadened or narrowed by their upbringing. The numbers indicate that single or divorced parents—however caring and dedicated—are unable, on average, to broaden those capacities as much as married parents can."[40] There is much discussion today of income inequality in the United States, but from a child's perspective, no disparity is greater than the one felt by children lacking stable, loving—and, ideally, two-parent—households.

### Low Income, Dim Prospects

As crucial as the role of family is, it isn't everything. It can be hard to break out of poverty even when you do things right.

The question remains as to how to help the working poor, who struggle in ways that most of us can't imagine. This includes, as Max Ehrenfreund writes in the *Washington Post*, paying

> more for everything, from rolls of toilet paper to furniture. It's not because they're spendthrifts, either. If you're denied a checking account, there's no way for you to avoid paying a fee to cash a paycheck. If you need to buy a car to get to work, you'll have to accept whatever higher interest rate you're offered. If you don't have a car, the bus fare might eat up the change you'd save shopping at a larger grocery store as opposed to the local corner store.[41]

Economists call this dynamic the "ghetto tax." A Brookings Study found, for instance, that a TV that costs only $200 will end up costing a poor person who has to use a payment plan up to $700.[42] A big part of the problem is that 68 million Americans have either limited or no access to traditional banking services.[43] They pay more to cash checks and can't benefit from the financial planning assistance that banks offer.

Even poor people's own adaptability—usually a positive trait—can work against them, as Megan McArdle of the American Enterprise Institute pointed out. She discussed how many poor people adapt to "communal scarcity" by helping one another when they're doing well, with the expectation that the favor will be returned down the line. As a result, many miss out on opportunities—like going to college—because they're helping those close to them (with child care, for instance) or supporting them financially.[44]

It's no wonder, then, that poor children start life behind in the race and never catch up. The Southern Education Foundation reported that 51 percent of students in prekindergarten through twelfth grade in American public schools during the 2012–2013 school year were eligible for federal school lunch programs that provide subsidized or free meals—a proxy for poverty. Many public schools have had to adapt to a predominantly needy student population. Sonya Romero-Smith is a kindergarten teacher in New Mexico; 14 of her 18 students qualify for free lunches. "When they first come in my door in the morning," she told the *Washington Post*, "the first thing I do is an inventory of immediate needs: Did you eat? Are you clean? A big part of my job is making them feel safe."[45] Data from the National Assessment of Education Progress found that over 40 percent of variation in reading scores and 46 percent of variation in math scores is associated with childhood poverty rates.[46]

## DEPENDENCY AND CULTURE

While antipoverty advocates can point to real-world, external factors for the plight of the poor, the honest ones acknowledge that dependency and culture also play a major role—and nowhere is the dependency issue more pressing today than in the black community. The issue isn't just welfare and poverty programs; it's a whole range of government efforts that, arguably, have not helped blacks but set them back further. The result is that when we speak about the underclass, it is difficult to avoid talking about the problems of poor blacks.

In *Please Stop Helping Us: How Liberals Make It Harder for Blacks to Succeed,* Jason Riley rejects the fundamental programs in the liberal project to lift living standards for blacks. He argues that welfare programs have slowed the self-development needed for blacks to advance, that minimum-wage laws help those already employed to earn higher wages but price many other blacks out of the labor force, and that affirmative action has produced fewer black college graduates, particularly in the fields of math and science.

Even increased political representation has done little to advance black economic fortunes. From 1970 to 2001, the number of black elected officials in the United States grew from fewer than 1,500 to more than 9,000—that's progress, right? Yet from 1940 to 1960, before such political gains, the black poverty rate fell precipitously, from 87 percent to 47 percent; from 1970 to 2011, the rate barely budged, declining only from 32 percent to 28 percent.[47] Moreover, the 2008 economic recession and resulting stagnation hit blacks hard. In September 2011, black unemployment, at 16 percent, was double the white rate.[48] In May 2015, the national unemployment rate was 5.5 percent; the rate for blacks was 9.6 percent.[49]

Riley also highlights how the election of a black man to the presidency, while a tremendous step forward, creates a misleading impression about how blacks are faring overall. In fact, the Obama years have been hard ones for blacks economically. "The data is going to indicate, sadly, that when the Obama administration is over, black people will have lost ground in every single leading economic indicator category," said Tavis Smiley in 2013. "On that regard, the president ought to be held responsible."[50]

Hovering over this discussion is the uncomfortable but unavoidable issue of culture. Nationwide, black students lag behind whites in education, with black kids overrepresented among high school dropouts and students who fail to perform at grade level. Many explain this problem by claiming that black students have unequal access to academic resources, but Professor John Ogbu of the University of California, Berkeley, sees a different problem. He believes that the leading cause of the achievement gap between black and white students of the same socioeconomic background is culture—black culture.[51] Ogbu is the scholar who first spotlighted how many black students considered certain attitudes and behaviors—like studying diligently and speaking Standard English—to be "white." They worry that adopting such habits will alienate them from other blacks. Ogbu also found that teachers frequently passed black students not performing at grade level.[52]

Most black leaders tend to blame racism in the public education system rather than student behavior for poor outcomes; the black-white achievement gap, they say, results from "racist" standardized tests and "Eurocentric" teaching styles.[53] But they cannot explain the comparative academic success of other nonwhite students, including black immigrants. In 2007, a study published in the *American Journal of Education* found that immigrants make up more than a quarter of black students at the nation's top colleges and universities, despite accounting for just 13 percent of the population.[54]

"No matter how you reform schools, it's not going to solve the problem," Ogbu says. "There are two parts of the problem, society and schools on one hand and the black community on the other hand."[55]

One of the most troubling influences in the black community, especially among young people, is the hip-hop culture—at least, the portion of hip-hop music that glorifies violence, misogyny, and criminality. Unfortunately, this aspect of the music tends to get the most commercial attention and enjoy the most pervasive cultural impact. The music of Curtis "50 Cent" Jackson, a native of Queens, New York, is a good example. Between 2003 and 2007, he sold over 24 million albums worldwide. The rapper's accomplishments propelled him to the top of the music industry. Jackson's lyrics often describe his upbringing, especially his teenage years dealing drugs—experiences mirrored in black underclass culture throughout the country. In songs like "I Get It In," "I'll Still Kill," and "Straight to the Bank," 50 Cent offers terrible prospects for blacks, seemingly suggesting that their only opportunities lie in making money "off the street moving bundles and loads" and enjoying a measure of success by having "more whips than a runaway slave."[56] Needless to say, these songs do not encourage young black men to tackle their challenges through education, job training, and family commitment. Instead, the music of 50 Cent, and too much of hip-hop music generally, glorifies violence and amorality.

"Hip-hop is not just a style of music," writes Jeffrey Hicks of the National Leadership Network of Conservative African-Americans. "It is a culture borne [sic] of poor, inner-city life in America that has evolved into the rallying cry of those unable to negotiate the nuances of the mainstream. It now serves to glorify formerly stigmatized characteristics of the lower class, preventing the impetus for upward mobility."[57] Not everyone agrees, of course. Black intellectuals, including Cornel West and Michael Eric Dyson, are quick to defend rap and hip-hop as a legitimate black cultural expression. Dyson sees rappers as refining the art of "oral communication."[58]

Certainly one can point to some praiseworthy aspects of hip-hop culture: creativity and entrepreneurialism, for example. And it's no wonder that the wealth and success that the leading stars have attained would be such an attraction for young blacks. But the sobering fact remains that the values and themes of the most noteworthy hip-hop artists are destructive, and they help perpetuate cycles of poverty, crime, and failure.

The hip-hop debate connects with a broader, and ongoing, debate over personal responsibility in the black community, especially as it relates to poverty. Criticism of black culture for its role in keeping African Americans down has pitted conservatives against liberals and even liberals against one another. Front and center in this debate have been, on one side, President Obama, who stressed the need for personal responsibility in the black community (again, not as often as his conservative critics would prefer), and, on the other, black writers like Ta-Nehisi Coates. "From the president on down," Coates writes, "there is an accepted belief in America—black and white—that African American people, and African American men, in particular, are lacking in the virtues in family, hard work and citizenship."[59] Coates asks, "Is the culture of West Baltimore actually less virtuous than the culture of Wall Street?"[60]

The answer to that question is likely subjective, but Coates misses a fundamental fact: Wall Street can afford its questionable morality. West Baltimore cannot.

## SOLUTIONS

The longstanding, entrenched nature of poverty today, especially its intergenerational and cultural aspects, does not lend itself to top-down, programmatic solutions. To some extent, we have to acknowledge the immensity of the problem and the likelihood that turning around the fortunes of the underclass is a generational project. Still, even given the daunting nature of the problem, certain basic principles should be clear, and with them, some approaches that are likely to meet with a degree of success.

At the broadest level, the way forward is through efforts that combine personal responsibility with opportunity—the values piece meeting the policy piece. Every effort should be made to ensure that funds go not just to providing services but also to changing the structure and incentives of impoverished communities.

The federal government does have a role to play here—for example, by providing investment incentives for businesses to set up shop in depressed communities. Private investment in poor neighborhoods should be tax-incentivized—including, in the right circumstances, potentially waiving minimum-wage requirements. (We support raising the national minimum wage generally, but experimental enterprise zones should be free to waive these requirements if a compelling case exists to do so.) Some companies have already taken steps to reach out: Starbucks, for example, has opened 15 stores in poor and middle-class neighborhoods, including Ferguson, Missouri, where it looks to employ local youths "who are neither employed nor at school."[61]

Addressing the problems of the urban underclass also means understanding the "urban" part of that equation. As Jill Homan argued in the *New York Post*, politicians of all stripes need to understand cities better. Currently, Republicans only control four of the mayoralties in America's biggest cities.[62] We should support programs like Bob Woodson's Center for Neighborhood Enterprise, which emphasizes changing inner-city neighborhoods from the inside out through training programs to address joblessness and substandard education in poor communities, providing leadership development for heads of community organizations, and overseeing antiviolence monitoring programs.

We need an economic plan that balances well-considered government assistance with a commitment to free-market principles of opportunity and mobility—rather than a failed vision of uplift in which passive recipients remain perpetually dependent on government. "All persons should have the opportunity to go as high as their merit and determination can carry them," Jack Kemp said.[63]

As President Obama proposed in 2014, Congress should expand the Earned Income Tax Credit, which targets low- and middle-income

Americans. Expansion has won support from Democrats as well as Republicans like Senators Marco Rubio and Mike Lee, who made it central to their tax plan.

President Bill Clinton's welfare reform of 1996 substantially modified the Aid to Families with Dependent Children (AFDC) program, replacing it with Temporary Assistance for Needy Families (TANF), which imposed work requirements on able-bodied adults. TANF was a huge step forward—welfare rolls dropped by half after it was passed in 1996—but according to the Heritage Foundation, roughly half of all able-bodied TANF recipients are "idle" on the rolls today, collecting their checks without performing the necessary work. Part of this is due to problems in the design of TANF, but part is also an outgrowth of the Obama administration's weakening of work requirements. Obama has allowed the Department of Health and Human Services to grant work-requirement waivers to the states.[64] The result has been a substantial lessening of the amount of work hours required, undermining the program. New York mayor Bill de Blasio has pursued a similar policy in a city with a substantial welfare population.[65] We need to strengthen work requirements as a fundamental pathway out of poverty. Otherwise, we are only perpetuating dependency.

Paul Ryan's proposal for federal opportunity grants deserves serious consideration. As he writes, "These grants would consolidate up to 11 programs—such as food stamps, housing assistance and cash welfare—into one funding stream, and allow states to experiment with different ways of customizing aid. Families in need would have a choice about where and how they get assistance."[66] In exchange for such flexibility, recipients would face greater accountability on results. It makes sense for Washington to play a more limited role here, letting local governments and organizations tailor and customize programs as they see fit.

Poor Americans need expanded access to banking and credit services. Writing for the *New Republic*, David Dayen has shown that the U.S. Postal Service could integrate basic banking services into its current infrastructure. This would include checking account and debit card services, savings accounts, and small loan services. Estimates show that post offices could do this for 10 percent of what check-cashers or lenders charge.[67] We should also consider bonuses for moving money from checking accounts to savings, which would encourage capital accumulation. Norm Ornstein has proposed giving every newborn American baby a $1,000 grant into an investment account.[68]

Education reform remains central to fighting poverty. School choice and vouchers are both critical to this effort. We discuss vouchers and other school-choice mechanisms at length in chapter 7. To combat truancy, a problem plaguing public schools across the nation, we can emulate—on a national level—programs like the one started in Anaheim, California, which uses GPS-monitoring systems to track chronic absentees.[69] Students who were absent at least 10 percent of the time wear a GPS device and must check in with counselors five times daily. Mentors can then locate students if they are truant. San Antonio, Texas, put a similar program in place in 2008 and saw attendance rates climb to 97 percent among truant students.

We also have to turn our attention to the importance of summer jobs in building a better-skilled workforce. The private sector has helped show the way here. JPMorgan Chase's $250 million workforce skills initiative invests in summer youth-employment programs to help kids—especially from low-income families—learn the right skills to get jobs when they finish school.[70] Chase's program found summer jobs for 50,000 teenagers. Studies have found that for every year young people work, their income in their twenties rises 14 percent to 16 percent.[71] At a time when we're seeing a 40 percent decline in the youth summer-employment rate, we should create and support more initiatives like this one, which not only help prepare young people for the workforce but also foster character and good habits, lessening the chances that a young person will make bad choices.

We must encourage not only traditional educational opportunities but vocational training, apprenticeships, and mentoring programs as well. The federal government should double its investment in community colleges, from $2 billion to $4 billion annually. This is a modest investment compared with the amount the federal government spends on K–12 and higher education.[72] To encourage community colleges to ensure that their students graduate on time with a degree or certificate, Washington should base its allocation of resources on a "resources-for-performance" formula. Schools serving low-income and minority students could receive proportionally greater resources.

Finally, on the values side, there is no substitute for strengthening marriage.

"Marriage remains America's strongest anti-poverty weapon, yet it continues to decline," Robert Rector wrote in a Heritage Foundation report. "As husbands disappear from the home, poverty and welfare dependence will increase, and children and parents will suffer as a result."[73] We should encourage marriage in lower-income communities through tax benefits, counseling, and outreach. We should reform welfare laws that punish marriage; currently, benefits go down as family income increases. Additionally, Washington and the states should launch public information campaigns, similar to those warning of the dangers of smoking or skipping school, to help promote marriage among at-risk populations. New York mayor Michael Bloomberg was on precisely the right track with his much-maligned subway ads. We should have more of these—everywhere.

There's a broad misconception that unmarried fathers don't earn enough to support mothers and children, but 80 percent of the fathers studied in a Heritage Foundation report were employed at the time of their child's birth.[74] "If women who had children out of wedlock were married to the actual father of their child, their probability of living in poverty would be cut by two-thirds," Heritage concluded.[75] This is why programs like President Obama's fatherhood initiative, which gives men valuable training in parenting skills, are so important. Obama's My Brother's Keeper Alliance is also deserving of support: it raises money for local programs that will be devoted to education, reading, mentoring, job training, and other opportunities for young black and Latino men.

Finally, a prerequisite to helping the underclass in struggling communities is public safety and crime control. Policing in such communities must be vigorous and proactive but also responsible and community-oriented. This is especially important in light of recent conflicts between blacks and the police. There is no doubt that this is an issue of national importance—and that alleviating these tensions is essential to creating the conditions necessary for social improvement and advancement. We'll have more to say about this issue in chapter 6.

## CONCLUSION

"If the Negro in the ghetto must eternally be fed by the hand that pushes him into the ghetto, he will never become strong enough to get out of the ghetto," said Carter G. Woodson, originator of Black History Month, in 1933.[76] His insight remains relevant today. It was central to Jack Kemp's thinking as well. In a 2008 editorial in the *Wall Street Journal*, Kemp wrote,

> In my opinion, people of all colors and income levels don't hate the rich. They want to get rich. They're more interested in generating wealth than they are in redistributing wealth. They want to own property, educate their children and build a nest egg that can be passed on to their heirs. Unfortunately, some aren't able to access the same ladder of opportunity that is so readily available to the majority.[77]

This type of inclusive thinking has usually been central to the Democratic Party's agenda—but on poverty, especially since the 1960s, Democrats have not balanced their approach between assistance and opportunity. They have overemphasized assistance and undervalued opportunity and individual efforts, and as a result, millions of blacks and other Americans have remained in poverty, cut off from the American mainstream.

"Why do blacks keep voting for the same people?" Allen West asked in the wake of the 2015 Baltimore riots, pointing out that in most major cities—especially those with the highest black populations—Democrats are in charge.[78] The simplest answer to that question is that Republicans have been completely ineffective, if not disinterested, in appealing to blacks. It would be a good thing for blacks and the poor more generally if both parties competed seriously for their votes.

Whichever party is making the pitch, the fact remains that we have had no vision and no strategy for addressing the problems of the American underclass for too long. Specific policies can be debated, but the principles should be clear: we need to offer assistance in return for accountability and responsibility. We must also remain cognizant of the elements, both contemporary and historical, that make the black experience in America decidedly different. This will require leadership and political courage—qualities in short supply in American politics these days. But serious times in the past have brought forth serious American leaders. We hope that this will be the case again soon, for the sake of millions of citizens locked out of the American dream.

CHAPTER 5

# The Racial Divide

There's not a black America and white America and Latino America and Asian America; there's the United States of America.
—Barack Obama, 2004[1]

The charge of racism is proving to be an effective strategy for Democrats.... Having one's opponent rebut charges of racism is far better than discussing joblessness.
—Mary Frances Berry, former head, Civil Rights Commission[2]

Black-white relations are worse now than in most living Americans' memories.
—Dennis Prager[3]

It's not just pop culture. It's our heritage, our past. And it's our present.
—Anika Noni Rose, cast member, *Roots* remake[4]

A mericans of a certain age remember well the television phenomenon that was *Roots*, the 1977 miniseries that dramatized the African American story in America, a saga from slavery to freedom. The series brought home to millions of white Americans the horrors of slavery, including the unforgettable scene of parental separation when a child was sold to a different slave master. *Roots* came about after a decade and a half of African American political awakening, the achievements of the civil rights movement, and the death of Martin Luther King. It felt like a summation.

Some were puzzled, then, when, in 2016, the series was remade on the History Channel. Even some of the first series' stars, like Cicely Tyson, expressed regret that the original, which she considered "a classic," was being tampered with. Rapper Snoop Dogg also expressed skepticism.

"They just want to keep showing the abuse that we took hundreds and hundreds of years ago," he said on Instagram, apparently weary of entertainment about historical black victimization.[5]

Those who watched the new *Roots* might see the truth in his observation. The new *Roots*, one critic wrote, was "more passionate, more sweeping," and "considerably angrier" than the original. And it rejected the original's effort to see itself "rather pointedly as an American story, as if to reassure white viewers that it would be involving for them, too."[6] "Good" or at least marginally benevolent white characters were removed. Some of the violence left off-camera in the original was brought into full focus in the remake—including scenes that seemed politically pointed, as in the shooting of a runaway slave in the back.

"I don't think I need to say how relevant that is to right now," said actor Malachi Kirby, who plays Kunta Kinte in the remake. "These things happened. *And they're happening today*."[7] His words were echoed by Anika Noni Rose, who plays Kunte's daughter, Kizzy. "It's not just pop culture," she said. "It's our heritage, our past. *And it's our present*."[8]

They were referring, of course, to high-profile shootings of black men in recent years by police officers, though they made no effort to distinguish the many cases in which the officers were forced by circumstances to discharge their guns from the comparatively fewer ones where cops made mistakes or committed crimes. But in the climate of our times, the notion that blacks are under assault is widely held to be true.

It's hard to divorce the new *Roots* from this mood of racial adversity and hostility that seemed so characteristic of the late Obama years—and which culminated, in many ways, in July 2016. In a single week, the videos documenting the police shootings of Alton Sterling in Baton Rouge and Philando Castile in St. Paul were made public, and at a subsequent Black Lives Matter protest in Dallas, five police officers were killed by an anti-white, anti-cop gunman. Seven more police officers were injured, along with two civilians, before the attacker was executed by a robot-delivered bomb. Five days after the massacre, a *New York Times*/CBS poll reported that Americans' views of race relations had reached their lowest ebb since the Rodney King riots of 1992.[9]

The irony of the *Roots* remake is that it appears in the final year of what most blacks watching the first *Roots* in 1977 would have believed impossible—a black presidential administration. "That a black man has been the master of the White House for the past six years does indeed reflect and reinforce a remarkable socio-psychological transformation in the American racial scene," writes Randall Kennedy.[10] He's right, but you wouldn't know it by the racial mood of the country. Race relations in the United States have reached their lowest point in a generation. In every sense, the national racial divide is sharp and bitter and troubling—and, given everything we have achieved in race relations over recent decades, appalling.

President Trump has many challenges to face, but he should be aware that racial reconciliation deserves a prominent spot on the to-do list. Feelings of racial bitterness and division run deep and wide today, and they threaten our national unity, even our survival.

## THE DIVIDE

Don't take our word for it that Americans are more racially divided after the Obama presidency than before. Listen to what Americans themselves are saying, through what they tell pollsters.

When President Obama was elected in November 2008, two-thirds of the electorate thought that race relations were "generally good."[11] By July 2015, 60 percent of Americans—majorities of both blacks and whites—said in a *New York Times*/CBS News poll that they thought race relations were "generally bad," and 40 percent thought they were getting worse.[12] One year later, following the July 2016 violence in Louisiana, Minnesota, and Texas, *New York Times*/CBS News reported that 69 percent of Americans viewed race relations as "generally bad," and 60 percent saw them as getting worse.[13]

Granted, the 2015 *Times*/CBS poll was taken in the light of the horrific shooting in Charleston, South Carolina, when a white man, Dylan Roof, entered a black church and opened fire with a handgun, killing nine people; the 2016 poll was taken in the light of the Dallas massacre. Both were blood-curdling instances of racial violence, and both shook the nation to its core. So attitudes were bound to be gloomy when the polls were taken. However, these poll results are no outliers. Consider:

A *Bloomberg* politics poll released in December 2014 found that only 9 percent of Americans thought race relations had improved since Obama took office, as compared with 53 percent who think they've gotten worse and 36 percent who think they've stayed the same.

At the end of 2014, a *Wall Street Journal*/NBC News poll showed that about half of those who thought race relations were good when Obama took office didn't think this any longer.[14]

A January 2015 Fox News poll found that 62 percent think race relations have gotten worse under Obama, whereas only 19 percent who think they've gotten better.[15]

In January 2015, Gallup found that 62 percent of Americans felt "somewhat dissatisfied" or "very dissatisfied" with the state of race relations; only 40 percent had said so in 2008.[16]

In March 2015, CNN found that only 15 percent of respondents agreed that race relations had improved under Obama—down from 32 percent in 2009—and that 39 percent felt they had worsened, up from just 6 percent in 2009.[17]

Results from a September 2015 Rasmussen survey showed that only 20 percent of Americans thought Obama had "brought Americans of different races closer together." Forty-seven percent thought Obama had "driven those of different races further apart instead."[18]

These views exist despite the measurable evidence of progress that America has made, which even most respondents in a *New York Times*/CBS News poll acknowledged: 71 percent said that the United States was making headway in reducing or eliminating racial discrimination.[19] Obama himself provides the most dramatic evidence, of course, of that progress, especially politically: in 1965, there were no black senators or governors and just six black congressmen. By 2015, there were 44 black congressmen, two black senators, and a black governor.[20] Attitudes improved, too, as can be seen in the increased tolerance and approval for interracial marriage—once a forbidden subject. Approval of interracial marriage has doubled from 1983 to 2014, and the actual practice of marriage between the races is on the rise, too.[21]

Closer to the present, Gallup's tracking poll found in April 2016 that now one in three Americans worry a "great deal" about race relations in America. Concern has gone up across all groups. Black Americans have consistently been more concerned, but from 2012 to 2014, only 31 percent of blacks said they were worried a great deal about race relations. Now it's more than 50 percent. For whites, the number is nearing 30 percent.[22]

There is one other point of perspective on where we currently are: in 1981, four years after the first *Roots* played on network television, an ABC/ *Washington Post* poll asked Americans, "On a national basis, do you think today there is more, less or about the same amount of anti-black feeling among whites as compared to 4 or 5 years ago?" Twenty-seven percent said more, 41 percent said less, and 27 percent said the same. In the same poll, people were asked to name "the most important problem facing this country today." *One percent* answered "race relations/civil rights."[23] In several 2016 Gallup surveys, 5–7 percent of respondents answered that way. And even among those who don't name race relations as *the* top issue in the country, as we have seen, majorities see things going downhill.

How could this be? With all the progress we have made economically, socially, and culturally, not to mention the world-historical election of Obama himself, how could race relations in the United States be getting worse—markedly worse—or at least be perceived to be worse among most people? There is blame enough to go around, but if Obama himself is looking for an answer to the question, he should start by looking in the mirror.

## OBAMA THE DIVIDER

In 2014, President Obama argued in an NPR interview that America was then less racially divided than in 2009, when he took office. "I actually think that it's probably in its day-to-day interactions, less racially divided," he told host Steve Inskeep.[24] "It's understandable the polls might say, you know, that race relations have gotten worse—because when it's in the news and you see something like Ferguson or the Garner case in New York, then it attracts attention."[25] He seemed to be suggesting that Americans feel worse about race relations not because they are worse but because we talk about them more. And he argued that the situation would get better as the economy continued to improve. But he was wrong.[26]

The problem with Obama's argument is that when it comes to something like race relations, perception *is* reality to a considerable degree: how people feel about relations between blacks and whites is going to shape how they conduct themselves—not to mention how they answer survey questions. What Obama seems unlikely to admit is that the much-touted promise of his presidency—that he would help lead America to a new era of racial healing and understanding—has not been kept. Not even close.

The natural questions are, "Why?" and "Who's to blame?" The answer to the first question is fairly simple. Instead of seeing genuine gains to social and racial harmony from Obama's presidency, the United States has instead moved backward on race relations, with the result that Obama left office with a much more contentious, hostile, and suspicious climate in this area than when he came in. The answer to the second question is more complex. But anyone who thinks that President Obama himself is not a big part of the reason for these failures either hasn't been paying attention or is not willing to acknowledge the history of these years.

Obama was never shy about blaming his Republican critics and adversaries—and they do bear responsibility for what has occurred. We'll turn to them in a moment, but what about the president himself? He occupied the bully pulpit of the White House, he had an unrivaled communications platform, and he had the credibility and appeal, when he took office in January 2009, to be the leader on positive racial change and relations. Did he fulfill that responsibility?

Again, we have to answer: not even close.

His administration consistently pursued policies that elevate race and ethnicity to the forefront of importance. That was apparent from the get-go with his Justice Department, led by the nation's most divisive attorney general since John Mitchell, Eric Holder, who sent a message right away about his priorities when he refused to prosecute a case of voter intimidation. On Election Day 2008, the New Black Panther Party bullied and frightened voters at polling places in Philadelphia. The incident, though isolated, was appalling, and it deserved the highest level of seriousness from the Justice Department, which is tasked with protecting the voting rights of all Americans. But Holder pointedly refused to prosecute the three Black Panther Party members implicated in the case.[27] Christopher Coates, former voting chief for the DOJ's Civil Rights Division, later suggested that Holder backed off prosecution under pressure from the NAACP.[28]

In education, Obama put race first in favoring preferential treatment for blacks over more academically qualified whites and Asians in college admissions. At the pre-college level, concerned about racial disparities in school discipline, he pushed school districts to practice a double standard, thus ensuring that black students—no matter their disciplinary record—could face penalties at more "proportionate" rates. His Fair Housing program threatened to supersede community autonomy by forcing localities to build low-income housing, even in areas where housing prices were out of reach for most middle-class people.[29] He went after banks for lending discrimination based on sketchy evidence, ramped up hate-crimes prosecutions, and cultivated a DOJ that took a "hostile" attitude toward race-neutral application of the Voting Rights Act.[30] Obama also had Holder go after states with voter-ID laws, which the administration suggested were racist—though such laws enjoyed majority support among every demographic group.[31] And in fact, black voter turnout has increased in states with such laws.[32]

Beyond these far-reaching, substantive policies, more visibly and symbolically, Obama set a communications style that consistently tweaked Americans on the subject of race. In February 2009, Holder branded Americans "essentially a nation of cowards" when it comes to race relations. "Though this nation has proudly thought of itself as an ethnic melting pot," Holder said, "in things racial we have always been and continue to be, in too many ways, essentially a nation of cowards. Though race related issues continue to occupy a significant portion of our political discussion, and though there remain many unresolved racial issues in this nation, we, average Americans, simply do not talk enough with each other about race." It was remarkable to hear the highest law enforcement official in the land take such a confrontational posture on such a sensitive topic. Also remarkable was the implication that Americans suffered from insufficient race talk, at a time when college campuses had whole courses of study dedicated to ethnic and racial experience, when movies and books covered race issues regularly, and when Holder himself was delivering his remarks to mark an event that itself signified Americans' recognition of race—Black History Month.

In the Obama administration, no issue seemed too far removed from race. Railing against environmental degradation, Van Jones, who served briefly in the administration as "green jobs czar," racialized this issue too, blaming "white polluters and the white environmentalists" who were "essentially steering poison into the people-of-color communities."[33] Health and Human Services Secretary Kathleen Sebelius invoked the civil rights movement in speaking out against opponents of Obamacare. She compared the battle to "the fight against lynching and the fight for desegregation."[34] Even Vice President Biden, a normally congenial soul, told a black audience that Republicans wanted to "put y'all back in chains."[35]

Obama's own public statements were often divisive. From the beginning, he showed a tendency to wade into still-developing news events, making premature judgments. The first hint came early, in July 2009, when Obama saw fit to opine on a confrontation between Harvard professor Henry Louis "Skip" Gates—an African American—and Cambridge police. Gates had locked himself out of his home and was hovering around his own front porch, seeking a way to get in. A neighbor, who obviously didn't know or recognize Gates, called the police, thinking him a prowler. The police arrested Gates, who asked if he was being taken in for "being a black man in America."

That was enough for Obama, who, at a press conference, said that the Cambridge police had "acted stupidly." He went on to tie Gates's arrest to the "long history in this country of African-Americans and Latinos being stopped by law enforcement disproportionately."

But the Gates incident was far from being so cut-and-dried. A committee in Cambridge later determined that fault for the incident extended to all sides. Moreover, the arresting officer was highly commended and even taught a course on racial profiling at the police academy. Sheepishly, Obama then backed off, praising the officer and saying that he would like to have him to the White House for a beer. The ridiculous "beer summit" then followed, with Obama, Gates, the officer, and Vice President Biden sitting around a table and talking.[36]

Nothing made the president's racialist lens clearer, however, than the Trayvon Martin case. In March 2012, the 17-year-old Martin, an African American, was shot dead by George Zimmerman, a neighborhood watch volunteer, in Sanford, Florida. Martin was unarmed, but he had been engaged in a physical struggle with Zimmerman when Zimmerman, who was armed, shot him. The circumstances will always remain murky, but Zimmerman had seen Martin walking around the neighborhood and, not recognizing him, had called 911. He was told to do nothing else, and he should have listened to that advice. Instead, he approached Martin, and whatever transpired between them resulted in the scuffle, with Martin pounding Zimmerman on the pavement. Zimmerman, fearing for his life, he said, pulled his gun out and shot Martin. Zimmerman's face and the back of his head showed cuts and abrasions.

The case quickly became a cause célèbre as another instance of white racism taking the lives of young black men—even though Zimmerman was a Hispanic man. (The *New York Times*, clearly eager for the racial angle, invented a new category, calling Zimmerman a "white Hispanic.") Later investigation, not to mention a high-profile trial, would determine that under the laws of Florida, Zimmerman had reasonable cause to fear for his life under the circumstances. He was acquitted.

Obama did not wait for the trial or even the arraignment to put a stake down. Speaking at a presidential press conference after Martin's death, he said, "If I had a son, he would look like Trayvon." The strange comment was interpreted in any number of ways, but was clearly meant as a statement of solidarity with the victim and his family—a highly inappropriate injection of presidential involvement into a local, and still-developing, story. When Zimmerman was acquitted a year later, Obama lectured the nation on race, reminding listeners that some years earlier, he could have been Trayvon.

He didn't stop there. The Community Relations Service (CRS) of Holder's Justice Department organized protests in Sanford, helping bring the case to national attention. CRS volunteers even escorted college students on a protest march. Here was a criminal trial just beginning to unfold, and the highest law enforcement authorities in the land were choosing sides and organizing political agitation.[37]

A little-noted aspect of the division Obama has fostered is the organizing group that he started, the well-funded Organizing for Action. OFA, formerly known as Obama for America, is designed to outlive the Obama presidency. According to Paul Sperry of the Hoover Institution, OFA had trained more than 10,000 organizers as of the end of 2015, and these organizers are training perhaps two million youths in activism and street demonstrations. As Sperry notes, "Through social media, they mobilize flash mobs against 'biased cops,' 'climate-change deniers,' 'Wall Street predators' and 'gun extremists.' They hold rallies against conservative foes of gay marriage, LGBT rights, abortion and amnesty for illegal immigrants."[38]

In autumn 2015, most Americans watched with some befuddlement as a series of racial protests broke out on college campuses, most notably at the University of Missouri and at Yale. The issues ranged from murky allegations of swastikas in bathrooms, hearsay accounts of racial epithets yelled from passing cars, and the innocuous email of a Yale official arguing that students ought to be free to wear whatever Halloween costumes they wish, though they should, of course, keep commonsense sensitivities in mind. These "incidents" led to outbreaks of mass protest often indistinguishable from mass hysteria, including the shutting down of free speech, the resignation of a college president, a football strike, and a host of demands for black-studies programs and the like. Where was all this activism coming from?

Some blamed overly sensitive millennials, others craven college officials; some truth lies in both of those explanations. But OFA is another piece of the puzzle. It has a strong presence on college campuses, where it holds regular "organizing summits." It follows logically that such cadres will eagerly look for issues on which to take action. We can probably expect much more of the same in the years ahead on our college campuses, which have become incredibly adverse environments for free speech and expression.

Obama betrayed the promise of his famous 2004 speech at the Democratic National Convention, which brought him to national renown by calling for an America beyond Red and Blue, an America united by the notion of being one people, one country. "There's not a black America and white America and Latino America and Asian America," he said then. "There's the United States of America."[39] By contrast, Obama's consistent approach as president was to pit blacks against whites for political gain. Turning his eyes from the predominant causes of black suffering—fatherlessness, poor educational levels, crime, and welfare cultures—he used the most powerful pulpit in the land to suggest to blacks that racism remains an everyday scourge for black Americans, a crushing obstacle to their progress in America.

Racism is not gone, of course; we may never be free of it. But the primary obstacles black America faces are more material—they are economic, educational, social, and moral. At some level, Obama must know this; or perhaps he has genuinely convinced himself that this isn't true. Either way, the net effect of his presidency was to exacerbate racial, social, and political divisions in the country—and to betray every hope that the nation's first black president might help lead us farther down the road to racial reconciliation. Instead, we've gone backward.

What has made it all worse—and no doubt factored in, to some degree, in causing it—has been the failure of Republicans to unify

Americans on these issues as well. "Failure" is at times too kind a word for Republican behavior—at their worst, they have been all too willing to play with racial fire, at least rhetorically, and they have played no small role in widening the divisions we face.

## REPUBLICAN DIVIDERS

It is hard to do justice to how badly the Republican Party handled its defeat in 2008. Republicans reacted as if they hadn't just lost an election—an election that they eminently deserved to lose, by the way—but as if an alien takeover had conquered the United States. They seemed first shocked by their ouster from power and then infuriated, and their fury fell on Barack Obama. Was this simply the unsporting reaction of a political party displaced from the White House, or did it have deeper roots—racist roots?

We're not fond of the national tendency to diagnose racism in public figures for off-target statements or political views. Racism is a serious charge, and one ought only to make it when strong evidence justifies the claim. But let's consider this objectively: Did Republicans conduct themselves in ways that could fairly be called unifying or divisive?

Was it unifying or divisive when many on the right questioned Obama's patriotism, loyalty to the country, and place of birth?

Was it unifying or divisive when the Tea Party movement arose just weeks after Obama's inauguration, fashioning itself as a national movement to reclaim America?

Was it unifying or divisive when, after a white kid got beat up on a school bus by black kids in St. Louis, Rush Limbaugh told his millions of listeners that such incidents could be expected from now on in "Obama's America"—and no major Republicans spoke out against this demagoguery?

Unifying or divisive? A South Carolina congressman yells out during a presidential speech to a joint session of Congress, "You lie!"

Unifying or divisive? The governor of Arizona, who disagrees strongly with Obama on border security, greets him at an airport tarmac by baring her teeth and pointing her finger in his face, as if he were her an errant high school student?

Unifying or divisive? House Speaker John Boehner denies Obama's request to speak before a joint session of Congress in September 2011, the first time in history such a presidential request had been refused?[40]

These and other incidents didn't just show disrespect for Obama, they also suggested a lack of sensitivity to the genuine historical uniqueness of someone in Obama's place as the nation's first black president. They showed zero awareness, or concern, about the understandable instinct that millions of blacks might feel to regard the president protectively, or that the history we all share might require some care in how one addresses certain matters. Their tone, words, and actions, from the very beginning, could not have helped, by conveying to blacks their contempt not just for Obama but for the notion that race still carries sensitivities in American life. It has been profoundly disappointing—and divisive—to watch.

Note how we haven't once cited examples of genuine Republican criticism of the president in this discussion; there has been plenty of that, too, and in our view, there is nothing to say about it. Liberals have too often dismissed substantive Republican criticisms of Obama as subterranean racism. For the most part, however, critiques of Obamacare, the stimulus, the president's foreign policy, his regulatory regime, or other policies have been just that—policy critiques. Even Newt Gingrich's much-derided criticism of Obama as "the food stamp president" was wrongly regarded as racist, even when the very critics of the comment cited the fact that more whites are on food stamps than blacks. Gingrich's point was that the administration's policies weren't creating jobs but were putting more and more Americans on government benefits—a perfectly valid argument.

Of course, by the time Gingrich made that comment, it was 2012, Obama was running for reelection, and much bitterness had already come to pass. Gingrich himself had contributed to it. Remember what he said in 2010, after viewing Dinesh D'Souza's documentary *America at Risk*? "What if [Obama] is so outside our comprehension, that only if you understand Kenyan, anti-colonial behavior, can you begin to piece together [his actions]? That is the most accurate, predictive model for his behavior."[41]

Here, Gingrich was playing on a common theme among Obama critics on the right—that he is somehow foreign, not American, alien to this country's political traditions. Again, consider the broader context of Obama's presidency and, regardless of your take on his policies, reflect on what his ascension to the presidency means to this country's history.

Yet Gingrich and other Republicans essentially said that Obama was an interloper who didn't belong in the American tradition. How can such arguments lead to anything other than racial bitterness and division?

And then there came the presidential campaign of 2016, when the Republican Party nominated Donald Trump as its standard bearer—to be sure, against the wishes of mainline Republican officials and insiders, along with a vast portion of the established conservative commentariat. Republican primary voters, however, gave Trump more votes than any GOP candidate has ever garnered in the modern primary system. For Democrats and liberals, Trump's ascension was further proof that Republicans were racist, because they had nominated a racist candidate.

We will withhold judgment on whether Trump is legitimately ethnically or racially biased. What is at issue here though, again, is divisiveness. During the primary season, Trump's strongest support came in areas with the greatest degree of racial polarization, and he has certainly been an extraordinarily divisive candidate.

At times, Trump's divisiveness has indeed crossed the racial line.

The two most notorious moments for Trump were these: announcing his candidacy in June 2015, he lambasted Mexico for problems at the border. "When Mexico sends its people, they're not sending their best," Trump said. "They're sending people that have lots of problems, and they're bringing those problems with us. They're bringing drugs. They're bringing crime. They're rapists. *And some, I assume, are good people.*"[42] Trump was making a genuine point about the border—there is no dispute that the illegal immigration problem is also a drugs and crime problem— but he did it so crudely that he sent an adversarial message to Hispanics, generalizing the behavior of a criminal element to the entire population.

Even worse, in February 2016, after he was endorsed for president by longtime Klansman David Duke, Trump refused to decline the endorsement—even after Jake Tapper gave him at least three chances to do so in a CNN interview. "Will you unequivocally condemn David Duke and say that you don't want his vote and that of other white supremacists in this election?" Tapper asked. Trump's response:

> I don't know anything about David Duke, OK? I don't know anything about what you're even talking about with white supremacy or white supremacists. So I don't know. I mean, I don't know—did he endorse

me or what's going on? Because I know nothing about David Duke.
I know nothing about white supremacists. And so you're asking me
a question that I'm supposed to be talking about people that I know
nothing about.[43]

Trump's response was utterly absurd on its face. David Duke has been
well known in the United States for at least 25 years. Trump's reluctance
to disavow Duke on Tapper's program suggested that he was not willing
to risk losing the support of white voters who think along these lines.
(Trump did disavow Duke's support shortly afterward.)

Not exactly a unifying moment.

Of course, Trump's rise, as we said earlier, came against the wishes
of the Republican establishment; and thus, his willingness to stir the pot
on sensitive issues has to be seen as an expression not of the Republican
leadership but of a substantial portion of the electorate itself. After one
peels away the layers of the various Trump controversies, a stark fact
remains clear about the Trump coalition: it is made up significantly of
people who feel disempowered, economically vulnerable, and yes, often
resentful—though this resentment is not at all solely confined to matters
of race. Indeed, as studies during the Obama years have shown, white
America isn't doing so great, either—economically or otherwise. A 2015
study by two Princeton economists, widely reported in the media, showed
that death rates for middle-class and working-class white Americans—
unlike every other demographic group in the United States—were rising,
and that this increased mortality was being driven by alcoholism, drug
abuse, and suicide. These causes suggest not a major health problem, like
heart disease, but despair.[44] For millions of American whites, the claim
that their skin color somehow gives them "privilege"—as race protestors
like to claim—would be laughable.

And herein lies the great tragedy of the Obama years and the failure
not only of the president but of his Republican opposition: during an
eight-year period that saw a genuine but very limited economic recovery,
the wages and economic opportunity for most in the working and middle
classes advanced barely at all. Blacks have made virtually *no* economic
progress under Obama; whites, except for those in the upper-income
brackets, have fared hardly better. When blacks and whites increasingly
should be making common cause, and the country most needs a unifying

message of economic opportunity and national renewal, we have gotten instead a harvest of racial animus and division.

It has hurt the country greatly, further torn our tender social fabric, set us back politically and economically, and left a daunting challenge for the next president. Shame on all the dividers in American political life who have contributed to it.

## LOOKING FORWARD

Americans of all races were inspired by the reaction of Charleston, South Carolina, to the horrific mass shooting of 2015—especially that of the victims' families, who refused to turn to anger but instead offered forgiveness and prayers for the shooter's soul. Their devout faith informed their conscience in this case and helped foster more positive relations in the wake of such awful events. This remarkable magnanimity not only demonstrates, again, the healing benefits for our society of religious faith, but also, perhaps even more hopefully, suggests that everyday Americans of all races want very much to live in harmony with one another.

We believe that the spirit of Charleston is broadly true of America. Problems remain, of course, and people holding racially hateful views certainly exist (even if Donald Trump isn't aware of them). Yet any objective evaluation of American society must concede that the strides our society has made in racial tolerance are not only vast and remarkable but unmatched anywhere else.

The problem lies, by and large, with our political leaders. The toxic racial politics of the Obama years will take some effort to heal. Perhaps, with a new president and new political circumstances, a chance at starting fresh presents itself. Clearly, we need to reshape the dialogue. President Trump should stress and stress again that we are all Americans and that one standard will apply to everyone. Moreover, while some of us take pride in our racial or ethnic identity, our large-group identity—as Americans—should be what unites us all.

We need a president—and a Congress—who will push, both in policy and rhetoric, themes of national unity and common purpose; principles of fairness and opportunity for all; and a staunch refusal to sort people into groups or to give aid and comfort to those who would divide us, whether they're the white supremacists whom Donald Trump wouldn't disavow or the Black Lives Matter and campus protestors who use racial bullying and extremism to garner power for themselves. Such people are dividing the country, and Americans—black and white—need to stand together and say "Enough." Our truest enemy is division among ourselves.

The tragedy of Barack Obama's presidency is that its historic promise was squandered willfully by choices that too often reflected a racial analysis of problems that were not exclusively racial, or not racial at all, but in fact transcended race—the problems of a neighborhood watchman frightened by crime, or the timeless problem of a cop menaced by an out-of-control young man (black or white, it doesn't matter) who simply forced him to defend himself. It is America's tragedy that the nation's first black presidency will be remembered for such deterioration in race relations and increased suspicions and anger between the races.

But that's over now. We have to look ahead and leave the ashes behind us.

# CHAPTER 6

# Crime, Policing, and Incarceration

Americans who suffer from an addiction need help, not moral condemnation.

—RICK PERRY[1]

They lock us up in the name of public safety but then they release us and at that point we're more of a menace than we were when we went in.

—ADRYANN GLENN, RELEASED PRISONER[2]

There is a lot of truth in the notion that jails and prisons are graduate schools of crime.

—NEWT GINGRICH[3]

Readers of this book probably don't need reminders that in recent years, tensions between police and urban communities, especially minority communities, have run high. One of the most prominent stories of the late years of President Obama's term in office was the series of high-profile shootings of blacks by police officers, followed by massive protests—and not infrequently, rioting and disorder—in the cities where these incidents took place. This cycle of tragedy and outrage, followed by more tragedy, seemed to reach a crescendo in July 2016, when two police shootings of black men, one in Minneapolis and one in Baton Rouge, were followed by the assassination of five police officers in Dallas by an enraged black man.

For years, critics, especially on the left, have alleged that urban police forces have in effect declared war on black men; they argue that blacks are killed disproportionately by police, that black men exist in society with a target on their backs, and that racism infects most big-city police forces (even forces composed heavily of black cops). Critics also allege that blacks are improperly incarcerated, at higher rates than other groups, and that in fact much of our criminal justice system is endemically unjust, handing out draconian sentences to harmless, nonviolent offenders, effectively ruining their lives and rendering them unable to reenter normal life.

These allegations arise from genuine pain and suffering of minority communities. Anyone who knows much about the history of the United States knows that the relationship of the police and black Americans has been a story of pain and abuse, sorrow and tragedy. Memories are long. Older blacks still carry with them memories of mistreatment or disregard at the hands of law enforcement, and many blacks today allege that things haven't changed much. Even when a close study of the evidence shows that police are doing a better job today than they ever have, the next terrible incident is usually enough to reactivate these emotions.

We cannot change that history, of course, only move forward into a time that we hope will be more mutually understanding, respectful, and harmonious for all parties. When all is said and done, however, we believe that as volatile as the police issues have been in recent years, the broader issue is less about policing than about how to rehabilitate those who have been incarcerated and will be getting out. We say this because, while we strongly agree that police and the black community have some fences to mend, statistically speaking, the problems are not nearly so profound as they are often portrayed as being. Some incidents in recent years have been truly terrible, but a wealth of data makes clear that there is no police "war" on blacks; blacks are not killed by police disproportionately to other groups; and the black crime rate, which dwarfs that of whites and other groups, explains much of the heavy interaction between black Americans and police—interaction that often results in tragic or at least contentious episodes.

We will briefly review the sources of black grievance against police, including episodes of recent years, and then outline the realities behind much of today's political rhetoric: specifically, having to do with the crime rate in the black community and the profiles of most of the population in prison and jail. We will then turn to what we see as the true issue going forward: we are very good at punishing offenders for serious crimes and very bad at rehabbing and preparing prisoners for life after incarceration. This is especially critical at a time where we are releasing more prisoners with shortened sentences and when many of our incarcerated population are dealing with mental illness and drug addiction. A number of promising bipartisan alternatives exist for addressing necessary criminal justice reform, especially with regard to reintegrating ex-cons into society by making them more employable.

To be clear, we have no interest, as some libertarian-minded reformers do, in the decriminalization of legitimate crime or in lax sentences for those guilty of grievous crimes, or in permissive, lax policing, for that matter. On balance, over the last 25 years, what is sometimes called "the policing revolution" has saved countless thousands of lives, many of them black. But we do believe—as the great, now-retired chief of the NYPD, William Bratton, also believed—that police can calibrate and modulate their practices to be less intrusive without diminishing their effectiveness, keeping streets safe while also respecting the community and showing sensitivity to a long and painful history between blacks and police. That history is real; those who would deny it are not likely to be part of the solution. At the same time, the crime rate is real, too, and those who wish to pretend that cops are cruising black communities looking for people to oppress are also not likely to find answers to our problems. We do believe that rehabilitation, for those capable of it, should be pursued more vigorously and expansively.

## POLICING AND BLACK AMERICANS

As most readers know, recent years have been traumatic ones for relations between police officers and the black community. In 2016 alone, major stories included the deaths, at the hands of police officers, of Alton Sterling in Baton Rouge and Philando Castile in Minneapolis, both in July, and the deaths of Terence Crutcher in Tulsa and Keith Lamont Scott in Charlotte, both in September. Each incident was different. In some cases, the police had plausible claims for their actions. In the case of Castile's death, at least from what we know so far, there seems to be no plausible defense for the officer's use of deadly force. These incidents and others over recent years—such as the 2014 shooting death of 17-year-old Laquan McDonald in Chicago—have formed a growing list of high-profile public exhibits for those who demand police reform and argue that police racism results in what amounts to a war on blacks.

In some of these cases, too, the police have not helped their cause by their bungled or, frankly, deceitful manner of handling the incidents. The Chicago police, for example, went public with a story that McDonald had assaulted four police officers and posed a physical threat to CPD officer Jason Van Dyke, who began shooting McDonald and didn't stop until he had emptied his cartridge. But the dashboard video of the incident made clear that Van Dyke was not in any danger, especially since McDonald was armed only with a knife, not a gun, and was walking away from the officers before Van Dyke unloaded his clip into McDonald's chest. And the video itself only became public more than a year after the incident, after the Chicago Police Department finally consented to its release. No wonder they resisted doing so: the video contradicted almost every point of the department's official narrative. Van Dyke was charged with first-degree murder the day before the video was released. The Chicago Police Department's handling of the McDonald incident was an institutional failure at ever point, from the shooting itself to its public explanations for it, and public confidence has suffered as a result.

Blacks also have reason to resent the prerogatives enjoyed by police officers involved in some of the worst incidents. Michael Slager, the former South Carolina police officer charged with murder in the shooting death of Walter Scott, an unarmed black man, after a traffic stop, was released from prison on bail while he awaits trial. Slager's shooting of Scott, who was running away as the officer fired, was captured on video, and it's hard to find a starker instance of outright police abuse of deadly force—Scott didn't even have a knife, and he was fleeing, yet still he was killed. "Looking at the film that I saw, every time I look at it, it makes me cry," said Scott's father. "When I go down to the graveyard, the only thing I see there is a pot sticking in the ground with flowers in it." Speaking of Slager, he said, "If you let him out, he's gonna go home and look at his wife and children."[4]

In the old days, many big-city police forces paid little to no political price for abusive or powerhouse practices in black neighborhoods; conversely, police also were free to ignore crime in black neighborhoods, keeping white enclaves of big cities safe but shrugging at violence in black areas. Blacks had little political voice to make themselves heard about police mistreatment—whether from excessive force or outright neglect— and the resentment simply festered, sometimes exploding in urban riots, which dot the history of American cities throughout the twentieth century, from Harlem in 1943 to Los Angeles in 1965 to the unrest we saw in cities like Baltimore, Milwaukee, and Charlotte in 2016. The difference between 2016, though, and earlier eras is that in the intervening time, police have made controlling crime in black neighborhoods and safeguarding black lives and property a top priority, especially in places like New York City. But the combination of a long and unhappy history, a political orientation among many black leaders to be skeptical of police, and the continued trail of tragic incidents has left relations between blacks and police uneasy at best.

Not surprisingly, blacks take a more skeptical view of police than whites or other groups. A National Bar Association poll found that 88 percent of blacks think they are treated unfairly by the police and 59 percent of whites feel blacks are treated unfairly.[5] The perception gap is starker in the South, where 90 percent of blacks feel this way and just 55 percent of whites. The difference is much narrower in the Northeast, where 74 percent of blacks say police treat blacks unfairly compared with 63 percent of whites.[6] The story isn't that clear-cut, though. Some two-thirds of whites believe the police are misunderstood by blacks, and more than 50 percent of blacks agree. These figures change based on region, with a low of 35 percent of blacks agreeing that the police are misunderstood in the Northeast.[7]

While it's safe to say that today's police are better trained and more aware than police have ever been, that doesn't mean they don't have a long way to go in terms of interacting with minority communities, especially in certain police departments. The harshest critics—some even former cops themselves—see the problem of police as massive and pervasive. "On any given day, in any police department in the nation, 15 percent of officers will do the right thing no matter what is happening," writes Redditt Hudson, who served in the St. Louis police department for five years. "Fifteen percent of officers will abuse their authority at every opportunity. The remaining 70 percent could go either way depending on whom they are working with."[8] Those proportions seem hard to believe—nearly three-quarters of all police officers are empty vessels, easily led into either moral or immoral behavior, depending on circumstance? But even if Hudson's math is wrong, he is surely right to warn that some proportion of officers can be vulnerable to having their worst instincts activated—unless a healthy institutional culture and positive role models are present within the department. The NYPD, the nation's biggest and best police force, has both; many other urban police forces (like, say, Baltimore's) do not.

Black anger at police, which launched the protest group Black Lives Matter in 2012, reached a horrible crescendo in July 2016 when, just days after the Castile and Sterling shootings, Micah Johnson, an Army veteran who had served in Afghanistan, opened fire at a Black Lives Matter–organized march in Dallas protesting the recent shootings. Johnson targeted cops, and he did his grisly work well: he killed five officers and wounded nine. The attacks stunned the nation and prompted widespread support and sympathy for police officers. But the underlying tensions remained, and in September 2016, after the killing of Keith Lamont Scott, Charlotte erupted in several nights of disorder and violence.

The new climate has many police officers feeling that they wear a target on their backs—and, as a result, many are pulling back from proactive policing. Chicago mayor Rahm Emanuel, facing a soaring murder rate, told CNN "officers themselves were telling me about how the news over the last 15 months have impacted their instincts—do they stop, or do they keep driving? When I stop here, is it going to be my career on the line?"[9] Emanuel's point is part and parcel of what's been referred to as the "Ferguson effect," wherein upticks in crime are associated with slowdowns in policing for fear of backlash. Sam Dotson, chief of police in St. Louis, which saw a 17 percent increase in crime in the first half of 2015, offered that "in part, it can be attributed to tensions associated with recent police shootings and the associated publicity."[10]

By July 2016, the aggregate homicide rate in the nation's 56 largest cities had risen nearly 17 percent.[11] Whether or not one agrees that the policing pullback has contributed to or even caused the homicide spike, the numbers are real enough. And they point to the uncomfortable realities about crime and policing that, even allowing for black pain and suffering and the scars of history, cannot be denied: blacks and police have so many interactions because the crime rate in the black community is so high.

## CRIME AND PUNISHMENT: THE REALITIES

It goes without saying that each and every policing incident should be taken individually and evaluated as unique. Certainly, cases continue to present themselves in which police officers make tragic misjudgments or simply abuse their authority, sometimes with deadly results. But looking at data on crime, policing, and race makes clear that, despite these tragic or outrageous incidents—too many, to be sure—there simply is no war on blacks being conducted by cops.

Police critics, claiming that blacks are targeted by police, usually cite what sounds like a glaring disparity: blacks are only 13 percent of the United States population but make up 26 percent of police shooting victims. What they leave out is the black crime rate.

According to the Bureau of Justice Statistics, 52 percent of homicides committed between 1980 and 2008 were committed by black offenders.[12] In 2008, the offending rate for blacks was seven times higher than for whites.[13] FBI data reveals that between 2011 and 2013, nearly 39 percent of people arrested for murder, manslaughter, rape, robbery, and aggravated assault were black.[14] Yet African Americans make up just 13 percent of the American population.[15]

In New York City, blacks commit 75 percent of all shootings, though they make up only 23 percent of the city's population. By contrast, whites make up 34 percent of the New York City population but commit just 2 percent of the shootings.[16] This breakdown is typical in cities around the United States. In the nation's 75 largest counties, blacks make up about 15 percent of the population—but they account for 62 percent of robberies, 57 percent of murders, and 45 percent of assaults.

Yet, despite these crime numbers, recent studies have powerfully rejected evidence of police racial bias in police shootings—especially a study from Harvard's Roland Fryer, no right-winger, who evaluated 1,000 cop shootings and concluded that there was *zero* evidence of racial bias. Federal crime statistics, along with a *Washington Post* database on police shootings, show that 12 percent of white and Hispanic homicide victims die at the hands of cops; just 4 percent of black homicide victims are killed by cops. That's especially significant considering that 6,000 blacks were murdered in 2014—more than whites and Hispanics combined. The overwhelming majority of these black victims are killed by other blacks.[17]

These are the facts on policing and crime rates. They are drawn from federal statistics, comprehensive databases, and extensive studies.

We wish to be clear: we do *not* believe that these numbers mean that everything is okay between the black community and police, or that police shouldn't work to do their jobs better and more sensitively when dealing with minority communities. Nor do we believe that these statistics mean that the cases in which police *do* make terrible misjudgments or abuse their power should be shrugged off, chalked up to a statistical anomaly. No: every life matters, and the families of men like Philando Castile have every right to demand justice. And police and their supporters must understand that, even with these numbers, many, many people in black communities feel aggrieved with the police for one reason or another. Statistics don't tend to help with those problems; outreach, changes in behavior, and reforms to policing practices do.

That said, we have to reject the narrative that the prevalent danger to black men in America is the police. This is simply false. The prevalent danger is crime, not law enforcement.

The same goes for a related narrative: that legions of black men are being locked up in our "prison-industrial complex" largely for racial reasons. This accusation has been levied even from the highest officials. In July 2015, when President Obama visited a federal penitentiary in Oklahoma, he told reporters, "These are young people who made mistakes that aren't that different than the mistakes I made and the mistakes that a lot of you guys made."[18] A few months earlier, Hillary Clinton argued that

> there is something profoundly wrong when African-American men are far more likely to be stopped by the police and charged with crimes and given longer prison terms than their white counterparts. There is something wrong when trust between law enforcement and the communities they serve breaks down.... We must urgently begin to rebuild bonds of trust and respect among American between police and citizens.[19]

The Manhattan Institute's Heather Mac Donald, who has for years cited figures on racial disparities in crime, argues that President Obama and criminal justice reform advocates are way off the mark with these claims. Most Americans locked up for a serious length of time are locked up for good reason, she maintains. One of the most common claims of the anti-incarceration advocates is that American prisons are swelling with nonviolent drug offenders, but Mac Donald took apart this argument in a 2015 *Wall Street Journal* editorial:

The state-prison population (which accounts for 87 percent of the nation's prisoners) is dominated by violent criminals and serial thieves. In 2013 drug offenders made up less than 16 percent of the state-prison population; violent felons were 54 percent and property offenders 19 percent. Reducing drug-related admissions to 15 large state penitentiaries by half would lower those states' prison count by only 7 percent, according to the Urban Institute.

In federal prisons—which hold only 13 percent of the nation's prisoners—drug offenders make up half of the inmate population. But these offenders aren't casual drug users; overwhelmingly, they are serious traffickers. Fewer than 1 percent of drug offenders sentenced in federal court in 2014 were convicted of simple drug possession, according to the U.S. Sentencing Commission. Most of those possession convictions were plea-bargained down from trafficking charges.[20]

That's certainly a different picture than Obama paints.[21]

If you look at the breakdown of crime by race, the picture gets even more muddled for many reform advocates. Hispanics account for 48 percent of drug offenders sentenced in federal court; blacks make up 27 percent and whites 22 percent.[22] In defending Mac Donald, Scott McConnell writes in the *American Conservative*, "People may not like the fact that blacks are arrested in disproportionate numbers, but this is due far more to disproportionate rates of criminal behavior than to racist police officers. It's a fact that most people probably know and yet prefer not to state, which results in a stilted and not particularly honest national debate about policing."[23]

It's also critical to note that the argument that we are facing an unprecedented mass incarceration crisis in America relies on comparisons with European countries that leave crime rates out of the analysis. Anti-incarceration advocates lament the fact that we have 2.3 million people behind bars in the United States, 1 million of them black;[24] they point out that while the United States is home to just 5 percent of the world's population, it accounts for fully 25 percent of the world's incarcerated population.[25] Those figures look damning, and they seem to support the advocates' contention that the American incarceration rate makes the United States an outlier among the world's other advanced nations, which have much lower rates of imprisonment.

But, again, the question—what about the crime rate?—goes unasked in these analyses. As Mac Donald points out, the American crime rate is *seven* times higher than the aggregate rate of 21 advanced Western nations plus Japan.[26] Moreover, "contrary to the advocates' claim that the U.S. criminal-justice system is mindlessly draconian, most crime goes unpunished, certainly by a prison term," she writes.

> For every 31 people convicted of a violent felony, another 69 people arrested for violence are released back to the streets, according to a 2007 analysis of state courts by the Bureau of Justice Statistics. That low arrest-to-conviction rate reflects, among other things, prosecutors' decisions not to go forward with a case for lack of cooperative witnesses or technical errors in police paperwork. The JFA Institute estimated in 2007 that in only 3% of violent victimizations and property crimes does the offender end up in prison.[27]

Taken together, these numbers should humble critics of policing practices and incarceration. Let's face it, when it comes to things that we're proud of in the United States, none of us is going to cite the more than two million people we have living behind bars. Yet most of them committed serious crimes to get there.

This bring us to what we believe should be our focus when it comes to imprisonment: not the fact that legions of people are there unjustly—though some are—but, rather, the fact that we do such a poor job at rehabilitation, job training, and providing opportunities for those who will eventually be released. This is especially vital in the current climate, with state and federal moves to lessen sentences and even release prisoners early. We will have more people emerging from incarceration in the years ahead—but what are they emerging into, and what prospects will they have? If we don't find positive answers, they will soon be back where they started.

## INCARCERATION AND REHABILITATION

"Of course I had burned all my bridges," David Hudgens said soon after his release from prison. "Just the shame of asking the driver, 'can I ride for free?' because I had no money. Just basic transportation." Hudgens was dropped off at a metro stop in Northern Virginia with nowhere to go and no money. He knew he had to get to a shelter. But how?

Hudgens found a bus driver standing outside on his break and told him his story. Was he embarrassed? Yes. But the driver gave Hudgens a ride, though only to the next bus. A second driver let Hudgens on without money for the fare and got him to a shelter in Fairfax County, Virginia, where he was to live until he got back on his feet. It was a few miles' walk to the probation office, to the Social Security office, and anywhere that he might apply for a job. And during those walks there was plenty of time for doubting his chances at making it on the outside. "When I was in the shelter and walking out there on a hot sunny day, three miles to Social Security, there were thoughts," Hudgens told Think Progress. "I can do just a little criminal activity. Get some money. And I'm just thankful that I didn't."[28] Having spent a good portion of two decades in and out of jails and prisons, Hudgens was determined never to go back.

But the difficulties of his circumstances, once the doors of the prison opened, make clear the challenges facing those trying to start over on the outside. It's all too easy to fall back into familiar habits. Prison's "revolving door" is very real. Ultimately, this is the greatest challenge that our criminal justice system faces.

As Katy Steinbruck, director of programs for Offender Aid and Restoration of Arlington, a reentry nonprofit, puts it, "Just not having a plan, not having a place to be. You gravitate toward survival. And that makes you vulnerable. There are definitely people on the streets who are gonna take advantage of that. And then boom, you've done all this work pre-release to reduce somebody's risk and it skyrockets the second they step away from the facility." She continued, "When things start going wrong, typically they started going wrong right away. And if things start going wrong initially, that places you in a really high-risk category."[29]

Rudolph Norris was one of 22 lucky nonviolent drug offenders who had their sentences commuted by President Obama as part of his push to shorten sentences in the summer of 2015. (The commutations end the sentence but preserve the conviction.) At 58, Norris became a free man after spending over ten years in various prison libraries studying federal drug law and pursuing his release. His case made its way to a George Washington University Law School clinic, where he found a student to assist him. Today, they refer to Norris as the Miracle of Morgantown.[30]

But that doesn't mean that being on the outside will be easy. Far from it.

"He's going to be fighting for his life. It's going to be hard as hell, but he has to be willing to do whatever it takes. It's not going to be up to him what that is. He won't decide how long he's going to have to do it. He'll have to have some faith," Courtney Stewart, founder of the Reentry Network for Returning Citizens, told the *New York Times*.[31] Stewart works with ex-prisoners as they look for jobs, housing, and mental-health services, if needed. "It was terribly hard when I first got out," said Richard Martin, a recovering drug addict who went to jail two decades ago for felony drug possession. "You feel like the civilized world doesn't really want me, and maybe they're right, I should be with people like me."[32] Martin found that most private employers wouldn't even look at his application, a key reason that 60 percent of ex-convicts face long-term unemployment.[33] He eventually became a teacher but had his license revoked after the state found out about his conviction. Ultimately, he earned a master's degree and now works in the nonprofit sector. But he's one of the lucky ones.

It is our challenge as a society to ensure that we have as many Rudolph Norrises as possible. We are moving forward with criminal justice reform which will include, as a central plank, reducing and commuting sentences for inmates. Obama's release of 6,000 federal inmates in October 2015[34] and another 61 in March 2016[35] will happen more regularly. As Hillary Clinton put it at a rally at Clark Atlanta University, "People who have paid their dues to society need to be able to find jobs. We believe in second chances, don't we?"[36]

The question is how we can make sure those second chances lead to success. Perhaps the greatest challenge to reforming the system is making sure that ex-inmates can get a job and reintegrate into society. "Through the inescapable stigma it imposes, a brush with the criminal-justice system can hamstring a former inmate's employment and financial opportunities for life," Matt Ford writes in the *Atlantic*. "Mass incarceration's effects are not confined to the cell block.... The effect is magnified for those who already come from disadvantaged backgrounds."[37]

This is especially true when you consider the rates of recidivism in America. In 2014, the Bureau of Justice Statistics released information on recidivism from 2005. The figures show that nearly 67.8 percent of 404,000 prisoners tracked from across 30 states were re-arrested within three years. The re-arrest rate jumps to 77 percent within five years.[38] Just over 50 percent were re-arrested within the first year after release.[39] Blacks have the highest recidivism rate after five years, at almost 81 percent, compared with 73 percent among whites and 75 percent for Hispanics.[40]

Not being able to get a job is a central factor in high recidivism rates. A study of Missouri's prisoners found that re-incarceration rates were halved for former inmates with full-time jobs.[41] Some 70 million Americans have some type of arrest or conviction on their records. That means that each day, thousands are faced with the dilemma that Tamisha Walker, who spent six months in jail on arson charges, faced when applying for a job at Burlington Coat Factory: Do you check the "yes" box on a job application when it asks if you've ever been convicted of a crime?[42] California has passed a law requiring state employers to ask this question only after an applicant meets the basic requirements for the job.[43] San Francisco has extended this policy to private employers. This "ban the box" approach has gained federal support as well, with Obama directing federal agencies to delay inquiries into applicants' records until later in the process.[44] The next few years should see tremendous gains in ex-convicts' ability to get decent jobs thanks to state and federal support for banning the box.

But succeeding isn't just about having a job; you've got to be healthy, too. Another area in need of crucial improvement is that of mental health and drug addiction, issues that we have handled very poorly up until recently.

## MENTAL HEALTH AND DRUG ADDICTION

"We're using jails and prisons as a substitute for a properly functioning mental health system,"[45] says Senator Al Franken, a co-sponsor of the Justice and Mental Health Act. A study by the National Research Council supports Franken's assertion: 64 percent of jail inmates, 54 percent of state prisoners, and 45 percent of federal prisoners reported mental-health concerns in 2006.[46] The report found that there are ten times more mentally ill Americans in prisons and jails than in state psychiatric hospitals— a direct result of the movement in the 1950s to deinstitutionalize mental health, which led to the presence of thousands of mentally ill people on the streets, while others were wrongfully incarcerated.[47] By 2015, an Urban

Institute Report found that more than half of all inmates in jails and state prisons have a mental illness: 55 percent of male inmates and 73 percent of female inmates. The most common problem is depression followed by bipolar disorder. What's more, "only one in three state prisoners and one in six jail inmates who suffer from mental-health problems report having received mental-health treatment since admission."[48]

The odds of a seriously mentally ill individual being imprisoned rather than hospitalized are 3.2 to 1. E. Fuller Torrey, founder of the Treatment Advocacy Center, calls the lack of treatment for mental illnesses in our prison system "inhumane." Torrey adds, "If societies are judged by how they treat their most disabled members, our society will be judged harshly indeed."[49] A study of 132 suicide attempts in a county jail in Washington found that in 77 percent of the cases, the individual in question had a "chronic psychiatric problem." One schizophrenic man in New York spent 13 years of his 15-year sentence in solitary confinement.[50]

Drug addiction is rampant in our prisons: 65 percent of the 2.3 million Americans in the system meet criteria for substance-abuse addiction. "Our prison system does little more than teach addicts how to be better addicts," writes addiction psychiatrist David Sack in the *Washington Post*. He continues, "Inmates are likely to find a drug trade as active as the one outside prison walls. Many is the time I've listened sadly as family members have consoled themselves about a loved one's incarceration by saying, 'At least he'll have to quit using now.' If only."[51]

Addicts get little help from within the system. The National Center on Addiction and Substance Abuse at Columbia University found that only 11 percent of inmates with substance addictions got treatment in federal, state, or local prisons.[52] "No wonder that more than half of inmates with addiction histories relapse within a month of release,"[53] Sack writes.

## SOLUTIONS

Obviously, the subjects of policing, crime, and incarceration are intimately related. For years, debates around these topics have been polarized and largely fruitless, in no small part due to America's political polarization. The Left tends to see police conspiracies against blacks; the Right often is reluctant to criticize police officers unless their wrongdoing is so blatant (and evident on video) that it cannot be denied. The Left often sees our prison system as a gulag in which thousands of people are unjustly locked up; the Right often is resistant to even sensible sentencing reforms and other legal reforms as being "soft on crime." Recent years have seen some promising convergences between the Right and the Left on prison and sentencing reforms—on the police and crime, less so. But improvement is possible in all areas.

## Policing

As we have indicated in this chapter, we tend to believe that policing reform is a matter of making adjustments, not wholesale, radical change. The best model for doing so is the career of the NYPD's retiring police commissioner, Bill Bratton, a pioneer in using computerized technology called Compstat (short for "comparative statistics") to drive down crime rates by mapping arrest and patrol activity. In celebrating Bratton's impact on policing, which cannot be underestimated, Juan Williams writes, "Bratton's innovative approach to policing has driven the nation's crime rate to historic lows; changed the way Americans accept being constantly monitored, even videotaped in public."[54] Even liberal New York mayor Bill de Blasio, who often clashed with Bratton, touted him as someone "whose contributions to our city and law enforcement not only here, but across the nation are literally inestimable and extraordinary."[55]

But Bratton was more than just a visionary crime fighter. In the latter stages of his career, he also showed a growing awareness of the importance of community buy-in, of police work's essential component of public and even political management, of the responsibilities that police face in a democratic society to be accountable and sensitive. He showed that there is a way to preserve proactive policing while reducing impositions on daily life—especially in his moving away from the tactic known as "stop and frisk," detested by many black New Yorkers and practiced heavily under Bratton's predecessor, Ray Kelly. And Bratton did this while still getting top results, keeping crime low and even driving it lower.

Bratton managed to present an appealing face to the broader community, including to minorities, while also letting his rank and file know that he had their backs. In a powerful editorial just after retiring, Bratton writes,

Officers now live in a transparent world, with continual monitoring by cellphones, dashboard cameras and body cameras, which sometimes reveal genuine wrongdoing but also can lead to second-guessing of officers' actions by politicians and the public. You have to show them you care about them, their safety, job satisfaction and careers. And you have to prove it by making fundamental changes in management, equipment, working conditions, training, discipline and operations.[56]

Beyond creating this kind of environment in police forces and the reforms regularly discussed, like requiring all officers to wear body cameras and putting smartphones in their hands, Bratton recommends additional policing reforms, including:

- providing six months of field training and work with community partners for new officers;
- giving instruction on de-escalating confrontations and treating people, including criminals, with respect and fairness;
- matching homeless people with the services they need;
- applying a less arrest-driven approach to emotionally disturbed people;
- instituting a neighborhood-based policing program that localizes police work.[57]

These are guidelines every police force would be smart to take on board and, indeed, many across the nation have emulated Bratton's example. Overall, Bratton's legacy will be one of lowering crime rates in an effective and socially constructive way. Going forward, he is the model thinker and practitioner for police forces around the nation looking to improve their effectiveness, reduce social tensions, and build and deepen community relationships, especially among minority citizens. And nowhere does he say that police should stop policing.

### Fighting Recidivism

Prisoners who can work at jobs while incarcerated get a leg up on life in the outside world, in addition to gaining a sense of purpose. "I made $1.75 a day in prison and I never felt exploited," Chandra Bozelko wrote in the *Wall Street Journal*. Bozelko, a former inmate at maximum-security York

Correctional Institution in Niantic, Connecticut, continued, "My prison work assignment actually made me feel like a human being. Every other woman with whom I worked felt the same way."[58] A Manhattan Institute study found that "rapid attachment" to employment reduces recidivism by 20 percent. "Getting and keeping a job requires more than just vocational training; an ex-offender needs to get along in the workplace, too, and that's what prison work assignments teach," Bozelko said.

There is ample evidence that education and vocational training in prisons cuts down on recidivism. A 2013 RAND Corporation report shows that for every $1 investment in prison education, incarceration costs are reduced by $4–5 in the first three years after release.[59] Those who participated in some prison-based educational program were 43 percent less likely to re-offend.[60] According to Lois Davis, who headed the study, "Prisoners who participated in academic or vocational education programs had a 13% better chance of finding employment than those who did not. And prisoners who participated specifically in vocational training programs were 28% more likely to be employed after release from prison than those who were left out."[61]

Failure to invest in education and job-skills rehabilitation programs makes it more likely that the 60,000 ex-offenders who reenter society each year will become re-offenders. By gaining essential skills, ex-convicts will radically improve their job prospects and other future opportunities. Without such programs, many ex-convicts will face dim economic prospects.

A key component here, in prison and out of prison, is education. Evidence suggests that taking courses in prison reduces recidivism. Currently, however, only a privileged few prisoners get to take classes. At Attica, for instance, only 1 percent of prisoners are enrolled in a privately funded program to get associate's degrees.[62] New York governor Andrew Cuomo announced plans to expand private education programs by allocating $1 billion of the $3 billion corrections budget to them, but his proposal ran into stiff political resistance. It's understandable that law-abiding taxpayers, many of whom can't afford college themselves, would resent paying for prisoners' education. The best bet is to use the free online courses provided by companies like Coursera.

For ex-cons, the barriers to entering the "real world" after prison are high indeed. We support the "ban the box" campaign not only for federal employers but for private employers as well. This would mean removing "have you been convicted of a crime" only from the opening application, not subsequent follow-ups. Inquiries into an applicant's criminal history will not be banned full stop but will come later in the process. It would help 70 million American ex-convicts get their foot in the door of potential employment.

Judges should be encouraged to evaluate more requests for expunging convictions for non-serious offenses. This is becoming more common for nonviolent offenders and should be considered more regularly so that offenders are able to reenter society and get jobs. As one judge put it, "I sentenced her to five years of probation supervision, not to a lifetime of unemployment."[63]

Incentives should be provided for employers to hire ex-convicts. In Los Angeles County, for instance, local, state, and federal entities give priority to bids from contractors who employ people coming out of jail.[64] In conjunction with banning the box, this should help those released from prison reintegrate into society. It is also welcome news that the Department of Education has allocated $8 million over three years to fund skills-training programs. Thirty communities will provide tech and coding training to former prisoners.[65]

Sensible reforms that could help ex-cons reintegrate into society extend beyond jobs to housing arrangements. The Obama administration has issued new guidelines for when arrest records can be used for housing eligibility. A series of smaller initiatives from the Obama administration will also make it easier for prisoners to live in subsidized housing by mandating that arrest records cannot be the sole reason to turn down applicants or the sole cause of evicting tenants.[66] This policy emulates a New Orleans law wherein a criminal record is no longer an automatic trigger for rejection for public housing.[67]

### Reforming Youth-offender Laws, Reducing Unjust Laws

"The biggest impediment to civil rights and employment in our country is a criminal record," write Republican senator Rand Paul and Democratic senator Cory Booker, cosponsors of a sentencing-reform law. "Our current system is broken and has trapped tens of thousands of young men and women in a cycle of poverty and incarceration."[68] Their bill focuses

on raising the age of criminal responsibility to 18 and expunging or seal-
ing the records of juveniles who commit nonviolent crimes before they
turn 15. They also want to give "eligible nonviolent criminals" the right to
have their criminal records sealed so that they won't show up in employer
background checks.[69] Their bill is worth supporting.

Today, ten states try youths under the age of 18 in adult criminal
court. Former Speaker of the House Newt Gingrich, a longtime supporter of criminal justice reform, offers that states "have done a poor
job of taking this gap into account in their sentencing codes. They might
condemn teenagers to life in prison without the opportunity for parole,
for instance, for crimes they committed when they were 14 or 15 years
old."[70] Although we can't let criminal activity slide, we also shouldn't treat
children as adults, locking them away for life terms. "People who commit offenses before their capacities are fully formed," Gingrich writes,
"deserve a second chance—an opportunity for a parole hearing if they
mature, rehabilitate, and pay serious restitution to their victims and to
the community."

More broadly, we should also reduce the number of laws—especially
federal laws—that lead to prison sentences. The number of federal laws
has risen from 3,000 in the early 1980s to over 4,450 by 2008;[71] violators
are often locked up for transgressions they didn't even know existed.
Congress should play a more active role in vetting new criminal laws
and taking a skeptical view of new criminal offenses or penalties—while
repealing unjust laws. Meanwhile, at the state level, between 2000 and
2010, 17 states reduced their number of prisoners while also reducing
crime, and conservative states like Texas led the way.

## CONCLUSION

Now is the time to seize bipartisan enthusiasm to address crime in
America, our criminal justice system, and, perhaps most critically, the
prospects for successful lives after prison for ex-convicts. We can't think
of a time in the last several decades where these issues were as prominent in the public mind as they are now. The efforts on both sides of the
aisle to reform sentencing laws and make greater assistance available to
prisoners, from mental-health services to job training, show clearly the
potential that exists for substantial achievements.

More broadly, while the specifics may remain contested, the principles should be clear for how to proceed on issues of crime, policing, and incarceration: continue America's long-running success against crime by maintaining the policing revolution that enabled it, but innovating new approaches that cause less social friction and abuse; continue to prosecute and punish serious crimes, but think constructively about lessening penalties or even changing laws regarding offenses for which incarceration does more harm than good; and make rehabilitation, job training, and network-building fundamental practices for those released from prison and trying to start a new life.

# CHAPTER 7

# Educational Failure

The school system doesn't want to change, because it serves the needs of the adult stakeholders quite well, both politically and financially.

—Joel Klein[1]

A lot of people say you shouldn't talk of education as a business, but the reality is, it is a business.... My idea [is] that parents should have hundreds of choices, whereas currently if they go to the public school system, they have one, maybe two. They have precious few choices. Once you open up competition, the choices will be abundant.

—Bob Luddy, chairman, Franklin Academy[2]

Few leaders better represent innovation in urban schooling than Geoffrey Canada. The charismatic New Yorker devoted his career to improving educational outcomes for underclass American children, especially minorities. Through his work heading the Harlem Children's Zone (HCZ) between 1990 and 2014, Canada transformed a family-oriented community center into a model for national education reform.

Growing up in the South Bronx, Canada sensed the need for profound education reform. He went on to design programs that combated the culture of poverty and offered support to those lacking the choice and opportunity that more affluent Americans enjoy. In the inner city, Canada points out, many saw it as "a rite of passage for boys to go to reform schools" and subsequently to "end up going to prison."[3] By contrast, the HCZ and its national partners focus on "working hard, focusing on college, being responsible," and "delaying pregnancy and childbearing until you're a professional."[4] HCZ students typically outperform an average white student in the New York City public school system in math and have narrowed the black-white achievement gap in language arts.[5]

Canada seeks to "make sure our education system prepares our students to fill every quality job that our economy produces....If we get those two things right—plentiful jobs and Americans with the skills to fill them—we can recapture the American Dream for generations to come," he says.[6]

Canada is an inspiring figure, but we're a long way from achieving his dream for all American kids. Most Americans agree by now that our education system is a failure. We spend an average of $10,768 per pupil on primary and secondary education annually, more than any other OECD country except Switzerland.[7] In fact, the United States has *doubled spending on education* over the past 40 years—but test scores in reading, math, and science have remained stubbornly flat.[8]

School dropout rates, especially in poor areas, are staggeringly high; we're creating generations of unemployable people. Our failures have already caused a massive skills gap in the American economy, at both ends of the range; low-income, poorly educated people are often unemployable. And if you're looking for an explanation for why America has the world's largest prison population, look no further. American taxpayers pay far more to incarcerate inmates for four years than it would have cost to educate those inmates properly when they were in elementary school. Meanwhile, in Silicon Valley, firms are constantly importing foreigners to do the high-tech development work for which not enough Americans are qualified. Why hasn't pouring more money into the system worked?

Because the system itself is the problem.

Nothing less than a total educational overhaul is needed in the United States. There is no single, silver-bullet solution, but vouchers, charters, private options, and rigorous standards, among other worthy solutions, all have their virtues. In this chapter, we'll examine a range of options centered on the premise of market-based education, with parents in the driver's seat—a premise that could not just reform American education but remake it. But remake it from what? Let's first review the sorry state of American schooling.

## FALLING BEHIND IN THE EARLY GRADES

Start where the education system begins: with early-age and elementary-grade schooling. Here, the progress of fourth-graders and eighth-graders in reading and math is regularly monitored by the National Assessment of Educational Progress (NAEP), known as "the nation's report card" and the "gold standard" in measuring students' achievement and readiness. On the surface, there is some good news to report. Over the past 40 years, reading scores rose by 6 percent among 9-year-olds and 3 percent among 13-year-olds. Math scores rose by 11 percent among 9-year-olds and 7 percent among 13-year-olds.[9] As we will see, American education is at its best, by far, in the early grades.

But NAEP studies over the last 20 years show student progress slowing, and in fact progress was greater in the years before President George W. Bush's No Child Left Behind (NCLB) in 2003 than it has been since.[10] For over a decade now, NCLB has been a lightning rod of debate in education circles: its critics believe that the law forced teachers to prioritize test-taking and thus emphasize certain content that will appear on the tests at the expense of other, perhaps more vital, material.[11] And with all the law's incentives toward higher test results, the tests themselves, critics charged, were designed around questions that measured the ability to recall facts, rather than deeper thinking or analytical abilities. By making test scores such a high-stakes game, NCLB's incentives even encouraged—unintentionally—test-score inflation (if not outright cheating) as states raced to meet NCLB's "proficiency" requirement.[12]

Over more than a decade, NCLB has produced nominal improvement in test-score performance but also raised serious questions about genuine knowledge and readiness. And American students' performance trends steadily downward from eighth grade on, by both domestic and international measurements—especially the Programme for International Student Assessment (PISA), a widely respected triennial international survey that tests the skills of 15-year-old students in mathematics, science, and reading in over 70 countries, including the United States.

In the most recent PISA assessment, in 2015, the United States ranked 24th in reading and 36th in math.[13] Students in other nations are improving their PISA performance, but U.S. students are performing worse. Data from just a few years ago shows that one-quarter of American students failed to reach "Level 2" in math proficiency on the PISA, compared with just 10 percent of students in Canada, Korea, Shanghai, and Singapore failing to reach that benchmark.[14] Only 2 percent of U.S. students reached the highest performance level on the PISA math assessment—compared with 3 percent of students in most OECD countries and as much as *30 percent* of students in top performers like Singapore, Hong Kong, and Shanghai.[15]

To get a sense of the gap, consider that the average math score for Shanghai students was 613 (compared with the OECD average of 494), the average reading score was 570 (OECD average: 496), and the average science score 580 (OECD average: 501). The United States, meanwhile, lagged behind the OECD average in all three areas. U.S. students scored on average 481 in math, 498 in reading, and 497 in science.[16]

Some critics dismiss the importance of PISA by claiming that the high poverty rate among American students drives U.S. scores down. Certainly, America's 20 percent child-poverty rate is a factor here. Yet if poverty were the determining factor, how could the United States rank behind countries like Vietnam, which has a poverty rate of 79 percent?

No wonder former Secretary of Education Arne Duncan called our PISA results a "picture of educational stagnation."[17] Duncan's words were echoed by Angel Gurria, secretary-general of the OECD. "This is not only a great loss to the American economy, it's obviously a very great consequence to people's future," he said. "Poor educational performance limits access to employment and widens social inequality."[18]

As American students move through high school, things get worse.

## HIGH SCHOOL STAGNATION, COLLEGE REMEDIATION

There is one other age group for whom NAEP measures educational progress: 17-year-olds. Over the last 40 years, this cohort has *shown no improvement whatsoever on standardized tests*. Reading and math scores for 17-year-olds have not moved at all.[19]

Optimists like to point to U.S. high school graduation rates as a bell-wether indicator for whether our children are ready to move on to college or professional or trade education. And on the surface, things look good: the high school graduation rate in the United States reached an all-time high of 81 percent in the 2012–2013 school year.[20] High school graduation rates have risen 1.3 percent annually since 2006; if this rate is maintained, U.S. high schools will reach a graduation rate of 90 percent by 2020.[21]

Sounds good, right? But these statistics put the United States near the bottom of the OECD's 2014 list of high school graduation rates for developed countries.[22] And the average number ignores the great disparities that exist in graduation rates from state to state. For example, while Virginia and Maryland both have above-average graduation rates (84 and 83 percent, respectively), the nearby District of Columbia only has a graduation rate of 59 percent—well below the national average.[23]

Drill down farther and you see that among different groups of students, the disparities in graduation rates are vast: White students graduate at an 86 percent rate, Hispanic students at 76 percent; black students, however, graduate at just 68 percent.[24] (A McKinsey study found that U.S. annual GDP could increase by as much as $525 billion if the achievement gap between white students and black and Hispanic students were closed.[25]) Girls graduated at substantially higher rates than boys, 84 to 77 percent.[26] And some 1.1 million American high school students drop out every year.

The dropout rates, along with the lagging test scores, no doubt have many causes, but surely one of them is that American high school students are less engaged by their schoolwork than their counterparts in other countries.[27] Surveys show that American high school students find school boring and uninspiring; some critics see high school as a holding pen for young adults who have left the rigors of their elementary years behind and are marking time, trying to determine whether they will go to college.

No wonder, then, that American students show a growing college-readiness gap.[28] About 21 million students attended a college or university during the fall semester of 2014, an increase of about 5.7 million students since 2000.[29] More than two-thirds of high school graduates were enrolled in an institution of higher learning in 2014, according to the Bureau of Labor and Statistics.[30]

But fewer and fewer can do the work.

About *one-half* of all students at less-selective four-year colleges and universities require remedial work in English or math. (At two-year colleges, the figure is closer to 75 percent.) Only 4 percent of black students and 11 percent of Hispanic students finish high school ready for college in their core subjects.[31] Even students who have completed college-prep curricula often require remedial work in various subjects.

ACT Inc., which administers the ACT college entry exam, reported that just 26 percent of high school students who took the text in 2014 met college-readiness benchmarks in math, science, English, and reading.[32] Individually, 64 percent of students met the benchmarks for English, 44 percent met the benchmarks for reading, 43 percent for mathematics, and only 37 percent for science, though the science score represents a substantial boost since 2010..[33]

These numbers are abysmal for an advanced nation.

"It is concerning that while we keep calling this up and trying to address it, we're not making great progress," says ACT president Jon Erickson, speaking about the college readiness of high school graduates in 2013. "We get some small signs that we start to get optimistic and celebrate about, and then it takes a quick slide back a point or two."[34]

Several explanations have been offered for this alarming situation. Two-thirds of college professors report that what is taught in high schools does not adequately prepare students for college.[35] Some suggest that the problem lies with the college-prep standards, which are generally formulated without input from colleges and universities. Thus, high school teachers often teach to standards matching the SAT and ACT tests, which are used as gauges for college admission but are not reliable guides of college readiness. Others say that high schools improperly gauge student preparedness.

Perhaps the remediation figures wouldn't be so alarming if these students caught up successfully and went on to graduate—yet only 10 percent do.[36] And remedial education isn't the only problem with the college graduation picture. Consider:

- While the United States has one of the world's highest rates of college entry among advanced nations, its college *completion* rate is the worst among such countries. More than one-third of U.S. students entering full-time, two-year colleges drop out after one year; about one in five students at four-year colleges do the same.[37]
- The vast majority of college students don't earn their degrees within four years. At most public universities, only 19 percent of students earn a bachelor's degree in that space of time.[38]
- Even at more selective state universities, only 36 percent of students graduate in four years.[39]

- Nationally, less than 10 percent of public four-year institutions graduate more than half of their students within four years.[40]
- Only 5 percent of full-time community college students earned an associate's degree within two years.[41]

In today's economy, college degrees have never been more crucial to getting a job with a decent wage. In the next decade, approximately 63 percent of jobs in the United States are expected to require a college degree—meaning that the workforce will need 22 million new college-educated employees. The United States is expected to fall short of this number by 3 million graduates.[42] Even President Obama's $60 billion community college plan, which would offer free tuition, won't do anything to change the underlying problem with graduation rates.[43]

"They're too focused on efficiency and not enough on quality," says Debra Humphreys, a spokeswoman for the Association of American Colleges and Universities, on criticism that college students do not complete school in time. "Yes, we have a huge completion problem, but we also have a problem that a lot of students graduated without learning what they need."[44]

It's no surprise then, with college readiness lacking and graduation rates lagging, that *career* readiness also suffers among young people. In a 2008 survey, more than three out of four employers reported that new employees with four-year college degrees were deficient in basic knowledge and applied skills; nearly half of businesses employing recent high school graduates said that these workers weren't prepared for their jobs.[45]

"It's a huge issue for society. It's a huge issue for the individual students who are spending more money on tuition than they need to," says Matthew Chingos, author of *Crossing the Finish Line: Completing College at America's Public Universities*. "The longer they wait to graduate and get a job, those are extra years of their careers when they're in college and not working and not making money."[46] Not only are they are often not making money by virtue of being unemployed, but also, even when they are employed, they often face staggering student loan debt.

## UNAFFORDABLE COLLEGE TUITION

"As a nation, we need more college graduates in order to stay competitive in the global economy," says Arne Duncan. "But if the costs keep on rising, especially at a time when family incomes are hurting, college will become increasingly unaffordable for the middle class."[47] Duncan is too modest; college tuitions have been unaffordable for years.

In 2013, the average annual tuition at four-year, private colleges or universities was $40,917; at a public four-year college, it was $18,391. Those figures are up 14 percent and 20 percent, respectively, in five years.[48] In the past 30 years, college tuition has exploded by 1,120 percent.[49] The class of 2014 had an average student loan debt of $33,000.[50] The total U.S. student loan debt now exceeds *$1.3 trillion.*[51]

Combine the high cost of obtaining a college degree, the weak job prospects for young people (and stagnant wages), and the fact that millions of young (and jobless) college graduates are up to their eyeballs in debt, and you can see why the younger generation of Americans don't share the optimism that prevailed in past eras.

So that's a succinct summary of our education picture: failing schools, especially in urban areas serving minority students; stagnating test-score performance and poor proficiency levels, even among affluent students; mounting numbers of college students who need remedial assistance; low college graduation rates; skyrocketing college costs; and, even among those who do complete college, weak career readiness.

## WHAT DO WE DO ABOUT IT?

Today's education system is built to serve the economy and job market of the past.[52] We are stuck in old models that no longer serve us.

The fundamental and overriding priority is this: we must remake our education system along market principles that empower parents as educational consumers and make the education of their children the only goal—not the protection of jobs or the preservation of lavish, taxpayer-supported benefits. In the end, for American education to be saved, it must be saved from the American education *system*—and realigned along aggressive, even radically market-oriented lines. In education, we share the goal of the libertarian Cato Institute, which hopes to see state-run schools give way to a "dynamic, independent system of schools competing to meet the needs of American children."[53]

True education reform, let alone education transformation, begins with parental choice and empowerment. Random-assignment studies show overwhelmingly that parental choice in education improves students' academic outcomes; no study exists demonstrating that parental choice harms a child's education.[54]

Under that heading, a range of reforms exist, all of which would put more autonomy and decision-making power in the hands of parents. We do not believe that these reforms alone can address every ill that plagues our public schools, but we do believe that without them—or without, most specifically, the fundamental principle of parental choice—school reform in the United States will remain illusory.

## *Vouchers and Scholarship Tax Credits*

School vouchers are the most widely known reform and have been around for a few decades. They have staunch critics and proponents. Under a typical voucher system, parents would receive the monetary equivalent of their child's per-pupil expenditure for the school year in the form of a voucher, which the parent could then use to send the child to a school of his or her choice. Voucher supporters point out that parents want the best education for their children and will pick the best possible schools to send them to. Not only will their child get a better education, but also the poorly performing schools will feel the pressure of losing enrollment and either take steps to perform better or shut down. Vouchers would bring market forces to the school system, proponents say, with parents as the consumers driving market patterns.

Opponents say that vouchers will only divert resources (that is, money) from already struggling public schools; vouchers will help a small subset of the student population while ensuring that the vast majority go to schools even weaker than before. The critics tend to dismiss claims that competition will improve public schools, and they worry that sending kids to private (and sometimes parochial) schools with public funds violates the constitutional separation of church and state.

These issues have been adjudicated for years in the courts, including the Supreme Court, with mixed results. The high court in 2002 upheld an Ohio voucher system, seeming to clear away constitutional barriers to voucher programs; but in 2006, the Florida Supreme Court struck down what would have been a statewide voucher system. (Florida has maintained, however, its Tax Credit Scholarship Program, which offers tax credits to corporations that contribute to organizations providing vouchers to children from low-income families. Research has shown that Florida schools at risk of losing students to private schools have improved their performance.)[55]

At the legislative level, Democrats tend to oppose vouchers, while Republicans support them. In 2009, congressional Democrats let Washington's voucher program for inner-city students, the D.C. Opportunity Scholarships Program, expire. It was reauthorized in 2011, and then again in 2017. Obama had leveled off its funding, despite studies showing that the program boosts student graduation rates by as much as 21 percent and encouraged parents to search for new schools in the proactive and engaged way that many search for a new car or a new house.[56]

Clearly, vouchers remain highly contested political terrain—though 66 percent of mothers with school-aged children nationwide support universal vouchers and 69 percent support tuition tax-credit options.[57] The political battles are not likely to be resolved anytime soon. That means that other measures are needed to empower parents.

Perhaps the most promising of these are scholarship tax credits (STCs), which grant full or partial refunds of state taxes for individuals against donations they make to nonprofit scholarship organizations. The nonprofits help families enroll their kids in schools of their choice.

"In contrast to vouchers," the Cato Institute says, "which distribute funds contributed from a compulsory tax, STCs entail private funding from voluntary contributions." Indeed, donations to the scholarship organizations are voluntary—and the organizations have more freedom to pick the schools for which they provide scholarship aid. STCs, then, in Cato's words again, not only "enhance the freedom of conscience of parents by helping parents choose a school that aligns with their values and educational preferences" but also "preserve the freedom of conscience of taxpayers in a manner consistent with America's founding ideals."[58] Currently, about 200,000 students in 14 states use STCs, which are proving popular with parents.[59]

## Education Savings Accounts

Another promising recent alternative is education savings accounts, also known as empowerment scholarship accounts and commonly abbreviated as ESAs, which act as a form of educational choice for those opting out of public schools. Currently, two states—Florida and Arizona—employ ESAs for students who opt out of public school.[60] Under this arrangement, states redirect 90 percent of the money they would have spent on a student at a public school into their ESA. The accounts—which parents access through a debit card—can be used not just for tuition at a private school but also to pay for tutors, textbooks, homeschool curricula, online classes, and more.[61] And parents can choose to save unused ESA funds for college tuition.[62]

Arizona was the first state to offer ESAs, in 2011, originally limiting the program to special needs children but then expanding it broadly. Over 70 percent of parents in Arizona's ESA program report being "very satisfied" with their children's educational experience. State enrollment in the program has nearly doubled over the past year.[63] In 2014, Florida enacted its own ESAs, now called Gardiner Scholarships. ESAs are catching on nationally.

Whether it's ESAs, STCs, traditional school vouchers, or some as-yet undersigned option, in our view the fundamental reality remains the same: we need expanded parental choice and market competition in education. In 1955, Milton Friedman became the first to voice the idea of vouchers. Plenty of debates have come and gone since then, but the great economist's words remain as relevant today as ever:

> Let the subsidy be made available to parents regardless [of] where they send their children—provided only that it be to schools that satisfy specified minimum standards—and a wide variety of schools will spring up to meet the demand. Parents could express their views about schools directly, by withdrawing their children from one school and sending them to another, to a much greater extent than is now possible.[64]

## Charter Schools

"Up in Harlem," says Stephen Brill, author of *Class Warfare: Inside the Fight to Fix America's Schools*, "there's a building where on one side of the building there's a conventional public school, and unfortunately those kids perform the way the stereotype would say. On the other side of the building—the same community, in fact often the siblings of the kids on the public school side—kids are performing the same way as kids in Scarsdale, one of the wealthiest suburbs of New York. It doesn't prove that all charter schools are good. It doesn't prove anything other than the fact that we don't have to tolerate this problem. We can fix it."[65]

Brill was talking about Success Academy Harlem I, a New York City charter school that shares a building with P.S. 149, a traditional public school. Both schools' student bodies are overwhelmingly composed of children from disadvantaged socioeconomic circumstances—yet their results differ dramatically. At Harlem I, 86 percent of students are proficient in reading; 94 percent are proficient in math. Meanwhile, only 29 percent of P.S. 149 students reached proficiency in reading and just 34 percent in math.[66] "If all 32 schools in the Success Academy network made up a single, large school, it would rank seventh out of the 3,560 New York State schools in math," write Jared Meyer and Diana Furchtgott-Roth. Ninety-four percent of Success Academy students are proficient in math and 64 percent are proficient in English-language arts, compared with 35 percent and 29 percent, respectively, on average, for New York City public schools.[67]

Success Academy is just one example of the promise of charter schools—public schools that are independently run and generally free of the restrictions imposed on traditional public schools. About 2.3 million American students—4 percent of primary-education students[68]—attend more than 6,000 charter schools operating around the United States.[69]

Not every charter school gets results like Success Academy. Some have failed and closed, and management problems have dogged others. But taken overall, charters have left standard public schools in the dust. Research from distinguished Stanford University economics professor Caroline Hoxby reveals that students attending charters would make up 86 percent of the fabled "Scarsdale-Harlem achievement gap" in math and 66 percent in reading—Scarsdale being one of the wealthiest neighborhoods in metro New York and Harlem one of the poorest. Hoxby also found that a disadvantaged student attending a charter would, by the end of eighth grade, score 30 points higher on a standardized math test than a peer who stayed in a traditional public school.[70]

There's more: a study by Mathematica Policy Research compared students who had won admission to schools through the charter lottery with those who had applied for the lottery and lost. It found that KIPP schools— a charter network serving students in 20 states and Washington, D.C.—produce, over three years, the equivalent of *11 additional months of learning* in mathematics for students.[71] The report also found that students in KIPP schools spent between 35 and 53 additional minutes on their homework per night than they would have in a public school. And KIPP eighth-graders go to college at *twice the national rate* of low-income students.[72] Harvard University's Paul E. Peterson, an education policy expert, believes that American students could be "competitive with the highest-scoring countries in the world" if we dramatically increase charter school enrollment.[73]

Charter schools' leading critics are just who you would imagine: public school officials and teachers. They charge that charters are an escape route for white, middle-class families to escape failing urban schools—though data demonstrate that charters serve primarily poor and minority students.[74] In fact, a slightly higher proportion of charter school students come from families in poverty than those in traditional public schools. In big-city school districts like New York, charters' student populations are overwhelmingly minority.[75]

Moreover, the unions' resistance flies in the face of parental support for charters in minority communities. Among African Americans, support for charters runs at greater than three to one, while among the general public, it's two to one.[76]

At the moment, there is far more demand for charters than the schools can accommodate. In 2014, over 70,000 students in New York City applied for 21,000 available places in charter schools.[77] Selections are made on a lottery system; the lucky few escape their neighborhood's failing public school, while the others are stuck there. The situation was dramatized in the 2011 documentary *Waiting for Superman*. Nationally, more than one million young people have entered their names on waiting lists.[78]

In New York, the battle between traditional public schools and charters has been contentious, but not every city has set the two options against one another. Spring Branch, a Houston school district, demonstrates how charters and more traditional public schools might work together constructively. KIPP and YES Prep, two successful charter networks, opened schools with their own personnel within the same building as a traditional public school—a common practice, known as co-location, that helps charters save money and find space. In Spring Branch, the KIPP and YES Prep teachers shared ideas and programs with the public school teachers—and the public school offered access to extracurricular activities that charter students often lack. Richard Barth, KIPP's CEO, says that such collaborations are becoming more common.[79]

In short, charters work and should be supported aggressively. No, they cannot be a cure-all to what ails American schools—the very fact that they don't have enough seats for all the students who want to attend them makes that clear. Many charter critics hated *Waiting for Superman*, feeling that it painted a rosy picture of the lucky lottery students while downplaying those who get left behind. Without question, having lotteries that choose some kids and leave others behind is a painful process—yet it only magnifies the failures of those traditional public schools. It is *this* failure, not the imperfections of charters, that is the real problem.

### The Private Option

Bob Luddy is the CEO of North Carolina–based CaptiveAire Systems, a $300 million private manufacturer of commercial kitchen-ventilation products. CaptiveAire is one of the fastest-growing private companies in the United States. In 1998, Luddy, a passionate advocate for education, founded the Franklin Academy, one of North Carolina's first charter schools. Like many charters, Franklin started small, but it has since grown to enroll 1,650 students in five locations, offering kindergarten to eighth grade and a high school. Franklin's waiting list is nearly as large as its student body.

But Luddy wasn't satisfied. Successful as Franklin was, as a public charter, it was still subject to much of the pressures that charter schools face, whether from public administrators, politicians, or lobbyists. For Luddy, the only enduring answer is a massive expansion of private schooling—but in a way that is affordable and accessible for parents. What Luddy sought to do was create private schooling along the lines of a successful product—something that people wanted and needed and could afford; and perhaps most important, if they didn't like the product, they could choose another.

Luddy then founded St. Thomas More Academy in Raleigh, a private, college-preparatory high school that follows a classical-education curriculum, and Thales Academy in Raleigh—which he envisions as the first in a network of affordably priced private schools offering high-quality K–12 education. Thales students not only outperform traditional public school students on standardized tests; they beat out charter school students, too. Yet Thales charges tuition of $5,300 for kindergarten through fifth grade and $6,000 for sixth through twelfth—rates well below what almost any other private school costs.

"A lot of people say you shouldn't talk of education as a business, but the reality is, it is a business," Luddy says. But he means this in the sense that a proprietor wants to provide what his customers need. "My idea was that parents should have hundreds of choices, whereas currently if they go to the public school system...they have precious few choices. Once you open up competition, the choices will be abundant."[80]

Luddy is now looking to take his model national. If he succeeds, he will have advanced the cause of parental choice and educational democracy immeasurably, while also reminding us of the foundational role that philanthropists have often played in American history and social life.

## Teacher Accountability

As noted above, we'd like to see an entirely different, market- and incentive-based educational system take hold in the United States. In the meantime, though, commonsense improvements need to be pursued—reform should not be held up while we wait for a revolution. The kids in our schools today won't be kids anymore when and if things change as radically as they need to. In the meantime, they need something better than what they're getting, and that starts with holding teachers accountable for the results they get in the classroom, especially the unionized teachers in public schools, who have resisted every attempt to measure their effectiveness.

"The single most important factor in determining [student] achievement is not the color of [students'] skin or where they come from," said presidential candidate Obama in 2008. "It's not who their parents are or how much money they have. It's who their teacher is."[81] No wonder American public school students are struggling so much—too many of those teachers put their own interests first, ahead of their students.

Even some Democrats are recognizing the corrosive influence of teachers' unions. Governor Andrew Cuomo of New York has pushed for accountability in New York schools, seeking to reform the teachers' unions' onerous work rules and to institute some form of accountability for teacher performance.[82] The governor presides over a state education

system in which, in 2014, 96 percent of teachers were rated "effective"—
while only 38 percent of the state's high school graduates were prepared
for college.[83] It doesn't take much insight to see that something is wrong
with that picture.

Pushback against teachers' unions has occurred elsewhere as well.
Los Angeles County judge Rolf M. Treu ruled California's teacher tenure,
dismissal, and layoff laws unconstitutional on grounds that they negatively impacted both poor and minority students by permitting "grossly
ineffective teachers" to continue working in schools.[84] In his decision,
Treu agreed with the plaintiffs' argument that the tenure laws violated
California students' right to an equal education.

At present, public school teachers, unlike professionals in almost
any other field, don't face meaningful evaluation of their performance.
Their progress is simply measured by weighting professional credentials.
Teachers need to get certified and earn a degree from an education college. If they go on to get advanced degrees, they get higher salaries and
are judged all the more "effective" in the classroom. Typically, 98 percent
of teachers in a given public school system are judged "satisfactory" in
their work.[85]

An extensive body of research now demonstrates that teacher effectiveness varies widely, both from school to school and within schools. For
students, being assigned to a good or bad teacher can mean as much as a
grade level's worth of achievement over an academic year. The research
also makes clear that professional credentials correlate little with teacher
effectiveness. Whether a teacher has an advanced degree tells us nothing
about whether he or she is effective in the classroom.[86]

Teacher effectiveness measures can and should be instituted in every
American public school. A good model can be found in New Haven,
Connecticut, where a union leader is actually leading the effort: David
Cicarella, president of the New Haven Federation of Teachers, oversees
a yearlong evaluation process for public school teachers. In 2009, New
Haven's teachers agreed as part of a new contract to comply with the
evaluation system, which scores teachers on classroom performance
and their students' ability to master subjects. It didn't take long for the
accountability measure to show consequences: in 2011 and 2012, 62
teachers left the New Haven school district after receiving poor evalu-
ations—and Cicarella didn't try to reinstate them. Meanwhile, the New

Haven school district's graduation rate rose from just 58 percent in 2009 to 71 percent in 2012. Even more impressive, the percentage of New Haven public school students meeting or exceeding goals on state tests rocketed from 31 percent in 2009 to 54 percent in 2012.[87] It's hard to attribute such dramatic short-term gains to anything other than a new commitment to teacher accountability.

Once some kind of teacher-measurement system is instituted, schools should also explore offering financial incentives to high-performing teachers to move into low-performing schools. The Institute of Educational Studies conducted a study in which just one or two high-performing teachers were moved to a low-performance school. The teachers had a huge impact, improving the test scores of *entire grades*.[88] This experiment makes painfully clear how important good teachers are. Of course, moving top teachers to failing schools, even with financial incentives, probably won't be practical on a large scale. The only scalable alternative is to find ways to improve the performance of teachers in the low-performing schools, through mentoring—again, from high-quality teachers—and training programs.

Simply put, instead of setting the barrier for teachers on entry— where once you're in, you're "satisfactory" and nearly impossible to dislodge—the system should be realigned to focus on ongoing teacher effectiveness. In every other field of endeavor, we don't hire people and then keep them on for years without ever assessing whether they are doing a good job. It makes no sense—unless you're in the teachers' union.

The unions resist all teacher accountability measures, and understandably so. Since the unions' goal is to protect all teachers' jobs, regardless of how awful a teacher performs, it stands to reason that they would fight these measures furiously. And they have.

In short, every reform, large and small, that would weaken the teachers' unions' stranglehold on education policy should be explored. Most fundamentally, parents must be able to take their school funding elsewhere and send their child to another school.

## WHAT ABOUT STANDARDS?

The lagging performance of American schoolkids on standardized tests, and our continued loss of ground internationally, sparked multiple efforts over the last few decades to design a comprehensive system of rigorous educational standards—and to enforce testing mechanisms designed to evaluate our progress. Both President Bush's No Child Left Behind and President Obama's Race to the Top were motivated by these goals; both programs have their defenders and critics. Race to the Top was a $4 billion federal program that would award grants to public school systems that showed successful reform and innovation, accountability measures, and the adoption of common standards.

By the time Race to the Top came around, "standards" generally meant the Common Core—a unified set of standards in mathematics and literacy for students across the United States, designed to make sure that all American students reach college or the workforce with a consistent degree of preparation.[89] The Common Core is not a curriculum, however. It is rather a framework for standards to guide curriculum.

However modest the program may sound, as most readers of this book will already know, the Common Core has become one of the most contentious issues in American education since the standards were completed in 2010 and states began adopting them. The topic became hotter still when Race to the Top tied state grants to Common Core adoption, provoking an outcry against an overly coercive federal role in determining state standards. Worse, as Common Core standards were adopted in states around the country, teachers, students, and especially parents came to oppose them.

The Common Core story has been a painful one for education reformers on all sides. On the one hand, the broad national agreement on a system of rigorous, content-based educational standards seemed like a leap forward, a belated if welcome acknowledgment of the insights of great education reformers like E.D. Hirsch, who have long argued that content-rich education—especially for children from underprivileged homes—was the key to educational proficiency and later-life success. Yet the devising and especially the implementation of the Common Core have exhibited the same top-down, one-size-fits-all, coercive administrative and governmental directives that have characterized our failing education system as a whole.

At this point, the Common Core seems like one of those increasingly rare issues that unite broad sections of the Right and the Left—everyone hates it, for different reasons. For the record, we support the *goals and intentions* of the Common Core—principally, its emphasis on a rigorous, content-rich curriculum—but we agree that its implementation, its compulsory nature, and above all, its design by bureaucrats at the expense of input from teachers and educators are fatal flaws. It is more than likely that, given the draining political battles that have been fought over the Common Core and the tarnished reputation that national standards have acquired as a result, there won't be much appetite to try again. This would be a mistake. American schools need ambitious, measurable standards. The tragedy of the Common Core is to discredit, in the eyes of millions of Americans, the essential truth of that insight. But we must keep trying.

## GETTING CONTROL OF COLLEGE TUITIONS

College-loan debt is a problem hanging over the futures of millions of college graduates (and many others who have attended college but not graduated). So far, Washington's efforts to alleviate this problem have been middling at best. President Obama's main contribution was to advance a free community college initiative—on the idea that making it easier for people to get two-year associate's degrees will help them both in the workforce and in attaining an eventual four-year degree. But as many critics point out, the community college grants aren't targeted to those most in need; millions of middle-class students would benefit from the grants, too, which also don't go toward defraying expenses for materials and living costs. And as we have seen, community college hasn't shown itself to be a ladder to success—especially with graduation rates so dismal. A better option would be to increase means-tested Pell Grants, which, like vouchers, can be put toward educational options of the individual's choice.

Millions will still choose the traditional four-year college route, where costs have become so prohibitive that a generation of graduates (and non-graduates) faces decades of debt. The progressive Left has offered some bold solutions, though they tend to be short on practicality. Senator Elizabeth Warren wants students to get the same zero-interest rates for their loans as banks enjoy. The problem with such a scheme is that it won't force the schools to do anything about their cost structures. Offering students low interest rates will only encourage colleges to pile on their costs.

Fortunately, states are taking steps with innovative ideas. In Oregon, for example, the state legislature has passed a plan called Pay It Forward, Pay It Back, which would make tuition free at public universities and community colleges in the state. The catch? Students would sign contracts agreeing to pay a percentage of their future earnings to the state—regardless of whether they move out of state in the meantime. Many have noted that states often see little benefit from their massive investments in higher education; the Oregon plan would at least ensure that some of this money comes back to the state. However, the Oregon plan has a crucial flaw: it has a set time limit for the students' payments. Once they reach the end of that term, no matter how much they have paid back, their obligation is completed. Another free-tuition program, the Tennessee Promise, is similarly flawed, but at least these efforts try to attack the incentive structure in higher-ed costs.[90]

Former Texas governor Rick Perry proposed the most innovative solution to tuition costs. In 2011, Perry announced what he called his $10,000 degree challenge, asking public and private colleges and universities to design degree programs that cost $10,000 or less in *total*. To achieve this, the governor suggested that they "leverage web-based instruction, innovative teaching techniques and aggressive efficiency measures."[91] The challenge is optional, but many Texas schools have already sought to innovate, including some with degree programs in STEM, cybersecurity, and other employment-ready fields. And out of Perry's challenge grew the Texas Affordable Baccalaureate Program (TABP), through which students can earn bachelor's degrees in applied science and "organizational leadership," mostly online. The three-year program has a total price tag of between $13,000 and $15,000. Van Davis, a Texas higher-education official, says, TABP is "changing the way we deliver education."[92]

As Perry's approach shows, the answer to controlling college costs is not more loans or lower interest rates but simply more affordable options. And it seems likely that the states, not Washington, will take the lead in such an effort.

## CONCLUSION

American education is in need of reform across the board, so plans to remake the system would include many components, including an emphasis on school and teacher accountability (such as performance-based pay); the importance of high-quality, content-rich curricula; and giving parents a full range of education choices, including vouchers and charter schools. But the overarching principle that should guide these reforms is that of a market-based education system that empowers parents as the primary decision-makers. Parents almost universally desire the best education their children can get. They have a direct stake in their children's educational success.

Whether it's massively expanding public education along charter school lines, giving all parents the ability to send their children to better schools, or a massive buildout of affordable private school options on the model developed by visionaries like Bob Luddy, the bottom line remains the same: the American education system must be reformed along market lines. Its consumers— children and their parents, especially those of modest means—have been ill-served for generations. No goal is more important to our future than the revival of our education system. If we fail to educate the next generation of American children, it will hardly be possible to say that we have a future at all.

CHAPTER 8

# The Hollow Economy: Inequality and the Loss of Mobility

America's wealth gap between middle-income and upper-income families is [the] widest on record.

—RICHARD FRY AND RAKESH KOCHAR[1]

Because there's so much inequality, people born near the bottom tend to stay near the bottom, and that's much more consequential than it was 50 years ago.

—LAWRENCE KATZ[2]

I am not an economist, but one likely reason for the dismal labor-force participation is that many U.S. assistance programs act more like work replacements than work supports.

—ROBERT DOAR[3]

We see Ph.D.s from Harvard teaching as adjuncts, factory workers making minimum wage when they might have made middle-class wages before.

—JOSH CLINTON, VANDERBILT UNIVERSITY[4]

The problem is, 80 percent of the American people are still living on what they were living on the day before the [2008 financial] crash. And about half the American people, after you adjust for inflation, are living on what they were living on the last day I was president 15 years ago. So that's what's the matter.

—BILL CLINTON[5]

In April 2016, President Obama sat with Andrew Ross Sorkin for an extended conversation about his economic record, published in the *New York Times*. Sorkin, a journalist, *Times* columnist, and author of the best-selling *Too Big to Fail*, found the president expansive in discussing his economic policies and decisions—and defiant in defending them.

"I actually compare our economic performance to how, historically, countries that have wrenching financial crises perform," Obama said. "By that measure, we probably managed this better than any large economy on Earth in modern history."[6]

This was grandiose, even by Obama's standards. Why, Sorkin asked him more than once, with an economic recovery in full swing—and one that had some real numbers worth celebrating—did so many Americans, probably a majority, feel that things weren't getting any better, that they might even be getting worse?

People's outlook on the economy, the president replied, was shaped by "what they hear." Meaning? "If you have a political party—in this case, the Republicans—that denies any progress and is constantly channeling to their base, which is sizable, say, 40 percent of the population, that things are terrible all the time, then people will start absorbing that."[7] It wasn't all the Republicans' fault, he allowed; he had had to make political choices, like choosing to pursue Obamacare over other stimulus projects.

But Obama did acknowledge, as Sorkin put it, that the public's economic unease was "not without empirical basis." Household incomes in real dollars were $4,000 less than when Bill Clinton left office. Millions had left the work force permanently. Income inequality continued to grow.[8]

It's easy for a Republican critic of Obama to scoff at his economic self-assessment, but the fact remains that, by the traditional empirical figures by which voters once judged presidents, his record *does* show genuine achievement. Yet at the same time, the nation's economic malaise is real, not imagined. And that is what makes this economic moment almost unique in our history: both things are true at once.

When Obama sat down with Sorkin, the nation had seen a record 73 consecutive months of job growth—the longest ever—adding up to 14.4 million jobs in all, another record. Unemployment stood at 5 percent, after peaking at 10 percent during Obama's first year in office. The U.S. economy, unsatisfactory as it seemed, had grown at a better rate than its first world competitors. Moreover, the stock market has boomed; as of August 2016 the NASDAQ has increased over 350 percent and the Dow Jones Index over 230 percent.[9] Home prices and industrial production have grown by 15 percent.[10] In May 2016, new home sales hit an eight-year high.[11]

No wonder Obama told Americans during his 2016 State of the Union address, "Anyone claiming that America's economy is in decline is peddling fiction."[12]

Yet the reality of the Obama economy was that the outwardly positive figures obscured a darker picture under the surface. Legislators and elites see the economy one way; ordinary Americans tend to experience it differently. The truth is, the economy has recovered mostly for the wealthy. Real income growth for the top 1 percent of earners has increased by 35 percent over the last six years; this wealthiest-of-the-wealthy cohort has amassed about 91 percent of the gains produced since the recession. Everyone else, on aggregate, has only seen a 0.08 percent increase—basically nothing.[13] And millions have fallen behind, working lower-paying jobs or part-time jobs, or dropping out of the workforce altogether.

Obama touted his job numbers, and he was entitled to do so—any president would—but the facts weren't convenient. Millions of middle-class Americans find themselves downwardly mobile, many at ages at which it will be impossible to turn things around. Nearly eight years into the official "recovery" from the Great Recession, we seem to have settled into an era of slow economic growth and low-paying jobs. Economic mobility in America, once the vibrant engine that powered generational uplift and rising standards of living, is petering out. We are moving toward an American version of a caste system, where those with advantages tend to hold on to and expand them over time.

In this chapter, we'll examine how our economy has stopped working for millions of Americans. While millions of jobs have been created, the vast majority of them are low-paying. We'll spotlight the anemic rate of growth that Obama's economic policies have generated and how it cannot foster broad-based recovery and prosperity. For proof, look no further than the hollowing out of the middle class, once the defining demographic of the American electorate, but today so insecure and embattled that politicians have stopped even using the term in their campaigns. And we'll look underneath the well-documented crisis of income inequality, where the gaps between rich and poor—and between rich and moderate-income people—are indeed vast and troubling, but where the real problem is the freezing up of economic mobility, the very heartbeat of the American dream.

And yet, we aren't powerless: ideas and solutions exist that can help us turn the tide. We need fresh policies that cut across partisan divides to the heart of the problem, and we'll take a look at some of the most promising ones at the end of this chapter.

## SLOW GROWTH, LOW-PAYING JOBS

At the core of the problem with the Obama economic recovery was slow growth—the slowest, quarter over quarter, of any American economic recovery in half a century, with an annualized growth rate of 2.24 percent, compared with the post-1960 recovery average of 3.97 percent.[14] Bureau of Economic Analysis data shows that average GDP growth in the first two quarters of 2016 was just 1 percent, down from 2.4 percent in 2015.[15] And it's also a big comedown from even the relatively modest 2.6 percent growth of the last quarter of 2014.[16]

The administration's defenders were quick to point to the brutal winter of 2015 as a culprit in slowing consumer spending and exports, but we've had tough winters before and grown through them. And the slow-growth Obama economy transcended the seasons. In fact, during Obama's first five years in office, the economy grew at a slower rate—averaging just 1.3 percent annually—than any other time since just after World War II. If we omit the recession that followed the end of World War II in 1945 and 1946, the American economy's growth rate under Obama was the worst dating back to Herbert Hoover in 1932.[17]

The problem with slow growth is both obvious and subtle. The obvious problem is that the slower an economy grows, the fewer jobs get created and the fewer new businesses formed. More subtly, slow growth represents lost wealth—and in the Obama recovery, that translates to nearly $1.7 trillion, according to calculations by economists Joel Griffith and Stephen Moore. Even more starkly, Griffith and Moore compared Obama's growth performance with that of Ronald Reagan in the 1980s. Reagan's 23-quarter recovery averaged a remarkable 4.8 percent annualized growth, more than double Obama's, producing more than $2 for every $1 of economic growth. Obama's "Reagan recovery gap," Griffith and Moore estimated, was $2.48 trillion.[18]

Yet, while the broader economy has grown at sluggish or near-nonexistent rates, those in the financial sector or other elite positions in the economy have done just fine. The financial industry, the stock market, and other major corporate concerns landed on their feet from the 2008 financial meltdown—with a big assist from Washington. Fed policy pumped money into the credit markets and helped fuel a recovery—of a sort.[19] Financiers Kevin Warsh and Stanley Druckenmiller call it a "balance sheet recovery," pointing out how Fed policy proved massively more beneficial to those of higher income: "No wonder most on Wall Street applaud the Fed's unrelenting balance-sheet recovery strategy. It's great news for those households and businesses with large asset holdings, high risk tolerances and easy access to credit. Yet it provides little solace for families and small businesses that must rely on their income statements to pay the bills."[20]

In late 2015, the Federal Reserve raised the interest rate by 0.25 percent, a sign of faith that the economy was back on track after the financial crisis.[21] But the successes of higher-income individuals and groups with substantial capital didn't translate into job creation or wage increases for most Americans. It follows that the traditional indicators of a robust economy only tell part of the story. The stock market in particular is not a reliable barometer of the overall economy, since stocks are driven in part by the Fed's interest-rate policy.

As for the jobs recovery, consider that the percentage of working-age Americans in the workforce reached a 38-year low in 2015.[22] Several commentators have given this phenomenon a name: "the disappearing American worker." It refers to those who have given up on finding employment in tough economic times.[23] And while it's true that we saw some modest gains in the labor-force participation rate in early 2016— employment in January through June 2016 grew by an average of 170,000 Americans each month[24]—the rate is only half a percentage point higher than the 38-year low we faced at the end of 2015.[25]

By Stephen Moore's estimates, more than seven million Americans would have been in the labor force had they not either stopped looking for work or, as is the case for many young workers, never started looking. These underlying statistical realities must be kept in mind when evaluating the steadily dropping unemployment rates under President Obama.[26] No wonder the unemployment rate keeps going down; in calculating the figure, the Labor Department doesn't count people who aren't actively looking for jobs.

One factor that may have exacerbated this trend was the Obama administration's expansive attitude toward food stamps. Under Obama, the average food stamp benefit jumped by as much as 25 percent per recipient. And the administration has also made it easier to qualify for the program. Between 2010 and 2012 alone—as the recession had officially ended and unemployment was declining, albeit slowly—food stamp enrollment swelled by an incredible seven million people.[27]

For those who find work, many of the new jobs pay far less than those that were lost. Most job growth occurred in lower-paying sectors such as accommodation, retail, and food services, resulting in a 23 percent "wage gap" between jobs gained and those lost during the recession.[28] Since 1999, annual household income has declined for every age cohort; adjusted for household size, it has fallen by about $5,000.[29]

In short, wage growth has not tracked with job growth. Average private-sector earnings are staying barely ahead of the overall rate of inflation and well behind the rate of price increases of staple items like meat, energy, and transportation. In fact, some states with the lowest unemployment rates also have the lowest rates of wage growth. One of the most timeless economic principles—that wages rise as unemployment falls—has been turned on its head throughout the post–Great Recession recovery.

Consider the situation in Boston, where almost all the jobs lost in the recession had been recovered by September 2015, but more than 85 percent of the jobs added since 2009 pay less than $38,000 per year. And as in the rest of the country, most of the job gains have come in low-paying sectors like food service, home health care, and janitorial services.[30] It follows that while a lower unemployment rate and recent jobs reports suggest that more Americans are finding work, these measurements hide the true status of the American workforce. A survey of unemployed adults conducted in mid-2014 found that half of respondents had "completely given up" looking for a job, with one respondent explaining, "After searching for four years and being unsuccessful, I am tired of trying."[31] Many of those dropping out of the job search are young workers, causing labor-force participation to rise among older workers as it falls in the other age categories.[32] This means that older workers need to be retrained to continue their careers—and that younger workers start their careers behind on job skills and experience.[33]

Add it up, and you have what is probably the defining American social and economic problem of our time: the crisis of the middle class.

## THE VANISHING MIDDLE CLASS

"Things have changed a lot. The decks have been stacked against not only the lower class but also the lower middle class," said Michael Herdmann, a 54-year-old retired public-works employee from Fairview Park, Ohio. Voices like Herdmann's tell the true story of what's going on in the American economy.

A few years ago, Lisa Land, working customer service at a local textile factory in small-town North Carolina, considered herself middle class. Land was laid off in 2008 and moved in with her ailing father. She now survives on his Social Security checks and her adult daughter's help with the grocery bills. In the past, she says, "We wouldn't have a lot of money, but we had everything that we needed. Now, there's really no extra for anything. No vacation. No dining out. No stuff like that."[34]

Land's story is hardly unique. Americans who thought of themselves as middle class now find themselves not only struggling to make ends meet but needing government assistance as well. More than 23 percent of Americans reported living in a family that received some of sort of welfare under Obama, up more than 17 percent from the last year of George W. Bush's presidency.[35] These aren't all lazy people who don't want to work (though there are, as always, people living off assistance for those reasons). The majority are hardworking Americans who can't find a decent-paying job, people who lack the skills to stay competitive, people who didn't have savings before the recession hit.

"The 'middle-class squeeze,'" writes William Galston, "once a debatable slogan, is now a demonstrable fact."[36] He cites data from the Center for American Progress showing that, in inflation-adjusted dollars since 2000, "rents have risen by 7 percent, medical care by 21 percent, child care by 24 percent and higher education by an eye-popping 62 percent."[37]

"It was like all our money was being eaten up by bills and interest," Aja McClanahan, a 35-year-old Chicago resident said.[38] She and her husband live paycheck to paycheck while they pay off student loans, car notes, and credit card debt. "I'm scared to death of my car," another woman told the *Huffington Post*. She can't afford any mechanical work if something goes wrong. Another man said, "Both me and my wife make less than $10 an hour, we have two young daughters." A young woman commented, "I'm usually very lucky if I can walk out with $20 in tips on a lunch shift." From another: "I'm almost 40 years old and I've never made more than $20,000 a year."

"[I'm] getting by on less than $10 an hour, getting by on nothing. As Blanche Dubois would say, I'm getting by on the kindness of others," a woman sobbed. A young father commented, "I'm a single parent with a 6-year-old child. I've been out of work. I have one more day inside my apartment before I have to leave." Another woman sums up the reality for many Americans: "I have been struggling [for seven months] without unemployment. They're going to turn my electricity off tomorrow. I have trouble keeping food on the table for my family and I have worked since I was 15 years old. I have always worked full time."[39]

Connie Ogletree, 55, makes $7.25 an hour at a McDonald's in Atlanta. "It was 40 years ago that I had my first fast-food job, at Dairy Queen," she says. "This is my second."[40] In between, she worked as an executive assistant. "When you go into a fast-food restaurant, you want to be sure the people in the back are doing the best job they can," she said. "You want them not to be worried about missing a day if they're sick, to be able to go to a child's play at school or a P.T.A. meeting. I'd like a vacation once a year, but my employer doesn't offer that, or sick days."[41]

John D'Amanda's story is similar. D'Amanda owned a window-washing company for over two decades and made about $30,000 a year from it. However, during the Great Recession, his business collapsed.[42] D'Amanda now works at McDonald's, earning $9.25 an hour. At this wage, he's "barely able to afford" paying the $350 rent to share a small bedroom with a roommate.[43]

While life for those working these low-paying jobs can often look bleak, many are grateful for their situations, like Jason Pappas. In the mid-2000s, Pappas was making over $40 an hour as an iron worker, but building projects slowed down during the recession and he found himself unemployed. Pappas now works as a truck driver, making just *half* of his previous hourly wage. Despite this pay cut, he is grateful to have steady employment at this time and is happy to have a job that pays the bills.[44] Pappas has the right attitude, even if his situation is depressingly common.

"I think there's great honor in working," says Bernadette Feazell, a pawn shop employee in Austin, Texas. "I work hard. And frankly, it's not because I think I'm worth $9 an hour."[45]

With stories like these, it shouldn't be surprising to learn that, between 2000 and 2013, each of the 50 states saw its share of middle-class families shrink. Today, middle-class families in Wisconsin and Ohio make up less than half of those states' populations.[46] Pew data tracked from 1971 through 2014 found that in most U.S. industries, middle-income workers make up a smaller and smaller percentage of the labor force. For example, the communications industry has lost almost 20 percent of middle-income workers, business services jobs 17 percent, and construction jobs 10 percent, among other fields.[47] At the same time, the top 0.1 percent in the United States have the same amount of wealth as the bottom 90 percent.[48]

"Even when you're working your tail off," President Obama said in a speech at Northwestern University, "it's harder than it should be to get ahead.... Our economy won't be truly healthy until we reverse the much longer and profound erosion of middle-class income and jobs."[49] He's right. And this is the fundamental disconnect between the recovery the president touts, on the one hand, and the way millions of Americans feel about their prospects, on the other.

## INCOME INEQUALITY AND THE LOSS OF MOBILITY

With the middle class stagnating so chronically, income inequality in the United States has reached levels not seen in decades—and perhaps, by some measures, since the Great Depression.

In a landmark December 2014 study, the Pew Research Center found that the wealth gap between upper- and middle-income Americans has increased during the economic recovery. "In 2013," Pew reports, "the median wealth of the nation's upper-income families ($639,400) was nearly seven times the median wealth of middle-income families ($96,500), the widest wealth gap in 30 years."[50]

Simply put, the American middle class has cratered over the last three decades. Lower-income and median-income families are essentially in the same position they were in back in the early 1990s (in inflation-adjusted dollars), while those at the upper rungs of the income ladder are racing ahead. Upper-income families have doubled their median wealth since 1983. They took a hit during the Great Recession, but they have begun to regain that lost wealth. The wealth gap continues to grow.[51]

Polling data shows that Americans are aware of it. A 2015 Gallup poll reflects that 67 percent of Americans are dissatisfied with the way income and wealth are distributed in the United States, while only 31 percent are satisfied.[52] A more expansive *New York Times* survey makes clear that the American people are worried about income inequality and, moreover, that they share broad agreement that the government has some responsibility to address it. Nearly six in ten respondents to the *Times* survey said the government should do more to address the wealth gap—though the concerns split sharply along party lines, with only three in ten Republicans saying so, while nearly eight in ten Democrats do.[53] Still, taking the results in aggregate, the *Times* poll reveals some stark realities.

"Which comes closer to your view?" the poll asked. "In today's economy, everyone has a fair chance to get ahead in the long run, or in today's economy, it's mainly just a few people at the top who have a chance to get ahead?" Sixty-one percent said "just a few people at the top have a chance to get ahead."

"Do you feel that the distribution of money and wealth in this country is fair, or do you feel that the money and wealth in this country should be more evenly distributed among more people?" the survey asked. Two-thirds—66 percent—said that distribution should be more even.

"Do you think the gap between the rich and the poor in the United States is getting larger, getting smaller or has stayed the same?" Again, two-thirds—67 percent—said it was getting worse.

"Do you think the gap between rich and poor in this country is a problem that needs to be addressed now, a problem but one that does not need to be addressed now or not a problem?" Sixty-five percent said that the problem needed to be addressed now.[54]

Many Americans say the problem is urgent because they feel their hold on financial security slipping. A 2015 Pew study asked participants to define "financial security." They defined it as "consistent and modest. It means families have enough to pay the bills, have a little left over for savings and have few worries about making ends meet."[55] Yet, using that definition, only half of households in America are reportedly financially secure, despite the improvements in the economy. And in more specific areas, it's worse: 83 percent said they worried about "lack of savings," 71 percent about "not enough money to cover savings," and 69 percent about "not enough money to retire."[56]

"We are paying a high price for the inequality that is increasingly scarring our economy—lower productivity, lower efficiency, lower growth, more instability—and the benefits of reducing this inequality, at least from the current high levels, far outweigh any costs that might be imposed," writes Nobel laureate Joseph Stiglitz in his book, *The Price of Inequality*.[57] Stiglitz suggests that reducing inequality should be a goal not just for the sake of fairness but also to drive economic growth. He points out that in the decades after the end of the Second World War, when inequality in America was lower than it is today, the U.S. economy grew faster.[58] But things have deteriorated sharply since 1980, with the wealthy copping more and more of the gains—so much so, in fact, that Stiglitz now believes that "to a large extent, the American Dream is a myth."[59]

Erin Currier from Pew Charitable Trusts expands on Stiglitz's view: "Forty-three percent of those raised in the bottom fifth of the income ladder remain there a generation later," she writes, "and 40 percent of those raised at the top stay there. Just 4 percent raised at the bottom rung of the income ladder make it to the top a generation later, highlighting the unfortunate truth that rags-to-riches stories are more common in movies than in reality."[60]

These figures represent a real challenge to the notion of an American dream, and they put into perspective the most challenging consequence of the wealth and opportunity gap: the loss of economic mobility. In fact, economic mobility, not inequality, is the true economic issue in the United States today. We should see inequality as a consequence, not as a cause or issue in itself. The root of the problem is that the American economy has transformed itself in such a way that it continues to reward those at the upper range of the income scale—and their children, who benefit from better educational and work opportunities—while making it harder and harder for those closer to the bottom to work their way up.

The difference between the two concepts is best demonstrated by the way they are talked about in a policy sense. Discussions about income inequality usually lead to calls for redistribution of wealth—higher taxes on the wealthy, hikes to the minimum wage, and the like. By contrast, a focus on mobility centers on increasing economic opportunity and fostering wealth creation. Income inequality, such as what we see in the United States today, is certainly worth time and effort to understand; but more often than not, it inspires static, statist remedies. Economic mobility engenders a push for making our economy more dynamic and democratic in its distribution—not of wealth but of opportunity. And that's precisely what we need in order to get America back on track.

And yet, even here, our work is cut out for us. Because Americans don't just have negative views of the income gap; like Stiglitz, they are also growing more skeptical that the American dream of ascent and improvement really exists. The feeling that it's extraordinarily difficult, maybe impossible, to get ahead is driving a very uncharacteristic economic pessimism in the United States.

Here, returning to the Pew study that asked about financial security is instructive. "What we found is people have changed in terms of their perceptions of whether upward mobility from the bottom is possible," said Pew research manager Diana Elliot. "In 2009, nearly 4 in 10 Americans felt it was common for someone to work hard and become rich. This has dropped to just 23 percent of Americans who think that way. There is growing recognition that upward mobility from the bottom is challenging."[61]

These sentiments might be most pervasive among young people in America. In our own study of millennials, by a ratio of 52 percent to 34 percent, young people didn't believe they have the same chance at success as previous generations. Nearly half (48 percent) don't feel that society offers the right opportunities so that through hard work anyone can get ahead. More than half believe that it's impossible to get ahead without connections, while only 18 percent believe that society is open and fair to everyone.

And yet, for all of this public skepticism, it is important to stay focused on the mobility theme. While many Americans object to income inequality simply on the grounds of fairness, as we have seen in these poll numbers, Americans are not and have never been a jealous people. Sure, we're consumerist and capitalist. We want to be able to have the latest gadget or the chance to get away. But as long as we see ourselves getting ahead, and have confidence that our children will do better, we don't usually spend much time worrying about those who earn more. When inequality and lack of opportunity become so stifling that your chances of rising—even when you're working two or three jobs—seem miniscule at best, though, the perspective is bound to change. In our view, it is this reality that explains the poll numbers on inequality. What Americans are really saying is that they want *opportunities*—better-paying jobs, a chance at raises, a chance to better their economic circumstances and put some money away. If they get that, they won't lose sleep about the hedge-fund director or CEO making $100 million.

A 2015 *Wall Street Journal* survey reinforced this point of view. In it, by a 68 percent to 28 percent margin, respondents said that they were more worried about "middle and working class Americans not being able to get ahead financially" than they were about "the income gap between the wealthiest Americans and the rest of the country." This preference held for all age and income groups, across party lines, and for men and women. It is mobility and opportunity—the American economic creed, in essence—that is really at issue.

## WHAT DO WE DO ABOUT IT?

It's clear that the American economy needs serious reform. We can't keep doing the same thing and hoping that the results will be different.

In part, Americans' frustration owes to the mismatch between rhetoric and reality in the White House. On the one hand, President Obama often highlighted inequality and its effects. In the 2014 State of the Union, for example, he said, "Inequality has deepened. Upward mobility has stalled. The cold, hard fact is that even in the midst of recovery, too many Americans are working more than ever just to get by—let alone get ahead." Yet, since then, he has more often boasted about his economic recovery, even as the fundamental realities haven't changed. Republicans haven't exactly been Churchillian in their economic leadership, either.

But we do *need* economic leadership, and soon, if the American dream of mobility and self-improvement are not to become nostalgic memories. Our view, in brief, is this: the only way to alleviate both economic stagnation and the massive gap in income and opportunity is to make the American economy once again the engine of upward mobility and wealth creation that it has been for most of the last 100 years. If we can recapture the robust growth of past eras, we will see better-paying jobs across all income groups; better opportunities for young workers; stronger economic security for families; and, not incidentally, firmer ground for federal finances, from entitlements to budgeting, since tax revenues will soar. The way to capture all of it is not to redistribute wealth but to create more wealth by enhancing growth.

And to do that, we must embrace market-based solutions, even if those solutions intersect with and are sometimes tempered by government measures. Below we set out a series of ideas and proposals that might help us get there. What unites them all is a focus on dynamism, not dictates; flexibility, not ideological obsession; and equality of opportunity, not equality of outcome.

## Comprehensive Tax Reform

We support comprehensive tax reform to help drive this economic recovery, both for individuals and families and for businesses. The American tax burden on families and businesses has been too heavy for too long, and the American tax code is staggeringly complex and difficult to comply with.

Consider this: estimates by the IRS Taxpayer Advocate Service (TAS) suggest that the massive paperwork associated with filing taxes costs Americans approximately $160 billion a year. The tax code runs 76,000 pages[62] and four million words; Americans spend more than three billion hours per year computing their taxes.[63]

Not even the IRS itself can give reliable advice on how to comply with the tax code. In 2002, TAS conducted a review of its telephone hotlines and found that incorrect answers were provided to over a quarter of taxpayer questions. The report further noted that, even though less than 10 percent of people prepare their own taxes, the IRS help lines received some 110 million calls a year.[64]

It is high time we simplified things and lightened the load.

There is no shortage of proposals to do so. When he was a Republican presidential candidate, Governor Chris Christie of New Jersey suggested simplifying the tax system down to just three brackets, with the top rate being no higher than 28 percent—where it stood after the enormously successful 1986 tax reform signed by President Ronald Reagan—and the bottom rate reduced to a single digit. To compensate for any lost revenue and ensure that the reform would be revenue-neutral, Christie proposed eliminating or capping a broad range of deductions and credits. Most Americans would need about 15 minutes to do their taxes under such a plan, he said.

An even more dramatic proposal, put forth by conservative advocates ranging from the Heritage Foundation to Steve Forbes, is a single income-tax rate: a national flat tax. A flat tax, its proponents argue, would liberate the government to collect taxes free of distortions (and deductions) while offering taxpayers a simple system and freeing up money for private investment. It's easy to imagine the boon to personal savings and economic investment—and, yes, consumer spending, too—that would result from giving all Americans a single low tax rate. Forbes suggests that Americans should be offered a choice: pay taxes under the current system or pay under the national flat-tax rate. He and other flat-tax champions have no doubt about which choice most Americans would make.

Perhaps the most audacious idea of all—and our favorite—is a fundamental shift in our system, from taxing income to taxing consumption. The value-added tax, or VAT, which taxes our consumption of goods and services, has already been adopted in many of the world's leading democracies. In the *Wall Street Journal*, Reihan Salam explained how, under a VAT formulated by Columbia law professor Michael J. Graetz, we would see the VAT amount that we paid on the receipt for everything we purchase. Opponents of a VAT argue that it is regressive, hurting people of modest incomes on what they spend, but Graetz's plan solves that problem by using VAT revenue to exempt most households from income taxes entirely: "Unless you're earning more than $50,000 as a single person, $75,000 as a head-of-household filer or $100,000 as a married couple," Salam writes, "you will no longer have to pay income taxes. That means that 120 million of today's 145 million income-tax returns will no longer need to be filed."[65] And Graetz offers other adjustments for people of low incomes, satisfying Salam that this VAT "won't soak the poor." The plan, under Graetz's projections, would raise as much revenue through the VAT as under the current code. Salam believes that it would make the United States more attractive for foreign investment, allow it to slash corporate taxes, and, perhaps best of all, erode Washington's ability to hide spending via the tax code.

These are just sample plans of possible avenues that would reduce the rate of taxation of individuals and families. For our purposes, the specifics of any one plan are less important than the broader principles: tax rates should be lowered, tax brackets should be simplified, the tax base should be broadened (by eliminating or capping deductions)—all of which would not only make revenue for Washington more predictable and steady, but would also lighten the load on American families, improve financial prospects, and pump fuel into investments and innovation in the economy.

The overarching principles: pro-family, pro-growth, pro-opportunity.

The same premises apply to business and corporate taxes. The United States currently suffers under the heaviest corporate taxes in the industrialized world, a burden that smothers innovation and expansion while reducing jobs or sending them overseas. If American corporations don't hire Americans, they will hire people somewhere else. No one sheds tears for Lockheed Martin or Walmart, but they employ tens of thousands of Americans, most of whom have families.

Our corporate tax rate should be reduced from its current 35 percent down to at least 25 percent, if not lower (Donald Trump proposed 15 percent). This will prompt domestic investment.[66] We should also eliminate the policy of taxing American firms with overseas operations twice; they should be taxed only in the country where they earned the revenue. Rubio and Lee also suggest that firms should be able to deduct 100 percent of their expenses for new equipment, infrastructure improvements, or other upgrades. If we're going to keep more jobs here, as well as the innovation that drives new jobs, we've got to lighten the load on the American private sector.

To that end, we need to reduce needless federal regulations and impose a stringent review process on all new ones. We have strangled too many businesses with an overzealous regulatory approach. We have also unduly hurt ourselves with wrongheaded, counterproductive, or simply poorly managed regulations and policies in three key areas that have a profound effect on our economic future: energy, immigration, and infrastructure. We will discuss these areas in detail in chapter 9.

### Boosting Lower-income Workers

Pedro Gamboa wakes up at 3 am every day to work as a baggage handler at JFK airport for $10.10 an hour. "It's not enough. You have to be a magician to survive on that," he said. "Once you pay your bills, there is nothing left in your pockets."[67]

Gamboa is not alone. According to data from 2014, more than 10 percent of Americans who work full-time remained poor, and 25 percent of private-sector jobs now pay less than $10 an hour.[68] Here we confront one of the paradoxes of our current economic situation: Even when we succeed in creating jobs, how can we ensure that they pay enough?

For many Americans across the political spectrum, one answer is obvious: raise the minimum wage, which is currently $7.25 an hour. A Hart Research poll from early 2015 found that 75 percent of Americans support raising the federal minimum wage to $12.50 by 2020. This includes 92 percent of Democrats, 73 percent of Independents, and 53 percent of Republicans.[69] President Obama supports an increase as well. Raising the minimum wage to $10.10, he said, would "lift wages for nearly 28 million Americans across the country. We're not just talking about young people on their first job. The average minimum-wage worker is 35 years old. They work hard, often in physically demanding jobs."[70]

Obama's position enjoyed broad support: over 600 economists, including seven Nobel laureates, signed a letter in 2014 supporting the increase to $10.10, citing 64 studies that showed no discernible impact on employment from minimum wage increases.[71] The letter states that the "weight of evidence" shows that "increases in the minimum wage have had little or no negative effect on the employment of minimum-wage workers, even during times of weakness in the labor market."[72] In one survey, nearly 60 percent of small business owners supported an increase and said that it would increase purchasing power and benefit the economy.[73]

So, clearly, raising the minimum wage is a no-brainer, right? Not quite.

To be clear, we support a modest increase in the minimum wage to $10.10 that Obama and many others have called for—but *not* the dramatic hike to $15 an hour that activists and others have called for and which the City of Los Angeles adopted in 2015.

More broadly, we have concerns about overemphasizing a minimum-wage increase compared with other reforms that will likely prove more productive and beneficial.

"I don't have anything against raising the minimum wage but I don't think you can do it in a significant enough way without creating a lot of distortions," Warren Buffett said at an annual shareholders' meeting for his company, Berkshire Hathaway. Those distortions, he said, "would cost a whole lot of jobs."[74]

Of course, the "distortions" that Buffett points out don't mean that there wouldn't also be benefits from raising the minimum wage—and perhaps the benefits would outweigh the costs. But there *would* be costs. Some employers would not hire at the new minimum, and in those cases, workers who could have earned $7.25 an hour will earn nothing, since they won't have a job. Still, we're comfortable with arguing that the minimum wage, which hasn't risen since 2009, should at least be moderately higher.

That doesn't solve the larger issue, though. Buffett argues that an even more effective means of helping those of low income is to increase the Earned Income Tax Credit (EITC), which, unlike the minimum wage, has no labor-market effects. The EITC is a tax refund paid to those of low income; the payments diminish as their incomes increase. Importantly, the EITC is structured so as to avoid disincentives: in other words, when workers' wages increase (thus lowering the amount they get from the EITC), they still comes out ahead on income. Where raising the minimum wage produces winners and losers—at least some lost jobs—the EITC produces only winners.

At the end of the day, neither reforming the EITC nor raising the minimum wage is likely to work an economic revolution in the fortunes of those of lower income. To do that, too many other factors, social and otherwise, need to change as well, from education to family structure. But these reforms, especially boosting the EITC, would go some way to a more equitable economy and give a hand up to those working at its bottom rungs.

"Everyone who is willing to work should have a reasonably decent livelihood in a country like the United States," Buffett says.[75] It's hard to argue with that.

Furthermore, it's critical that we make increased investments in workers' training and education. We too often ignore the benefits of vocational training in favor of arguing that all Americans should go to college. But college isn't the answer for everyone. Government should incentivize companies to expand apprenticeship programs and put more of their own in place, as well as ensure that high schools are promoting vocational training as an option and organizing their own internship opportunities.

## Tax-incentivized Empowerment Zones

It's clear that the problems of America's inner cities remain profound. Studies show that children born to low-income families in America's most distressed cities will earn markedly less over the course of their lives than children from similar backgrounds in surrounding areas.[76] Inner cities are increasingly home to populations with little hope of breaking inter-generational cycles of poverty, crime, and hopelessness. The American dream of upward mobility is an abstraction, at best, in such places.

Republican Jack Kemp, the late congressman, vice presidential candidate, and secretary of Housing and Urban Development (HUD), had a radical notion of how to help resuscitate America's most distressed cities. During his tenure as HUD secretary under President George H.W. Bush, Kemp created the Empowerment Task Force, which sought to target tax incentives to specific areas to encourage growth and employment.

"By giving people access to capital and allowing them to take ownership of assets," said Kemp, "entrepreneurship will be encouraged and the cycle of poverty can begin to be broken."

While Kemp was unable to get funding from a Democratic Congress, the idea of empowerment zones lives on. Kentucky senator Rand Paul has become a proponent of what he calls "Economic Freedom Zones" and frequently cites Kemp as the inspiration for the idea. Says Paul, "Economic Freedom zones—areas of reduced taxes—are different than a government stimulus. Economic Freedom Zones encourage businesses and individuals which the market has already selected."[77] Unlike traditional government stimulus, empowerment zones are effective because they ensure that the tax breaks lead directly to capital and that capital stays where it is created to benefit the community.

In January 2014, President Obama created what he called "Promise Zones" in San Antonio, Philadelphia, Los Angeles, southeastern Kentucky, and the Choctaw Nation in Oklahoma. They function in the same way Kemp's empowerment zones would have: they apply targeted tax incentives to promote growth and employment where they are most needed.

Empowerment zones could help rehabilitate distressed areas. By creating areas that have favorable tax policies, offering tax credits for living within the area, and even suspending certain federal guidelines—including minimum-wage laws, where doing so would stimulate jobs—as an incentive for employers, we can create the opportunity-driven stimulus these areas need. We should give the Department of Housing and Urban Development and Department of Agriculture (which together oversee today's empowerment zones) greater authority to create and manage empowerment zones and devise more favorable tax policies.

We should also tie empowerment zones to our immigration policy. By guaranteeing immigrants citizenship after a number of years living in distressed areas (such as Detroit), the federal government would provide an incentive for individuals to go into these areas and begin rehabilitating the local economies. Former New York mayor Michael Bloomberg floated this notion, imagining a system in which the federal government would assign immigrants to a distressed city for seven years, at the end of which the immigrant would earn American citizenship.[78]

### Pro-family Policies

Of the developed countries in the world, only one doesn't have paid maternity leave: the United States.[79] Many women are forced to drop out of the labor force entirely when they have children. Fully 47 percent of the American workforce is composed of women, yet studies show that they get paid less over the course of their careers than men. These policies are bad for families and for the economy.

A number of policies act as disincentives to marriage. First, there's a marriage penalty tied to means-tested public benefits. When two people on public assistance get married, they often incur a big cut in assistance. Further, the EITC, mentioned earlier, is tied to households instead of individuals. If two individuals who qualify for the EITC get married, they would experience a loss of income—again, a marriage penalty. If the EITC were transformed into a wage subsidy, two low-income earners could get married without a penalty.[80]

In a powerful 2015 *Wall Street Journal* op-ed, Senators Marco Rubio and Mike Lee emphasized the benefits of tax reform for American families. Rubio and Lee proposed whittling the tax brackets down to just two—35 percent and 15 percent—and putting an end to "the unfair treatment of our ultimate investor class: America's moms and dads." They proposed eliminating the marriage penalty—under which married couples pay higher tax rates than they would have had they filed separately—but also what they call the "parent tax penalty," referring to how parents have to bear both the costs of senior entitlement programs (through the payroll tax) and the cost of raising children. Parents in effect pay twice for their benefits. Rubio and Lee suggested a new, $2,500-per-child tax credit to offset these costs.

Indeed, raising a child in America can cost upward of $17,000 per year;[81] the current Child Tax Credit is simply insufficient. Increasing the amount of money individuals have on a per-child basis through a tax credit will provide enormous relief.[82]

## CHANGING THE GAME

We've seen some legitimate economic improvements since the end of the Great Recession. But we still have a long way to go. We have a severe income inequality crisis and a critical one of mobility. Our nation has broadly lost faith in the American dream. The majority of new jobs don't pay enough. The middle class is hollowing out, the wealth gap has widened during the recovery, and majorities don't benefit from an improved economy. A feeling of hopelessness has submerged the American spirit.

The solutions that we've put forward are firm departures from the pervasive notion that redistribution is the key to recovery. The way out is economic growth, pure and simple. "Solving almost all of America's problems hinges on re-establishing robust economic growth," writes John H. Cochrane of the Hoover Institution. "Over the next 50 years, if income could be doubled relative to 2% growth, the U.S. would be able to pay for Social Security, Medicare, defense, environmental concerns and the debt. Halve that income gain, and none of those spending challenges can be addressed. Doubling income per capita would help the less well off far more than any imaginable transfer scheme."[83]

To foster that growth, we need sound policies that depart from the zero-sum game of winners-and-losers politics and that help everyone get ahead—individuals, families, businesses. Washington has a key role to play here, sometimes with big new initiatives—like investments in our infrastructure and energy exploration. More often, though, Washington can best contribute by undoing the effects of wrongheaded policies that have tamped down opportunity and weakened the economy's momentum.

Beyond strictly economic policies, however, the answer to a broader-ranging American recovery lies in another policy area: education. So much of what needs to be done to decrease inequality and promote mobility starts with education reform. Brookings data show, for instance, that the median income of working men between the ages of 30 and 45 who never graduated high school fell 20 percent over the last two and a half decades.[84] In the next chapter, we'll explore a range of options that might not reform American education but actually remake it—and give millions of Americans a real chance at the kind of economic opportunity and success that we once viewed as our birthright.

## CHAPTER 9

# America's Competitive Decline— and How to Reverse It

If it were a country, U.S. regulation would be the world's tenth-largest economy.
—WAYNE CREWS, COMPETITIVE ENTERPRISE INSTITUTE[1]

What needs to be done to restore growth is very straightforward. And that's change the U.S. corporate tax system. It... [holds back] investment. And investment, in turn, is what creates GDP growth and jobs.
—FREDERICK SMITH, CHAIRMAN AND CEO, FEDEX[2]

If I owned a place in Pennsylvania, I wouldn't be thinking of closing. I would be thinking of expanding.
—MARIAN SZAREJKO, OWNER OF MARIAN'S PIZZA SHACK IN WINDSOR, NEW YORK[3]

America's infrastructure crisis is really a maintenance crisis.
—ERIC JAFFE, CITYLAB[4]

Sometimes it seems that the only area where America still leads the world is pop culture. When it comes to cable dramas, hip-hop stars, Hollywood movies, the Super Bowl, and reality shows, the United States remains the undisputed superpower. Outside the realm of entertainment, though, our struggles are mounting up, as the nation that once paced the world in production and innovation seems increasingly to lag behind.

It's hard to find a more symbolic example than what's occurring in Indian Land, South Carolina, where a Chinese textile manufacturer, Keer Group, runs a cotton mill and employs American workers whom it struggles to train to its exacting standards.

"They're quick learners," says Ni Meijuan, a manager at the plant, of the American trainees, "but they have to learn to be quicker." She complains of the American workers' tardiness and of their productivity, which so far doesn't measure up to the Chinese workers she saw back home. "I have to be patient," she says.[5]

There is a positive angle on the Keer Group story, since the Chinese presence in South Carolina is part of a shift in manufacturing economics that is driving up costs in China and bringing back some manufacturing jobs to the United States. Jobseekers in Indian Land rushed to snatch up these positions as they became available. Still, it's hard for Americans past a certain age to read such stories and not think, The Chinese are training *us* how to make things? Bernie Sanders and Donald Trump made this sense of displacement a centerpiece of their presidential campaigns.

Indeed, we have become accustomed for years to such stories about the decline of American preeminence, whether it be our loss of industrial leadership, our failure to educate our citizens for a twenty-first-century economy, our inability to keep our own companies from shifting their operations—and their financial holdings—abroad, or our declining workforce participation. Without significant reforms to our regulatory, tax, and legal landscape, we will continue to lose ground.

In an important article from the March 2012 *Harvard Business Review*, "The Looming Challenge to U.S. Competitiveness," Michael E. Porter described what he called the nation's "incipient competitiveness problem," which he believes helped cause the Great Recession. As Porter sees it, our woes include

> levels of government debt not seen since World War II; health care and primary education systems whose results are neither world-class nor reflective of the large sums spent on them; and a polarized and often paralyzed political system (especially at the federal level) that makes decisions only when facing a crisis. In micro competitiveness, eroding skills in the workplace, inadequate physical infrastructure, and rising regulatory complexity increasingly offset traditional strengths such as innovation and entrepreneurship.[6]

Porter goes on to describe the results of a survey he conducted with hundreds of Harvard Business School alumni on America's current and future competitive situation. The results were sobering. Nearly two-thirds of the respondents saw the United States falling behind other competitive or emerging economies. The skill levels of the American workforce were widely viewed as declining. The survey did acknowledge that America maintains special strengths in "entrepreneurship, higher education, and management quality," but warned that these strengths were threatened by weaknesses in other areas.[7]

Others have zeroed in on more specific competitive deficiencies. One of these is overregulation. In 2013, Deloitte's Global Manufacturing Competitiveness Index rated the United States the third-most competitive country in the world for manufacturing—trailing China and Germany—and projected that we would slip to fifth place by 2018.[8] Business executives polled in the survey put a high priority on a country's legal and regulatory climate, describing "stability and clarity in legal and regulatory policies" as most important.[9] These qualities do not characterize the American system today.

We should be worried. But while our problems are serious and our challenges mounting, the situation is far from unsalvageable. In fact, if the United States could fix a few underlying problems, it could be positioned for yet another surge in economic power.

Throughout much of our modern history, America has outpaced the world, not just in economic growth and opportunity but also in innovation. We haven't yet lost that status, but our primacy is threatened, by competitors such as China as well as by our counterproductive, even destructive policies in key areas. No single chapter on such a broad topic can cover it all, and we don't claim that this survey is comprehensive. But here we will examine two areas where we seem to be almost willfully holding ourselves back—regulation and tax policy—as well as three others where, with a different mindset and some commonsense reforms, we could foster enormous growth and opportunity: energy, immigration and workforce policies, and infrastructure.

## THE REGULATORY CRUSH

It all starts with a regulatory framework so overgrown that it is choking our free-enterprise system. Ask average Americans if they're overtaxed, and they'll probably say yes—regardless of their party affiliation. Each year, Americans send about $1.4 trillion in taxes to Washington.[10] What few of us know is that, dollar for dollar, we pay even more in regulatory costs. By a recent estimate, those add up annually to $1.9 trillion.[11]

"If it were a country, U.S. regulation would be the world's tenth-largest economy," writes Wayne Crews, author of a yearly report from the Competitive Enterprise Institute on federal regulations. The red tape adds up to an average burden per household of $14,976 per year.[12] These onerous regulations have long been a source of concern for voters, and leaders often use excessive regulation as a political target.

"There are 12 different agencies that deal with exports," Obama said in his 2012 State of the Union address. "There are at least five different agencies that deal with housing policy. Then there's my favorite example: the Interior Department is in charge of salmon while they're in fresh water, but the Commerce Department handles them when they're in saltwater. I hear it gets even more complicated once they're smoked."[13] Those words got an appreciative chuckle, but during Obama's tenure, the rate of regulation only increased.[14] Obama reigns as the all-time regulatory champion among presidents, as measured by the number of pages added to the *Federal Register* each year. The two highest totals ever—in 2010 and 2011—came in Obama's first term, and five of the six highest annual totals came under Obama. Keep in mind that these are *new* rules, not replacements or revisions—so the *Federal Register* grows, seemingly infinitely.[15]

Six federal agencies account for roughly half of all federal regulations: the Departments of the Treasury, Commerce, Interior, Health and Human Services, and Transportation, and the Environmental Protection Agency (EPA).[16] These overreaching institutions consistently smother public- and private-sector efforts to innovate.

It seemed like a pretty simple idea, for example, to the citizens of Alaska to build a road connecting King Cove, a remote town in Alaska, to Cold Bay, a key commercial center in Alaska and home to Cold Bay Airport. The road would have provided access to an all-weather airport for King Cove, where medical evacuations had sometimes failed due to dangerous weather, leading to deaths or serious injuries. But the Department of the Interior killed the proposal, citing environmental concerns, particularly to local birds.

"I cannot fathom why the Fish and Wildlife Service prioritized a perceived risk to birds over an existing threat to human life," said Alaska's then-governor, Sean Parnell.[17]

Misplaced environmental concerns often drive the regulatory over-reach that has so often denied citizens needed infrastructure improvements. In Granite City, Illinois, where severe flooding is a regular fact of life, the Army Corps of Engineers had recommended, through eight commissioned studies spanning many years, the construction of lakes and channels to divert the floodwaters. Yet from 1965, when the first study was commissioned, to 1990, nothing had been done.

That's when Steve Lathrop, a Granite City resident, bought a city dump in his neighborhood and invested $100,000 to turn it into a lake. He even constructed several houses around the lake, improving the area further. It seemed like a fine example of proactive American ingenuity—until the courts stepped in, ruling that the dump constituted a "wetland" under existing regulations and insisting that Lathrop undo the entire development. The court made this decision in spite of the fact that, when Granite City had recently flooded again and required federal funds for disaster relief, Lathrop's neighborhood, saved by the lake, sustained little damage. In 1994, the court referred Lathrop to the EPA for prosecution. Fortunately, the EPA declined to pursue it.

Lathrop didn't give up. He invested another $200,000 for a permit to develop new wetlands on the adjacent land. But a decade and a half later, he is still waiting for that permit. Twenty-three years after buying the dump and trying to improve his neighborhood—and protect the lives and property of his neighbors—Steve Lathrop has been driven into bankruptcy.[18]

Lathrop exemplifies the target that the regulatory state so often seeks to crush—the independent operator pursuing ambitious goals. This is especially true in the private sector, where small businesses remain the lifeblood of the American economy. But small businesses take it on the chin from Washington regularly, reeling annually under seemingly countless new rules. In 2014, some 3,541 new regulations were passed, with 659 of them expected to have an impact on small businesses.[19] The next year, 2015, saw an all-time high of 81,111 pages of rules, proposed rules, and notices added to the *Federal Register*.[20] The cost of regulatory compliance is 36 percent higher for small businesses than large ones.[21] The Small Business Administration estimated that the cost of complying with federal regulations in 2008 was roughly $1.75 trillion.[22] The impact of federal minimum-wage increases and mandatory paid sick leave is sure to increase that figure.

The smaller the business, the costlier the regulations. Businesses with fewer than 20 employees paid an average of $10,585 per employee to comply with regulations, compared with $7,755 for businesses with more than 20 employees.[23]

Stories like these are epidemic around the United States, and they'll probably get worse before they get better, since the Dodd-Frank Act extended financial regulations to small businesses that had previously only been applicable to larger companies.[24]

## THE DODD-FRANK TRAIN WRECK

Dodd-Frank itself is a good example of how our regulatory state, often designed with good intentions, becomes a job-killing, business-destroying monster. Passed and signed into law in 2010, Dodd-Frank was meant to curb the abuses and systemic inefficiencies that had led to the financial crisis. Yet it doesn't really put an end to the "too big to fail" mentality that helped create the crisis. What it does instead is create yet another new, massive, and imperious regulatory authority: the Consumer Financial Protection Bureau (CFPB), tasked with protecting consumers from predatory financial institutions. Supposedly set up to protect ordinary Americans, the CFPB is almost entirely unaccountable, and its regulatory discretion is enormous.[25]

Dodd-Frank also adds to the *Federal Register* 14,000 pages of new regulations—28 times longer than *War and Peace*.[26] The staggering volume of new regulations will impose immense costs on financial institutions. The House Financial Services Committee determined that it would cost firms at least $27 billion and absorb more than 2.2 million annual work hours to comply with the *first 10 percent of the regulations*.[27] The regulatory costs will be passed down to consumers, too: retail banking costs have soared since the passage of the act, hitting low-income families especially hard.[28]

And much of Dodd-Frank hasn't even been implemented yet. By July 2015, the five-year anniversary of the bill's passage, 79 of the law's 390 proposed requirements had missed their deadlines for being either enacted or formulated.[29] Why? Because the act required federal agencies to write new regulations at an unprecedented pace, creating a pile-up of new rules. For instance, the act required the SEC and the Commodity

Futures Trading Commission (CFTC) to write over 140 rules in a single year—compared with the 10 substantive rules the SEC had written in 2005 and 2006 and 11 that the CFTC had written during the same period.[30] Dodd-Frank is a textbook example of regulatory overreach.

## NEAR-TERM AND LONG-TERM REGULATORY REFORM

While there is no question that we must rethink our entire regulatory approach—especially the almost biological growth of new regulations, year after year after year—we also shouldn't lose sight of the smaller or more incremental fixes that could make a real difference now in people's lives and businesses. At minimum, we should apply rigorous cost-benefit analysis to any contemplated new regulation, and we should also periodically review existing regulations—many of which have become counterproductive or obsolete. We should also, as the Heritage Foundation recommends, mandate that all new major regulations formulated by agencies be approved by Congress; that legislation pending before Congress be subject to regulatory-impact analysis; that all regulations come with a "sunset" date for expiration or reauthorization; and that "independent" agencies be subject to executive-branch regulatory review.[31]

But more broadly, relief can only come through recognition that, as the Cato Institute puts it, "there is no greater impediment to American prosperity than the immense body of regulations chronicled in the *Federal Register*."[32] That's certainly the case in the energy industry, where the United States is working with one arm tied behind its back.

## UNTAPPED ENERGY

For all its economic struggles of recent years, the United States has something to cheer about: a burgeoning energy sector that has revitalized the economies of states that have embraced new opportunities and new technologies. States with thriving energy economies—especially Texas, Oklahoma, Utah, Louisiana, West Virginia, and North Dakota—have some of the fastest rates of job creation in the country. And in North Dakota, shale gas—derived from hydraulic fracturing, or "fracking"—has brought to this sparsely populated state a twenty-first-century version of a gold rush.

"Welcome to Boomtown USA," reads a sign that greets visitors entering Williston, North Dakota, where less than a decade ago 12,000 people lived. Today, the population is 40,000, with newcomers arriving from around the world to take fracking jobs. Williston's unemployment at the end of 2014—1 percent—was the lowest in the United States. Even with the recent drop in gas and oil prices, most residents are sanguine about the future, believing that the technology and the demand it creates is here to stay.

Williston's growth mirrors that of North Dakota generally. The state's economic growth since 2008, when it started fracking, has been phenomenal. North Dakota leads all states in its per capita GDP growth, and it has the nation's second-lowest unemployment rate (after Nebraska). According to the latest projections, population has increased by nearly 13 percent since 2010.[33]

And yet, in other states with available reserves of shale gas—especially California and New York—we are barely scratching the surface of what we can do in the energy sector. New York and California are both sitting on massive reserves of shale gas that, for now, are going untapped, due to political resistance against fracking. Both those states have massive numbers of unemployed residents.

California is engaged in a long-running political battle over fracking that has resulted in several local bans on the practice. Greens want Governor Jerry Brown to ban fracking statewide, but so far Brown has refused. Brown, a Green pioneer—he pushed for sustainable technologies in the 1970s—cites studies showing that the safety and environmental risks of fracking are minimal. With Brown's support, the state passed regulations putting some limits on fracking but essentially allowing it to go forward.

Still, opposition is intense. Last year, Beverly Hills became the first city in California to ban fracking. Marin County, Oakland, and Culver City have all passed resolutions calling for a statewide ban on the practice.[34] Friction continues to grow between industry groups, environmentalists, and local residents to determine whether California will ramp up its shale oil operations or heavily curtail them.

The key battleground is the Monterey shale, which is estimated to hold as much as 500 billion barrels of oil, though only a small portion of this oil is believed to be extractable—perhaps as few as 600 million barrels, with existing technologies. Greens like to point to these recent estimates to justify their call for a ban, but "existing technology" is the operative term here. Given the ingenuity that drillers already have shown in perfecting hydraulic fracturing, we shouldn't doubt that they can devise still more effective ways of getting more oil and gas. Yet, unless fracking gets under way seriously in the Monterey shale, California will probably never see a fracking boom—and it is a state that desperately needs one.

So does New York, especially in its Southern Tier, along the border it shares with Pennsylvania, where communities have become hollowed out by unemployment rates among the nation's worst. Along that shared border, New York is sitting on massive deposits of gas in the Marcellus shale. But in December 2014, Governor Andrew Cuomo signed a statewide ban on fracking, with no exceptions, closing the door (at least for now) on an economic opportunity that could revitalize his high-unemployment, high-tax state in one stroke. Why the ban? The pressure from activists, especially the New Yorkers Against Fracking Coalition, was too great.

Fracking is by far the best economic hope for this depressed region. According to a study conducted by New York State, going ahead with hydraulic fracturing would have directly created 17,634 construction jobs and 7,161 production jobs, and indirectly created 29,000 jobs in other sectors. "Given the likely economic ripple effects—which would have spread into the Rochester, Syracuse and Utica-Rome areas as well—shale gas production was by far the most promising potential growth engine for a vast swath of Upstate New York," said the Empire Center for Public Policy.[35] Instead, Southern Tier residents inhabit a ghostly economic landscape.

"There are no jobs here," says Marian Szarejko, the owner of Marian's Pizza Shack in Windsor, New York, in Broome County. "Business has gone down so much that I am dipping into my savings just to keep this afloat. If I owned a place in Pennsylvania, I wouldn't be thinking of closing. I would be thinking of expanding."[36]

"The Southern Tier is desolate," agrees Jim Finch, Republican town supervisor for Conklin, a town in the area. "We have no jobs and no income. The richest resource we have is in the ground."

And if Cuomo won't let them get at it, they just might secede from the state. Shortly after Cuomo announced the fracking ban, Conklin and 14 other New York towns joined forces to pursue an effort to secede from New York and join Pennsylvania—where fracking is legal. The New Yorkers complain that the fracking ban is preventing them from monetizing their own resources, limiting access to jobs, tax revenue, and income. In Pennsylvania, the average fracking-related job pays $62,000.[37] "Everybody...has new cars, new four-wheelers, new snow-mobiles....They have new roofs, new siding," says Finch.[38]

Fracking is not the only energy area in which the United States could improve its economic prospects. In 2015, after Congress passed a bill approving the Keystone XL Pipeline, President Obama vetoed it, citing environmental concerns. In our view, this is a mistake. Even a State Department analysis conceded that the pipeline would create over 40,000 jobs, directly and indirectly, and would add $3.4 billion to GDP. Pipelines have long been shown to be the safest means of transporting oil and gas, with the fewest accidents, injuries, and fatalities,[39] and the State Department also concluded that Keystone posed minimal environmental risk.[40]

On energy policy, President Obama consistently made the wrong choices. It's foolhardy to turn our nose up at tens of thousands of well-paying jobs. This is why it is more critical than ever to pay attention to organizations like the scientist-founded Environmental Defense Fund, which wants to work with regulators to make fracking safer.[41] That's the realistic—and growth-oriented—approach we need.

## SEIZING THE ENERGY OPPORTUNITY

Consider what the United States stands to gain by fully exploiting its fracking opportunities. Thanks in part to the revolution of shale gas, America has become, over the last decade, the world's largest energy producer. Shale gas production grew by 51 percent between 2007 and 2014. Shale oil production has grown even faster. Technology for extracting both continues to improve, boosting barrel-per-day counts.[42]

Shale gas has created jobs in an economy where job growth remains sluggish; between 2007 and 2012, the oil and gas industry added 135,000 high-paying jobs. The benefits have been felt broadly, from Texas to Arkansas, Pennsylvania, Ohio, and elsewhere, and also among Americans who lack college educations. By some estimates, the shale gas boom could create over 1.7 million permanent jobs in the United States.[43]

And we are uniquely positioned to take advantage of these opportunities. Though shale formations exist around the world, only three countries—the United States, Canada, and China—have been able to produce gas in large volumes. Right now, even without New York's participation and the lagging participation of California, the United States is producing approximately 1.3 billion cubic meters of gas annually, dwarfing Canada (113 million cubic meters) and China (17 million cubic meters). No other country with shale gas possesses our advantages—the technological know-how, the infrastructure, the private-sector capabilities and private-property rights, the capital.[44]

And there is another benefit to be had, one that extends far beyond our national boundaries and beyond concerns about local economies and jobs: shale gas could have a major impact on international politics—in ways that benefit the United States. Consider that in 2011, America ran a negative trade balance for oil, to the tune of $354 billion; by 2020, that's projected to be a $5 billion surplus. In 2011, we were a net importer of hydrocarbon products; two years later, in 2013, we became a net exporter, with a positive balance of two million barrels a day. Some of the United States' leading global adversaries—Russia, Iran, and yes, the Islamic State—depend heavily on hydrocarbon exports. None have access to shale gas or oil. The possibilities here seem self-evident.[45]

We have to overcome our resistance to expanding domestic production and our passive acceptance of the Environmental Protection Agency's job-killing regulations. Not only has overregulation by the EPA stifled oil and gas exploration; it has also conducted a war on coal, which provides most of the power in the United States.[46]

Most Americans by now share a general concern over environmental pollutants and the potential drawbacks of energy exploration. Yet the remediation of such effects has never been more advanced or more successful. Safety and environmental concerns are real, but the truth is this: no one does energy more safely or more conscientiously than the United States. The opportunities before us are transformative and the risks controllable. Embracing the American energy economy could singlehandedly transform our economic prospects, especially for the middle class.

Another energy area where we're doing ourselves no favors is nuclear power. Though we supply more electrical power through nuclear energy than any other nation, we haven't seriously built nuclear capacity since the 1970s. Most of the 72 reactors under construction around the world are being built in Asia.[47] In the United States, nuclear power's reputation has never really recovered from the Three Mile Island disaster of 1979—but that was a lifetime ago in terms of safety technology. Even the 2011 Fukushima tragedy in Japan happened in large part because the reactors were built using outdated technology—not current technology, which prevents meltdowns or steam explosions.[48]

But since Three Mile Island, nuclear regulation in the United States has all but shut down new plant construction. Many U.S. nuclear energy companies moved their operations to countries like France that are friendlier to nuclear power.[49] And most new nuclear opportunities are going to China and Russia.

"If the world is serious about shifting to low-carbon energy, nuclear energy is the most direct path," writes Eric McFarland, a director at the Dow Centre for Sustainable Engineering Innovation. "Nuclear power is the densest (in watts per square meter of land) and safest (in deaths per joule) form of energy known to man."[50] It is also affordable, especially in the United States. Nothing is preventing the United States from jumping full-bore back into the nuclear game.

Obama always presented himself as a man of reason and rationality, a forward-thinker not bound to the ways of the past, a leader eager to turn a page into a new future. On energy, he systematically failed to do this, whether through his resistance to fracking, his hostility to nuclear power, or his refusal to build out the Keystone XL Pipeline. President Trump should regard seizing the energy future as synonymous with seizing the *American* future.

## THE WORKFORCE WE NEED

We won't be able to seize any future, energy-related or otherwise, if we don't upgrade the American worker's skills and competitiveness.

In a 2013 Deloitte study, manufacturing executives called "talent-driven innovation" the most important driver of competitiveness in manufacturing. They emphasized that the quality of a nation's scientists, engineers, and researchers, along with the availability of skilled labor, is the key driver of a nation's ability to succeed in manufacturing.[51] The key skills needed for high-tech manufacturing jobs, as well as jobs in industries such as bioscience, engineering, energy, medical, technology, and other such fields, are commonly called STEM skills—that is, those requiring a science, technology, engineering, or math degree. In a high-tech, super-competitive economic marketplace, these are the skills more and more people will need.

And not just in high-tech fields. Even entry-level manufacturing and other jobs increasingly require STEM skills. Roughly one-half of the workforce in aerospace, for example, is made up of skilled workers who hold two-year diplomas. In southwest Washington, where unemployment is over 10 percent, paper mill employers said that most job applicants lacked the necessary math, language, and computer skills to be hired.[52]

By now, the United States has become well known for its poor performance on international assessments of educational outcomes, with STEM skills lagging particularly badly. We rank 52nd in the quality of our math and science education, according to the World Economic Forum.[53] We are failing to educate and train American workers.

The problem is more complex than it first appears, however. America *does* have a STEM crisis, but not in all areas. It depends on which STEM areas you're looking at.

For example, there is a vast oversupply of STEM students seeking life-sciences PhDs, but not enough students seeking doctorates in mechanical and systems engineering. There is high demand for—and supply of—computer engineers at all levels and a good supply of STEM bachelor's degrees in general.[54] We certainly need more STEM graduates, but we need to match them better to the labor market. We should encourage businesses and universities to work together to make sure that today's STEM graduates are well-trained and flexible enough to do tomorrow's jobs.

We also tend to overlook STEM positions that don't require bachelor's degrees—such as those in advanced manufacturing and construction. Millions of STEM jobs require only a certificate or associate's degree, or have no formal qualification at all, yet require the numeracy and critical-thinking skills associated with STEM degrees. In order to fill these jobs, we need programs that make vocational training readily available. We also need to improve math education across the board.[55]

Ultimately, the STEM challenge mirrors our education challenge in general—and the solution is better education and training. Our long-range goal should be a vastly greater number of Americans equipped with the education and skills that lead to well-paying STEM jobs, particularly in areas important to the national interest—such as defense or health care. In short, we should focus on the quality, not just the quantity, of STEM education. This will require more STEM graduates but also a reworking of the education-to-job pipeline that makes these degrees useful.

In the meantime, though, when we have companies and jobs that require high-skilled workers, we must continue to bring in the skilled immigrants who have always provided an injection of innovation and dynamism to our economy. And that means fixing the situation with H-1B visas—a flashpoint in our current politics that needn't be so contentious. If we want a competitive economy, we need these visas and we need to resolve the political infighting that is going on around them.

In a recent Business Roundtable survey, the United States ranked second to last among advanced economies in competitive immigration policies. America's poor performance had a good deal to do with our cap on H-1B visas, which are granted to U.S. businesses so that they can employ foreign workers temporarily in "specialty" occupations such as biotechnology, chemistry, medicine, mathematics, or other technical fields. The H-1B visa cap means that the United States is missing out on a host of skilled workers in specialized fields. Too often, exceptional young people graduate American colleges and are forced to leave because their visas expire at the end of their education. They return to their home countries instead of staying and working in America.

The current system is a mess. For one thing, demand for the visas dramatically outstrips supply. In 2015, the congressionally mandated cap on H-1B visas, 65,000, was met *within a week* of the visas being made available. The cap has not been raised because an increase has been tied to a broader immigration overhaul.[56] Many engineers at U.S. universities are foreign students, and the shortage of visas means that most have to return home when they complete their educations, rather than getting jobs at U.S. tech companies and eventually becoming citizens. Leaders at tech companies say that they need more H-1B visas so that they can recruit these top graduates.

"Like Google, Intel and others, we recruit from top U.S. engineering universities and graduate programs," says Alice Tornquist, vice president of government affairs at Qualcomm. "Nearly half of the STEM graduates from these U.S. universities will need visas to stay in the United States after completing their education."[57] H-1B visas are also vital to small businesses, which have less staffing flexibility to make up for skills gaps.[58]

So why not dramatically expand the number of visas available, as numerous high-tech companies like Google and Facebook advocate?

Well, for one thing, the H-1B visa process is easily abused. Critics say that many visas are being taken not to bring over highly educated talent and improve the workforce; rather, they are being used to allow U.S. companies to outsource IT to companies staffed by foreign workers who have no intention of staying here. Tata and Infosys, for example, are the two largest users of H-1B visas—and both are outsourcing firms based in India.[59] Other critics argue that H-1Bs are abused by U.S. companies like Microsoft and Facebook to *import* workers from overseas—again, usually from India—who work for low wages. The workers are sent back after three years with no expectation that they will settle in the United States, and a new crop is brought in. This practice not only depresses wages for highly skilled U.S. workers but also disseminates expertise to foreign competitors.[60]

Still, though these flaws are real and serious, most objective observers concede that the United States still needs skilled labor from abroad. Practically no one is advocating that we junk the H-1B visa program or even downsize it—the realistic option seems to be to reform it and then expand it. Until American STEM talent becomes more geographically flexible and better matched to the needs of employers, there will be gaps in the talent pool. The H-1B program offers an opportunity to import labor to fill these gaps, but we should fix the program to prevent companies from voluntarily hiring foreign labor when local talent is available.

Solutions might include more stringent requirements for the type of labor that is imported—we could prohibit outsourcing firms, for example. We could also institute requirements that H-1B workers be paid equivalently to American talent—lessening the motivation for firms to select them on a purely cost-cutting basis and undoing the wage advantage they currently enjoy against our own workforce.

Innovation in the United States has long been tied to entrepreneurialism, but in recent years, that classic American habit has lagged. Research shows that educated immigrants play a disproportionately large role in high-impact entrepreneurial activity; we need to provide incentives for talented people to stay here. In their book, *Better Capitalism*, Robert Litan and Carl Schramm argue that the United States should give green cards to all foreigners coming to America to study science, technology, engineering, or math.

But the H-1B visa problem, which relates to the STEM problem, is part of a broader problem—that of the education, training, and preparedness of the American worker. We don't have to wait until students are in four-year colleges to start addressing our deficiencies. If our community colleges could perform better on graduation rates for students in STEM-related areas, our STEM workforce would get a boost.[61]

And we could start earlier than that. Some high schools already have incorporated advanced vocational skills, such as masonry, welding, and robotics, into their curricula. Some believe that a "new shop" movement might be taking shape in our high schools.[62] For example, at Indian Springs High School in San Bernardino, California, students can graduate with certificates in high-skill trades, such as health care and medical technology, logistics and transportation, and manufacturing.[63] Blackstone Valley Regional Vocational Technical High School in Massachusetts, which has a 93 percent graduation rate, specializes in vocational training, ranging from plumbing to automotive trades to engineering.[64] These are promising efforts that should be replicated and expanded.

In the end, solutions to the STEM/skills/workforce problem lie entirely under our own control. We should not be surprised that skilled foreign workers exploit the employment opportunities they find here, or that American companies look abroad for the workforce they need. Until we can educate, train, and develop the American workers of tomorrow to be the best in the world, we will continue to rely on highly skilled workers from overseas—and such reliance will always leave our own citizens less economically secure.

## THE INFRASTRUCTURE CRISIS: WHAT IT IS AND WHAT IT ISN'T

"Time for some traffic problems in Fort Lee," an aide to New Jersey governor Chris Christie infamously said in September 2013, before giving orders to close one of the traffic lanes to the George Washington Bridge during the evening rush hour. The shutdown, motivated by a political feud the Christie administration was having with the Fort Lee mayor, had the intended effect: a massive traffic jam ensued, infuriating commuters and area residents. They only became angrier when the truth came out that the entire thing was politically motivated; Bridgegate became a scandal.

But from an infrastructure perspective, the conditions that Bridgegate created are far from unusual in heavily trafficked commuting corridors all around the United States. What required political chicanery to create in Fort Lee arises organically every day around the nation, the product of a swelling population and aging public infrastructure that is no longer state of the art and capable of operating at a world-class standard. Jam-ups, closures, long commutes, breakdowns, and limited options are some of the characteristics of our public infrastructure system—a system that, after the United States built its Interstate Highway System in the 1950s, was the envy of the world.

But the 1950s was a long time ago. In 2013, the American Society of Civil Engineers famously gave U.S. infrastructure a D-plus grade. The weakest areas were aviation, drinking water supply, roads, transit, and sewage treatment.[65] Americans see problems with public infrastructure everywhere they look.

In Maryland, the Baltimore and Potomac tunnels are 140 years old, their construction dating back to the Civil War. Trains must slow down to 30 miles per hour, max, to pass through safely. Transit workers keep an eye on the tunnel for trouble.

"If they see things that are repairable, they fix them," said Steve Chan, a 61-year-old chairman of a local riders' council. "If they see something that is a safety concern, they'll shut it down. But long term? We need the tunnel rebuilt," Chan says.[66]

The Northeast Corridor, with the heaviest commuting traffic in the United States, is living on borrowed time before a major infrastructure collapse. The rail system carries 750,000 riders daily, most on Amtrak but also on multiple commuter train lines such as Metro-North. Up and down the line, the signs of vulnerability, gridlock, and risk are everywhere. New Jersey Transit riders were delayed for most of an entire workweek because of malfunctioning overhead wires; thousands of people were stranded in stations, or on trains, for hours. At one point, a frustrated rider, tired of hearing another Twitter update on the delays, observed that it would be "easier to alert us when there aren't delays."[67]

Under the Hudson River, New Jersey and New York are connected by two passenger train tunnels over a century old. In the often clogged Northeast Corridor, many view the Hudson tunnels as the worst choke point of all. They need to be replaced as soon as possible for efficiency, productivity, and safety—yet the familiar battles over budgets, costs, and politics have prevented anything from getting done.

According to a report from the Northeast Corridor Infrastructure and Operations Advisory Commission, a shutdown of the Northeast Corridor for *one day* would cost $100 million in congestion, reduced productivity, and other effects.[68]

"We're seeing two trends converging in an extraordinary way," said Thomas Wright, president of the Regional Plan Association. "Ridership is hitting all-time highs on the Northeast Corridor at the same time that the system is just too brittle and does not have the ability to withstand heat waves, storms and other incidents."

Trouble on the rails only sends more people onto the roads, and New York, Connecticut, and New Jersey commuters endure punishing daily drives to their jobs, especially when work is located in New York City. Mayor Michael Bloomberg proposed congestion pricing in 2007, but it didn't get through the city council. Even if New York adopts congestion pricing, it won't change the fact that the roads, highways, and bridges are in serious need of refurbishment or replacement. In New York, one of Governor Andrew Cuomo's aides called the Tappan Zee Bridge the "hold your breath bridge."[69]

In Los Angeles, meanwhile, the roads "are the most deteriorated in the United States, costing drivers more than $800 a year," the *Los Angeles Times* reported in 2013.[70] Everyone knows about the famous Los Angeles problems with gridlock, but fewer people know that the Los Angeles area has an emerging crisis with aging water pipes, which badly need to be replaced, as they are over a century old. The State of California is meanwhile expending billions on an infamous boondoggle, the California Bullet Train, which will probably cost upward of $43 billion while doing little to alleviate the congestion in travel between Los Angeles and San Francisco.

It will cost money to modernize our transportation, water, and energy infrastructure. Advocates point out that we spend only about 2.4 percent of GDP on infrastructure—half of what we devoted in the 1960s.[71] Yet as bad as all that sounds, the real problem is not that we don't spend enough but rather that we don't spend well.

The most common error is prioritizing glamorous, super-expensive new projects over commonsense repairs. A study of state infrastructure spending from 2004 to 2008 found that states spent 57 percent of their infrastructure budget on expansion projects—even though these projects, when completed, would add up to only 1.3 percent of roads. The states spent a mere 43 percent of their funding on 98.7 percent of the roads.[72]

In state after state, what we often see is transportation departments "willing to break the bank on gold-plated highway flyovers designed to shave 40 seconds off a half-hour commute, while neglecting important bridges and other assets that present real risks," as Angie Schmitt writes on Streetsblog.[73] Until this dynamic changes, expect American infrastructure to continue to struggle, especially as compared with some of our international competitors. But it doesn't have to: as with the energy sector, when it comes to infrastructure, we have everything we need to make things work again. What we need is the vision and leadership to put the right plans into practice.

## REBOOTING OUR INFRASTRUCTURE

Today's popular infrastructure consensus is that the United States needs a massive new buildout of public infrastructure—new bridges, highways, high-speed trains, and the like. The truth is, we don't need a NASA-like investment in new projects. On the contrary, we need a NASA-like investment in repairing, improving, and upgrading the infrastructure we have in place. This doesn't mean we shouldn't do some new building. By all means, if we really need it—especially in urban areas seeing robust population growth—we should build. But in many, even most cases, what we usually need is to repair, improve, or upgrade what we already have.

That's not what you tend to hear out there. Many liberals love the idea of high-speed rail and lambaste the United States for being the only major industrialized nation without a high-speed rail system. Obama called for a national infrastructure bank early in his presidency, and his 2009 stimulus package contained funding for some state and local infrastructure projects. Democrats and even Republicans have repeated the call over recent years for a federal effort of infrastructure upgrade and renewal. The call for massive, ambitious new infrastructure funding was exemplified in Bernie Sanders's proposal to spend $1 trillion over five years on infrastructure—roads, bridges, rail, water systems, electric grids, you name it. Sanders says that his plan would also create 13 million jobs.

Generally speaking, though, a Washington-driven agenda for infrastructure doesn't have a good track record, either in successful projects or in cost control. And too many Democrats (and some Republicans) look at infrastructure projects as jobs programs. Creating jobs can certainly be a byproduct of infrastructure investment, but it shouldn't be the organizing principle. Rather, we need to make our infrastructure decisions based first on what we actually *need*—for our economy, for the efficient transport of residents to and from their jobs, and for safety and well-being. This would include bridges and ports, power grids, tunnels, airports, highways, and yes, schools.

"Our infrastructure investments must work to support the American people, not the other way around," says civil engineer Chuck Marohn, who has shown skepticism about the consensus of many in his profession—and their political allies—for massive new infrastructure spending projects.[74]

And on that principle, it's important to note, high-speed rail, among other ideas, is a nonstarter. Obama's whole vision for high-speed rail only covered 8,500 miles and would have covered about 1 percent of U.S. passenger travel. His own transportation secretary, Ray LaHood, conceded that building out the plan would cost more than the entire Interstate Highway System—which runs 48,000 miles and connects every state on the American mainland. High-speed rail is a chimera, and a costly one at that.[75]

Here's something you won't hear from the conventional-wisdom crowd: for the most part, the United States has the infrastructure it needs *already in place*—we just need to improve it. Consider that we have 2.7 million miles of paved roads, 140,000 route-miles of rail lines, 600 commercial and thousands of non-commercial airports, as Cato's

Randal O'Toole notes. Instead of looking at these assets as aging dinosaurs that need to be replaced, we just need to upgrade them. We can do this because new technologies have emerged that will improve what we already possess.[76]

O'Toole points out, for instance, that the emerging self-driving cars will "at least double road capacities," as they will improve on human reaction times. Upgrades to our air traffic control system, which has become antiquated, will improve air travel times; bigger airplanes will carry more people at no additional cost to infrastructure. "For speed," O'Toole reminds us, "planes are twice as fast as high-speed trains yet cost far less," and "for the cost of a few miles of high-speed rail, we could double the throughput of airport security, saving travelers millions of hours per year." The same goes for the car itself: emerging metropolises in the United States will be better served by four-lane highways, which can move multiples of the people carried by any high-speed rail system, and at lower cost. And cars, not only through the self-driving technology but also through improvements like collision-avoidance systems, are becoming safer than ever.

"We don't need to impoverish ourselves to keep up with the neighbors," O'Toole writes. "We just need to maintain and efficiently use the infrastructure we have, making expansions where necessary but relying mainly on new technologies to use it ever more effectively."[77] And along these lines, we should take full advantage of public-private partnerships (P3), which can significantly reduce the cost burden for taxpayers generated by infrastructure projects.[78] P3 projects have already borne fruit around the country, put in practice by governors and mayors who, often struggling with tapped budgets, have reached out to private investors and groups to build or manage public infrastructure—everything from toll roads and water systems to airports and bridges.[79]

"America's infrastructure crisis is really a maintenance crisis," says Eric Jaffe of CityLab.[80] The sooner repairs are made, the cheaper they are; every $1 in preventive maintenance saves $4 to $10 in more complicated fixes. We need to redirect spending toward road repair and preservation and away from expensive new projects, except for those rare few that are truly needed. We need a comprehensive short- and long-term infrastructure upgrade plan, driven largely at the state and local level, to get American infrastructure into the twenty-first century.

## THE GREAT SUFFOCATOR: THE UNITED STATES CORPORATE TAX CODE

Most Americans are familiar with the burdens of income taxes and the way the system has become so complex that it is impossible to understand. And of course, most Americans think their taxes are too high. But what many don't realize is that the same complaints are applicable to our system of corporate and business taxation.

In 2014, the nonpartisan Tax Foundation ranked the United States' tax regime 32nd out of 34 nations that it reviewed for business competitiveness—ahead of Portugal and France but behind nations ranging from Estonia to Mexico to the United Kingdom. The United States suffered particularly because of its high corporate tax rate and its worldwide system of taxation. The foundation also highlighted the inefficiencies in the United States' local and state property taxes and its high top marginal rate for individuals.[81]

It's difficult to overstate the impact our tax system has on enterprise, innovation, and entrepreneurialism. Look no further than the confiscatory rates, distortions, and misguided incentives embedded in the United States corporate tax code. We have the highest rate of corporate tax in the world. The federal rate is 35 percent, and states charge an additional 4.1 percent on average, for a combined rate of 39.1 percent. By comparison, OECD countries charge 25 percent, on average. Even European welfare states have lower corporate rates, and many of the United States' most important trade partners, such as Canada and the United Kingdom, have recently reduced their rates to become more competitive.[82]

But here's the catch: most U.S. companies don't pay the full statutory rate. Exploiting loopholes, credits, and the like, companies pay an average of 12.6 percent, according to the Government Accountability Office.[83] However, a separate study, by PricewaterhouseCoopers, found that the United States has the highest *effective* tax rate, with companies being burdened, on average, at 30.9 percent in 2012.[84] Either way, our system encourages businesses to avoid compliance and to keep profits and investments abroad.

We tax overseas profits when they are repatriated—thus motivating American multinationals, like Apple, to store the lion's share of their assets offshore, rather than reinvesting them at home. Apple has billions stashed overseas, much of it in Ireland, where it negotiated a 2 percent rate, far below the country's 12 percent statutory rate.[85] To add insult to injury, Apple regularly issues debt in the United States to pay its shareholders dividends—though it could easily pay these costs out of its overseas holdings.[86]

Apple has plenty of company in its manipulation of the U.S. federal tax code. In a five-year study of 288 consistently profitable Fortune 500 companies, Citizens for Tax Justice found that 93 percent paid less than 10 percent a year on average. Boeing, General Electric, Priceline.com, and Verizon paid literally no federal income taxes at all.[87]

In short, Apple and many other American firms are withholding taxes from the United States by manipulating the code or by storing much of their profits overseas. This keeps Apple's capital from doing any good here at home, whether in spurring investment or creating jobs. These firms' behavior shouldn't be condoned—they should pay the taxes the law requires them to pay—but neither should we fail to recognize that the draconian American corporate tax system triggers this behavior.

Avoiding the American corporate tax monster is also the motive behind "tax inversions," which briefly became a political flashpoint during the 2012 and 2014 election seasons. The term refers to situations wherein American firms merge with overseas companies and become subject to the tax rules of the overseas firm. Since overseas tax rules for companies tend to be more favorable, the U.S. firms have strong motive to do this—and they can do it, so long as the deal stipulates that the overseas company is acquiring the U.S. one, not the other way around.

The combined tax inversions of the past decade are estimated to have cost the U.S. Treasury $2 billion annually.[88] President Obama has sought new rules that would limit acquisitions of American firms clearly motivated by tax avoidance—mandating, for example, that the acquiring foreign company be at least half the size of the U.S. firm. But the symptom itself is less important than the underlying problem: the American tax code is extraordinarily burdensome and anticompetitive. It would be hard to conceive of a more dramatic illustration of this than American firms' willingness to let themselves be acquired by foreign companies in order to lessen their tax burdens.[89]

## TAX REFORM NOW

It is high time that the United States stopped working against itself in its policies of corporate taxation. We should reduce the statutory corporate rate to no more than 25 percent while closing loopholes where possible, and we should adopt a territorial tax system that minimally taxes profits made overseas. In addition to its role in reviving our economy, tax policy has a role to play in a resurgence of American innovation. We should make the R&D tax credit permanent and allow repatriation of capital. And Obama's hike of the capital gains tax should be rolled back to 15 percent.

In a ferociously competitive global economy, American corporate tax rates are anticompetitive. That we have retained so much of our competitive edge up to now, despite this burden, is testament to the ingenuity, innovation, and quality that American companies continue to produce. But the time to protect those strengths is now—not after it begins to erode any more than it already has.

## PRO-GROWTH, OPPORTUNITY-BASED REFORM

Any single chapter on American competitiveness and innovation cannot hope to cover all the areas that have an impact on our long-term economic prospects. In this chapter, we have highlighted five areas in serious need of reform—areas in which a changed mindset and changed policies could have dramatic positive effects. But there is no shortage of other areas that we should be concerned about. These include overly restrictive intellectual property practices, especially the extortionist practice of "patent trolling," which forces innovative companies to pay huge sums to fight specious legal claims of patent infringement; the long-overdue need to streamline and change FDA approval protocols for new drugs, and indeed the agency's entire approval framework, as we move into an era of genetic, customized treatments that are ill-suited to one-size-fits-all evaluation; and making it easier to open small businesses. In addition, we must protect the openness, accessibility, and innovation of the greatest asset the American economy has enjoyed over the last 20 years—the Internet. By that we mean that President Trump must roll back the steps that President Obama has taken at the agency level to impose "net neutrality." We should reinstate—and perpetuate—an open Internet.

In short, we support policies that are pro-growth, forward-looking, and opportunity-based, with government as an enabler and partner, not a hindrance. Perhaps no area exemplifies this need more than American health care, to which we now turn.

CHAPTER 10

# The Health Care
# and Entitlements Albatross

Time is running out. If Mr. Obama doesn't act soon to control costs, escalating costs may ultimately threaten the sustainability of his coverage expansion—and his entire health-reform legacy.
—Ezekiel Emanuel and Topher Spiro[1]

Insurance without access to medical care is a sham. And that is where the country is heading.... The harsh reality awaiting low-income Americans is dwindling access to quality doctors, hospitals and health care.
—Scott W. Atlas, physician and senior fellow,
Hoover Institution[2]

Obamacare, meaning the operating model that undergirded the law that Congress passed and President Barack Obama signed with great fanfare—is dead, and it will not be revived. What remains is fitful chaos.
—Kevin Williamson[3]

On March 23, 2010, in a crowded White House East Room, President Obama signed the Patient Protection and Affordable Care Act (PPACA) into law, ensuring "the core principle that everybody should have some basic security when it comes to their health care."[4] The president was surrounded by his Democratic allies, such as the then House Speaker Nancy Pelosi and Vice President Joe Biden, and Americans whose experiences had dramatized the urgency of health care reform: 11-year-old Marcelas Owens of Seattle, whose mother had died without health insurance; Connie Anderson, whose sister, suffering from cancer, struggled to pay ever-higher health insurance premiums; and Victoria

Reggie, widow of Ted Kennedy, who had worked his entire career to establish a system of national health insurance.

"Now it is a fact," said Montana senator Max Baucus. "Now it is law. Now it is history. Indeed, it's historic."[5] Obamacare *has* been historic; it represents the first time in American history that the federal government has attempted to mandate that Americans purchase health insurance. But by 2016, a majority of Americans viewed Obamacare as a failure. The law's problems are manifold, not only its enormous price tag but also its ineffectiveness. Recent Central Budgeting Office (CBO) projections suggest that the law will only cover 45 percent of the uninsured, even when fully implemented.[6] Millions have lost their insurance due to the law's stringent and stifling coverage requirements. Its fiscal sustainability remains very much in doubt.

Of course, the problems with American health care didn't start with the Affordable Care Act. The ACA was a response to the crisis in the American health care system that has been worsening with each passing decade. As Obamacare was debated, the United States ranked 37th in the world in health care quality and fairness according to the World Health Organization—behind every other major first world country. U.S. health care spending continued to skyrocket—from $256 billion in 1980 to $2.6 trillion in 2010. Health care spending has reached 16 percent of GDP, compared with between 5 and 8 percent in other first world countries; administrative costs account for 22 percent of health care outlays in America, compared with just 5 to 7 percent in advanced nations. For all this, tens of millions of Americans go uninsured. Up to 60 percent of bankruptcies now stem from medical costs.[7]

Compounding our health care challenges is a broader crisis of entitlement costs—especially for Medicare and Social Security. In 2016, the Office of Management and Budget (OMB) found that Social Security will represent a $938 billion federal outlay. This represents more than a 5.2 percent increase from $891 billion in 2015 and is projected to increase by another 5.6 percent to $991 billion in 2017.[8] Medicare costs are predicted to jump by over 18 percent in the next four years up to $689 billion annually.[9] It's no surprise that estimates show both programs going bankrupt in the next decade without serious reform.

There can be no dispute that one of the United States' most pressing needs is finding comprehensive solutions to the challenges of management, delivery, and especially cost of our health care and entitlement systems.

Liberals and conservatives agree on one fundamental thing: the system remains in crisis. For many on the left, the solution is to improve Obamacare; others, further left, believe that only a Canadian-style, single-payer system can resolve the inequities and inefficiencies (there were polls with support as high as 58 percent for single payer[10]). Some on the right, particularly the Freedom Caucus, still want to repeal Obamacare, though this effort has already failed once—spectacularly, in March 2017—and would only lead to more disruption and chaos in the system. The ill-fated Republican repeal plan, the American Health Care Act, would have led to as many as 14 million uninsured Americans by 2018 and approximately 24 million fewer insured Americans over the next decade.[11] In addition, the AHCA's allowance for states to discontinue their expansion of Medicaid eligibility would have had potentially devastating long-term consequences as well.

Other reform plans, from the center and rightward, are more focused on pursuing fixes and remedies to the law. We're more in line with this latter group. Polls show that pluralities of Americans want Obamacare fixed, not repealed. It seems that one of President Trump and House Speaker Paul Ryan's greatest failures in proposing the American Health Care Act was that they did not recognize this fact. Speaker Ryan only came to accept it after he withdrew the AHCA bill from the House floor, saying, "I don't know what else to say other than Obamacare is the law of the land" and "we're going to be living with Obamacare for the foreseeable future."[12]

The demise of the AHCA was a severe blow to President Trump and the Republican Party, which had promised for seven years to repeal Obamacare. But their political failures aside, Republicans don't deserve the image they acquired during the Obama years as obstructionists with no health care ideas. On the contrary, Republicans are brimming with reform proposals, many of which we'll explore here. We're interested most in those that are patient-centered, put individuals in charge of their health care choices, and open up markets while driving down costs. This chapter will explore the options that exist between a doubling down on Obamacare's statist model and an all-out repeal—in short, a restructuring of our system that emphasizes affordability, choice, and competition.

## HOW DID WE GET HERE?

Before we get to the problems with American health care—particularly with Obamacare—and how to solve them, it's worth reviewing briefly how our health care system evolved to this point. Some background on the forces that have shaped the industry from the beginning gives insight into the obstacles for reform today.

Health insurance as we know it began in the United States in the years leading up to World War II. In the 1930s, several hospitals came together and formed the American Hospital Association, which became Blue Cross. By 1939, one million Americans were covered in Blue Cross networks. During the war years, employers used health benefits to attract workers since salaries were capped and the labor force contracted. By 1946, Blue Cross plans were available in 46 states.

The tensions that would define the system took shape early on. Initially, Blue Cross plans had set premiums so that they were in accordance with the health needs of a geographic area. But private and commercial insurance providers entering the market after the war adopted "experience ratings," whereby they offered their services to firms with healthier and cheaper-to-insure employees. Therefore, the commercial providers could offer lower prices. As healthier individuals exited Blue Cross plans, less healthy groups became more expensive to insure, reinforcing the problem. Thus was born a key problem in modern health care: insurers could keep prices down by favoring healthy individuals over those more likely to become sick.

In 1965, Congress passed Medicare, which provided coverage for most Americans over the age of 65. Hospitals had to accept Medicare, though physician participation was voluntary. At the same time, the federal government created Medicaid as a means-tested program for Americans who couldn't afford health care. Each state could design its own eligibility standards.

Despite these steps, costs kept rising. In the early 1970s, the Nixon administration made an ambitious attempt to establish a national system for health insurance. Nixon's attempt, like Harry Truman's in the 1940s, failed to get off the ground. The 1970s did see the rise of health maintenance organizations (HMOs), which aimed to provide incentives to promote healthy living and preventive care, reducing costly expenditures for emergency care. Preferred provider organizations (PPOs) were an offshoot of HMOs; they offered coverage within a network of "preferred" physicians. As HMOs and PPOs took hold, employers let their employees choose between different plans so that they could reach a balance between choice and price.

In the early 1990s Bill Clinton tried to create a national health care system. His effort also failed. By this time, many Blue Cross organizations were broadly restructured. Some went bankrupt, while others merged with their private competitors or were acquired, leading to significant market consolidation, which has continued. Today, a small number of companies dominate the industry.

### A Gold-plated but Troubled System

What did it all add up to? The world's best health care system, according to its defenders; the world's most expensive and least equitable, said its detractors. In the United States, unlike in most other advanced nations, health care coverage was not guaranteed; millions went without insurance, seeing doctors only when absolutely necessary and using emergency rooms as their fallback. These "free riders"—so called because by law doctors cannot refuse treatment to a sick patient—helped drive up rapidly rising costs in the system, decade after decade. The United States contends poorly against other rich countries in most health metrics, including life expectancy and infant mortality, in spite of having the most expensive health care system in the world.[13] A 2009 OECD study found that Americans spend, on average, $8,713 on health services each year, well over twice the OECD average. Americans pay more money per procedure and also had more procedures performed, even in cases where the need was dubious.[14] In 2016, health care prices rose 6.5 percent, increasing faster than the rate of inflation.[15] Furthermore, PwC's Health Research Institute predicts that health care costs will continue to increase at the same rate as 2016, leading to a 13.4 percent increase by the end of 2018.[16]

Its legions of uninsured citizens made the United States unique among the world's advanced nations. In 2010, 49 million Americans, or 16.3 percent of the population, were uninsured. The ranks of the uninsured included those without sufficient income to purchase private insurance but who exceeded the income requirement to qualify for Medicaid; they also included people who could not obtain coverage due to preexisting medical problems, which made them too expensive to insure. Of those who chose not to buy insurance, most were young, healthy people who felt that the expense did not justify its benefits.

It's important to note that critics of our health care system have been around a long time—and they haven't all been on the left. After all, as Obamacare's defenders often point out, the framework for the ACA came from a conservative plan first articulated by the Heritage Foundation in the early 1990s. But left or right, liberal or conservative, the critiques of our system have tended to fall into one of two categories: the system is insufficiently regulated and needs more oversight, or the system is over-regulated and needs to unleash market forces.

The more-regulation advocates want to prevent insurers from offering shoddy plans and from refusing to cover individuals with preexisting conditions. They would bar hospitals and doctors from performing needless tests and procedures. And they would force consumers to do their part too, by mandating that healthy Americans buy coverage and thus expanding the insurance pool to drive down costs.

The competing explanation is that the market is overregulated—again to the detriment of consumers. According to the Cato Institute, the cost of health regulations exceeds the benefits by $169.1 billion each year. Minimum-coverage requirements on plans prevent health insurers from offering minimal but adequate services that people could afford. In this heavily regulated industry, medical litigation accounts for every tenth health care dollar spent.[17] But perhaps the most damaging of all regulations is the one that would be simplest to overturn—the ban on interstate purchase of health insurance, which protects local insurance companies from competition and inflates prices.

### Enter the Affordable Care Act (Obamacare)

The primary aspiration of the ACA was to expand coverage. According to the CBO, the ACA would cover 34 million Americans who previously lacked health insurance. The second goal was financial: the ACA would cut the costs of health care by introducing efficiencies, saving more than $200 billion in the first ten years and over $1 trillion in the next decade.[18] The law's main provisions can be boiled down as follows.

*Guaranteed Issue.* The ACA prevents individuals from being denied coverage on the basis of any preexisting condition such as health status, gender, or age. In some states, prices of plans may not be set according to preexisting conditions.[19]

*Minimum Standards for Health Insurance Policies.* Insurance policies must meet a variety of new conditions regarding the services they offer. These include:

- Essential benefits. All plans must cover a very broad range of health services, from emergency services and hospitalization to maternity and newborn care, mental-health and substance-abuse treatment, prescription drugs, rehabilitative services, and more.[20]
- Coverage of young people. If a plan covers children, then it must cover them until they turn 26, regardless of their economic or marital status.[21]
- No more arbitrary cancellations or lifetime benefit caps. So long as individuals pay their premiums and don't commit fraud, and the insurer stays in business, insurers can't stop providing coverage.[22] Health providers can't put dollar-value caps on services that individuals use.[23]

*The Individual Mandate.* The most controversial aspect of ACA, the individual mandate requires individuals to obtain health insurance that meets the minimum requirements of the ACA. Individuals who can afford health coverage yet choose not to buy it will pay the higher of $695 per person, or 2.5 percent of their income in 2016, with the amount to increase with inflation.[24]

*Health insurance exchanges.* The ACA mandates the creation of online "health insurance marketplaces" where people who don't have insurance can sign up for it. States have the option of using a federal exchange website or designing their own websites.[25]

*Subsidies.* The ACA offers subsidies for families whose income levels are 100 percent to 400 percent of the federal poverty level. Subsidies are provided as "premium tax credits" and are automatically applied to people who seek insurance via the health care exchanges.[26]

*Medicaid Expansion.* Originally, the ACA mandated that states expand Medicaid to cover individuals making less than 138 percent of the federal poverty level. In the wake of recent Supreme Court decisions, this expansion has become optional on a state-by-state basis.[27] The ACA further changes the way that Medicaid and Medicare payments are made, requiring payment for results—say, a hip transplant—rather than for individual procedures (such as medical tests) that help reach the result, in the hope of reducing frivolous procedures that don't directly improve health outcomes.[28]

These are the central provisions of the Affordable Care Act, which has now been on the books for more than half a decade. After several delays, it saw the implementation of most of its important provisions. The law has a track record now, even if it's an incomplete one. Unfortunately, that record suggests nothing but trouble ahead.

### The Tragic Failure of Obamacare

Where to begin? Let's start with enrollments. In July 2016, the federal government stated that about 11.1 million people had enrolled in health insurance plans related to the ACA through the end of March.[29] Yet initial projections from the Congressional Budget Office, the Medicare actuary, and independent analysts were for *20 million enrollees*.[30] By the end of 2016, enrollments ran at less than half of initial promises.

"HHS [Department of Health and Human Services] believes some 19 million Americans earn too much for Medicaid but qualify for ObamaCare subsidies and haven't signed up," warned an October 2015 *Wall Street Journal* editorial. "Some 8.5 million of that 19 million purchase off-exchange private coverage with their own money, while the other 10.5 million are still uninsured. In other words, for every person who's allowed to join and has, two people haven't."[31] Worse, about half of the uninsured population are in the 18–34 demographic—the younger, healthier cohort depended upon to subsidize policies for the older and sicker. The goal was for about 40 percent of exchange enrollees to come from the 18–34 age group, but so far it lags at about 28 percent. That's a huge discrepancy.[32] So far, the young, healthy, and uninsured are opting to pay Obamacare's penalties, which are much more affordable than buying policies that these Americans have concluded they don't want or need.

Meanwhile, those signing up for Obamacare are skewing older and sicker—which, if you look at it optimistically, fulfills one of the goals of Obamacare: ensuring coverage for people who desperately need it. Fair enough. But without the countervailing participation of the young and healthy, this portion of the population can only drive costs up.[33]

"This is not surprising, exactly," writes Megan McArdle, "but it is perhaps somewhat disappointing. Subsidies or no, people who don't get a lot of value out of insurance don't seem to be buying it. As a result, the cost of the cheaper policies—the ones you'd expect the healthier folks to be buying, since they don't expect to use it much—is going to have to go up, because the average cost to cover the people who remain is higher than initially hoped."[34]

The much smaller enrollment figures have had a cascading effect on every other aspect of Obamacare. One of the ACA's most optimistic creations was the so-called health care co-op, a nonprofit health insurance plan that would supposedly steer clear of the abuses of private health insurers and prioritize patient health. But even nonprofits need income; the success of the ACA co-ops depended crucially on the ACA enrollment figures. In the fall of 2015, HHS announced that nearly half of the ACA co-ops—11 out of 23—would be going out of business by the end of the year.[35] More seem sure to follow. Though critics warned all along that the co-ops wouldn't prove economically viable, the previous Obama administration plowed ahead with their formation, supporting the co-ops with more than $1 billion in federal loans.[36] So far, the failures of the co-ops have cost half a million Americans their health insurance.[37]

Then consider the spiking premium costs—which are related to the reluctance of those younger Americans to enroll in Obamacare. According to information provided on healthcare.gov, nearly every state expects average premium increases of 10 percent or more for multiple plans—and some other plans are expecting much higher increases of as much as 50 percent. Health-finance professor Stephen T. Parente estimated that family plans in 2016 would average an 11.2 percent increase and another 9.2 percent in 2017. "After 2017," he wrote, "most ACA-compliant plans will likely fall into a pattern of annual premium increases of between 3%–6%, which will persist for the next decade and likely beyond."[38]

Already, the Affordable Care Act has made a mockery of its name with the rising out-of-pocket costs more and more Americans are paying. The nonpartisan Commonwealth Fund, a health research group, classifies anyone whose out-of-pocket health care costs amount to 10 percent or more of household income as "underinsured." And the organization now says that 23 percent of Americans between the ages of 19 and 64 meet that classification.[39] Nearly half of these adults, when running into trouble paying their medical bills, wind up depleting their savings.[40]

The out-of-pocket costs are going to keep spiking because deductibles are spiking as the ACA funnels more and more people into high-deductible plans. One reason for this is the ACA's so-called Cadillac Tax, a 40 percent levy on high-cost, employer-sponsored health plans expected to begin in 2018 that may affect as many as one in three employer plans—unless those companies change their plans before that can happen. Thus, with the Cadillac Tax looming, many firms are moving employees into high-deductible plans to share costs. In 2015, deductibles for individual coverage in employer-sponsored plans averaged $1,217. In the new ACA marketplaces, deductibles for most available health plans are even higher.[41]

Already, employees are seeing huge increases in their out-of-pocket costs. Average out-of-pocket costs for health plans on the ACA exchanges run more than 40 percent higher than pre-ACA plans.[42] More people are cutting back on their medical care as a result; others are having trouble paying the higher bills. The high-deductible plans do generally provide coverage for severe illness and other catastrophic costs, but the upfront costs are discouraging many from doing preventive medical care.

"If you make $30,000 and can find an affordable premium but still have a $5,000 deductible, that's not a great deal if you get sick," said ACA "navigator" Rachel DeGolia. "It doesn't make sense to me why we have to have these high deductibles. Maybe they exist because people need to have 'skin in the game,' but I haven't met people who overuse services. . . . I'm afraid the deductibles will be so high for some people that it will deter them from getting the care they need, even if they are insured."[43]

Family-practice physician Praveen Arla, from Hillview, Kentucky, echoed these concerns. He sees the ACA creating a reversal of health care fortunes, with long-uninsured patients, now covered under ACA, coming in to see him, while middle-class patients who once saw him regularly cut back on their visits. "It's flip-flopped," he says. He says that patients who get their health insurance through work are saying to themselves: "'My deductible is so high. I'm trying to come to the doctor as little as possible.' . . . They're really worried about cost."[44]

It doesn't help, either, that the ACA's affordability estimates are based on individual, not family coverage. The result is that family coverage was not factored in to these cost estimates, and the ACA's "family affordability glitch" has put such plans out of reach for many.[45]

## PRACTICAL HEALTH CARE REFORM

Defenders of Obamacare have long argued that critics of the law have no proposals of their own—except for outright repeal. While it is true that the Republican Party has wasted, in our view, enormous time, energy, and political capital trying to repeal the ACA, it is also true that proposals for reforming Obamacare have been plentiful and promising. Despite this plethora of ideas, the inability to come together and agree to a solution has so far thwarted Republican efforts to fix Obamacare. For the most part, the ideas Republicans have offered come from the political center and move rightward. We have surveyed a wide range of ideas and proposals, and we can say with confidence that sensible and promising ideas are out there. They should be tried, as the status quo in health care cannot sustain itself. This means that despite the Trump administration's initial failure in agreeing to a strategy to reform health care, we must try to reform Obamacare again.

Let's take a look at four key plans that have crucial components of this vision. The first two are more radical in seeking to replace Obamacare; the third and fourth look to reform the existing law. As we've said, we don't support the repeal of Obamacare, but that doesn't mean that proposals for "replacing" the law don't contain worthy components.

### *"Replacing" Obamacare*

The first plan, articulated in a 2012 *National Affairs* article called "How to Replace Obamacare" by James Capretta and Robert Moffit, seeks to replace the ACA with a system in which the government helps people afford insurance in the private market.[46] As Capretta and Moffit see it, the root of the problem in the private health care insurance market is federal tax policy. Employers are given an open-ended tax break for providing health benefits, which encourages them to make these benefits as generous as possible. Insurers and providers have little incentive to offer price-efficient plans.

The solution: get rid of the employer tax credit and transform it into a standard tax credit given to all Americans, regardless of employment status. The tax credit would be a standard amount, possibly scaled to income or phased out for the wealthiest Americans. Individuals could put the credit toward health care. Those who chose more expensive plans would have to pay the additional premiums beyond the credit; those who chose thriftier plans could pocket the unused portion of the credit.

Employers who economized on plans would no longer be penalized via a lower tax credit. Even more importantly, individuals would become active consumers who could choose the best plans based on price and quality. As a result, insurers and health-service providers would have a compelling incentive to offer insurance and care in the most efficient ways possible. And finally, individuals wouldn't be tied to their employer for health insurance—the credit would apply regardless of employment status.

Medicare and Medicaid would be reformed along similar lines. Medicaid has a host of problems, but two main issues overshadow the rest. First, whenever health services' prices rise, Medicaid subsidies rise with them, meaning that the programs are not sensitive to market forces and give no incentive to treat patients efficiently. In fact, they often encourage unnecessary care. And second, because Medicaid pays physicians and hospitals at low rates, it often does not provide good service; many physicians refuse Medicaid patients entirely.

The potential solution, provided that leaders can forge bipartisan support on incorporating market-driven approaches into reform plans, is to move people off of Medicaid and into the private insurance market. Why is the private insurance aspect so important? Because for quality and accessibility, private insurance is vastly superior to public insurance. Under the ACA though, Medicaid rolls are growing at three times the rate of private insurance. Medicaid enrollment is slated to grow from 107 million in 2013 to 135 million by 2018. Against this backdrop, Democrats are going to have to engage in some tough conversations about the role of block grants.

"Insurance without access to medical care is a sham," wrote physician Scott Atlas in the *Wall Street Journal*. "And that is where the country is heading.... 55% of doctors in major metropolitan areas refuse new Medicaid patients. The harsh reality awaiting low-income Americans is dwindling access to quality doctors, hospitals and health care."[47] Doctors are refusing Medicare patients, too. Atlas continues: "Of the many negative effects of the Affordable Care Act, the increasing unaffordability of private insurance might be the most damaging."[48]

Private insurance premiums under current conditions will no doubt continue to rise—unless, as Atlas urges, we take steps to "revive and expand" private health insurance. The most important of these steps is to reduce the ACA's constrictive regulatory requirements—especially its onerous coverage mandates. "Modifying ObamaCare," he writes, "to give everyone the option of lower cost, high-deductible plans restores insurance to its fundamental purpose—protection from significant, unexpected expenses."[49] Atlas wants to see private insurance access improved for the most vulnerable: Medicaid recipients. A few states, such as Arkansas and Iowa, have added a "private option" for Medicaid recipients to use their funding to put toward purchasing private insurance via the exchanges. This reform should be made universal.[50]

Perhaps the most comprehensive reform to Obamacare is offered by Avik Roy, president of the Foundation for Research on Equal Opportunity. Roy claims that his Universal Exchange Plan, or UEP, would insure 12 million more Americans than Obamacare by 2025 while controlling costs and improving quality—without an individual mandate.

Here, briefly, is how it would work. The UEP would preserve some features of the Obamacare exchanges while significantly reducing regulations, including the minimum-coverage requirements. It would also allow plans that require higher-deductible payments than those currently available under ACA. These changes would allow a broader range of plans and increase innovation. The UEP would also expand access to health savings accounts (HSAs). It would preserve such ACA protections as the requirement that insurance be priced and provided regardless of preexisting conditions or gender. Finally, the subsidies that the ACA uses to help needy families afford their premiums would be converted into HSA contribution subsidies, allowing families to save the value of subsidies that they don't need in any given year.

The UEP would repeal the employer mandate, which requires that employers of a certain size offer health insurance to individuals working 30 hours a week or more. The UEP would create a division in Medicaid between "acute" Medicaid patients—those requiring traditional insurance for hospital stays and doctor visits—and "long-term" Medicaid patients, who require nursing homes, in-home care, hospice, or the like. The federal government would fully fund all acute Medicaid care via block grants, while states would be responsible for long-term care. States would gain considerably more flexibility in administering Medicaid.

On the Medicare side, Roy's plan would raise the Medicare eligibility age by four months each year, returning Medicare to its original purpose as a benefit for those nearing their final years. Individuals would maintain their present insurance until they reached the new eligibility age. Medicare would achieve permanent fiscal solvency.

Needless to say, policy analysts have been promising savings and dream-like results from their plans for as long as we have had policy analysts. So Roy's projections have to be evaluated skeptically. Yet his plan is sensible and holds out real hope for fixing the American health care crisis.

### Reforming Obamacare

A third plan, more modest yet perhaps more practical, bears consideration: the National Center for Policy Analysis puts forth a set of moderate reforms that would encourage work and reduce bureaucracy.[51] This "reforming Obamacare" plan aims to refine the ACA and make it work better on its own terms, particularly in regard to four key problems. These are:

*The ACA benefits insurers rather than people.* Under the ACA exchanges, insurers have an incentive to design plans that meet the legal requirements but are not beneficial to patients. Evidence suggests that they are doing so wherever possible—for instance, drugs for cancer, HIV, and multiple sclerosis almost always demand the highest copays. This problem persists because Obamacare subsidies go to insurers, not to individuals. *Solution:* merge all ACA subsidies into a single account and distribute it to families, allowing them to decide how to allocate money between premiums and direct payments for health services.

*The exchanges are too bureaucratic.* The health care exchanges remain confusing, buggy, and expensive to operate. The federal government levies a 3.5 percent "user fee" on insurers to pay for it, the cost of which is likely passed on to consumers. *Solution:* allow private companies to operate online exchanges that work better and don't cost taxpayers anything. These private exchanges already exist, but they can't sell insurance directly, as the ACA tax credits are available only via government exchanges. This restraint should be abolished.

*Obamacare mandates drive up costs.* The ACA forbids making price distinctions by age and gender, even though these factors have a real impact on premium costs. It requires that people buy coverage for medical events that are extremely unlikely to befall them. *Solution:* reduce ACA mandates, especially age bands.

*The employer mandate is counterproductive and discourages work.* The ACA punishes employers that don't offer health insurance to employees working over 30 hours a week. *Solution:* end the employer mandate.

A final reformist plan comes from a conservative, David Frum, known for his sometimes unconventional thinking. Frum wants conservatives to accept that Obamacare is probably here to stay and that it responds to a real need in the market for reform.[52] He says that Republicans should focus on changing how the law is implemented to make it more effective. Coming from reasonably close to the political center, Frum's solution leaves Obamacare largely intact.

Frum has three core recommendations. First, he suggests fixing the funding mechanism. The ACA is funded by forcing young, healthy Americans to pay for services for old, sick Americans by requiring them to buy coverage they don't need. The subsidies should come from a broad-based tax, rather than one on just a small part of the population. Right now, Obamacare is funded in the same way as all liberal programs— increased taxes on the rich—and this is neither economically sound nor politically sustainable.

Second, Frum argues for more state autonomy. Obamacare provides full federal funding for the Medicaid expansion through 2016, with the federal portion falling to 90 percent in 2020 and decreasing thereafter. As states are asked to take on more of the costs of the expansion, Obamacare should give states more say in how the programs are run, rather than forcing them to accept every federal dictate.

Finally, Frum argues, like others, for ending the employer mandate. In addition to requiring individuals to buy health insurance, the ACA also forces employers with more than 50 employees to provide plans for those who work more than 30 hours a week. This facet of the law was delayed until January 1, 2016, but it will encourage employers to reduce hours in order to escape the mandate or to offer bare-bones coverage to employees. The employer mandate doesn't help anyone get coverage, since these employees have access to the exchanges in any event. All it does is reduce the availability of full-time work. It should be scrapped.

## THE ENTITLEMENTS CRISIS

Speaking to Bloomberg TV & Radio in March 2016, former Federal Reserve chairman Alan Greenspan was asked if he was optimistic about the state of the United States and the global economy. "No," he said. "I haven't been for quite a while. And I won't be until we can resolve the entitlement programs. Nobody wants to touch it. And that is gradually crowding out capital investment, and that's crowding out productivity, and it's crowding out the standards of living. Where do you want me to go from there."[53]

Greenspan's gloom is well founded. The 2016 annual figures on the state of Medicare and Social Security show that these programs will start to spend more than they earn by the end of the decade.[54] Medicare's hospital insurance trust fund will "exhaust its reserves by 2028," leaving 55 million Americans without coverage.[55] Social Security faces insolvency in 2034. Forty-nine million Americans collected retirement benefits in the last year; another 11 million claimed disability.[56]

When Greenspan says "nobody wants to touch it," he means those in political office or running for political office. Cutting entitlement programs has been the third rail of politics for years, and the 2016 presidential campaign did nothing to change that. Hillary Clinton consistently called for expanding Social Security[57]—a standard Democrat position — and Donald Trump blazed a new path for recent Republican nominees by vowing not to cut entitlements. "I'm not going to cut Social Security like every other Republican and I'm not going to cut Medicare or Medicaid," Trump said on the campaign trail.[58]

Politicians have been dodging the implications of long-term entitlement costs for many years, at least, and arguably for a generation. One of the dreaded allegations in American politics across many years of campaigns has been "my opponent wants to cut Social Security." And yet, if *something* isn't done to control costs—call it cutting or use some other word—Social Security and Medicare may not survive. And that has implications for tens of millions of Americans.

Take Denise Scott, a 64-year-old woman who was forced into early retirement due to health problems. Denise said she felt "blessed" that her medication was "relatively inexpensive" and that Medicare covered everything when she first retired. But that didn't last long. Her health plan hiked its premiums, and she recently discovered that she'd have to pay the difference between the Medicare subsidy and the new premium rate. A social-service counselor helped her find a new plan that was premium-free, and Denise enrolled in it.[59] But many others are not so lucky—and it's not like Denise is out the woods. Her new plan could change, too, as plans have changed on millions of Americans since the passage of Obamacare.

When people think of the fiscal worries about Social Security, they usually think of elderly recipients, understandably enough—they're the ones who would be affected immediately should coverage be rolled back. But in the broader sense, the real Social Security question concerns millennials, many of whom believe that the program won't be there by the time they retire. There's a reason former senator Alan Simpson called elderly voters who oppose Social Security reform the "greediest generation." They stand staunchly opposed to any reforms, even when some could feasibly take a reduced payout to ensure that the program remains solvent. Indeed, as David Bass, a millennial, argues in the *American Spectator*, "In the coming years, my generation, the Millennials...will bankroll a retirement scheme for our elders that we ourselves will never participate in, at least not in the same way.... Millennials will pay into a system for decades but see no benefits (at worst) or reduced benefits (at best)."[60]

The most frustrating aspect of the entitlements crisis is that good plans have been put forward to fix it but have gone nowhere in Washington.

Remember this? "We're going to need the help of citizens who've served this country in extraordinary ways in the past and are continuing to do so in their spare time. I'm looking forward to having them as partners in order to get this done,"[61] President Obama said when he announced the National Commission on Responsibility and Reform, commonly known as Simpson-Bowles. Obama asked Bill Clinton's former chief of staff Erskine Bowles and former senator Alan Simpson to head this bipartisan task force to come up with policies that would address our spiraling debt and deficit and put us on a sustainable fiscal path.

And they did, fashioning a plan that would have cut the deficit by $4 trillion over 12 years by balancing spending cuts with tax hikes, ensuring all Americans would have to make some sacrifice.[62] Its key features included ending the Bush-era tax cuts for those with incomes over $125,000; balancing $2.6 trillion in tax increases over ten years with $2.9 trillion in spending cuts; and raising the Social Security retirement age to 68 in 2050 and 69 in 2075.[63]

Simpson-Bowles also proposed constructive Medicare reforms on the beneficiary side.[64]

The genius of Simpson-Bowles was in its balance. Democrats may not have liked the changes to entitlements, but they loved the rise in domestic spending and the higher taxes on the wealthy. And both sides could agree that cutting the deficit by $4 trillion was an outstanding result. When the Simpson-Bowles report was released, it was greeted in Washington with tremendous praise from legislators on both sides of the aisle.

And then it died. The report failed to meet the 14-vote threshold to go to Congress for approval. And today, neither the report nor others inspired by it have passed thus far.

This is remarkable when you consider the overwhelming support for the plan. Our firm, Schoen Consulting, did polling for the Campaign to Fix the Debt (the new name for the National Commission on Responsibility and Reform) and found that by an overwhelming margin—80 percent to 8—respondents supported the plan. Further, as Doug Schoen wrote at the time in an article for *Forbes*, "The plan stood up to scrutiny. When we gave specifics of the plan—including arguments against it that included cuts to Medicare and Social Security—support dropped, but remained between 56 percent and 65 percent favorability. Opposition to the plan never increased above 24 percent."[65] He continued, "What does this mean? . . . Americans are prepared for both entitlement reform and perhaps even higher taxes. They support limiting tax deductions and sacrificing some of their Medicare and Social Security benefits to ensure that we can balance the budget and reduce our debt and deficit."[66]

That's something you never hear on Capitol Hill: that Americans want to protect entitlement programs—for themselves and future generations—and that they're prepared to make some sacrifices for that to happen. And yet, even with a rock-solid fiscal-reform plan in hand, which enjoyed substantial bipartisan backing and immense support from the electorate, the federal government in Washington couldn't get it done. And half a decade later, here we are, with all the same problems unaddressed and continuing to metastasize. Our political leaders just aren't serious about debt and deficit reduction or entitlement reform. Few areas of our national life more starkly illustrate what we called, in an earlier chapter, the failure of politics.

### Our Health Care and Entitlement Future

"Obamacare, meaning the operating model that undergirded the law that Congress passed and President Barack Obama signed with great fanfare—is dead, and it will not be revived," wrote *National Review*'s Kevin Williamson in 2015. "What remains is fitful chaos."[67] There is no question that the ACA faces deeply uncertain prospects. That shouldn't mean, however, that the prospects more broadly for health care *reform* are bleak: on the contrary, the law's myriad problems could provide the setting from which we make a new beginning. One problem up to now, though, is that too much of the debate around this broader idea of health care reform gets subsumed as "Obamacare" debates. Dyed-in-the-wool conservatives despise Obamacare as a big-government solution to a primary challenge in modern society: health care. Dyed-in-the-wool liberals defend Obamacare as a central plank in a progressive vision for a better society.

Our view is focused less on ideology than on pragmatism: What works? The challenge of affordable, accessible health care isn't going away, and Obamacare as currently designed doesn't meet that challenge. From our point of view, it is less important to endorse any single plan than to articulate the broad principles that should underpin reform. These include:

- Ending the employer mandate that requires employers to provide insurance to all full-time workers, since it discourages the creation of full-time jobs;
- Replacing insurance subsidies with fixed-amount credits that can be used toward insurance premiums or health services, giving people greater choice and encouraging competition between insurers;
- Giving states more administrative leeway to implement the law as they see fit;
- Reducing the minimum requirements, which force people to

buy care they don't need, and ending the requirements of price equality by age and gender, which have the same effect and raise premiums for everyone;

- Adopting reforms that encourage the purchase of private insurance—including moving able-bodied Medicaid recipients to private coverage and ending the ban on interstate purchase of insurance.

Before we make headway on dramatic health care reform, we need a broader acknowledgment that the system—including Obamacare—has failed. The only way to save American health care is to open up markets. Within that principle, much flexibility and room for compromise exists, but until we recognize it, our health care system will continue its downward spiral, causing needless personal suffering and imposing debilitating financial costs.

The same kind of out-of-the-box thinking is needed to reform our entitlement programs. Surely other plans will be advanced in coming years, and if they manage to strike a balance between costs and benefits, as the Simpson-Bowles plan did (in both its 1.0 and 2.0 versions), we'll support them. Other clear-eyed proposals include the Heritage Foundation's Social Security "flat-benefit" plan, under which benefits for the wealthiest 9 percent of recipients would be slowly reduced—yet those same recipients would see their benefits restored in the event of financial reversals.[68] Proposals like this would make Social Security what it was meant to be: a social insurance plan for those who truly need it.

But regardless of whose plan it is, when it comes to our foundational entitlement programs and the broader health care system, the obstacle to reform is not lack of ideas or solutions. The sole obstacle is political will.

# CHAPTER 11

# National Security Emergency

It is better to lead from behind and to put others in front, especially when you celebrate victory when nice things occur. You take the front line when there is danger. Then people will appreciate your leadership.
— President Barack Obama[1]

Not acting can be every bit as consequential as acting.
— Richard Haas, president, Council on Foreign Relations[2]

"The president of the United States lands with all the majesty of Air Force One, waiting to exit the front door and stride down the rolling staircase to the red-carpeted tarmac," Charles Krauthammer wrote in September 2016. "Except that there is no rolling staircase. He is forced to exit—as one China expert put it rather undiplomatically—through 'the ass' of the plane."

Krauthammer continued:

If the Chinese didn't invent diplomatic protocol, they surely are its most venerable and experienced practitioners. They've been at it for 4,000 years. They are the masters of every tributary gesture, every nuance of hierarchical ritual. In a land so exquisitely sensitive to protocol, rolling staircases don't just disappear at arrival ceremonies. Indeed, not one of the other G-20 world leaders was left stranded on his plane upon arrival.

Did President Xi Jinping directly order airport personnel and diplomatic functionaries to deny Barack Obama a proper welcome? Who knows? But the message, whether intentional or not, wasn't very subtle. The authorities expressed no regret, no remorse and certainly no apology. On the contrary, they scolded the press for even reporting the snub.

No surprise. China's ostentatious rudeness was perfectly reflective of the world's general disdain for President Obama.[3]

Krauthammer was referring to Obama's arrival in China for a G20 summit, and he went on to chronicle other slights, not just of Obama but of American power itself, in recent years: Vladimir Putin keeping Secretary of State John Kerry waiting for three hours in 2013; Russian fighter jets buzzing our ships in the Baltic Sea, and one Russian fighter coming within *ten feet* of an American military jet; China's illegal expansion into the South China Sea, despite (toothless) American warnings; the Obama administration secretly airlifting $400 million in ransom cash to Iran to free hostages; and perhaps the ultimate image of American humiliation from the Obama years, the sight of ten American sailors, captured and made to kneel by the Iranians, who dutifully photographed and video-recorded the scene. And when the sailors were released, Secretary of State Kerry *thanked* the Iranians.

In short, as Donald Trump assumed the presidency, the United States faced a daunting task of recapturing respect around the world, especially from our rivals and adversaries. Obama's "lead from behind" approach has failed, especially in the crucial areas discussed in this chapter: military and nuclear preparedness, China's aim to supplant the United States as the world's preeminent power, Russia's power push, the proliferation of global terrorism, and cyber warfare. President Trump must reassert vigorous American foreign policy in the service of our ideals and national interests.

Obama failed to maintain American military standards and downsized and downgraded the U.S. military. His administration fundamentally altered the "standard for American military adequacy from winning two wars to winning one and attempting to deny an aggressor his objectives or punish him severely in the second,"[4] according to analyst Daniel Goure. The United States Army has reached its smallest size since before World War II. Rear Admiral Thomas Moore, the Navy's executive officer for its carrier program, notes that the United States will now be dependent on partnerships with allied navies in order to take "the strain off America's shrinking defense budgets."[5]

Throughout Obama's presidency, China moved aggressively not only in the Asia-Pacific but also throughout the world. The Obama administration watched idly as Beijing asserted sovereignty over contested islands and adjacent waters throughout the East and South China Seas.[6] The Chinese threaten the peace and stability of our allies in Asia, especially Japan and the Philippines, and the security of American commercial interests. China has also pursued an expansionist economic agenda. Beijing boasts a vigorous purchasing power now overtaking that of the United States,[7] magnified by its establishment of the Asian Infrastructure Investment Bank, or AIIB. In March 2015, multiple European allies publicly brushed off American pleas not to join the bank and instead became founding members.[8]

Meanwhile, Russian president Vladimir Putin continues to wreak havoc in Ukraine, where he has been violating international law regularly since his 2014 annexation of Crimea. U.S.-led sanctions have done nothing to thwart Russia's aggression. As former director of the Defense Intelligence Agency and retired Lieutenant General Michael Flynn put it, Obama has been "playing checkers while Putin has been playing chess, combining tactics with strategy and looking several moves ahead."[9] When it comes to the Ukraine conflict, though, Flynn acknowledges that the Russian president "has simply knocked the pieces off the board."[10]

China and Russia are on the move just as the threat that Americans worried most about after 9/11 seems newly invigorated: Islamic terrorism, both abroad and at home. Obama won the presidency in large part by running against George W. Bush's disastrous invasion of Iraq, but Obama now bears the blame for what became of Iraq after Bush left office—at a time when the troop surge had brought relative stability to that country. Obama's hasty drawdown of American troops from Iraq in 2011 created a power vacuum that led to the rise of ISIS, which has become a mortal threat in the region and a grave national security challenge for the United States. And Obama's efforts to prop up Iraqi military forces have proved fruitless, at least up to now.

We also face nuclear threats. America has made vast and dangerous nuclear concessions to the autocratic Iranian regime. A framework worked out in early 2015 all but assures that Iran will have nuclear capability within a decade. It's not a stretch to imagine America's weak stance setting off a new nuclear arms race in the Middle East. Following in Iran's path, Saudi Arabia, a Sunni Muslim nation threatened by Shia Iran's rising power, might develop nukes of its own. And the threat from North Korea continues to mount. In September 2016, the outlaw state conducted its second nuclear test of the year,[11] its fifth since 2006.[12] A January 2015 South Korean defense white paper declared that North Korea has a long-range missile capable of threatening the United States.[13] In the face of these challenges, Obama's ambitious plan to reach "nuclear zero"—a world without nuclear weapons—has functioned essentially like a private fantasy: the United States is dismantling its nuclear deterrent in a world with more nuclear players than ever before.

Last but not least, we are under constant cyber attack from China, Russia, and Iran. In 2012, Secretary of Defense Leon Panetta gave a grim speech warning about the likelihood of a "cyber-Pearl Harbor." He warned that "an aggressor nation or extremist group could use these kinds of cyber tools to gain control of critical switches. They could derail passenger trains, or even more dangerous, derail passenger trains loaded with lethal chemicals. They could contaminate the water supply in major cities, or shut down the power grid across large parts of the country."[14] Those dangers have only increased in the years since, and, as we have seen, Russian cyber hackers have even tried to tamper with American politics, in their hacking of email systems from the Democratic Party, which were released before the party's convention.

On all these fronts—cybersecurity; the challenge of newly aggressive nation-states like China and Russia; and the continued threat of Islamic extremism, both at home and abroad—the Obama administration presided over a massive weakening of America's national defense and a diminishment of its leadership role in the world. President Trump faces a daunting task of repair and renewal—starting with the American military itself.

## AMERICA'S MILITARY AND NUCLEAR RETREAT

As new threats surface around the globe, it makes sense to assume that the world's leading powers would be strengthening their national defense postures. That's certainly what Russia and China are doing. In 2015, China boosted its defense budget by 10.1 percent, to $145 billion.[15] Russia's defense budget reached a record-high $81 billion, equivalent to 4.2 percent of the nation's GDP.[16]

By contrast, the United States is scaling back its defense expenditures and has been doing so steadily since 2010.[17] In 2015, the Heritage

Foundation released its first annual "Index of U.S. Military Strength," which evaluates the capabilities of each branch of our armed forces. The study found that, with the exception of the Air Force, all the branches are operating at "marginal" strength levels.[18] The American military is the smallest it has been since before World War II. In March 2016, the U.S. Army's total active-duty force stood at 479,172 soldiers, the smallest American force since 1940, a year before the Japanese attack on Pearl Harbor brought the United States into the war and prompted a massive mobilization.[19]

"We are getting dangerously small,"[20] said General Lloyd Austin, U.S. commander of Central Command, in March 2016 testimony to the Senate Armed Services Committee. In the same meeting, General Joseph Votel, commander of Special Operations Command, said that the U.S. Army is at "high risk" because of the decline in forces.[21]

The U.S. Navy is being asked to play a larger role in ensuring American primacy in the Pacific, but it lacks the ships needed to achieve that goal. The Navy is "on a budgetary path to 260 ships or less," according to a report in the recent *Quadrennial Defense Review*, which believes that the requirements are "somewhere between...323 and 346 ships...and an even larger fleet may be necessary if the risk of conflict in the Western Pacific increases."[22] Former Navy secretary John Lehman sees the current fleet as "far too small to effectively protect this country's vital interests in the Pacific, Atlantic, Mediterranean, Persian Gulf and Arabian Sea."[23]

Though it got the only reasonably encouraging grade from the Heritage Foundation report, the Air Force faces similar problems. Air Force Chief of Staff General Mark Welsh said that readiness levels have been seriously compromised. "The Air Force will need eight to 10 years to restore 'full-spectrum readiness' for its air and space forces," Welsh says.[24]

Hovering over this discussion is the lingering effect of sequestration, which stipulated that failing to take meaningful steps toward debt reduction would trigger an automatic $1.2 trillion cut across federal departments—including defense—over ten years. Sequestration went into effect in 2013, and it has been a calamity ever since, particularly for the defense budget. Sequestration doesn't provide for tailored cuts to specific programs; it is a blunt tool that cuts spending proportionally across the board. So if a vital weapons platform costs a certain amount to build, there is suddenly 10 percent less money to build it with, regardless of its importance.

One other crucial area of the United States' defense umbrella—nuclear weaponry—is reeling from President Obama's wrongheaded and potentially calamitous distaste for the very concept of nuclear deterrence. Obama made this opinion clear starting with his first major foreign policy speech in Prague in 2009, when he spoke of "America's commitment to seek the peace and security of a world without nuclear weapons."[25] He has steadily built down the American arsenal, even as Russia and China increase theirs. He speaks of a world without nuclear weapons, seemingly unwilling to confront the reality that nukes have probably prevented World War III more than once since 1945.

Most dangerously, Obama embraced a doctrine of "no first use"—meaning that the United States would not, under any circumstances, initiate the use of nuclear weapons in any conflict. You don't have to be Clausewitz to understand the incentive that such a doctrine would provide for aggression. If Vladimir Putin, for example, wanted to move aggressively into the Baltics or elsewhere in Eastern Europe, and he knows that under no circumstances will American nukes come into the picture, then his calculations could focus entirely on whether NATO forces could stop him in time. ("We now have the nuclear capacity to confront NATO in Europe," a Russian academic close to Putin said at a 2015 Paris think tank event.[26]) An American no-first-use nuclear posture would simply concede this entire strategic area to our adversaries.

American citizens have grown comfortable living in a world of American primacy—one which is, for us, largely stable and free of immediate danger. But none of that will last without continued investment in the instrument which maintains it: the military. It is absolutely vital that President Trump conduct a vast overhaul of military budgeting and put our armed forces—and yes, our nuclear arsenal—back on a competitive path so that we don't lose any more ground, especially with our adversaries advancing without hesitation.

## RISING CHINA, RECEDING AMERICA

U.S. Defense Secretary Ash Carter "wasn't as tough as I'd expected," a Chinese military leader boasted after June 2015's Shangri-La security summit in Singapore.[27] The Chinese have reason to feel bold. They have gone further than ever before in asserting their territorial claims in the South China Sea. They're not just asserting control over the Spratly Islands, a group of more than 750 reefs, cays, and islands; they have even started building new islands.

China is taking over reefs and developing them into manmade bases with runways that can support military flights. "I want to reaffirm that this construction is well within the scope of China's sovereignty and it is justified, legitimate and reasonable," said Sun Jianguo, deputy chief of the General Staff Department of the People's Liberation Army (PLA). "In spite of the sufficient historical and legal evidence and its indisputable claims of rights and interests, China has exercised enormous restraint, making positive contributions to peace and stability of the region and the world at large."[28]

Not quite, says American admiral Harry Harris, commander of United States Pacific Command, likening China's activities to building a "great wall of sand."[29] Harris said China is engaged in "unprecedented land reclamation," an effort to build artificial lands by "pumping sand on to live coral reefs—some of them submerged—and paving them over with concrete. China has now created over four square kilometers of artificial landmass." Despite Chinese protestations that the work is "necessary construction," it's clear that the projects are expansionist. Steve Tsang, professor of Chinese studies at the University of Nottingham, sees the threat this way: "If China should successfully claim all of the Spratly islands, it would transform most of the South China Sea, one of the most important maritime routes in the world, into a 'Chinese lake.'"[30]

China's neighbors Vietnam, Japan, the Philippines, Indonesia, and Taiwan have expressed concerns over this mounting aggression. And over the last few years, Japan and India have beefed up their military capacity in response. According to the *Wall Street Journal*, India has established a "new mountain corps for deployment along its Himalayan boundaries," is "testing ballistic missiles with a range of over 3,000 miles, which could strike inside China," and is beefing up its military capacity. For its part, Japan has increased its defense budget by 2 percent and set up its first amphibious unit.[31]

Carter had harsh words for the Chinese at the Shangri-La summit. He called for an "immediate and lasting halt" to the development of the Spratly Islands into Chinese bases. And he also emphasized that the United States will "fly, sail, and operate wherever international law allows, as U.S. forces do all around the world."[32] But China does not appear concerned about American retaliation. Perth USAsia Centre, a foreign policy think tank, conducted a poll in March 2015 that showed 86 percent of the Chinese public believes that the PLA is capable of taking control of the South China Sea; 87 percent said the same about the East China Sea.[33] Beijing declared an air-defense identification zone (ADIZ) in the East China Sea in 2013, and there are signs they may do so on the South China Sea as well.

Such confidence is consistent with Xi Jinping's vision for China under his rule, a concept he refers to as the China dream, by which he means the rejuvenation of Chinese society, with a strong focus on the military and economic might. From a military standpoint, this means to Xi a philosophy of what he calls "active defense." In 2016, speaking on the 95th anniversary of the Chinese Communist Party, Xi told his listeners that "creating an army that corresponds to the international status of our country is a strategic goal. We should put together economic and defense development, modernize the army to make it contemporary and standardized.... We should comprehensively promote the military reform to create an army that will be disciplined and able to win."[34] Xi's goal is a new regional order, with China dominant.

Case in point: the Chinese Ministry of Defense's first policy document in two years, a white paper called "China's Military Strategy." The white paper is "a blueprint for achieving slow-motion regional hegemony," says Patrick Cronin, director of the Asia-Pacific Security Program at the Center for a New American Security. "It asserts a confidence backed by growing capability on land and increasingly at sea. While it calls for balancing China's territorial 'rights' with 'stability,' there should be little doubt from its neighbors that China is building a maritime force to assert the former."[35]

Finally, consider this warning from Australian strategic scholar Hugh White, author of *The China Choice*, who warns Americans not to be complacent about a worst-case scenario: a war with China. "Remember," he writes, "the stakes are high for both sides. This is a contest over the future of the Asian order, and we should not for a moment assume that China is any less committed to building a new order than we are to preserving the old one."[36] Not everyone sees the situation as gravely as White does, but most informed Asia observers would agree that the American response to the China challenge so far has been wholly ineffective.

## THE RUSSIAN PUSH

If one could apply a single timeworn phrase to describe President Obama's foreign policy, it might be "too little, too late." We saw this in Syria with his supposed red line that never came to be, despite Syrian president Bashar Al-Assad's use of chemical weapons on his own people. And the same description applies to the crisis in Ukraine. Since its 2014 annexation of Crimea, all Russian involvement in Ukraine has been illegal, by both international and domestic Russian defense standards. But despite rebukes from Obama and German chancellor Angela Merkel, among others, Russia has only become further emboldened.

Many Obama critics argue that the president's "lead from behind" foreign policy doctrine, which debuted in Libya in 2011, played a crucial role in precipitating the Ukraine crisis.[37] The administration viewed Putin's aggression in Ukraine differently than many experts, commentators, and military personnel. When Russia stepped up its military involvement in August 2014, six months after the crisis began, Obama was asked whether the moves constituted an invasion. No, he said, Russian actions were merely "a continuation of what's been taking place for months now"—implicitly accepting what Putin had done.[38] As the Ukraine crisis continues to drag on, Obama largely responded by calling on Russia to negotiate a peaceful solution, despite its ongoing violations of ceasefire agreements.[39] At every stage, Putin moved too quickly and decisively for American officials, whose indecision left allies vulnerable.

"While the wolf is eating the sheep, there is no shepherd to come to the rescue," said Turki al-Faisal, former head of Saudi Arabia's General Intelligence and ambassador to the United States.[40]

Our inept response to Putin has wide-ranging implications beyond Ukraine. Consider Russia's role in the Syrian civil war, where Russia "emerged as a spoiler, blocking further progress on disarmament and defending Syrian dictator Bashar Assad's continuing use of chemical weapons," according to Russia expert Stephen Blank.[41] After first suggesting that Assad had crossed his "red line" with the use of chemical weapons, indicating that retaliation was imminent, Obama backed down, taking refuge in a diplomatic option based around, of all things, a Putin peace proposal. On Syria, Putin played the Obama team like a fiddle, always at least one step ahead of his American foes, who were often made to look foolish. In March 2016, Putin put the administration back on its heels with his sudden announcement that Russian forces were leaving Syria; administration officials were left literally speechless. It turned out that Putin was just spinning a slight reduction of Russian forces into a major milestone.[42] Day to day, month to month, year to year, the Russian leader leaves his U.S. adversaries blindsided.

Putin also came out on top from the U.S. nuclear deal with Iran, a deal that Moscow supposedly supported—yet Russia went forward with the sale of an $800 million air-defense system to Tehran. And again, Obama's response was demoralizing. "I'm not surprised given some of the deterioration in the relationship between Russia and the United States," he said, "and the fact that their economy is under strain and this was a substantial sale."[43]

Russia has also moved to support anti-American regimes in our backyard. In 2014, Putin forgave 90 percent of Cuba's Soviet-era debts in an attempt to gain influence dangerously close to the United States.[44] And in early 2015, Putin met with Venezuelan president Nicolas Maduro to discuss their countries' economies, especially the oil price plunge since economic sanctions took effect. Putin has singled out Venezuela as Russia's "reliable partner" in Latin America.[45]

President Obama always said he was comfortable with America living in a multipolar world. And indeed, such a world is now a reality, whether we like it or not. But the former president confused multipolarity with abdication of American leadership. Nothing demonstrated this disconnect more starkly than Obama's abject response to Russian aggression. Obama was not willing to go beyond U.S. economic sanctions in responding to Putin—and those sanctions, while they continue to have some effect, are not nearly enough to counter Putin's unabashed desire to regain control of Ukraine and, eventually, to dismantle NATO.

Just as Hugh White warns the West that we might be on course for war with China, former British general Sir Alexander Richard Shirreff, who once served as NATO deputy commander, argues in his book *War with Russia* that, to escape encirclement by NATO, Putin could seize territory in eastern Ukraine (which he in fact has already done), open up a land corridor to Crimea, and invade the Baltics, starting with Latvia. Such a scenario would ignite a war that "could so easily go nuclear," warns U.S. admiral James Stavridis, former supreme allied commander of Europe, in the book's foreword.[46] Shirreff believes this nightmare scenario can be avoided if NATO gets large enough forces pre-positioned in the Baltic States. But here again, Obama's policies left the United States vulnerable—especially his nuclear reluctance. "Be under no illusion whatsoever," Shirreff writes. "Russian use of nuclear weapons is hardwired into Moscow's military strategy."[47]

Of course, Putin might help bring about the fall of NATO in less dramatic fashion. Among the electorate of many Western countries, support for institutions like NATO and the EU is dwindling. During the U.S. presidential campaign, Donald Trump infamously claimed that he wouldn't necessarily agree to come to NATO countries' defense—at least, not until they had first "fulfilled their obligations to us."[48] Such sentiments give Putin political leverage, which is magnified by his growing support among nationalist, anti-NATO, anti-EU parties across Europe.

By August 2016, Putin had put in place more than 100,000 troops in Crimea, in the Donbas, and around the Russia-Ukraine border.[49] The question hanging over this and every conflict scenario: if an attack occurred, would NATO invoke Article 5, calling on all members to come to the defense of a member under attack? And if Article 5 proves to be just a piece of paper, wouldn't that spell the end of NATO, then and there?

The bottom line is this: for eight years under President Obama, the United States had no coherent policy vis-à-vis Vladimir Putin and his expansionist plans. Moreover, the 2016 presidential campaign made clear that neither candidate had much to offer either. Hillary Clinton defended her role in the Obama administration's disastrous Russian "reset"; Trump suggested that he might turn a blind eye to Putin's aggression. As this book goes to press, it's hard to feel any optimism about the American posture toward Russia in the years ahead.

## THE UNDECLARED CYBER WAR

Shortly before the 2016 Democratic National Convention, a cache of 20,000 emails by party insiders appeared on Wikileaks. The messages revealed the role of the Democratic National Committee (DNC) in the election's primary process, confirming the allegations of Bernie Sanders supporters that the party establishment was working against him and had favored Hillary Clinton all along.[50] Most intelligence experts believe that Wikileaks got the mails from Russian cyber hackers. Whether the Russians conducted the attack to explicitly support Republican nominee Donald Trump, as Democrats claimed, or simply timed the release of the emails to maximize the disruption they would cause, the reality remains that Russia has attempted to influence an American presidential election.

The hack of the DNC was profoundly disturbing, and it led some Democrats to say, after Hillary Clinton's defeat, that the Russians had "hacked" the election. To be sure, there is no evidence that the Russians tampered directly with any U.S. voting systems. But it's hardly implausible that they could do so in the future. After all, Russian hackers had already had success in previous years tapping into White House and State Department email systems, the latter being described as "the worst ever" cyber intrusion against a federal target.[51]

Cyber warfare perfectly complements Russia's growing military operations. "Russia certainly has been more active than any other country in terms of combining cyber-attacks, or cyber-operations, with physical operations," says Jeffrey Carr, a web security specialist and author of *Inside Cyber Warfare*. "The Russia-Georgia war of 2008 was a perfect example of a combined kinetic and cyber operation."[52] During that conflict, Russian hackers expertly attacked Georgia's Internet infrastructure to cripple access to government websites, cutting off information to citizens. It was the first time that a traditional war was conducted in tandem with a cyber attack.[53] And it could happen again. As Carr adds, "The U.S. government has not kept current on Russian technical advancements which means that we cannot estimate capability accurately."[54] Indeed, we seem continually surprised by Russian capabilities.

Cyber attacks are listed as the principal national security threat to America in the *Worldwide Threat Assessment of the U.S. Intelligence Community* report that director of National Intelligence James Clapper presented to the Senate Armed Services Committee in 2015.[55] Indeed, CrowdStrike, a cybersecurity firm, recorded over 10,000 Russian intrusions at companies across the globe in the first four months of 2015 alone. The reason for the rise? "They're coming under a lot of pressure from the sanctions—their financial industry, their energy industry and they're obviously trying to leverage cyber intrusion and cyber espionage to compensate for that," said CrowdStrike cofounder Dmitri Alperovitch.[56] National Security Agency veteran Will Ackerly adds, "I think that the calculus for them has changed. It seems that they're definitely behaving dramatically different in that regard."[57]

Russia is the source of at least one-third of all viruses and malware spread throughout the world, and its cybercrime industry runs through an estimated $2 billion annually.[58] The conditions in Russia are perfect for cybercriminals, as the country's technological infrastructure provides necessary access and the cadre of highly skilled mathematicians and computer engineers are capable of launching highly sophisticated attacks. The incentives to carry out these attacks are compelling as well, especially against the United States, where hundreds of millions of dollars lie behind corporate firewalls.

But while Russia is the global leader in cybercrime, FBI director James Comey notes that the Chinese are the greatest perpetrators of such crimes against the United States. The average cost of cybercrime for U.S. retail stores more than doubled from 2013 to 2014.[59] For a time, U.S. and Chinese officials had been working together to combat certain types of online crime, including money laundering, child pornography, and drug trafficking, but that cooperation stopped after the indictment of five Chinese military members in May 2014 for hacking defense companies such as Boeing in addition to working with other Chinese hackers to "steal manufacturing plans for defense programs, such as the F-35 and F-22 fighter jets."[60]

Indeed, on the military front, as defense expert Bill Gertz writes, "China is considered the major cyber weapons threat to U.S. weapons systems. Over the past decade, Chinese military hackers have penetrated major defense contractors involved in cutting edge weapons systems, including the fifth generation F-35 Joint Strike Fighter."[61] Analysts say that by gaining access to F-35 plans, the Chinese could disrupt the aircraft's electronics.

Chinese president Xi Jinping announced in early 2014 that he was seeking to make China a "cyber power."[62] Admiral Michael Rogers, head of U.S. Cyber Command and the NSA, testified before Congress that China already has the capability to shut down the U.S. power grid with a cyber attack.[63] And China is increasing its funding for cyber warfare. According to one American official, "There is now data we have that suggests that they have redirected as much as 20 to 30 percent more funding to cyber than they have in previous years."[64]

The Obama administration's initial strategy for dealing with Chinese cyber attacks depended largely on diplomatic pressure—and a certain degree of naiveté. "We expect them to follow international norms and abide by international rules," Obama said of the Chinese in early 2013.[65] That strategy evolved to include limited sanctions against individuals and groups.[66] In early 2014, the administration briefed the Chinese military leadership on Pentagon plans to defend against cyber attacks, including those coming from China.[67] According to the *New York Times*, "The idea was to allay Chinese concerns about plans to more than triple the number of American cyber warriors to 6,000 by the end of 2016," in the hope that China would "give Washington a similar briefing about the many People's Liberation Army units that are believed to be behind the escalating attacks on American corporations and government networks."[68]

Surprise! China didn't reciprocate.

China and Russia are not our only concerns in cyberspace. Belarus and other Eastern European nations are serious players. In 2013, at least 40 companies, including Apple, Facebook, and Twitter, were victims of malware attacks originating with a gang of Eastern Europe hackers.[69] "Eastern European malware is so elegantly crafted as to be the 'Faberge eggs' of the malware world," wrote Trend Micro, a cybersecurity firm, in a report.[70]

Iran is in the game, too. In March 2016, Attorney General Loretta Lynch announced a federal indictment against seven Iranian hackers for conspiring to hack "civilian targets in the United States financial service industry, that in total or in all, in sum cost the victims tens of millions of dollars," Lynch said.[71] Iranians were also behind a hack of Saudi Aramco, the state-owned oil and gas company, in which they erased information from 30,000 computers.[72] And they targeted U.S. banks with denial-of-service attacks in 2012, forcing website shutdowns.[73]

## ISIS AND RADICAL ISLAM

Few readers of this book will need much reminder about the mounting tide of terrorism in the West and around the world. The last several years have been stark ones on this front, as savage, ruthless terror attacks have roiled leading Western cities. At the same time, in the Middle East, while ISIS has suffered setbacks, it continues to exact a breathtaking toll of savagery and terror, and there is no sign of a Western strategy for its ultimate defeat.

The danger of terror attacks in Western cities has never been greater—and France has been ground zero for such attacks. Starting with the 2015 attack at the offices of satirical magazine *Charlie Hebdo*, France has been repeatedly attacked by radical Islamic terrorists. The November 2015 Paris attacks represented a sophisticated and coordinated effort, unlike the "lone wolf" attacks the country was accustomed to seeing. The attacks wrought terror across Paris, with three teams of terrorists ultimately killing 130. On Bastille Day 2016, another terrorist struck in Nice, killing 84 by driving a truck through a crowd celebrating the holiday.

In the United States, "homegrown" terrorists have struck with deadly success—especially in June 2016 in Orlando, where Omar Mateen shot and killed 49 at a gay nightclub. In December 2015, Syed Rizwan Farook and Tashfeen Malik slaughtered 14 in San Bernardino. Intelligence analysts have pointed to homegrown terrorists as the looming domestic threat in the United States. San Bernardino and Orlando indicated that the threat was becoming more real.

President Obama never acted as if he truly believed this, however. To the very end, he minimized the threat of ISIS and radical Islamic terror, even as the carnage piled up. Obama's lack of conviction about the threat from ISIS and radical Islam shows in his rhetoric and his political choices. As many conservatives lamented, the president simply refused to call ISIS radical Islamic terrorists. Symbolically at least, this sent a terrible signal—suggesting that the president cared more about offending ISIS than about defeating them. After the *Charlie Hebdo* massacre in January 2015, Obama, alone among major Western leaders, refused to travel to Paris for the march that took place after the attack, which drew more than two million people, including more than 40 world leaders. Obama's comments at the 2015 National Prayer Breakfast—where he condemned religious violence but warned Westerners not to "get on our high horse," because such religious violence is part of our own (often centuries-old) past, even as present-day ISIS atrocities dominated the front pages—also proved exasperating.

Since Obama always believed that ISIS was not as serious a threat as, say, climate change, it's not surprising that his administration never formulated a coherent strategy to defeat the group overseas. "I don't want to put the cart before the horse. We don't have a strategy yet," he said at a press conference in August 2014.[74] A year later, little had changed. "We don't yet have a complete strategy" about how to counter ISIS in Iraq, the president said at a June 2015 G7 summit in Germany, "because it requires commitments on the part of the Iraqis," referring to difficulties in recruiting enough Iraqis to fight ISIS.[75] It's true that the Iraqis are the most critical component in the ground war against ISIS, but it's also clear that Obama never sent an unambiguous message of commitment to fighting ISIS—and backing up the Iraqis brave enough to join him. Why should the Iraqis trust American words at this point?

Many officials blame the rise of ISIS on our hurried withdrawal from Iraq in 2011. Leon Panetta argued that "a small U.S. troop presence in Iraq could have effectively advised the Iraqi military on how to deal with al-Qaeda's resurgence and the sectarian violence that has engulfed the country."[76] Hillary Clinton voiced a similar concern regarding Obama's hesitation to arm the moderate Syrian rebels.[77] General David Petraeus, chief architect of the Iraq surge, was also candid in 2015 remarks to the *Washington Post*.

"What has happened in Iraq is a tragedy—for the Iraqi people, for the region and for the entire world," Petraeus wrote.[78] "It is tragic foremost because it didn't have to turn out this way. The hard-earned progress of the Surge was sustained for over three years. What transpired after that, starting in late 2011, came about as a result of mistakes and misjudgments whose consequences were predictable. And there is plenty of blame to go around for that."[79]

Though Obama refused to concede that he was wrong in leaving Iraq prematurely, his later actions suggested that he grudgingly realized the need for American action. He sent several hundred American troops to Iraq, where some would embed with Iraqi units and help in the fight against ISIS.[80] But Obama's move only raised more questions. Why was he only increasing the troop level now, and why so slowly? How many more would be needed? By refusing to take decisive action against the Islamic State before it became such a potent force, Obama compromised the security of the Middle East. "This is yet another example of the kind of grudging incrementalism that rarely wins wars, but could certainly lose one," said Senator John McCain, a fierce critic of the administration's Iraq policy.[81]

Even in their limited form, allied efforts against ISIS have borne some fruit: the group has lost substantial territory that it once held in Iraq and Syria.[82] Yet if there is anything that we should have learned by now from our fights against al-Qaeda and ISIS, it is that territorial and military victories, if not followed up with sustained efforts, will prove temporary. In August 2016, Muhammad al-Adnani, a founding member of ISIS, was killed in an American airstrike in northern Syria. But al-Adnani's words of a few months earlier make clear the scope of the challenge that we face in fighting radical Islam: "Do you think, America, that defeat is by the loss of towns or territory? Were we defeated when we lost the cities in Iraq and retreated to the desert without a city or a land? . . . True defeat is losing the will and desire to fight."[83]

No one believes that ISIS has lost that. We are in a very long-term battle.

In such a protracted fight, Obama didn't help matters with his poor management of our alliances. The administration failed to leverage Egypt in the fight against ISIS. Egyptian president Abdel Fattah el-Sisi should be a natural ally of Washington's against ISIS—he is a staunch anti-Islamist—yet he has had to weather constant U.S. criticisms about his crackdowns on extremists. Obama didn't even back Egypt's strikes against ISIS militants. In May 2015, Saudi Arabian king Salman pulled out of Obama's summit of Gulf Arab states at Camp David at the last minute, humiliating an American president who had confirmed the visit just a day before.[84] The move was widely interpreted as a statement of Saudi dissatisfaction with Obama's nuclear deal-making with Iran. And U.S.-Israeli relations under Obama were strained, to put it politely.

We seem perpetually caught off-balance. A further example is the troubled negotiations over the Iranian nuclear program. Israeli prime minister Bibi Netanyahu made it clear that he opposed the nuclear deal, arguing that it offered far too many concessions to Iran and endangered the Israeli future. For his part, in May 2015 President Obama conceded that the Iranian regime sponsors terrorism. He said, "Iran clearly engages in dangerous and destabilizing behavior in different countries across the region. Iran is a state sponsor of terrorism. It helps prop up the Assad regime in Syria. It supports Hezbollah in Lebanon and Hamas in the Gaza Strip. It aids the Houthi rebels in Yemen."[85] Yet the president formalized the Iranian nuclear deal anyway.

In short, we face a range of terrorist threats that we have shown no capacity to combat effectively, let alone defeat. Our confused and sometimes frankly dishonest posture cannot continue indefinitely without major repercussions, including a major terror attack at home in the United States. President Obama meant well, but his foreign policy proved calamitous, largely due to his determination to call an end to George W. Bush's War on Terror—no matter the cost. Now those costs are coming due. President Trump will have to restart President Bush's War on Terror, though probably by another name.

## LOOKING FORWARD

As Obama's presidency reached its end, our national security challenges appeared daunting, even insurmountable. They do not have to be the latter. First and foremost, the United States must retire its eight-year policy of leading from behind, which only provided our adversaries with open running room to pursue their interests. Not just our posture but also our choices must change, beginning with our national defense preparations.

Our military must be rebuilt to secure American global interests. The needs extend across the board—Army, Navy, Air Force, Marines, equipment, systems intelligence, you name it. A particularly pressing need, especially with regard to the Chinese challenge in the Pacific, is fleet size—that is, shipbuilding and capacity. Continuing the development of the most advanced military aircraft will also support this critical need. The new F-35 will play an essential role in intelligence gathering and defensive posturing against China.

History and human nature argue against Obama's naïve assumptions and his reckless insistence that the United States can maintain its current level of security without a substantial nuclear stockpile—let alone with a no-first-use policy. Everything that we know about the checks and balances between nation-states tells us that, in walking back our nuclear arsenal and renouncing first-strike deterrent options, Obama made the United States more vulnerable, not safer. In February 2013, 20 foreign policy experts wrote the president an open letter urging him to reconsider his nuclear disarmament agenda. We share their views. Whereas President Trump faces complicated choices in several areas, in nuclear policy, the choice, at least at the outset, should be relatively simple: reverse Obama's nuclear drawdown by restoring our nuclear strength, especially via our nuclear "triad" of land-, sea-, and bomber-delivered weapons; and renounce any intention of pursuing a no-first-use policy.

### Countering China

Chinese audacity in the South China Sea is made easier by sharp cuts in U.S. military budgets; our military must be rebuilt to secure American global interests, as noted.

The United States must recognize and support its multiple regional partners—especially India, Japan, Vietnam, the Philippines, and South Korea—in efforts to counter China. We should empower the Association of Southeast Asian Nations (ASEAN) to be the region's preeminent authority on peaceful cooperation. America must be the first outlet for defense resources. For example, Boeing believes that it possesses the capabilities in "intelligence, surveillance and reconnaissance platforms that may meet Vietnam's modernization needs."[86] By helping Vietnam and its neighbors secure these systems, the United States can restrain Chinese expansion projects.

The United States and its partners should impose a moratorium on China's rogue island-building projects. China must recognize international maritime law. We can do this by sharply increasing support for the annual Operation Pacific Angel, which brings humanitarian aid and U.S. assistance in civil-military operations to Asia-Pacific nations.

Through the leadership of the Navy's Seventh Fleet, the United States should conduct biannual naval exercises with regional allies. By building up our regional allies' hard naval power and engaging them in mutual adherence to international maritime law, we can persuade China to respect the same standards. More broadly, the Chinese must recommit to the requirements of the U.N. Convention on the Law of the Sea and offer to complete reports on the environmental impact of their naval actions, as the convention dictates, and make additional efforts to rectify their egregious violations. We should also bolster military partnerships with all Trans-Pacific Partnership nations to form the bedrock of a coalition working to counter China.

The United States must push for economic liberalization through-out the region. While the Chinese engage in predatory trade tactics, the United States should establish a genuine free-trade zone with controlled tariffs and subsidies. To its credit, the Obama administration boldly pushed for passage of the Trans-Pacific Partnership (TPP). "China wants to write the rules for the world's fastest-growing region," the president said. "Why would we let that happen? We should write those rules." Exactly. The TPP would have incorporated 40 percent of global GDP into a free-trade zone that excluded China, but President Trump, during his first week in office, signed an executive order formally abandoning the agreement, which was awaiting congressional approval. Trump expresses a strong preference for bilateral, not multilateral, trade agreements.

Finally, the United States should deepen ties with India, the world's largest democracy. We should support Prime Minister Narendra Modi's ambition to bolster border infrastructure to make it easier to move troops and equipment to contested areas in India's northern region, near main-land China. We should strengthen economic and military deals, such as the ten-year agreement between India and the United States to develop protective gear against chemical and biological weapons, as well as deals for the United States to build jet engines and an aircraft carrier for India.[87]

### Standing Up to Russia

President Trump and other G7 leaders must be unequivocal on the illegal-ity of the Russian annexation of Crimea and of Russia's disguised involve-ment in eastern Ukraine.[88] Russian aggression must be made abundantly clear to the world. Ukraine's survival is at stake.

A legitimate ceasefire must be established—unlike the deceptive, dishonest deals that have been reached up to now, which have mostly served as pretexts for the Russians to continue destabilizing Ukraine. The ceasefire should impose proper controls for all parties involved, especially the Russian armed forces and Moscow-aligned separatists, to respect its provisions and procedures. Western powers should provide Kiev with sufficient defensive weapon systems in order to reassert its territorial integrity, including sovereignty over the Crimean peninsula.[89]

The June 2015 G7 summit underscored the necessity for the United States and Germany to coordinate efforts against Russia. Building barriers around access to foreign capital, targeting sanctions against the Russian energy sector, and more concerted work to weaken the ruble would all be highly effective. On the whole, the United States, while working closely with our allies, must not forfeit leadership of this objective to Germany or a small group of European partners.

Finally, to be clear: we support the arming of Ukrainian forces and Kiev-aligned resistance fighters by the United States and its allies—if not to win the fight in the field, then to bolster Ukraine's negotiating position. While military aid would be strictly designated for defensive use, stronger armaments would impose higher cost on future Russian aggression, especially breaches of the current ceasefire.[90]

## Defending Cyberspace

As the dramatic recent breaches have demonstrated, the United States must make a more conscious effort to recognize our "significant vulnerabilities."[91] Investigative authorities need the necessary resources to dig deeper into breaches, discover their source, and form actionable resolutions. In turn, government employees and other staff need to get up to speed on the nature of these threats. Similar protocols should apply in the private sector.

In terms of resources and technology, the United States Computer Emergency Readiness Team (US-CERT) must deliver on its mandate to get to the source of cyber breaches and uncover the culprits. The operational arm of the National Cyber Security Division (NCSD) of the Department of Homeland Security, US-CERT must defend American cyber leadership and serve as the world's foremost cyber-protection agency.

President Trump should call on both parties in Congress to commit to strong legislation on cybersecurity, requiring comprehensive investigations and upgrades of obsolete systems with modern networks equipped with US-CERT's "Einstein" intrusion-detection technology. Investment in proper infrastructure by both government agencies and private organizations will dramatically improve vigilance. More broadly, we should see cyber defense as national defense. The United States must lead in setting international legal standards and penalties for destructive cyber breaches and dangerous activity within private networks. Some cyber attacks are so severe that they amount to an effective declaration of war; others, such as Russia's tactics against Georgia in the 2008 war, amount to weapons of war. It's likely that we'll see a lot more of such tactics in the future. As globalization blurs lines between national economies and domestic politics, the integrity of a nation's most sensitive cyber networks must be maintained.

### A New War on Terror and Islamic Extremism

Effective opposition to Islamic extremism and global terrorism begins with the assertion that fundamentalist sects are wholly at odds with American values. President Obama always seemed to be more concerned with not offending Muslims in the United States and elsewhere, rather than calling out the adherents of radical Islamic extremism for their ideology and their murderous deeds. Our adversaries show no such equivocation; they openly curse the American way of life. We must respond with clear objectives and, crucially, clear language. Equivocating about who our enemy is puts us on the wrong foot from the start.

The United States must take the lead among Western coalition partners to increase military engagement in the struggle against ISIS. We need to improve intelligence gathering to identify critical targets and increase airstrikes through both surface-to-air missiles and bombing runs. Coalition nations should do more to train Iraqi forces and provide necessary equipment.

In addition to supporting Iraqi security forces, the coalition forces should arm other anti-ISIS forces—including supplying Sunni tribes and Iraqi Kurds. The United States should expand its current allotment of a limited number of missiles with a range of 300 meters to antitank missiles, with an effective range of 2,000 meters. Former Army vice chief of staff General Jack Keane notes that supporting militias and tribal forces helps reclaim lost territory and subsequently hold it.[92] Humanitarian support to refugees and other victims of ISIS should be stepped up in order to neutralize the Islamic State's argument that they are the only political force in the region that retains the power to protect.

We need to display America's interest in developing a future for Syria beyond ISIS tyranny or an Assad dictatorship. Washington should pursue a pact with moderate opposition forces to help them not only vanquish ISIS but also eventually depose Assad.

At home, American federal and state-level investigative authorities need to improve their vigilance against potential terror recruits in three ways: tracing suspicious behaviors on social media, monitoring suspicious travel arrangements, and empowering informants to assist in investigations. Each of these areas highlights traceable patterns to thwart those interested in materially supporting foreign terrorist organizations, especially ISIS. Federal authorities, especially the Departments of State and Homeland Security, should institute extensive visa and passport restrictions on Americans attempting to travel to nations with deep terrorist ties, namely Iraq and Syria, and their neighbors, like Turkey and Lebanon.

The United States can—and indeed, must—eradicate and defeat ISIS. This is not a group with which coexistence or even stalemate is possible. It shows every sign of being a death cult, a millennialist organization committed to dying for its beliefs and butchering all who stand in its way. Only total, unconditional defeat will suffice. To achieve this objective, we must first recognize what will be required to accomplish it: above all, honesty about the enemy, the threat it poses, and the nature of what is required to defeat it. We need new leadership.

When we do defeat ISIS, the United States must learn from history and not let its guard down or diminish its efforts at securing regional stability, fostering democracy where possible, and nurturing effective alliances. We should develop partnerships at the national, provincial, and community level throughout Iraq, Syria, and Afghanistan to make it less likely that young men fall into the vicious cycle of terror recruiting and to elevate their personal and familial status. By empowering these individuals to become global citizens, rather than radicalized recruits, the United States will make progress in stopping the spread of Islamic extremism.

## CONCLUSION

Never before in the modern era has the world seen such a diffusion of power—not just among states but also among non-state actors. In the pre–World War II era, power primarily existed in a state of multipolarity among European nations, America, and Japan; in the Cold War, as bipolarity between the United States and the Soviet Union; and in the post–Cold War era, as unipolarity during a brief age of American hegemony. Power today is much more fragmented and diffuse. The rise of non-state actors, the functional dissolution of borders in certain areas, and decreased state sovereignty in an increasingly globalized world all yield new threats. Terrorism, cyber war, and biochemical sabotage don't organize according to borders.

In the midst of all this turbulence, Barack Obama's experiment in leading from behind was revealed as a complete failure. It turns out that, in a multipolar world, American leadership is more important than ever. As Obama stood back, refusing to inject American power, and assuming somehow that the world could be self-governing, his failures became a mirror image of George W. Bush's: where Bush overreached, seeing few problems in the world that couldn't be solved through the vigorous assertion of American power, Obama has underreached, believing that most of the world's trouble spots would be better off with less American involvement. As Richard Haas, president of the Council on Foreign Relations, puts it, "Not acting can be every bit as consequential as acting."[93] The Bush and Obama presidencies make this truth tragically clear—and they remind us that there is no substitute for wise leadership and sound judgment.

CHAPTER 12

# The Endangered American Idea

Most Americans no longer know what America stands for. For them, America has become just another country, a place located between Canada and Mexico.

—DENNIS PRAGER[1]

I would not look to the U.S. Constitution, if I were drafting a Constitution in the year 2012. I might look at the Constitution of South Africa. That was a deliberate attempt to have a fundamental instrument of government that embraced basic human rights, had an independent judiciary.... It really is, I think, a great piece of work that was done. Much more recent than the U.S. Constitution.

—RUTH BADER GINSBURG[2]

When was the Civil War fought? What are the three branches of the U.S. government? What is the Electoral College? What does the First Amendment guarantee?

Don't ask Americans. They don't know.

In 2009, the Intercollegiate Studies Institute (ISI) randomly selected more than 2,500 adults to take its 33-question American history and civics survey. Nearly three-quarters of those taking it—71 percent—earned an average score of 49, for an "F" grade. More than twice as many test-takers knew that Paula Abdul had been a judge on *American Idol* than knew that the phrase "Government of the people, by the people, for the people" came from Lincoln's Gettysburg Address. Only half of those taking the test could name the three branches of government, and only a little more than half knew that it was Congress, not the president, that had the constitutional power to declare war.[3]

The ISI survey also revealed that an incredible 43 percent of those who had held elected office didn't know that the Electoral College elects the president. One in five thought that it either "trains those aspiring for higher office" or "was established to supervise the first televised presidential debates."[4]

It has become commonplace to note that Americans know little about their history or even about current events—unless you count reality TV or what is trending on Twitter. When he hosted *The Tonight Show*, Jay Leno regularly walked the streets of Burbank and asked ordinary Americans what they thought of items in the news. They knew almost nothing, and Leno was routinely able to make up fake news without being corrected.

Leno's vignettes were often amusing, and to many, Americans' lack of historical knowledge or awareness of current events is no big deal. Some even suggest that ignoring the news and politics is part of being a free people. That's true, up to a point. But when such ignorance impairs the ability of the people to make important decisions about our future, it's a problem. Moreover, when such ignorance is part of a broader trend toward deemphasizing or rewriting our history, undermining our founding principles, and denying the worth and uniqueness of American democracy, we're in different territory.

"Most Americans no longer know what America stands for," Dennis Prager writes. "For them, America has become just another country, a place located between Canada and Mexico."[5] The United States, founded on ideals of liberty, equality under the law, small government, and free enterprise, has spent much of its history believing that its adherence to these ideals made the nation special—even blessed. And since, from its inception, the United States offered most people opportunity and a standard of living unmatched anywhere else, Americans had good reason to feel that way. For most of our history, Americans believed firmly that the country was unique—and, yes, even superior.

Increasingly, Americans don't believe that anymore. That's why the history-test numbers are so important. They illustrate a larger trend: the decline of belief in the American idea, which encompasses not just the American dream of a better life, but also the conviction that America's principles are worth defending (or even knowing about) and the confidence that once came with living in the world's oldest constitutional republic and strongest (and richest) democracy.

The decline in such conviction, sharpest among the young, poses serious obstacles to our ability to solve the challenges we face ahead. Most great American achievements—breaking away from Great Britain, winning the Civil War, defeating the Nazis and the Japanese, walking on the moon—have been inseparable from the qualities of conviction, confidence, and unity. But if Americans stop believing in America, we will lack the cohesion to pursue such great common purposes, here or abroad. Our fractiousness and squabbling send a message to the world that we are not unified. Dissolution from within weakens our ability to fight against our adversaries and guard against threats. Lack of faith and conviction in who we are makes us vulnerable as a nation, no matter how economically or militarily powerful we may still be.

We are seeing this loss of conviction play out in three key areas: in a decline of educational efforts to inculcate the American idea; in a public loss of confidence in democratic ideals, from freedom of speech and democratic political norms to the free-enterprise system; and in the erosion of faith in American exceptionalism and the belief that America is a special country. Let's take them one by one.

## EDUCATION

In March 2015, students at the University of California at Irvine removed a U.S. flag from a common area of the student government office. Then six members of the Associated Students Council passed a resolution banning display of the flag in the office lobby. The resolution said that flags "construct cultural mythologies and narratives that in turn charge nationalistic sentiments" and "construct paradigms of conformity and set homogenized standards for others to obtain which in this country typically are idolized as freedom, equality, and democracy."[6] The students went on to note that "the American flag has been flown in instances of colonialism and imperialism" and that "a common ideological understanding of the United States includes American exceptionalism and superiority."[7] (A higher student panel voted to fly the flag again, though more than 1,000 students and many professors later signed a petition supporting the original ban.)

The UC Irvine student resolution showed a tendency common on many campuses today: a kind of tyranny of the minority devoted to utopian thinking, in which symbols, public spaces, and language itself must be untainted by the imperfections of human behavior—an impossibility, as anyone past adolescence should know.

Most people shrug off these episodes, but they have proliferated enormously on college campuses in recent years. The targets are not just the flag but also the symbols and personages of American history—and the impulses, again, often involve efforts to eradicate reminders of unpleasant histories. Students at Princeton, for instance, lobbied to remove Woodrow Wilson's name from their School of Public and International Affairs. The students objected to the 25th president's record on race, especially his re-segregation of federal government employment. Wilson's racial views, which included support for the Ku Klux Klan, are indeed noxious, especially 100 years later, in a country that has achieved so much racial progress. The *New York Times* came out in favor of removing Wilson's name: "The overwhelming weight of the evidence argues for rescinding the honor that the university bestowed decades ago on an unrepentant racist."[8] But Wilson was a major influence on Princeton, not to mention on the United States and on the world. We cannot erase the parts of history that we don't like. Princeton chose to retain Wilson's name on the school and on a residential college.[9] After a similar battle, Yale retained the name of John C. Calhoun—supporter of slavery and states' rights—on one of its colleges, despite student outrage.

The heritage of slavery has been at the heart of many of these controversies. Both Yale and Harvard have stopped using the faculty name "master." Harvard was first to change the title "master" and replaced it with "faculty dean."[10] Yale now calls leaders of its residential colleges "head."

In August 2015, the University of Texas took down a statue of Confederate president Jefferson Davis and moved it to an institute on campus, the nation's largest collection of material depicting slavery. Statues of Robert E. Lee and Albert Sidney Johnston (Confederate generals) and John H. Reagan (Confederate postmaster general) stayed in place.[11] After students at Amherst College learned that Jeffrey Amherst had advocated the use of smallpox blankets on Native Americans, they changed the school's mascot from Lord Jeff to a moose.[12]

These efforts aren't limited to university campuses. Cities such as Albuquerque, St. Paul, Seattle, Minneapolis, and Portland have all renamed Columbus Day "Indigenous Peoples Day" in an attempt to reframe our history in terms of race, greed, and exploitation.[13] Such movements have been familiar for a few decades now. The quincentennial of Columbus's arrival in the Western Hemisphere, in 1992, sparked many protests and much discussion about proper commemoration.

We don't mean to suggest that these efforts are always wrongheaded. Many campus episodes, like the one at UC Irvine, are frankly cartoonish, and in many other instances, student activists are simply applying naïve judgments to complicated historical figures and events. In other cases, however—often involving the issue of slavery—a sensitive approach is justified. It is proper that we reexamine our past, that we never stop asking questions, and that we reevaluate based on new information or new arguments. But we cannot simply expunge the events and figures that have defined us because they sinned. We must incorporate our understanding of these sins into a broader narrative.

That's the approach Harvard president Drew Gilpin Faust has taken. Streets and buildings across Harvard are named after slaves. Faust, a Civil War historian, has resisted renaming buildings. "I feel quite strongly that we should not be trying to erase our history of names," Faust told the *Crimson*, the student newspaper, in 2016. "I think we're all going to be facing these questions, and the case that I would make is...about the importance of sustaining our history, not erasing it."[14] But Faust went on to accept the recommendation of a committee to change Harvard Law School's seal because it was the family crest of a slaveholder. Harvard also installed a plaque on a building on campus, recognizing the names of four slaves who lived and worked there.

In many other instances, however, college administrators have lacked Faust's firmness, learning, and sensitivity to apply a constructive standard to these debates. Too often, the mere discovery of "hypocrisy"—that some great figure from America's past held views or committed acts that we would now condemn—is grounds enough to take action. Activists call for renaming buildings, removing monuments, eliminating or creating academic programs—and defaming those who disagree with them.

Why have such movements increased in recent years? Certainly one reason is the nation's changing demographics, on campus and elsewhere. With minorities making up a greater share of the American population, more skepticism is being brought to bear on American historical figures. When this skepticism is fair-minded and constructive, we're all for it. Too often, it is simply motivated by resentment.

Another key reason—and one that explains in good part why so many of the activist students today don't seem to know much about their own arguments—is that American history and civics education has declined so dramatically.

Across the board, civics requirements in college are decreasing.[15] A survey by the American Council of Trustees and Alumni showed that only 18 percent of universities require students to take a course in U.S. history or government. The report also showed that less than 20 percent of U.S. college grads understood the meaning of the Emancipation Proclamation. Almost 10 percent thought Judge Judy was a Supreme Court justice.[16] A 2015 survey found that only 19 percent of Americans knew that the First Amendment guarantees freedom of religion and only 10 percent knew that it guarantees freedom of the press; 33 percent know nothing about it. Clearly, our education system has failed to teach the basics.

Not surprisingly, the college students are so ignorant because they haven't learned much about American history or government before showing up on campus. The National Assessment of Educational Progress's 2015 National Civics test showed that one in four high school seniors lacked "proficient" knowledge of civics. In United States history, 20 percent of fourth-graders were proficient in 2010, while just *12 percent* of high school seniors reached that standard.[17] No wonder college students show such extreme reactions when they discover—probably for the first time—that some bad things happened in American history. It's all news to them.

Young Americans simply don't learn about the country they live in and will someday govern to nearly the degree they once did. They also get little instruction in ethics and moral philosophy—the skills that might help, for instance, college students to make distinctions and judgments when faced with troubling historical information. Indeed, moral philosophy and civic education were once cornerstones of the curriculum at institutions like Harvard. Not anymore.[18]

It's hard to know how different things might be if our civic and historical instruction were better. But it's a pretty good bet that Americans would know more about their history and government than they do today. And it's also a good bet that they wouldn't be so ignorant about their fundamental freedoms—in some cases, even showing a disinterest in preserving them.

## LOSING FAITH IN FREEDOM OF EXPRESSION
## AND DEMOCRATIC IDEALS

It's not just history or civics that Americans don't know. They don't even seem to understand their fundamental freedoms. As noted above, a 2015 survey found that depressingly low numbers of Americans understood even baseline concepts like what freedoms are guaranteed by the First Amendment. With such a flimsy base of knowledge, it should be no surprise that Americans are less attached to the principle of free speech and more willing to violate it.

Here again, college campuses are ground zero. Campus efforts in recent years to rename buildings or remove historical symbols are related to a broader trend: an assault on freedom of speech and the free exchange of ideas. It has become routine for colleges and universities to disinvite scheduled commencement speakers, for example, after student groups protest their selection. The brave and eloquent champion of Western freedoms, Ayaan Hirsi Ali, was disinvited from Brandeis University after one such protest. It was "deplorable," she said, "that an institution set up on the basis of religious freedom should today so deeply betray its own founding principles."[19] African American columnist Jason Riley, who writes boldly from a conservative perspective on race, was disinvited from speaking at Virginia Tech because of the mere possibility that there might be protests. (After being ridiculed, the university reversed itself.) Former secretary of state Condoleezza Rice agreed not to speak at Rutgers after not students but faculty members demanded that her invitation be retracted.[20] Conservative columnist George Will, after writing a column questioning campus-rape statistics, was disinvited from speaking at all-female Scripps College.[21]

Even when conservative-minded speakers do make it to campus, students are often unwilling to hear them out. Former New York City police commissioner Ray Kelly tried to speak at Brown, but his talk on crime prevention was canceled when he was booed off the stage.[22] And former New York mayor Michael Bloomberg, after telling University of Michigan graduates that "one of the most dangerous places on a college campus is the so-called safe space, because it creates a false impression that we can isolate ourselves from those who hold different views," was booed—neatly illustrating the very point he was making.[23]

College students increasingly seem to believe that the test of their political commitment is to shut down the political expression of those who disagree or who represent an opposing point of view. And they apparently believe that "freedom" means that they should be free from having to hear—whether in a formal speech or merely in a passing conversation—ideas and opinions that clash with their own. These alternative ideas, in fact, have increasingly come to be defined as threats to students' well-being.

It is this idea of free speech as a form of assault, as something from which we need to be sheltered, that underpins the movement to stamp out "microaggressions" and "triggers" that can traumatize students. The idea is twofold: first, just about anything can be offensive, a "trigger" that could open up emotional wounds—whether reading a novel in which a woman is raped, or having to learn about the slave trade, or even being asked in a social setting what one's ethnic background is (i.e., "are you Filipino?"). Second, since triggers are everywhere, we need the broadest possible protections from them—whether speech codes on campus, removal of troubling materials from college courses, or the shutdown of campus newspapers or publications that have repeatedly shown insensitivity to student trauma by publishing upsetting ideas. The antidote to triggers and microaggressions is the creation of "safe spaces," where no such "assaultive" ideas or expressions are permitted—including the flying of American flags, which might trigger feelings of inferiority or helplessness, thoughts about the slave trade, or reflections on the disinheritance of Native Americans. (Of course, the flag might also conjure pride in the ideas of equality, freedom of expression, and opportunity, but never mind. Triggers and microaggressions only seem to work in one direction.)

The expression of these ideas on campuses has become increasingly extreme and even thuggish. At Yale, a student protest broke out over an email from a faculty member's wife telling students that she thought it was okay to wear "culturally appropriative" Halloween costumes. In a video that went viral, a student screamed at her college master, refusing to let him speak. "Be quiet! Why the fuck did you accept the [master] position?" She looks as if she is going to hyperventilate. The faculty member, true to form in almost all such situations, stands there and takes it.[24]

And it hasn't just been students, either. Who can forget, for example, how a professor at the University of Missouri spearheaded the physical intimidation of a photographer with the student newspaper, who was trying to cover the protests? The photographer, Tim Tai, was surrounded by protestors chanting, "Hey, hey, ho, ho, journalists have got to go."[25] Melissa Click, a "professor of mass media," approached Tai, indicating that he should move on. "Who wants to help me get this reporter out of here?" Click shouted to the students. "I need some muscle over here."[26]

At the heart of these efforts is a fundamental rejection of the principle of free speech and the free exchange of ideas—principles foundational not only to American life but also to higher education. Ridiculing the call for "safe spaces," famed Harvard Law School professor Alan Dershowitz argued that "humorless" college students should either accept the free exchange of ideas on campus, or leave. "They want a safe space for their ideas, well fine, don't go to college," Dershowitz said in an interview in January 2016. "Don't go to universities. Universities are not gonna give you a safe space for your ideas. Your ideas are gonna be challenged. Whether they're ideas about sex, rape, consent, race, religion, terrorism—every one of your ideas are gonna be challenged."[27]

Jonathan Chait, a man of the Left always willing to speak his mind, has warned that these trends should not be dismissed as the silly behavior of undergraduates. "Even if it were the case that political correctness was totally confined to campuses, it would not make the phenomenon unimportant," Chait writes. "Colleges have disproportionate influence over intellectual life, and political movements centered on campuses can spread well beyond them." Besides, "to imagine p.c. as simply a thing college kids do relieves us of taking it seriously as a coherent set of beliefs.... Political correctness is a system of thought that denies the legitimacy of political pluralism on issues of race and gender."[28]

Unsurprisingly, given its prominence on campus, opposition to free speech has a strong generational angle. Millennials don't support free speech as robustly as earlier generations of Americans. A November 2015 Pew study found an incredible 40 percent of millennial respondents favored federal penalties for offensive speech about minorities.[29] The millennials are, in effect, the tip of the spear in a new way of looking at free speech. Since the Silent Generation, each succeeding cohort has weakened in its absolute support for free speech. Only 12 percent of Silent Generation respondents, for example, favored federal penalties for offensive speech about minorities—but 24 percent of baby boomers and 27 percent of Generation Xers did.[30]

Indeed, political correctness has extended far beyond the campus by now, to all areas of American life. Mozilla CEO Brendan Eich lost his job over his opposition to gay marriage. Eich was forced out of the company because he held political views that were deemed unacceptable. This chilling of free speech and expression has extended to Twitter and Facebook, where people in public life—from politicians to celebrities—write controversial tweets and then are forced by an electronic lynch mob to retract their statement, pull down the tweet, and apologize. Public institutions around the country are reluctant to put up Christmas decorations, lest they "offend" nonbelievers. High school sports coaches are threatened with disciplinary measures or termination for leading their kids in a voluntary prayer. Fewer and fewer people say "God bless you" after a sneeze. "Everything's so p.c.," said one New Hampshire voter. "And then the second you do say something, you're a racist."[31]

The residents of San Bernardino wish that someone had said something about Syed Farook and his wife, Tashfeen Malik. A neighbor of the soon-to-be-murderous couple noticed suspicious activity at their apartment, but didn't call the authorities because she didn't want to "racially profile" or "be called racist." She later said that she saw three or four "Middle Easterners" had recently moved into the apartment and were receiving a number of packages.[32] She said nothing. Similarly, no one at Fort Hood said anything about Major Nidal Hasan, who had spouted violent Islamic propaganda on the base, and even reached out to terrorist groups online—this behavior, too, was known—for fear of being accused of "Islamophobia." Hasan murdered 13 Americans and injured more than 30 in a 2009 shooting spree on the base. Political correctness and the stifling of free expression are not just threats to our values; they also cost lives.

Alas, as Democrats, we must concede that most of the energy for these kinds of efforts comes from the Left, not the Right. It is a troubling political legacy for Democrats to grapple with—but it is also, more importantly, a threat to our freedoms, of which freedom of speech is the most fundamental.

Hand in hand with the increasing contempt for free speech goes a loss of devotion to the ideals of democracy and to the conviction that democracy is the best available form of government. Once again, in this regard, we see a generational component.

We were very troubled by the survey results published by Roberto Foa and Yascha Mounk in Vox, partially based on their own research, showing that fewer Americans of the younger generation place importance on living in a democracy. This manifests itself in low approval for democratic institutions and openness to seemingly illiberal alternatives. Most remarkable was a chart mapping—by decade of birth, from the 1930s to the 1980s—what percentage of respondents said that it was "essential" to live in a democracy. More than 70 percent of those born in the 1930s said that it was; fewer than 30 percent of those born in the 1980s said the same. Conversely, another chart measured the percentage of Americans affirming the statement that democracy was "a bad way to run America." Of those born since 1970, 22 percent think that democracy is a bad way to run the country as opposed to 13 percent of those born in the 1950s and 1960s.[33]

Unsurprisingly, then, Americans—led by millennials—are more open to non-democratic alternatives, especially socialism. In 2010 and 2011, Pew found that Americans under 30 narrowly favored socialism over capitalism,[34] and that millennials were more likely, by 36 points, to favor big government, with lots of services, than older generations.[35] A 2011 GlobeScan survey found Americans less supportive of the free market than respondents in China and Brazil, and roughly on par with those in India.[36]

Some Americans even seem open to authoritarianism. "Most Americans are still horrified by the idea of living in an authoritarian regime, but the number of citizens who are open to some form of illiberal rule is going up," Foa and Mounk write. In 1995, when the World Values Survey asked Americans if they thought that "army rule" would be a "good" or "very good" thing, one in 15 Americans said yes. In 2015, one in six did.

What is at the core of these troubling trends? Certainly, some of the developments that we have chronicled in other chapters have contributed—especially Americans' loss of trust in institutions. And yet, it seems that we can peel back the onion to another layer. For just as the rewriting of American history and diminishment of our educational efforts is really the symptom of a broader push against freedom of speech and a loss of faith in democratic ideals and institutions, so, too, are these crises the outgrowth of something larger still: the loss of confidence, not just in this or that principle but in America itself, in what makes it exceptional, and in what its role in the world should be.

## THE END OF AMERICAN EXCEPTIONALISM?

American exceptionalism is the belief that the United States is set apart from other nations by its history, geography, and values: a nation founded on the ideas of self-government and equality, not tribal identities, set apart from the Old World, and governed as a constitutional republic. This uniqueness came to be seen by many as a mission, not only to our own people but also to the world; and in the twentieth century especially, the idea of American exceptionalism became a foundation of our foreign policy (for good and for ill). To believe in American exceptionalism, in some sense, united Americans. Most of us believed that America was special, and we were proud of the country and of our identification with it, whatever our criticisms.

This seems to be changing, and again, the change looks starkest among the young. A 2013 Public Religion Research Institute poll found that nearly two-thirds of Americans over 65 considered themselves "extremely proud to be an American," but among those under 30, less than two in five said the same. In 2011, Pew found that millennials lagged, by 40 points, those 75 and older in calling America the "greatest country in the world." And as we have seen, millennials' devotion to American principles like free speech and democratic governance also lags behind older generations.[37]

This waning belief is not confined to the young, however, or to those lacking education or opportunity. In fact, it goes right to the top levels of American life. Supreme Court justice Ruth Bader Ginsburg made headlines in 2012 when she told Egypt's Al-Hayat TV, "I would not look to the U.S. Constitution, if I were drafting a Constitution in the year 2012. I might look at the Constitution of South Africa. That was a deliberate attempt to have a fundamental instrument of government that embraced basic human rights, had an independent judiciary....It really is, I think, a great piece of work that was done. Much more recent than the U.S. Constitution."[38] Ginsburg seemed to be suggesting either that the American Constitution had become outdated or that it did not "embrace basic human rights" or provide for an independent judiciary. Very odd.

That a Supreme Court justice, whose job it is to interpret the American Constitution, thinks so poorly of it is certainly indicative. And Ginsburg isn't alone on the bench in this tendency. Her colleague, Anthony Kennedy, has spent decades citing international legal precedents in making case law—international precedents that, constitutionally speaking, are entirely irrelevant.

Ginsburg and Kennedy arrived at the Supreme Court in 1987 and 1993, respectively—long before Barack Obama made it to the White House. But to listen to Republicans tell it, it's Obama who played the key role in eroding the sense of American exceptionalism. To them, his signal comment came in 2009: "I believe in American exceptionalism," he said, "just as I suspect that the Brits believe in British exceptionalism and the Greeks believe in Greek exceptionalism."[39] In other words, American exceptionalism isn't very exceptional; every country feels that it is unique and special. This is actually demonstrably false; whether one accepts American exceptionalism or not, it is a national sentiment not found in other countries.

Elsewhere, Obama sounded as if he did recognize this. He rose to fame in 2004 saying that his distinctive personal story was only possible in the United States. The night he won the presidency in 2008, he told a massive crowd in Chicago's Grant Park, "If there is anyone out there who still doubts that America is a place where all things are possible, who still wonders if the dream of our founders is alive in our time, who still questions the power of our democracy, tonight is your answer."[40]

What really seems to gall conservative critics is Obama's skepticism about the broadly bipartisan foreign policy that dominated the Cold War era and afterward. "I believe in American exceptionalism with every fiber of my being," he told West Point's graduating cadets in 2014. "But what makes us exceptional is not our ability to flout international norms and the rule of law; it is our willingness to affirm them through our actions."[41] In this, he is not out of step with the broader public. The 2014 General Social Survey found that 64 percent of American adults agreed that "there are some things about America today that make me feel ashamed," and 70 percent agreed that "the world would be a better place if Americans acknowledged America's shortcomings."[42]

Obama's critics see the president as part of a vanguard trying to pull apart a multigenerational consensus about America's special place. "At the heart of the debate over Obama's program," Rich Lowry and Ramesh Ponnuru wrote in a 2010 *National Review* cover story, "is the survival of American exceptionalism."[43] Rudy Giuliani made headlines in 2015 when he told an audience, "I know this is a horrible thing to say, but I do not believe that the president loves America. . . . He wasn't brought up the way you were brought up and I was brought up, through love of this country."[44] Marco Rubio, speaking in 2015 at the Council on Foreign Relations, said that Obama had "demonstrated a disregard for our moral purpose that at times flirted with disdain."[45]

Obama's cautious—too cautious, in our view—foreign policy has prompted much of this critique. Robert Kagan has scored Obama for retreating from global engagement. The president, Kagan believes, does not have conviction in America's role as the beacon of freedom for the world and defender of democratic values. "Insofar as the shift in the geopolitical equation has affected the fate of democracies worldwide," Kagan writes, "it is probably the change in the democratic superpower's behavior that bears most of the responsibility. If that superpower does not change its course, we are likely to see democracy around the world rolled back further."[46]

Yet the allegations that Obama's foreign policy has eroded American exceptionalism overlook decades of previous erosion—especially dating back to the Vietnam War. It was that conflict, after all, that broke apart the postwar consensus on America's role in the world, a consensus that has never been reassembled. No less a player in that war than Henry Kissinger himself acknowledges Vietnam's role in weakening Americans' faith in their country's global leadership. "One of the most important casualties of the Vietnam tragedy was the tradition of American 'exceptionalism,'" he wrote. "The once near-universal faith in the uniqueness of our values—and their relevance around the world—gave way to intense divisions over the very validity of those values. . . . And those schisms have had a profound impact on the conduct of U.S. foreign policy ever since."[47] It didn't start with Obama.

Vietnam abroad, and Watergate at home, shattered the concept of American exceptionalism for millions, and no subsequent generation—not Generation X and not the millennials—has picked it up with anything like the unanimity of their forebears. As Peter Beinart argued persuasively in an important article in the *Atlantic*, in many ways Obama is not the cause of declining American exceptionalism—he is the *result*. As Beinart sees it, the three prongs of American exceptionalism were belief in organized religion, belief in America's special mission to spread freedom around the world, and belief that America was a society where anyone could advance with hard work.[48] But religion in America is declining, as we have chronicled; confidence in our global mission, as we've also seen, is nowhere near what it was; and faith in our free-enterprise system and in economic mobility has also been shaken, especially after the financial crisis of 2008. The bottom line: Americans don't believe in the country, its institutions, the American dream, or even the meaning and mission of America as they once did.

## WHAT TO DO?

This doesn't mean that we cannot go on and have success, that we cannot continue to advance the American idea in compelling ways, and most important, that we can't regain some of the special strengths that have defined us in the past—especially that long-running success at providing economic mobility for people of modest means. What it does mean, however, is that we're going to have to find a way to recapture the past—that is, past success—while looking firmly forward, probably with some refined idea of American exceptionalism that takes into account the changes we have undergone as a society. Americans have never been backward-looking—our future orientation has also been one of the key aspects of American exceptionalism. However we choose to proceed, we need to revive the American idea in the present and future, not try to restore older notions that, however venerable, have lost their appeal.

"Europe was created by history," Margaret Thatcher said. "America was created by philosophy."[49] Indeed, we don't talk about a British or a French or a German "idea"; these are countries that arose out of tribal identities to form distinct national federations. But the United States came into being from ideas, and it has always been a nation defined by ideas—freedom or equality or opportunity. Today, that American idea is endangered, and the problems that we have discussed in this book are a big part of the reason why.

At the simplest level, the crisis of American belief has much to do with the decline of economic opportunity. The American dream means many things, but it has always contained a crucial component of upward mobility. The fundamental change that would probably bring the greatest shift in our current attitudes would be the recovery of the American economy's ability to spread prosperity across the income spectrum, to enable people, generationally, to improve the lots of their families, and to give people a tangible—not just emotional—reason to believe that their children's circumstances will be better than their own. As we have seen, the decline of faith in the American ideal, both at home and abroad, has closely tracked the sense that economically, the United States skews financial gains to the few, the educated, the highly intelligent, and the privileged. This fatalistic view that we can't transcend our economic circumstances, and that the American economic system is rigged—as both Bernie Sanders and Donald Trump alleged—has profoundly damaged faith in the country and in its ideals.

Student debt, health care costs, an anemic recovery offering few good-paying jobs—the young have much to worry about. Add in our spiraling entitlement costs as well as the national debt, which President Obama more than doubled, and it's no wonder that they don't see a future as rosy as their parents and grandparents did. If we don't get control of these challenges, the young might do more than just flirt with socialism.

We must turn this around. In chapters 8 and 9, we offer a full range of proposals. We won't repeat them here, but they all involve the core principles of equal opportunity, fairness, entrepreneurialism, growth, and innovation—in short, a reembrace, via specific policies, of the traits that helped make the American economy the engine of world prosperity. In 2012, Mitt Romney ran for president under the motto "Believe in America." It was a good instinct, but saying it doesn't make it so. If millions of Americans, from millennials starting out in the workforce to middle-aged business managers trying to pay for college educations, start believing again that the future will be better, we will see belief in America rebound.

Our political dysfunction, of course, is also a major factor here. Why should Americans believe that their country is blessed and exceptional, when everything they see in Washington tells them otherwise? We see little hope of bipartisanship in the future. The political polarization that has hardened in recent decades looks certain to continue.

The failure of our political leadership makes it even more important that we recover a strong civics component in our schools and deep instruction in history. Understanding the Constitution and its protections should be mandatory class work in both high school and college. Not only should we know these things, as Americans, but an informed citizenry is one better able to explore political alternatives.

This applies to education more broadly, and not just in American civics: as we discussed in chapter 7, the cause of equal opportunity in education is a fundamental one for our future. And school choice, charter schools, and other educational options that empower parents are crucial to achieving this goal. Americans of the past, most growing up in modest circumstances, attended excellent public schools; they learned and advanced themselves, and they also appreciated the country and felt included in it. Our urban public schools today don't teach, don't inspire, and don't give poor children any reason to feel that they are part of the American project.

We have become too passive, too reliant on government and big institutions. The path forward to American renewal will likely involve heroic individual efforts of Americans themselves—in communities, in the military, in education, in churches and hospitals, in business. We need to regain the American hardiness that sought solutions to problems without asking for permission. And we need to put the culture of hypersensitivity into a deep freeze, on college campuses and elsewhere. More liberal thought leaders like Alan Dershowitz need to speak out against the abuse of "safe spaces" and protections for students on college campuses and beyond.

If America doesn't stand for freedom—of speech, of expression, of conscience—then America stands for nothing. Liberals and conservatives should join forces on this issue and tell those easily offended to get over it—and get over themselves.

At the same time, however, there is no substitute for presidential leadership—not to impose big-government policy solutions but to set a tone that fosters unity. The United States desperately needs a leader who will bring the American people back together—lower the social temperature, de-emphasize race, and press themes that emphasize that we are one people, not a collection of groups. Even if, as we all know, we don't share the same experiences, we are all Americans. If the United States can rediscover the economic formula to reenergize mobility, reeducate its young about the vitality of the nation's principles and institutions, and re-foster political themes of unity, we might yet see better days for national self-confidence and civic pride.

It is our contention that there is nothing wrong intrinsically with U.S. democracy that cannot be fixed. The many failures and crises that this book describes are not, in the end, failures of America's founding principles: they are, rather, failures of leadership. Hovering over all these disappointments has been the most destructive failure of all: our loss of faith in America itself. On the fate of this idea hangs the fate of every reform discussed in this book.

# AFTERWORD

As this book goes to press, the need for innovative, bipartisan solutions to the United States' spiraling set of problems is more urgent than ever. This is especially true because the unstable, volatile, dysfunctional nature of our politics shows no sign of abating; on the contrary, it continues to grow worse. Our worst fears, expressed in the chapter entitled "The Failure of Politics," seem to be confirmed.

Consider the Republican failure, in March 2017, to pass the party's long-planned repeal of Obamacare and put in its place the Paul Ryan–supported—and Donald Trump–supported—American Health Care Act (AHCA). If there was one consistent message that united an unraveling Republican Party during the Obama years, it was the repeal of the hated Affordable Care Act—and the promise to the American people that, if the GOP could only be granted the levers of power, it would abolish Obama's failing health care law. Instead, with all the pieces in place, Republicans gave a dramatic demonstration of failed governance. It turned out that it didn't matter whether they had both houses of Congress and the White House to boot. They lack consensus, coordination, and, frankly, competence. The failure of the AHCA was a fiasco for the president and his party and another reminder to the American people that Washington is broken.

The Democrats have been little better. Their refusal to consider an alternative to partisan warfare, even at the outset of a new president's term, was exemplified by their decision to filibuster Trump's nomination of Judge Neil Gorsuch to the Supreme Court. Gorsuch, though a staunch conservative, is universally respected. His nomination should not have prompted a scorched-earth response by Democrats, especially since it was likely that Trump would get another nomination somewhere down the road. Better to save the filibuster bullet for a more objectionable candidate; instead, by going to the mat in a futile, self-destructive battle against Gorsuch, the Democrats triggered the "nuclear option"—the long-threatened Republican plan to change Senate rules and do away with the filibuster. At long last, Republicans did so, and the Senate has been changed forever—and not for the better. Across-the-aisle cooperation will become an even more remote prospect in the future.

This deepening collapse comes at a time of great national anxiety about the economy, about the future of health care, about the stagnation of the American, about law and order in our cities, about a failing education system, about high pressures overseas, with the Trump administration's April 2017 missile strike against Syria igniting serious tensions with Russia and raising the terrifying specter of a broader conflict in the Middle East involving superpowers.

We cannot prevail in our many international challenges without muscularity and assertiveness of American leadership—but we also cannot prevail without cooperation between the parties. It was long said that partisanship stopped at the water's edge. That needs to be true again if we are to avoid catastrophic scenarios.

The only way forward in all these areas is for President Trump to pursue bipartisanship, as he has occasionally suggested he would do, and for Democrats—particularly those ten Democratic senators up for reelection in 2018 in states that Trump won—to push their party to build a bipartisan coalition on health care, tax reform, and infrastructure, in the manner of almost all major legislation in the past. We can do nothing without some form of consensus and cooperation, but partisanship poisons everything in Washington. We are in a paralyzed situation in which no American political leader enjoys broad-ranging public confidence.

Thus, in our view, this book could not be timelier. In each area that we have focused on, it is clear America has lost its edge and even its competitive position. We've tried to analyze the problems systematically, to talk about why America is in decline and what needs to be done. We have proposed a series of solutions that focus on values, ideas, and initiatives because we believe that without a focus on all three, America can't succeed. The revitalization of this country depends on a new willingness to embrace what is unique and special about America in terms of its cultural and religious values and also in terms of the can-do, vibrant spirit of the American people—a spirit that remains a source of optimism for millions, despite data showing widespread skepticism among Americans about supporting their retirement, paying for their aging parents' health care, or seeing their children surpass their own living standards or educational attainment.

The solutions we have tried to emphasize are those that don't focus merely on increasing federal spending. We came up with a series of cost-effective ideas in a variety of policy areas to demonstrate that the American people, working with a responsible federal government, can make the country work better—not as a battle between right and left but as a responsive country that unites around common values and supports commonsense policies, if these policies are shown to advance the greater good.

We see this book as urgent, involving a series of challenges that can't be ignored. Our national decline simply cannot continue indefinitely without causing irreversible damage. As we hope this book has demonstrated, the polarization in our politics, the extreme divisiveness of the 2016 presidential campaign, and the continued divided nature of our government mean that we cannot go forward without solutions that transcend partisan warfare. Our work also concludes, candidly, that there is no substitute for a reassertion of the American role globally and the revitalization of our military, weapons systems, and nuclear arsenal.

Our worldview is not ideological but practical. Our emphasis is on what works, regardless of where on the political spectrum it originates. We welcome feedback and responsiveness from people of goodwill who share our concerns about the country's future and who are willing to embrace some new ideas and reinvigorate some venerable and proven values. The future is unwritten: it remains in our hands to write. America's best days can still lie ahead. But there is much to be done.

# NOTES

## INTRODUCTION

1  Melanie Hunter, "Panetta: 'Biggest National Security Threat' to U.S. Is Total Dysfunction in Washington," CNS News, February 15, 2015, http://www.cnsnews.com/news/article/melanie-hunter/panetta-biggest-national-security-threat-us-total-dysfunction-washington.

2  Fareed Zakaria, "Are America's Best Days Behind Us?" *Time*, March 3, 2011, http://content.time.com/time/magazine/article/0,9171,2056723,00.html.

3  Michael Lind, "The American Century Is Over: How Our Country Went Down in a Blaze of Shame," *Salon*, July 12, 2014, http://www.salon.com/2014/07/12/the_american_century_is_over_how_our_country_went_down_in_a_blaze_of_shame/.

4  Kellan Howell, "Secret Service Flaws Laid Bare in Report over White House Fence Jumper," *WJLA*, April 19, 2016, http://wjla.com/news/nation-world/secret-service-flaws-laid-bare-in-report-over-white-house-fence-jumper.

5  Natalie Wexler, "Why Americans Can't Write," *Washington Post*, September 24, 2015, https://www.washingtonpost.com/opinions/why-americans-cant-write/2015/09/24/6e7f420a-6088-11e5-9757-e49273f05f65_story.html.

6  "NAEP Report Cards," *The Nation's Report Card*, http://www.nationsreportcard.gov/.

7  Ibid.

8  Kayla Webley, "ACT Scores Show 1 in 4 High School Grads Are Unprepared for College," *Time*, August 18, 2011, http://newsfeed.time.com/2011/08/18/act-scores-show-only-1-in-4-high-school-grads-are-ready-for-college/.

9  Ibid.

10 "Results from PISA 2012," Organisation for Economic Co-Operation and Development, 2012, http://www.oecd.org/pisa/keyfindings/PISA-2012-results-US.pdf.

11 Jillian Berman, "Watch America's Student-Loan Debt Grow $2,726 Every Second," *MarketWatch*, January 30, 2016, http://www.marketwatch.com/story/every-second-americans-get-buried-under-another-3055-in-student-loan-debt-2015-06-10.

12 Aimee Picchi, "Congrats, Class of 2016: You're the Most Indebted Yet," *CBS News*, May 4, 2016, http://www.cbsnews.com/news/congrats-class-of-2016-youre-the-most-indebted-yet/.

13 Betsy Mayotte, "Falling Student Loan Default Rates Still Challenge Borrowers," *U.S. News*, October 7, 2015, http://www.usnews.com/education/blogs/student-loan-ranger/2015/10/07/falling-student-loan-default-rates-still-challenge-borrowers.

14 "America's New Aristocracy," *Economist*, January 24, 2015, http://www.economist.com/news/leaders/21640331-importance-intellectual-capital-grows-privilege-has-become-increasingly.

15  Melanie Dostis, "Degree Alone Not Enough to Prepare Grads," *USA Today*, October 31, 2013. http://www.usatoday.com/story/news/nation/2013/10/31/more-than-a-college-degree/3324303/.

16  Meredith Kolodner, "Fewer Than One in Seven Community College Students Transfer and Get Bachelor's Degree—But There Is Hope," *Hechinger Report*, January 19, 2016, http://hechingerreport.org/how-often-do-community-college-students-who-get-transfer-get-bachelors-degrees/.

17  Donna Cooper, Adam Hersh, and Ann O'Leary, "The Competition That Really Matters," *Center for American Progress*, August 21, 2012, https://www.americanprogress.org/wp-content/uploads/2012/08/USChinaIndiaEduCompetitiveness.pdf.

18  Richard Arum and Josipa Roksa, *Academically Adrift: Limited Learning on College Campuses* (Chicago: University of Chicago Press, 2011).

19  Bob Herbert, "College the Easy Way," *New York Times*, March 4, 2011, http://www.nytimes.com/2011/03/05/opinion/05herbert.html.

20  Ibid.

21  Mary Ann Zehr, "NAEP Scores for 17-Year-Olds Flat Since 1970s," *Education Week*, April 28, 2009, http://blogs.edweek.org/edweek/curriculum/2009/04/scores_for_17yearolds_flat_sin.html.

22  "An Interview with the President," *Economist*, August 2, 2014.

23  Jason Furman, Maurice Obstfeld, and Betsey Stevenson, "The 2015 Economic Report of the President," White House, February 19, 2015, http://www.whitehouse.gov/blog/2015/02/19/2015-economic-report-president.

24  "Labor Force Statistics from the Current Population Survey," Bureau of Labor Statistics, last updated February 2015, http://data.bls.gov/timeseries/LNS14000000.

25  Patrick Gillespie, "Unemployment Falls to 4.9%, Lowest in 8 Years," CNN News, February 5, 2016, http://money.cnn.com/2016/02/05/news/economy/us-economy-january-jobs-report/.

26  Reuters, "New Claims for Jobless Aid Hit Lowest Level Since 2000," *New York Times*, January 29, 2015, http://www.nytimes.com/2015/01/30/business/economy/new-claims-for-jobless-aid-hit-lowest-level-since-2000.html.

27  Josh Zumbrun, "Have Most Economic Indicators Improved Under Obama?" *Wall Street Journal*, August 4, 2014.

28  Rich Miller and Steve Matthews, "The U.S. Economic Recovery—Long, Slow, but Still Going," *Bloomberg Business*, June 13, 2013.

29  Peter Coy, "America's Low-Paying Recovery: More Than Ever, Worse Wages," *Bloomberg Business*, August 11, 2014.

30  Ibid.

31  Annie Lowrey, "Recovery Has Created Far More Low-Wage Jobs Than Better-Paid Ones," *New York Times*, April 27, 2014.

32  "Labor Force Statistics from the Current Population Survey," *Bureau of Labor Statistics*, http://data.bls.gov/timeseries/LNS15000000.

33  "Labor Force Statistics from the Current Population Survey," *Bureau of Labor Statistics*, https://data.bls.gov/timeseries/LNS11300000.

34  "America's Wealth Gap between Middle-Income and Upper-Income Families Is Widest on Record," Pew Research Center, December 17, 2014, http://www.pewresearch.org/fact-tank/2014/12/17/wealth-gap-upper-middle-income/.

35  Dionne Searcey and Robert Gebeloff, "Middle Class Shrinks Further as More Fall Out Instead of Climbing Up," *New York Times*, January 25, 2015.

36  Michael E. Porter and Jan W. Rivkin, "The Looming Challenge to U.S. Competitiveness," *Harvard Business Review*, March 2012, https://hbr. org/2012/03/the-looming-challenge-to-us-competitiveness.

37  David Alexander and Andrea Shalal, "U.S. Defense Budget Focuses on Changing Security Environment: Carter," Reuters, February 2, 2016, http:// www.reuters.com/article/us-usa-defense-budget-idUSKCN0VB1HX.

38  Craig Whitlock and Greg Jaffe, "Obama Announces New, Leaner Military Approach," *Washington Post*, January 5, 2012, http://www.washingtonpost.com/ world/national-security/obama-announces-new-military-approach/2012/ 01/05/gIQAFWcmcP_story.html.

39  Rowan Scarborough, "U.S. Military Decimated Under Obama, Only 'Marginally Able' to Defend Nation," *Washington Times*, February 24, 2015, http://www.washingtontimes.com/news/2015/feb/24/us-military-decimated-under-obama-only-marginally-/.

40  Craig Whitlock and Greg Jaffe, "Obama Announces New, Leaner Military Approach," *Washington Post*, January 5, 2012, http://www.washingtonpost. com/world/national-security/obama-announces-new-military-approach/2012/01/05/gIQAFWcmcP_story.html.

41  Rowan Scarborough, "U.S. Military Decimated Under Obama, Only 'Marginally Able' to Defend Nation," *Washington Times*, February 24, 2015, http://www.washingtontimes.com/news/2015/feb/24/us-military-decimated-under-obama-only-marginally-/.

42  Ibid.

43  Ibid.

44  Ibid.

45  Shreeya Sinha, "Obama's Evolution on ISIS," *New York Times*, June 9, 2015, http://www.nytimes.com/interactive/2015/06/09/world/middleeast/obama-isis-strategy.html.

46  John Bolton, "Doubling Down on a Muddled Foreign Policy," *Wall Street Journal*, May 28, 2014, http://online.wsj.com/articles/john-bolton-doubling-down-on-a-muddled-foreign-policy-1401317355.

47  Michelle Ye Hee Lee, "Does the United States Really Have 5 Percent of the World's Population and One Quarter of the World's Prisoners?" *Washington Post*, April 30, 2015, https://www.washingtonpost.com/news/fact-checker/ wp/2015/04/30/does-the-united-states-really-have-five-percent-of-worlds-population-and-one-quarter-of-the-worlds-prisoners/.

48  Carl Hulse, "Unlikely Cause Unites the Left and the Right: Justice Reform," *New York Times*, February 18, 2015, http://www.nytimes.com/2015/02/19/us/ politics/unlikely-cause-unites-the-left-and-the-right-justice-reform.html.

49  "Offenses," Federal Bureau of Prisons, http://www.bop.gov/about/statistics/ statistics_inmate_offenses.jsp.

50  Paul Waldman, "Six Charts That Explain Why Our Prison System Is So Insane," *American Prospect*, August 15, 2013, https://prospect.org/article/six-charts-explain-why-our-prison-system-so-insane.

51  Ibid.

52  John S. Baker, "Revisiting the Explosive Growth of Federal Crimes," Heritage

Foundation, June 16, 2008, http://www.heritage.org/research/reports/2008/06/revisiting-the-explosive-growth-of-federal-crimes.

53  "One Nation, Behind Bars," *Economist*, August 15, 2013, http://www.economist.com/news/leaders/21583680-eric-holders-ideas-locking-up-fewer-americans-are-welcome-do-not-go-far-enough-one.

54  "What It Covers: Social Security," Heritage Foundation, http://savingthedream.org/what-it-covers/social-security/.

55  Tara Parker-Pope, "Too Much Medicare Care?" *New York Times*, July 25, 2012, http://well.blogs.nytimes.com/2012/07/25/too-much-medical-care/.

56  Theresa Tamkins, "Medical Bills Prompt More Than 60 Percent of U.S. Bankruptcies," CNN News, June 5, 2009, http://www.cnn.com/2009/HEALTH/06/05/bankruptcy.medical.bills/.

57  "Key Facts About the Uninsured Population," Kaiser Family Foundation, September 29, 2016, http://kff.org/uninsured/fact-sheet/key-facts-about-the-uninsured-population/.

58  "Confidence in Institutions," *Gallup*, June 1–5, 2016, http://www.gallup.com/poll/1597/confidence-institutions.aspx.

59  Nolan Feeney, "Violent Crime Drops to Lowest Level Since 1978," *Time*, November 10, 2014, http://time.com/3577026/crime-rates-drop-1970s/.

60  Jeffrey M. Jones, "In U.S., Confidence in Police Lowest in 22 Years," *Gallup*, June 19, 2015, http://www.gallup.com/poll/183704/confidence-police-lowest-years.aspx.

61  Frank Newport, "Gallup Review: Black and White Attitudes Toward Police," *Gallup*, August 20, 2014, http://www.gallup.com/poll/175088/gallup-review-black-white-attitudes-toward-police.aspx.

62  "Confidence in Institutions," *Gallup*, June 1–5, 2016, http://www.gallup.com/poll/1597/confidence-institutions.aspx.

63  Ron Fournier and Sophie Quinton, "In Nothing We Trust," *National Journal*, April 19, 2012, http://www.nationaljournal.com/s/65927/nothing-we-trust.

64  "Children in Single-Parent Families by Race," Kids Count Data Center, http://datacenter.kidscount.org/data/tables/107-children-in-single-parent-families-by#detailed/1/any/false/869,36,868,867,133/10,11,9,12,1,185,13/432,431.

65  "Marriage and Divorce," Centers for Disease Control and Prevention, http://www.cdc.gov/nchs/fastats/marriage-divorce.htm.

66  Pamela Engel, "Map: Divorce Rates Around the World," *Business Insider*, May 25, 2014, http://www.businessinsider.com/map-divorce-rates-around-the-world-2014-5.

67  Carol Morello, "Married Couples at a Record Low," *Washington Post*, December 14, 2011, http://www.washingtonpost.com/local/married-couples-at-a-record-low/2011/12/13/gIQAnJyYsO_story.html.

68  "Households and Families: 2010," United States Census Bureau, April 2012, https://www.census.gov/prod/cen2010/briefs/c2010br-14.pdf.

69  "Census Bureau Reports 64 Percent Increase in Number of Children Living with a Grandparent over Last Two Decades," United States Census Bureau, June 29, 2011, https://www.census.gov/newsroom/releases/archives/children/cb11-117.html.

70  Caroline May, "The Number of Babies Born Out of Wedlock in the US Is Soaring," *Business Insider*, February 21, 2012, http://www.businessinsider.com/the-number-of-babies-born-out-of-wedlock-in-the-us-is-soaring-2012-2.

71  Melissa Schettini Kearney and Phillip B. Levine, "Why Is the Teen Birth Rate in the United States So High and Why Does It Matter?" National Center for Biotechnology Information, Spring 2012, http://www.ncbi.nlm.nih.gov/pubmed/22792555.

72  David Gardner, "One in 15 Americans Now Officially Living in Poverty as Number Receiving Food Stamps Rises 8.1% in a Year," *Daily Mail*, November 3, 2011, http://www.dailymail.co.uk/news/article-2056864/Handout-nation-Food-stamp-map-America-reveals-hotspots-15-population-government-help.html.

73  Michael Snyder, "More Than 1 in 5 American Children Are Now Living Below the Poverty Line," *Economic Collapse*, June 10, 2010, http://theeconomiccollapseblog.com/archives/more-than-1-in-5-american-children-are-now-living-below-the-poverty-line.

74  Brady E. Hamilton and Paul D. Sutton, "Recent Trends in Births and Fertility Rates Through December 2012," Centers for Disease Control and Prevention, June 6, 2013, http://www.cdc.gov/nchs/data/hestat/births_fertility_december_2012/births_fertility_december_2012.htm.

75  Melanie Hunter, "Panetta: 'Biggest National Security Threat' to U.S. Is Total Dysfunction in Washington," CNS News, February 15, 2015, http://www.cnsnews.com/news/article/melanie-hunter/panetta-biggest-national-security-threat-us-total-dysfunction-washington.

76  Kevin Short, "The American Dream Is Dying: Poll," *Huffington Post*, June 6, 2014, http://www.huffingtonpost.com/2014/06/06/american-dream-impossible_n_5453854.html.

## CHAPTER 1

1  George Stephanopoulos, "Matthew Dowd: Secret Service, GSA Scandals Undermine Faith in Institutions," ABC News, April 22, 2012, http://abcnews.go.com/blogs/politics/2012/04/matthew-dowd-secret-service-gsa-scandals-undermine-faith-in-institutions/.

2  Seth Freed Wessler, "Middle Class Betrayal? Why Working Hard Is No Longer Enough in America," NBC News, March 16, 2015, http://www.nbcnews.com/feature/in-plain-sight/middle-class-betrayal-why-working-hard-no-longer-enough-america-n291741.

3  Marc J. Hetherington and Thomas J. Rudolph, *Why Washington Won't Work: Polarization, Political Trust, and the Governing Crisis* (Chicago: University of Chicago Press, 2015).

4  Jeffrey M. Jones, "Confidence in U.S. Institutions Still Below Historical Norms," *Gallup*, June 15, 2015, http://www.gallup.com/poll/183593/confidence-institutions-below-historical-norms.aspx.

5  "Direction of Country," *Real Clear Politics*, http://www.realclearpolitics.com/epolls/other/direction_of_country-902.html.

6  Chris Arnade, "Who Still Believes in the American Dream?" *Atlantic*, September 23, 2015, http://www.theatlantic.com/business/archive/2015/09/american-dreams-portraits/405907/.

7  Ariel Edwards-Levy, "Americans Aren't Sure Anything in America Works Anymore," *Huffington Post*, November 17, 2015, http://www.huffingtonpost.com/entry/america-future-survey_us_564bae1de4b045bf3df193bd.

8  Ibid.

9  Ibid.

10	Ted Johnson, "Bernie Sanders Rails Against 'Rigged' Economy at L.A. Rally," *Yahoo.com*, August 11, 2015, https://www.yahoo.com/movies/bernie-sanders-rails-against-rigged-economy-l-rally-062437663.html.

11	"Donald Trump Transcript: 'Our Country Needs a Truly Great Leader,'" *Wall Street Journal*, June 16, 2015, http://blogs.wsj.com/washwire/2015/06/16/donald-trump-transcript-our-country-needs-a-truly-great-leader/.

12	Chris Arnade, "Who Still Believes in the American Dream?" *Atlantic*, September 23, 2015, http://www.theatlantic.com/business/archive/2015/09/american-dreams-portraits/405907/.

13	Doyle McManus, "Is the American Dream Really Dying?" *Los Angeles Times*, May 20, 2015, http://www.latimes.com/opinion/op-ed/la-oe-0520-mcmanus-cruz-pessimism-20150520-column.html.

14	Tami Luhby, "The American Dream Is Out of Reach," CNN News, June 4, 2014, http://money.cnn.com/2014/06/04/news/economy/american-dream/.

15	Aaron Blake, "The American Dream Is Hurting," *Washington Post*, September 24, 2014, https://www.washingtonpost.com/news/the-fix/wp/2014/09/24/the-american-dream-is-hurting/.

16	Ibid.

17	"The American Dream," *Atlantic/Aspen Institute*, June 2015, https://www.scribd.com/doc/270133740/The-American-Dream?secret_password=1Rj95jqAHMgw9Cddc7Jq; Don Baer and Mark Penn, "The American Dream: Personal Optimists, National Pessimists," *Atlantic*, July 1, 2015, http://www.theatlantic.com/national/archive/2015/07/aspen-ideas-american-dream-survey/397274/.

18	Tami Luhby, "Who Still Believes in the American Dream? Blacks and Hispanics," CNN News, July 2, 2015, http://money.cnn.com/2015/07/02/news/economy/blacks-hispanics-american-dream/.

19	Ibid.

20	Tami Luhby, "Why Blacks Believe in the American Dream More Than Whites," CNN News, November 25, 2015, http://money.cnn.com/2015/11/24/news/economy/race-american-dream/.

21	Richard Eskow, "7 Facts That Show the American Dream Is Dead," *Alternet*, October 22, 2014, http://www.alternet.org/economy/7-facts-show-american-dream-dead.

22	Binyamin Appelbaum, "Family Net Worth Drops to Level of Early '90s, Fed Says," *New York Times*, June 11, 2012, http://www.nytimes.com/2012/06/12/business/economy/family-net-worth-drops-to-level-of-early-90s-fed-says.html.

23	Marianne Cooper, "The Downsizing of the American Dream," *Atlantic*, October 2, 2015, http://www.theatlantic.com/business/archive/2015/10/american-dreams/408535/.

24	Christopher Ingraham, "Guess Who's Losing Faith in the American Dream? Everyone," *Washington Post*, September 24, 2014, https://www.washingtonpost.com/news/wonk/wp/2014/09/24/guess-whos-losing-faith-in-the-american-dream-everyone/.

25	Josh Boak, "America's Crushing Surge of Student Debt Has Bred a Disturbing New Phenomenon," *Business Insider*, October 5, 2015, http://www.businessinsider.com/americas-crushing-surge-of-student-debt-has-bred-a-disturbing-new-phenomenon-2015-10.

26  Rep. Carolyn Maloney, "The Student Debt Crisis Solution," *Politico Magazine*, October 4, 2015, http://www.politico.com/magazine/story/2015/10/the-answer-to-the-student-loan-debt-crisis-213217.

27  Ron Fournier and Sophie Quinton, "How Americans Lost Trust in Our Greatest Institutions," *Atlantic*, April 20, 2012, http://www.theatlantic.com/politics/archive/2012/04/how-americans-lost-trust-in-our-greatest-institutions/256163/.

28  Jeffrey M. Jones, "Confidence in U.S. Institutions Still Below Historical Norms," *Gallup*, June 15, 2015, http://www.gallup.com/poll/183593/confidence-institutions-below-historical-norms.aspx.

29  "Trust in America: Recovering What's Lost," NPR, October 30, 2011, http://www.npr.org/2011/10/30/141844751/trust-in-america-recovering-whats-lost.

30  Jeffrey M. Jones, "Trust in Federal Gov't on Domestic Matters Edges to New Low," *Gallup*, September 24, 2015, http://www.gallup.com/poll/185876/trust-federal-gov-domestic-matters-edges-new-low.aspx.

31  Ibid.

32  Matthew Boyle, "Sen. Ben Sasse's Maiden Floor Speech: Since 'The People Despise Us All,' Why Even Have a U.S. Senate?" *Breitbart*, November 3, 2015, http://www.breitbart.com/big-government/2015/11/03/sen-ben-sasses-maiden-floor-speech-since-the-people-despise-us-all-why-even-have-a-u-s-senate/.

33  Jennifer Agiesta, "Poll: Most Americans Say Send Ground Troops to Fight ISIS," CNN News, December 7, 2015, http://www.cnn.com/2015/12/06/politics/isis-obama-poll/index.html.

34  Thomas McArdle, "Americans Doubt Obama's Plan, Resolve to Fight ISIS: IBD/TIPP Poll," *Investor's Business Daily*, April 5, 2016, http://www.investors.com/politics/ibdtipp-poll-distrust-on-what-obama-does-and-says-on-isis-terror/.

35  Marc Hetherington, "Trust in Trump Comes from Lack of Trust in Government," Brookings, September 16, 2015, http://www.brookings.edu/blogs/fixgov/posts/2015/09/16-republican-debate-hetherington.

36  Anthony Salvanto, "Why Don't Americans Trust Government?" CBS News, February 13, 2013, http://www.cbsnews.com/news/why-don't-americans-trust-government/.

37  Patrick Caddell, Scott Miller, and Bob Perkins, "It's Candidate Smith by a Landslide," *Huffington Post*, September 3, 2014, http://www.huffingtonpost.com/patrick-caddell/its-candidate-smith-by-a-_b_5552229.html.

38  Ibid.

39  Ibid.

40  "Trust in Government Plunges to Historic Low," *Edelman*, January 19, 2014, http://www.edelman.com/news/trust-in-government-plunges-to-historic-low/.

41  "Financial Trust Index," Chicago Booth/Kellogg School, December 2015, http://financialtrustindex.org/.

42  Andrew Dugan, "Americans Still More Confident in Small vs. Big Business," *Gallup*, July 6, 2015, http://www.gallup.com/poll/183989/americans-confident-small-big-business.aspx.

43  Jeff Zilka, "The State of Trust in Financial Services," *Edelman*, June 8, 2015, http://www.edelman.com/post/the-state-of-trust-in-financial-services/.

44  Andrew Dugan, "Americans Still More Confident in Small vs. Big Business," *Gallup*, July 6, 2015, http://www.gallup.com/poll/183989/americans-confident-small-big-business.aspx.

45  "Confidence in Institutions," *Gallup*, June 1–5, 2016, http://www.gallup.com/
    poll/1597/confidence-institutions.aspx.

46  Alap Naik Desai, "43 Percent Americans Don't Trust Banks—Here's
    Why It Makes Sense," *Inquisitr*, March 12, 2015, http://www.inquisitr.
    com/1917491/43-percent-americans-dont-trust-banks/.

47  Rebecca Riffkin, "Americans' Trust in Media Remains at Historical Low,"
    *Gallup*, September 28, 2015, http://www.gallup.com/poll/185927/americans-
    trust-media-remains-historical-low.aspx.

48  Jack Shafer, "The Public's Correct Not to Trust the Media," *Politico Magazine*,
    September 30, 2015, http://www.politico.com/magazine/story/2015/09/shafer-
    public-distrust-media-historic-lows-the-public-is-right-chris-cillizza-213208.

49  Ravi Somaiya, "Brian Williams Scandal Shows Power of Social Media," *New
    York Times*, June 21, 2015, http://www.nytimes.com/2015/06/22/business/media/
    brian-williams-scandal-shows-power-of-social-media.html.

50  Ibid.

51  Anita Balakrishnan, "Cruz: This Is Why the American People Don't Trust the
    Media," CNBC News, October 28, 2015, http://www.cnbc.com/2015/10/28/cruz-
    this-is-why-we-dont-trust-the-media.html.

52  James Taranto, "Thanks, Zack," *Wall Street Journal*, October 5, 2015, http://
    www.wsj.com/articles/thanks-zack-1444069559.

53  Jeffrey M. Jones, "Confidence in U.S. Institutions Still Below Historical
    Norms," *Gallup*, June 15, 2015, http://www.gallup.com/poll/183593/confidence-
    institutions-below-historical-norms.aspx.

54  Ibid.

55  Dan Merica, "Poll: America Losing Its Religion," CNN News, May 29, 2013,
    http://religion.blogs.cnn.com/2013/05/29/poll-america-losing-its-religion/.

56  Lydia Saad, "Confidence in Religion at New Low, but Not Among Catholics,"
    *Gallup*, June 17, 2015, http://www.gallup.com/poll/183674/confidence-religion-
    new-low-not-among-catholics.aspx.

57  Ron Fournier and Sophie Quinton, "In Nothing We Trust," *National Journal*,
    April 19, 2012, http://www.nationaljournal.com/s/65927/nothing-we-trust.

58  Frank Newport, "U.S. Confidence in Police Recovers from Last Year's Low,"
    *Gallup*, June 14, 2016, http://www.gallup.com/poll/192701/confidence-police-
    recovers-last-year-low.aspx.

59  Jeffrey M. Jones, "Confidence in U.S. Institutions Still Below Historical
    Norms," *Gallup*, June 15, 2015, http://www.gallup.com/poll/183593/confidence-
    institutions-below-historical-norms.aspx.

60  Byron Dobson, "Poll: Blacks, Whites Agree Police Treat Blacks Differently,"
    *USA Today*, September 9, 2015, http://www.usatoday.com/story/news/
    nation/2015/09/09/poll-blacks-whites-agree-police-treat-blacks-differently
    /71918706/.

61  Ibid.

62  Ibid.

63  Jason Millman, "This Is Obama's Explanation for Why You Might Not Get to
    Keep Your Doctor," *Washington Post*, March 14, 2014, https://www.
    washingtonpost.com/news/wonk/wp/2014/03/14/this-is-obamas-explanation-
    for-why-you-might-not-get-to-keep-your-doctor/.

64  "Confidence in Institutions," *Gallup*, June 1–5, 2016, http://www.gallup.com/
    poll/1597/confidence-institutions.aspx.

# CHAPTER 2

1 Walter Russell Mead, "A Drought of Ideas," *American Interest*, April 11, 2016, http://www.the-american-interest.com/2016/04/11/a-drought-of-ideas/.

2 Howard Kurtz, "Why the 112th Congress Was the Worst, and the Next One Won't Be Much Better," *Daily Beast*, January 3, 2013, http://www.thedailybeast.com/articles/2013/01/03/why-the-112th-congress-was-the-worst-and-the-next-one-won-t-be-much-better.html.

3 Dana Blanton, "Fox News Poll: Voters Show Anxiety About Guns, Terrorism," Fox News, June 29, 2016, http://www.foxnews.com/politics/2016/06/29/fox-news-poll-voters-show-anxiety-about-guns-terrorism.html.

4 Christopher Ingraham, "From 2004 to 2014, Over 2,000 Terror Suspects Legally Purchased Guns in the United States," *Washington Post*, November 16, 2015, https://www.washingtonpost.com/news/wonk/wp/2015/11/16/why-the-nra-opposed-laws-to-prevent-suspected-terrorists-from-buying-guns/.

5 "Confidence in Institutions," *Gallup*, June 1–5, 2016, http://www.gallup.com/poll/1597/confidence-institutions.aspx.

6 George Gao, "15 Striking Findings from 2015," Pew Research Center, December 22, 2015, http://www.pewresearch.org/fact-tank/2015/12/22/15-striking-findings-from-2015/.

7 Amber Phillips, "Time for a Political Revolution? Not Quite," *Washington Post*, September 14, 2015, https://www.washingtonpost.com/news/the-fix/wp/2015/09/14/americans-are-ticked-off-with-washington-but-they-arent-revolutionaries/.

8 Jim Geraghty, "A Dysfunctional Government, Top to Bottom," *National Review*, June 11, 2014, http://www.nationalreview.com/article/380066/dysfunctional-government-top-bottom-jim-geraghty.

9 Kate Pickert, "Report: Cost of HealthCare.Gov Approaching $1 Billion," *Time Magazine*, July 30, 2014, http://time.com/3060276/obamacare-affordable-care-act-cost/.

10 Paul C. Light, "Government's Most Visible Failures, 2001–2014," Brookings, July 14, 2014, http://www.brookings.edu/research/interactives/2014/paul-light-gov-failures.

11 Elisha Anderson, "People of Flint Speak: 'Nobody Should Be Living Like This,'" *Detroit Free Press*, January 17, 2016, http://www.freep.com/story/news/local/michigan/flint-water-crisis/2016/01/17/people-live-with-flint-water-crisis/78860228/.

12 Nicholas Kristof, "America Is Flint," *New York Times*, February 6, 2016, http://www.nytimes.com/2016/02/07/opinion/sunday/america-is-flint.html.

13 "Congressional Job Approval," *Real Clear Politics*, http://www.realclearpolitics.com/epolls/other/congressional_job_approval-903.html.

14 Patrick Caddell, Scott Miller, and Bob Perkins, "It's Candidate Smith by a Landslide," *Huffington Post*, September 3, 2014, http://www.huffingtonpost.com/patrick-caddell/its-candidate-smith-by-a-_b_5552229.html.

15 Howard Kurtz, "Why the 112th Congress Was the Worst, and the Next One Won't Be Much Better," *Daily Beast*, January 3, 2013, http://www.thedailybeast.com/articles/2013/01/03/why-the-112th-congress-was-the-worst-and-the-next-one-won-t-be-much-better.html.

16 Chris Cillizza, "Is Polarization Really All Republicans Fault?" *Washington Post*, April 30, 2012, https://www.washingtonpost.com/blogs/the-fix/post/

is-polarization-really-all-republicans-fault/2012/04/30/gIQAJXFAsT_blog.
html.

17 Tom McKay, "One Graph Shows Why Nothing Will Ever Get Done in
Washington," Mic.com, May 29, 2014, http://mic.com/articles/90127/
one-graph-shows-why-nothing-will-ever-get-done-in-washington.

18 Stephen Dinan, "114th Congress Breaking Gridlock, the Washington Times
Legislative Futility Index Shows," *Washington Times*, July 20, 2015, http://www.
washingtontimes.com/news/2015/jul/20/114th-congress-breaking-gridlock-
the-washington-ti/.

19 Shannon McGovern, "Why Congress and Washington Are So Dysfunctional,"
*U.S. News*, June 7, 2012, http://www.usnews.com/opinion/articles/2012/06/07/
why-congress-and-washington-are-so-dysfunctional.

20 Patrick O'Connor, "Poll Finds Americans Want Parties to Work Together,"
*Wall Street Journal*, November 19, 2014, http://www.wsj.com/articles/
wsj-nbc-poll-finds-americans-want-parties-to-work-together-1416439838.

21 Greg Sargent, "Morning Plum: Democrats Want Compromise. Republicans
Don't. That's Bad for Democrats," *Washington Post*, November 14, 2014, https://
www.washingtonpost.com/blogs/plum-line/wp/2014/11/14/morning-plum-
democrats-want-compromise-republicans-dont-thats-bad-for-democrats/.

22 Alexandra Jaffe, "Poll: Americans Predict More Gridlock in Full GOP Control
of Congress," CNN News, December 1, 2014, http://www.cnn.com/2014/12/01/
politics/poll-americans-gop-congress-control/.

23 Dave DeFusco, "GOP Most Responsible for Political Dysfunction," School of
Public Affairs at American University, May 14, 2014, http://www.american.edu/
spa/news/gridlock-conference-thomas-mann-2014.cfm.

24 Greg Sargent, "Morning Plum: Democrats Want Compromise. Republicans
Don't. That's Bad for Democrats," *Washington Post*, November 14, 2014, https://
www.washingtonpost.com/blogs/plum-line/wp/2014/11/14/morning-plum-
democrats-want-compromise-republicans-dont-thats-bad-for-democrats/.

25 Sahil Kapur, "Filibuster Opponents Have Gone Quiet Since Democrats
Lost the Senate," *Bloomberg Politics*, September 8, 2015, http://www.bloomberg.
com/politics/articles/2015-09-08/filibuster-opponents-have-gone-quiet-
since-democrats-lost-the-senate.

26 Ed O'Keefe and Phillip Rucker, "Gun-Control Overhaul Is Defeated in Senate,"
*Washington Post*, April 17, 2013, https://www.washingtonpost.com/politics/gun-
control-overhaul-is-defeated-in-senate/2013/04/17/57eb028a-a77c-11e2-b029-
8fb7e977ef71_story.html.

27 Brentin Mock, "Mapping How Guns Get Around Despite Background
Check Laws," *Atlantic Citylab*, October 22, 2015, http://www.citylab.com/
crime/2015/10/mapping-how-guns-get-around-despite-background-
checks/411946/.

28 W. Gardner Selby, "Jeremy Bird Says 90 Percent of Americans Want Mandatory
Background Checks for All Gun Purchases," *PolitiFact Texas*, October 5,
2015, http://www.politifact.com/texas/statements/2015/oct/05/jeremy-bird/
jeremy-bird-says-90-percent-americans-want-mandato/.

29 Art Swift, "Americans' Desire for Stricter Gun Laws Up Sharply," *Gallup*,
October 19, 2015, http://www.gallup.com/poll/186236/americans-desire-stricter-
gun-laws-sharply.aspx.

30 Louis Jacobson and J.B. Wogan, "Ryan and the Simpson-Bowles Commission: The Full Story," *PolitiFact*, August 30, 2012, http://www.politifact.com/truth-o-meter/article/2012/aug/30/ryan-and-simpson-bowles-commission-full-story/.

31 Doug Schoen, "The Compromise That Americans Want to Break the Budget Deadlock," *Forbes*, April 2, 2013, http://www.forbes.com/sites/dougschoen/2013/04/02/the-compromising-way-forward/.

32 Ibid.

33 Stephen Dinan, "Interceptions of Immigrants Stubbornly Low," *Washington Times*, January 9, 2013, http://m.washingtontimes.com/news/2013/jan/9/interceptions-immigrants-stubbornly-low/.

34 Stephen Dinan, "700 Miles of U.S.-Mexico Border Still Insecure, Congressional Investigators Say," *Washington Times*, January 3, 2015, http://www.washingtontimes.com/news/2015/jan/3/700-miles-us-mexico-border-still-insecure-congress/.

35 Jennifer Steinhauer, "Republicans Land a Punch on Health Care, To Their Own Face," *New York Times*, March 24, 2017, https://www.nytimes.com/2017/03/24/us/politics/house-republicans-health-care-paul-ryan.html.

36 Ezra Klein, "The Failure of the Republican Health Care Bill Reveals a Party Unready to Govern," Vox, March 24, 2017, http://www.vox.com/policy-and-politics/2017/3/24/15054446/gop-health-bill-ahca.

37 David Lawder and Steve Holland, "Trump Tastes Failure as U.S. Healthcare Bill Collapses," *Reuters*, March 25, 2017, http://www.reuters.com/article/us-usa-obamacare-idUSKBN16V149.

38 Kevin Liptak, "Trump: 'Nobody Knew Health Care Could Be So Complicated,'" CNN, February 28, 2017, http://www.cnn.com/2017/02/27/politics/trump-health-care-complicated/.

39 Joseph Burgo, "The Psychology of Unity After Tragedy," *Atlantic*, April 20, 2013, http://www.theatlantic.com/health/archive/2013/04/the-psychology-of-unity-after-tragedy/275158/.

40 David Blankenhorn, "Why Polarization Matters," *American Interest*, December 22, 2015, http://www.the-american-interest.com/2015/12/22/why-polarization-matters/.

41 Ibid.

42 John Podhoretz, "These Are the People Who Would Lead This Great Nation?" *New York Post*, April 16, 2016, http://nypost.com/2016/04/16/these-are-the-people-who-would-lead-this-great-nation/.

43 Dylan Stableford, "Majority of Americans Can't Fathom Supporting Trump or Clinton (or Cruz)," *Yahoo News*, April 19, 2016, https://www.yahoo.com/news/trump-clinton-cruz-majority-wont-support-143030280.html.

44 Matt Vella, "Bill Clinton's 3-Word Secret to Leading the World," *Time*, March 21, 2014, http://time.com/33349/bill-clintons-3-word-secret-to-leading-the-world/.

45 Walter Russell Mead, "A Drought of Ideas," *American Interest*, April 11, 2016, http://www.the-american-interest.com/2016/04/11/a-drought-of-ideas/.

46 Shannon McGovern, "Why Congress and Washington Are So Dysfunctional," *U.S. News*, June 7, 2012, http://www.usnews.com/opinion/articles/2012/06/07/why-congress-and-washington-are-so-dysfunctional.

## CHAPTER 3

1 George Washington, "Farewell Address—Transcription," *Papers of George Washington*, http://gwpapers.virginia.edu/documents_gw/farewell/transcript.html.

2 Patrick J. Buchanan, "The West Dies with Its Gods," *American Conservative*, April 26, 2016, http://www.theamericanconservative.com/buchanan/the-west-dies-with-its-gods/.

3 Peter Wehner, "Rebuilding a Marriage Culture in 21st-Century Black and Latino America," *National Review*, February 19, 2016, http://www.nationalreview.com/article/431544/soul-mates-religion-sex-marriage-book-review.

4 Michael Novak, "Crumbling Foundations—Why the Family Is Crucial to Civilization," *CatholiCity.com*, October 15, 2009, http://www.catholicity.com/commentary/mnovak/00062.html.

5 Dennis Prager, "America's Accelerating Decay," *National Review*, April 7, 2015, http://www.nationalreview.com/article/416543/americas-decay-speeding.

6 Family Policy Institute of Washington, "College Kids Say the Darndest Things: On Identity," YouTube video, 4:13, April 13, 2016, https://www.youtube.com/watch?v=xfO1veFs6Ho.

7 "Moral Issues," *Gallup*, May 4–8, 2016, http://www.gallup.com/poll/1681/moral-issues.aspx.

8 Justin McCarthy, "Majority in U.S. Still Say Moral Values Getting Worse," *Gallup*, June 2, 2015, http://www.gallup.com/poll/183467/majority-say-moral-values-getting-worse.aspx.

9 Patrick J. Buchanan, "The West Dies with Its Gods," *American Conservative*, April 26, 2016, http://www.theamericanconservative.com/buchanan/the-west-dies-with-its-gods/.

10 Justin P. McBrayer, "Why Our Children Don't Think There Are Moral Facts," *New York Times*, March 2, 2015, http://opinionator.blogs.nytimes.com/2015/03/02/why-our-children-dont-think-there-are-moral-facts/.

11 Dennis Prager, "America's Decay Is Speeding Up," *Dennis Prager Show*, April 7, 2015, http://www.dennisprager.com/americas-decay-is-speeding-up/.

12 Sarah Pulliam Bailey, "Christianity Faces Sharp Decline as Americans Are Becoming Even Less Affiliated with Religion," *Washington Post*, May 12, 2015, https://www.washingtonpost.com/news/acts-of-faith/wp/2015/05/12/christianity-faces-sharp-decline-as-americans-are-becoming-even-less-affiliated-with-religion/.

13 "America's Changing Religious Landscape," Pew Research Center, May 12, 2015, http://www.pewforum.org/2015/05/12/americas-changing-religious-landscape/.

14 Sarah Pulliam Bailey, "Christianity Faces Sharp Decline as Americans Are Becoming Even Less Affiliated with Religion," *Washington Post*, May 12, 2015, https://www.washingtonpost.com/news/acts-of-faith/wp/2015/05/12/christianity-faces-sharp-decline-as-americans-are-becoming-even-less-affiliated-with-religion/.

15 Ibid.

16 "America's Changing Religious Landscape," Pew Research Center, May 12, 2015, http://www.pewforum.org/2015/05/12/americas-changing-religious-landscape/.

17 Mary Wisniewski, "Americans Becoming Less Religious, Especially Young Adults: Poll," Reuters, November 3, 2015, http://www.reuters.com/article/us-usa-religion-idUSKCN0SS0AM20151103.

18  David Brooks, "The Next Culture War," *New York Times*, June 30, 2015, http://
    www.nytimes.com/2015/06/30/opinion/david-brooks-the-next-culture-war.
    html.

19  John Hinderaker, "Decline of Religion," *Center of American Experiment*, June
    30, 2014, http://www.americanexperiment.org/article/decline-of-religion/.

20  Donna St. George, "Holidays' Names Stricken from Next Year's Montgomery
    Schools Calendar," *Washington Post*, November 11, 2014, https://www.
    washingtonpost.com/local/education/christmas-stricken-from-school-
    calendar-afnter-muslims-ask-for-equal-treatment/2014/11/11/f1b789a6-6931-
    11e4-a31c-77759fc1eacc_story.html.

21  Mercedes Shlapp, "That's Me in the Corner," *U.S. News*, April 18, 2014, http://
    www.usnews.com/opinion/mercedes-schlapp/2014/04/18/the-decline-of-
    religion-will-hurt-america-in-the-long-run.

22  Jason Hanna and Steve Almasy, "Washington High School Coach Placed on
    Leave for Praying on Field," CNN News, October 30, 2015, http://www.cnn.
    com/2015/10/29/us/washington-football-coach-joe-kennedy-prays/.

23  Joan Desmond, "No Sunday Mass at Some Military Bases If Government
    Shutdown Continues," *National Catholic Register*, October 3, 2013, http://www.
    ncregister.com/blog/joan-desmond/no-sunday-mass-at-quantico-if-
    government-shutdown-continues.

24  Janet Levy, "Christianity Under Attack in America," *American Thinker*, October
    25, 2013, http://www.americanthinker.com/articles/2013/10/christianity_under_
    attack_in_america.html.

25  Todd Starnes, "School District Bans the Word 'Christmas' from Flyer," Fox
    News, December 2, 2015, http://www.foxnews.com/opinion/2015/12/02/school-
    district-bans-word-christmas-from-flyer.html.

26  Jason L. Riley, "Christian Belief Cost Kelvin Cochran His Job," *Wall Street
    Journal*, November 10, 2015, http://www.wsj.com/articles/christian-belief-
    cost-kelvin-cochran-his-job-1447200885.

27  Wendy Thomas Russell, "Column: Here's the Church; Here's the Steeple. Open
    the Doors—Where's All the People?" PBS News Hour, September 23, 2015,
    http://www.pbs.org/newshour/updates/heres-church-heres-steeple-open-
    door-wheres-people/.

28  "Public Sees Religion's Influence Waning," Pew Research Center, September 22,
    2014, http://www.pewforum.org/2014/09/22/public-sees-religions-influence-
    waning-2/.

29  Michael Lipka, "Is Religion's Declining Influence Good or Bad? Those Without
    Religious Affiliation Are Divided," Pew Research Center, September 23, 2014,
    http://www.pewresearch.org/fact-tank/2014/09/23/is-religions-declining-
    influence-good-or-bad-those-without-religious-affiliation-are-divided/.

30  Frank Newport, "Most Americans Say Religion Is Losing Influence in U.S.,"
    *Gallup*, May 29, 2013, http://www.gallup.com/poll/162803/americans-say-
    religion-losing-influence.aspx; Mercedes Shlapp, "That's Me in the Corner,"
    *U.S. News*, April 18, 2014, http://www.usnews.com/opinion/mercedes-
    schlapp/2014/04/18/the-decline-of-religion-will-hurt-america-in-the-long-run.

31  "Religion," *Gallup*, http://www.gallup.com/poll/1690/religion.aspx.

32  Rebecca Riffkin, "In U.S., Support for Daily Prayer in Schools Dips Slightly,"
    *Gallup*, September 25, 2014, http://www.gallup.com/poll/177401/support-daily-
    prayer-schools-dips-slightly.aspx.

33  Ibid.

34 George Washington, "Farewell Address—Transcription," *Papers of George Washington*, http://gwpapers.virginia.edu/documents_gw/farewell/transcript.html.

35 Mercedes Shlapp, "That's Me in the Corner," *U.S. News*, April 18, 2014, http://www.usnews.com/opinion/mercedes-schlapp/2014/04/18/the-decline-of-religion-will-hurt-america-in-the-long-run.

36 Christopher G. Ellison, John P. Bartkowski, and Kristin L. Anderson, "Are There Religious Variations in Domestic Violence?" *Journal of Family Issues* 20 (1997): 87–113.

37 "Religion in Prisons—a 50-State Survey of Prison Chaplains," Pew Research Center, March 22, 2012, http://www.pewforum.org/2012/03/22/prison-chaplains-exec/.

38 "Promoting the Positive: The Link Between Individual Religious Practice and Social Outcomes," Heritage Foundation, http://www.familyfacts.org/briefs/17/promoting-the-positive-the-link-between-individual-religious-practice-and-social-outcomes.

39 Arland Thornton, William G. Axinn, and Daniel H. Hill, "Reciprocal Effects of Religiosity, Cohabitation, and Marriage," *American Journal of Sociology* 98, no. 3 (November 1992): 628–651.

40 Lauren Fox, "The Science of Cohabitation: A Step Toward Marriage, Not a Rebellion," *Atlantic*, March 20, 2014, https://www.theatlantic.com/health/archive/2014/03/the-science-of-cohabitation-a-step-toward-marriage-not-a-rebellion/284512/.

41 Andrew Hough, "Having Faith 'Helps Patients Live Longer,' Study Suggests," *Telegraph*, October 6, 2010, http://www.telegraph.co.uk/news/health/news/8044586/Having-faith-helps-patients-live-longer-study-suggests.html.

42 Alex Daniels, "Religious Americans Give More, New Study Finds," *Chronicle of Philanthropy*, November 25, 2013, https://philanthropy.com/article/Religious-Americans-Give-More/153973.

43 Michael Novak, "Democracy and Religion in America," Catholic Education Resource Center, October 2, 2002, http://www.catholiceducation.org/en/culture/catholic-contributions/democracy-amp-religion-in-america.html.

44 Ibid.

45 Michael Novak, "How Christianity Created Capitalism," Acton Institute, May/June 2000, http://www.acton.org/pub/religion-liberty/volume-10-number-3/how-christianity-created-capitalism.

46 Michael Novak, "Democracy and Religion in America," Catholic Education Resource Center, October 2, 2002, http://www.catholiceducation.org/en/culture/catholic-contributions/democracy-amp-religion-in-america.html.

47 Matthew Continetti, "The Theological Politics of Irving Kristol," *National Affairs*, Summer 2014, http://www.nationalaffairs.com/publications/detail/the-theological-politics-of-irving-kristol.

48 Ibid.

49 Tom Wilson, "Irving Kristol's God," FirstThings.com, March 2015, http://www.firstthings.com/article/2015/03/irving-kristols-god.

50 Matthew Continetti, "The Theological Politics of Irving Kristol," *National Affairs*, Summer 2014, http://www.nationalaffairs.com/publications/detail/the-theological-politics-of-irving-kristol.

51 John-Peter Pham, "Why America Needs Religion," Acton Institute, September/

October 1997, http://www.acton.org/pub/religion-liberty/volume-7-number-5/why-america-needs-religion (page no longer available).

52   Ibid.

53   Gretchen Livingston, "Is U.S. Fertility at an All-Time Low? It Depends," Pew Research Center, February 24, 2015, http://www.pewresearch.org/fact-tank/2015/02/24/is-u-s-fertility-at-an-all-time-low-it-depends/.

54   Dennis Prager, "America's Accelerating Decay," *National Review*, April 7, 2015, http://www.nationalreview.com/article/416543/americas-decay-speeding.

55   Patrick J. Buchanan, "The West Dies with Its Gods," *American Conservative*, April 26, 2016, http://www.theamericanconservative.com/buchanan/the-west-dies-with-its-gods/.

56   Sabrina Tavernise, "Married Couples Are No Longer a Majority, Census Finds," *New York Times*, May 26, 2011, http://www.nytimes.com/2011/05/26/us/26marry.html.

57   Dennis Prager, "America's Accelerating Decay," *National Review*, April 7, 2015, http://www.nationalreview.com/article/416543/americas-decay-speeding.

58   "Children in Single-Parent Families by Race," *Kids Count Data Center*, http://datacenter.kidscount.org/data/tables/107-children-in-single-parent-families-by#detailed/1/any/false/869,36,868,867,133/10,11,9,12,1,185,13/432,431.

59   "When Marriage Disappears: The New Middle America," *State of Our Unions*, 2010, http://stateofourunions.org/2010/SOOU2010.php.

60   Ibid.

61   Ibid.

62   Kay Hymowitz, W. Bradford Wilcox, and Keleen Kaye, "The New Unmarried Moms," March 15, 2013, https://www.wsj.com/articles/SB10001424127887323826704578356494206134184.

63   Gretchen Livingston, "Fewer Than Half of U.S. Kids Today Live in a 'Traditional' Family," Pew Research Center, December 22, 2014, http://www.pewresearch.org/fact-tank/2014/12/22/less-than-half-of-u-s-kids-today-live-in-a-traditional-family/.

64   Gudrun Schultz, "Broken Family Structure Leads to Educational Difficulties for Children," LifeSite News, January 16, 2006, https://www.lifesitenews.com/news/broken-family-structure-leads-to-educational-difficulties-for-children.

65   Larry Bilotta, "18 Shocking Children and Divorce Statistics," *Marriage Success Secrets*, http://www.marriage-success-secrets.com/statistics-about-children-and-divorce.html.

66   Patrick F. Fagan, "How Broken Families Rob Children of Their Chances for Future Prosperity," Heritage Foundation, June 11, 1999, http://www.heritage.org/research/reports/1999/06/broken-families-rob-children-of-their-chances-for-future-prosperity.

67   "Family Structure and Welfare Dependency," Marriage and Religion Research Institute, http://downloads.frc.org/EF/EF14K20.pdf.

68   Ibid.

69   Robert Rector, "How Welfare Undermines Marriage and What to Do About It," Heritage Foundation, November 17, 2014, http://www.heritage.org/research/reports/2014/11/how-welfare-undermines-marriage-and-what-to-do-about-it.

70   Ibid.

71   James Pethokoukis, "Can Anything Really Be Done About Family Breakdown and American Poverty? A Q&A with Brad Wilcox," American Enterprise

Institute, March 11, 2014, http://www.aei.org/publication/can-anything-really-be-done-about-family-breakdown-and-american-poverty-a-qa-with-brad-wilcox/.

72 Frank Newport, "Majority Still Says Religion Can Answer Today's Problems," *Gallup*, June 27, 2014, http://www.gallup.com/poll/171998/majority-says-religion-answer-today-problems.aspx.

73 Ibid.

74 "U.S. Public Becoming Less Religious," Pew Research Center, November 3, 2015, http://www.pewforum.org/2015/11/03/u-s-public-becoming-less-religious/.

75 David Brooks, "The Big University," *New York Times*, October 6, 2015, http://www.nytimes.com/2015/10/06/opinion/david-brooks-the-big-university.html.

76 John-Peter Pham, "Why American Needs Religion," Acton Institute, September/October 1997, http://www.acton.org/pub/religion-liberty/volume-7-number-5/why-america-needs-religion (page no longer available).

77 W. Bradford Wilcox, Robert I. Lerman, and Joseph Price, "Strong Families, Prosperous States: Do Healthy Families Affect the Wealth of States?" American Enterprise Institute and the Institute for Family Studies, October 19, 2015, https://www.aei.org/publication/strong-families-prosperous-states/.

78 James Pethokoukis, "Can Anything Really Be Done About Family Breakdown and American Poverty? A Q&A with Brad Wilcox," *American Enterprise Institute*, March 11, 2014, http://www.aei.org/publication/can-anything-really-be-done-about-family-breakdown-and-american-poverty-a-qa-with-brad-wilcox/.

79 Michael Novak, "Crumbling Foundations—Why the Family Is Crucial to Civilization," *CatholiCity.com*, October 15, 2009, http://www.catholicity.com/commentary/mnovak/00062.html.

80 Ibid.

81 Peter Wehner, "Rebuilding a Marriage Culture in 21st-Century Black and Latino America," *National Review*, February 19, 2016, http://www.nationalreview.com/article/431544/soul-mates-religion-sex-marriage-book-review.

82 Michael Novak, "Crumbling Foundations—Why the Family Is Crucial to Civilization," *CatholiCity.com*, October 15, 2009, http://www.catholicity.com/commentary/mnovak/00062.html.

## CHAPTER 4

1 Dylan Matthews, "Everything You Need to Know About the War on Poverty," *Washington Post*, January 8, 2014, http://www.washingtonpost.com/blogs/wonkblog/wp/2014/01/08/everything-you-need-to-know-about-the-war-on-poverty/.

2 Nicholas Kristof, "The White Underclass," *New York Times*, February 8, 2012, http://www.nytimes.com/2012/02/09/opinion/kristof-the-decline-of-white-workers.html.

3 Jordan Fabian, "Obama Announces Fatherhood Initiative," *The Hill*, June 21, 2010, http://thehill.com/blogs/blog-briefing-room/news/104421-obama-announces-fatherhood-initiative-.

4 "Obama Criticizes Black Deaths by Police, Rioters and Society," *Chicago Tribune*, April 28, 2015, http://www.chicagotribune.com/news/nationworld/chi-baltimore-obama-20150428-story.html.

5  Mark Puente and Erica L. Green, "Mayor, Commissioner Denounce Work of Agitators," *Baltimore Sun*, April 25, 2015, http://www.baltimoresun.com/news/maryland/politics/bs-md-freddie-gray-march-pressers-20150425-story.html.

6  Allen West, "My Greatest Fear About the Baltimore Riots," *Allen B. West* (blog), April 27, 2015, http://allenbwest.com/2015/04/my-greatest-fear-about-the-baltimore-riots/.

7  Elizabeth Chuck, "Baltimore Mayor Stephanie Rawlings-Blake Under Fire for 'Space' to Destroy Comment," NBC News, April 28, 2015, http://www.nbcnews.com/storyline/baltimore-unrest/mayor-stephanie-rawlings-blake-under-fire-giving-space-destroy-baltimore-n349656.

8  Juliet Linderman, "Riots in Baltimore the Product of Anger, Deep Dysfunction," CNS News, April 28, 2015, http://www.cnsnews.com/news/article/riots-baltimore-product-anger-deep-dysfunction.

9  "Daniel Patrick Moynihan Interview," PBS, accessed March 27, 2017, http://www.pbs.org/fmc/interviews/moynihan.htm.

10  Marjorie Valbrun, "Was the Moynihan Report Right? Sobering Findings After 1965 Study Is Revisited," *Washington Post*, June 13, 2013, http://www.washingtonpost.com/local/was-the-moynihan-report-right-sobering-findings-after-1965-study-is-revisited/2013/06/13/80eac980-d432-11e2-b05f-3ea3f0e7bb5a_story.html.

11  Ibid.

12  Jack Kemp, "Jack Kemp in His Own Words," *Wall Street Journal*, May 4, 2009, http://www.wsj.com/articles/SB124139616039181855.

13  Poverty to Prosperity Program and the CAP Economic Policy Team, "Expanding Opportunities in America's Urban Areas," Center for American Progress, March 23, 2015, https://www.americanprogress.org/issues/poverty/report/2015/03/23/109460/expanding-opportunities-in-americas-urban-areas/.

14  Elizabeth Kneebone and Natalie Holmes, "U.S. Concentrated Poverty in the Wake of the Great Recession," Brookings, March 31, 2016, https://www.brookings.edu/research/u-s-concentrated-poverty-in-the-wake-of-the-great-recession/.

15  Sarah Gray, "6 Shocking Facts About Poverty in Baltimore," *Attn:*, April 28, 2015, http://www.attn.com/stories/1541/baltimore-poverty-facts.

16  Bruce Kennedy, "America's 11 Poorest Cities," CBS News, February 18, 2015, http://www.cbsnews.com/media/americas-11-poorest-cities/12/.

17  Dylan Matthews, "Everything You Need to Know About the War on Poverty," *Washington Post*, January 8, 2014, http://www.washingtonpost.com/blogs/wonkblog/wp/2014/01/08/everything-you-need-to-know-about-the-war-on-poverty/.

18  Louis Jacobson, "Are There More Welfare Recipients in the U.S. Than Full-Time Workers?" *PunditFact*, January 28, 2015, http://www.politifact.com/punditfact/statements/2015/jan/28/terry-jeffrey/are-there-more-welfare-recipients-us-full-time-wor/.

19  Michael D. Tanner and Charles Hughes, "War on Poverty Turns 50: Are We Winning Yet?" CATO Institute, October 20, 2014, http://www.cato.org/publications/policy-analysis/war-poverty-turns-50-are-we-winning-yet.

20  Jack Kemp, "Fighting a New War on Poverty," *Townhall*, May 25, 2007, http://townhall.com/columnists/jackkemp/2007/05/25/fighting_a_new_war_on_poverty.

21  Ibid.
22  Jack Coleman, "Juan Williams: Daniel Patrick Moynihan 'Had It Right' About Breakdown of the Black Family," NewsBusters, May 5, 2015, http://newsbusters.org/blogs/jack-coleman/2015/05/05/juan-williams-daniel-patrick-moynihan-had-it-right-about-breakdown.
23  Peter-Christian Aigner, "What the Left and Right Both Get Wrong About the Moynihan Report," *Atlantic*, April 16, 2014, http://www.theatlantic.com/politics/archive/2014/04/what-the-left-and-right-both-get-wrong-about-the-moynihan-report/360701/.
24  Louis Jacobson, "Facebook Meme Blame Great Society for Large Rise in African-American Fatherlessness," *PolitiFact*, March 25, 2014, http://www.politifact.com/truth-o-meter/statements/2014/mar/25/facebook-posts/facebook-meme-blames-great-society-large-rise-afri/.
25  "Children in Single-Parent Families by Race," Kids Count Data Center, accessed March 27, 2017, http://datacenter.kidscount.org/data/tables/107-children-in-single-parent-families-by#detailed/1/any/false/36,868,867,133,38/10,168,9,12,1,13,185/432,431.
26  Louis Jacobson, "Facebook Meme Blame Great Society for Large Rise in African-American Fatherlessness," *PolitiFact*, March 25, 2014, http://www.politifact.com/truth-o-meter/statements/2014/mar/25/facebook-posts/facebook-meme-blames-great-society-large-rise-afri/.
27  Roger Clegg, "Latest Statistics on Out-of-Wedlock Births," *National Review*, October 11, 2013, http://www.nationalreview.com/corner/360990/latest-statistics-out-wedlock-births-roger-clegg.
28  Jesse Washington, "Blacks Struggle with 72 Percent Unwed Mothers Rate," NBC News, November 7, 2010, http://www.nbcnews.com/id/39993685/ns/health-womens_health/t/blacks-struggle-percent-unwed-mothers-rate/.
29  "Single-Parent Families—Demographic Trends," *NetIndustries*, accessed March 27, 2017, http://family.jrank.org/pages/1574/Single-Parent-Families-Demographic-Trends.html.
30  "Single Mother Statistics," Single Mother Guide, accessed March 27, 2017, https://singlemotherguide.com/single-mother-statistics/.
31  Pam Fessler, "One Family's Story Shows How the Cycle of Poverty Is Hard to Break," NPR, May 7, 2014, http://www.npr.org/2014/05/07/309734339/one-familys-story-shows-how-the-cycle-of-poverty-is-hard-to-break.
32  Ibid.
33  George F. Will, "What Patrick Moynihan Knew About the Importance of Two Parents," *Washington Post*, March 13, 2015, https://www.washingtonpost.com/opinions/what-patrick-moynihan-knew-about-the-importance-of-two-parents/2015/03/13/2cdf9bae-c9a4-11e4-aa1a-86135599fb0f_story.html.
34  Jordan Fabian, "Obama Announces Fatherhood Initiative," *The Hill*, June 21, 2010, http://thehill.com/blogs/blog-briefing-room/news/104421-obama-announces-fatherhood-initiative-.
35  Terence P. Jeffrey, "Obama: 'There Will Never Be a Substitute For' Fathers; Obama's DOJ: Children Don't Need Fathers," CNS News, June 15, 2013, http://cnsnews.com/news/article/obama-there-will-never-be-substitute-fathers-obamas-doj-children-dont-need-fathers.
36  Raj Chetty and Nathaniel Hendren, "The Impacts of Neighborhood on

Intergenerational Mobility: Childhood Exposure Effects and County Level Estimates," May 2015, http://scholar.harvard.edu/files/hendren/files/nbhds_paper.pdf.

37 Francis Barry, "Liberals, Try Talking About Family Breakdown," *Bloomberg View*, May 5, 2015, http://www.bloombergview.com/articles/2015-05-05/liberals-try-talking-about-family-breakdown.

38 Ibid.

39 Michael Barone, "Can Family Breakdown in Low-Education America Be Reversed? Maybe," *Washington Examiner*, March 25, 2015, http://www.washingtonexaminer.com/can-family-breakdown-in-low-education-america-be-reversed-maybe/article/2561904.

40 Ibid.

41 Max Ehrenfreund, "This Powerful Reddit Thread Reveals How the Poor Get By in America," *Washington Post*, January 14, 2015, http://www.washingtonpost.com/blogs/wonkblog/wp/2015/01/14/this-powerful-reddit-thread-reveals-how-the-poor-get-by-in-america/.

42 Ibid.

43 Jess Spross, "Want to End Poverty in America? It's Pretty Simple," *The Week*, January 21, 2015, http://theweek.com/articles/534655/want-end-poverty-americaits-pretty-simple.

44 Ibid.

45 Lyndsey Layton, "Majority of U.S. Public School Students Are in Poverty," *Washington Post*, January 16, 2015, http://www.washingtonpost.com/local/education/majority-of-us-public-school-students-are-in-poverty/2015/01/15/df7171d0-9ce9-11e4-a7ee-526210d665b4_story.html.

46 Helen F. Ladd and Edward B. Fiske, "Class Matters; Why Won't We Admit It?" *New York Times*, December 11, 2011, http://www.nytimes.com/2011/12/12/opinion/the-unaddressed-link-between-poverty-and-education.html.

47 Jason Riley, *Please Stop Helping Us: How Liberals Make It Harder for Blacks to Succeed* (New York: Encounter Books, 2014), 21.

48 Ibid., 27.

49 Chico Harlan, "Why the Improvement in the Black Unemployment Rate Will Be Short-Lived," *Washington Post*, May 13, 2015, http://www.washingtonpost.com/news/wonkblog/wp/2015/05/13/why-the-improvement-in-the-black-unemployment-rate-will-be-short-lived/.

50 Noel Sheppard, "Tavis Smiley: 'Black People Will Have Lost Ground in Every Single Economic Indicator' Under Obama," NewsBusters, October 11, 2013, http://newsbusters.org/blogs/noel-sheppard/2013/10/11/tavis-smiley-black-people-will-have-lost-ground-every-single-economic.

51 Riley, *Please Stop Helping Us*, 44.

52 Ibid., 45–46.

53 Ibid., 47.

54 Ibid., 48.

55 Felicia R. Lee, "Why Are Black Students Lagging?" *New York Times*, November 30, 2002, http://www.nytimes.com/2002/11/30/arts/why-are-black-students-lagging.html.

56 "50 Cent Lyrics," AZ Lyrics, http://www.azlyrics.com/lyrics/50cent/straighttothebank.html.

57  Jeffrey Hicks, "How Hip-Hop Destroys the Potential of Black Youth," National Leadership Network of Conservative African-Americans, accessed March 27, 2017, https://www.nationalcenter.org/P21NVHicksHipHop90706.html.

58  Riley, *Please Stop Helping Us*, 52.

59  Jonathan Chait, "Barack Obama, Ta-Nehisi Coates, Poverty, and Culture," *New York Magazine*, March 19, 2014, http://nymag.com/daily/intelligencer/2014/03/obama-ta-nehisi-coates-poverty-and-culture.html.

60  Ibid.

61  DocMartin1, "Jack Kemp and Bob Woodson: Great Ideas!" *DocMartin1* (blog), July 18, 2015, https://docmartin1.wordpress.com/2015/07/18/jack-kemp-and-bob-woodson-great-ideas/.

62  Jill Homan, "How Republicans Can Win Urban Voters," *New York Post*, July 20, 2015, http://nypost.com/2015/07/20/how-republicans-can-win-urban-voters/.

63  Jack Kemp, "Jack Kemp in His Own Words," *Wall Street Journal*, May 4, 2009, http://www.wsj.com/articles/SB124139616039181855.

64  Robert Rector, "How Obama Has Gutted Welfare Reform," *Washington Post*, September 6, 2012, https://www.washingtonpost.com/opinions/how-obama-has-gutted-welfore-reform/2012/09/06/885b0092-f835-11e1-8b93-c4f4ab1c8d13_story.html.

65  Erin Durkin, "De Blasio Eases Work Requirements for Welfare Recipients," *NY Daily News*, October 3, 2014, http://www.nydailynews.com/news/politics/de-blasio-eases-work-requirements-welfare-recipients-article-1.1960571.

66  Paul Ryan, "A Better Way Up from Poverty," *Wall Street Journal*, August 15, 2014, http://www.wsj.com/articles/paul-ryan-a-better-way-up-from-poverty-1408141154.

67  David Dayen, "The Post Office Should Just Become a Bank," *New Republic*, January 28, 2014, https://newrepublic.com/article/116374/postal-service-banking-how-usps-can-save-itself-and-help-poor.

68  Norm Ornstein, "A Plan to Reduce Inequality: Give $1,000 to Every Newborn Baby," *Atlantic*, February 13, 2014, http://www.theatlantic.com/politics/archive/2014/02/a-plan-to-reduce-inequality-give-1-000-to-every-newborn-baby/283819/.

69  Jason Koebler, "Cities Take Aim at Truancy," *U.S. News*, March 4, 2011, http://www.usnews.com/education/high-schools/articles/2011/03/04/cities-take-aim-at-truancy.

70  Peter Scher, "Why Summer Jobs Matter," *Politico Magazine*, July 28, 2015, http://www.politico.com/magazine/sponsor-content/2015/07/why-summer-jobs-matter/.

71  Ibid.

72  "US Education Spending," accessed March 27, 2017, http://www.usgovernmentspending.com/us_education_spending_20.html.

73  Robert Rector, "Marriage: America's Greatest Weapon Against Child Poverty," Heritage Foundation, September 5, 2012, http://www.heritage.org/research/reports/2012/09/marriage-americas-greatest-weapon-against-child-poverty.

74  Ibid.

75  Ibid.

76  "Lifehack Quotes," Lifehack, accessed March 27, 2017, http://quotes.lifehack.org/quote/carter-g-woodson/if-the-negro-in-the-ghetto-must/.

77  Jack Kemp, "Jack Kemp in His Own Words," *Wall Street Journal*, May 4, 2009, http://www.wsj.com/articles/SB124139616039181855.

78  Allen West, "The Dirty Little Secret No One Wants to Admit About
    Baltimore," *Allen B. West* (blog), April 29, 2015, http://allenbwest.com/2015/04/
    the-dirty-little-secret-no-one-wants-to-admit-about-baltimore/.

**CHAPTER 5**

1  Barack Obama, "Transcript: Illinois Senate Candidate Barack Obama,"
   *Washington Post*, July 27, 2004, http://www.washingtonpost.com/wp-dyn/
   articles/A19751-2004Jul27.html.
2  Patrick H. Caddell and Douglas E. Schoen, "Our Divisive President," *Wall
   Street Journal*, July 28, 2010, http://www.wsj.com/articles/SB10001424052748703
   700904575391553798363586.
3  Dennis Prager, "The Immaturity of Supporting Hillary Clinton Because
   She's a Woman," *National Review*, June 21, 2016, http://www.nationalreview.
   com/article/436859/hillary-clinton-woman-card-identity-politics-are-bad-
   reason-vote-her.
4  Kevin Fallon, "'Roots' Returns for the Black Lives Matter Generation," *Daily
   Beast*, May 30, 2016, http://www.thedailybeast.com/articles/2016/05/30/roots-
   returns-for-the-black-lives-matter-generation.html.
5  Jonathan Bernstein, "Roots, Episode 1, Review: 'Brit Actor Malachi Kirby Is
   Exceptional in This Powerful Remake,'" *Telegraph*, June 1, 2016, http://www.
   telegraph.co.uk/tv/2016/05/31/roots-episode-1-review-brit-actor-malachi-
   kirby-is-astonishing-i/.
6  Matt Zoller Seitz, "The New *Roots* Is More Scathing and Pulls Fewer Punches,"
   Vulture.com, May 27, 2016, http://www.vulture.com/2016/05/tv-review-roots.
   html.
7  Kevin Fallon, "'Roots' Returns for the Black Lives Matter Generation," *Daily
   Beast*, May 30, 2016, http://www.thedailybeast.com/articles/2016/05/30/roots-
   returns-for-the-black-lives-matter-generation.html. Emphasis added.
8  Ibid. Emphasis added.
9  Kevin Sack and Megan Thee-Brenan, "Poll Finds Most in U.S. Hold Dim
   View of Race Relations," *New York Times*, July 23, 2015, http://www.nytimes.
   com/2015/07/24/us/poll-shows-most-americans-think-race-relations-are-bad.
   html.
10 Jamelle Bouie, "Why I Am Optimistic About the Future of Race Relations in
   America," *Slate Magazine*, December 31, 2014, http://www.slate.com/articles/
   news_and_politics/politics/2014/12/future_of_america_s_race_relations_
   why_i_am_optimistic_despite_ferguson.html.
11 Kevin Sack and Megan Thee-Brenan, "Poll Finds Most in U.S. Hold Dim
   View of Race Relations," *New York Times*, July 23, 2015, http://www.nytimes.
   com/2015/07/24/us/poll-shows-most-americans-think-race-relations-are-bad.
   html.
12 Ibid.
13 Ibid.
14 Reid J. Epstein, "Poll: Views of Race Relations Worse Than Before Obama
   Took Office," *Wall Street Journal*, December 17, 2014, http://blogs.wsj.com/
   washwire/2014/12/17/poll-views-of-race-relations-worse-than-before-obama-
   took-office/.
15 "Is America More Racially Divided Today Than 2008?" Fox News, January 5,
   2015, http://www.foxnews.com/transcript/2015/01/05/is-america-more-racially-
   divided-today-than-2008/.

16  Jason L. Riley, "The Wages of Racial Discord," *Wall Street Journal*, August 4, 2015, http://www.wsj.com/articles/the-wages-of-racial-discord-1438730963.

17  Ibid.

18  "Has Obama Widened the Racial Divide?" *Rasmussen Reports*, September 4, 2015, http://www.rasmussenreports.com/public_content/politics/general_politics/august_2015/has_obama_widened_the_racial_divide.

19  Mark Hanrahan, "Race Relations in U.S.: Many Americans Think Racial Divide Growing, Relations Getting Worse: Poll," *International Business Times*, July 24, 2015, http://www.ibtimes.com/race-relations-us-many-americans-think-racial-divide-growing-relations-getting-worse-2022879.

20  Anna Brown and Sara Atske, "Blacks Have Made Gains in US Political Leadership, but Gaps Remain," Pew Research Center, June 28, 2016, http://www.pewresearch.org/fact-tank/2016/06/28/blacks-have-made-gains-in-u-s-political-leadership-but-gaps-remain/.

21  Kyle Becker, "10 Charts Show How 'Racist' America Really Is," *Independent Journal Review*, 2014, http://www.ijreview.com/2014/04/133024-10-charts-show-racist-america-really/.

22  Philip Bump, "1 in 3 Americans Are Now Worried a 'Great Deal' About Race Relations," *Washington Post*, April 12, 2016, https://www.washingtonpost.com/news/the-fix/wp/2016/04/12/1-in-3-americans-are-now-worried-a-great-deal-about-race-relations.

23  Richard Morin and Dan Balz, "Shifting Racial Climate," *Washington Post*, October 25, 1989, https://www.washingtonpost.com/archive/politics/1989/10/25/shifting-racial-climate/e4ec2368-968b-4ddd-afe6-5685f4b3a8a6/.

24  Jesse Byrnes, "Obama: Nation 'Less Racially Divided,'" *The Hill*, December 26, 2014, http://thehill.com/homenews/administration/228113-obama-nation-less-racially-divided.

25  Jamelle Bouie, "Why I Am Optimistic About the Future of Race Relations in America," *Slate Magazine*, December 31, 2014, http://www.slate.com/articles/news_and_politics/politics/2014/12/future_of_america_s_race_relations_why_i_am_optimistic_despite_ferguson.html.

26  Steve Inskeep, "Here's Why Obama Said the U.S. Is 'Less Racially Divided,'" NPR, December 30, 2014, http://www.npr.org/2014/12/22/372557632/heres-why-obama-said-the-u-s-is-less-racially-divided.

27  Patrick H. Caddell and Douglas E. Schoen, "Our Divisive President," *Wall Street Journal*, July 28, 2010, http://www.wsj.com/articles/SB10001424052748703700904575391553798363586.

28  Arnold Ahlert, "How Obama Poisoned Race Relations in America," *Frontpage Mag*, July 25, 2013, http://www.frontpagemag.com/fpm/198280/how-obama-poisoned-race-relations-america-arnold-ahlert.

29  Jason L. Riley, "The Wages of Racial Discord," *Wall Street Journal*, August 4, 2015, http://www.wsj.com/articles/the-wages-of-racial-discord-1438730963.

30  Arnold Ahlert, "How Obama Poisoned Race Relations in America," *Frontpage Mag*, July 25, 2013, http://www.frontpagemag.com/fpm/198280/how-obama-poisoned-race-relations-america-arnold-ahlert.

31  Mario Trujillo, "Poll: 70 Percent Support Voter ID Laws," *The Hill*, May 16, 2014, http://thehill.com/blogs/blog-briefing-room/206300-poll-70-percent-support-voter-id-laws.

32  Riley, *Please Stop Helping Us*, 12–14.

33 Arnold Ahlert, "How Obama Poisoned Race Relations in America," *Frontpage Mag*, July 25, 2013, http://www.frontpagemag.com/fpm/198280/how-obama-poisoned-race-relations-america-arnold-ahlert.

34 Ibid.

35 Jake Tapper, "VP Biden Says Republicans Are 'Going to Put Y'all Back in Chains,'" ABC News, August 14, 2012, http://abcnews.go.com/blogs/politics/2012/08/vp-biden-says-republicans-are-going-to-put-yall-back-in-chains/.

36 Patrick H. Caddell and Douglas E. Schoen, "Our Divisive President," *Wall Street Journal*, July 28, 2010, http://www.wsj.com/articles/SB10001424052748703700904575391553798363586.

37 Arnold Ahlert, "How Obama Poisoned Race Relations in America," *Frontpage Mag*, July 25, 2013, http://www.frontpagemag.com/fpm/198280/how-obama-poisoned-race-relations-america-arnold-ahlert.

38 Paul Sperry, "How Obama Is Bankrolling a Nonstop Protest Against Invented Outrage," *New York Post*, November 14, 2015, http://nypost.com/2015/11/14/how-obama-is-bankrolling-a-non-stop-protest-against-invented-outrage/.

39 Barack Obama, "Transcript: Illinois Senate Candidate Barack Obama," *Washington Post*, July 27, 2004, http://www.washingtonpost.com/wp-dyn/articles/A19751-2004Jul27.html.

40 Helene Cooper and Jackie Calmes, "Obama Moves Jobs Speech After Skirmish with Boehner," *New York Times*, August 31, 2011, http://www.nytimes.com/2011/09/01/us/politics/01obama.html.

41 David Weigel, "What Was Newt Gingrich Talking About?" *Slate Magazine*, September 12, 2010, http://www.slate.com/blogs/weigel/2010/09/12/what_was_newt_gingrich_talking_about.html.

42 Washington Post Staff, "Full Text: Donald Trump Announces a Presidential Bid," *Washington Post*, June 16, 2015, https://www.washingtonpost.com/news/post-politics/wp/2015/06/16/full-text-donald-trump-announces-a-presidential-bid/.

43 Colin Campbell, "CNN Anchor Jake Tapper Asks Donald Trump 3 Times If He Would Condemn David Duke and the KKK," *Business Insider*, February 28, 2016, http://www.businessinsider.com/cnn-anchor-jake-tapper-donald-trump-david-duke-kkk-2016-2.

44 Gina Kolata, "Death Rates Rising for Middle-Aged White Americans, Study Finds," *New York Times*, November 2, 2015, http://www.nytimes.com/2015/11/03/health/death-rates-rising-for-middle-aged-white-americans-study-finds.html.

**CHAPTER 6**

1 Steven Teles and David Dagan, "Reforming Our Prison System," *Real Clear Books*, June 27, 2016, http://www.realclearbooks.com/articles/2016/06/27/reforming_our_prison_system_153.html.

2 Nicole Flatow, "The Prison Doors Open and You're Released. You Have No Money or Transportation. Now What?" *Think Progress*, June 21, 2015, https://thinkprogress.org/the-prison-doors-open-and-youre-released-you-have-no-money-or-transportation-now-what-442f6b067dfb.

3 Anthony Hennen, "Newt Gingrich Embraces Criminal Justice Reform: 'Prisoners Are Graduate Schools of Crime,'" *Red Alert Politics*, June 3, 2016, http://redalertpolitics.com/2016/06/03/

newt-gingrich-embraces-criminal-justice-reform-prisons-graduate-schools-crime/.

4  Catherine E. Shoichet and Chandler Friedman, "Walter Scott Case: Michael Slager Released from Jail After Posting Bond," CNN News, January 5, 2016, http://www.cnn.com/2016/01/04/us/south-carolina-michael-slager-bail/.

5  Byron Dobson, "Poll: Blacks and Whites Agree Police Treat Blacks Differently," USA Today, September 9, 2015, http://www.usatoday.com/story/news/nation/2015/09/09/poll-blacks-whites-agree-police-treat-blacks-differently/71918706/.

6  Ibid.

7  Ibid.

8  Redditt Hudson, "I'm a Black Ex-Cop, and This Is the Real Truth About Race and Policing," Vox, July 7, 2016, http://www.vox.com/2015/5/28/8661977/race-police-officer.

9  Ray Sanchez, "Chicago Mayor: Anti-Police Backlash Makes Officers 'Fetal,'" CNN News, October 16, 2015, http://www.cnn.com/2015/10/16/us/rahm-emanuel-police-comments/.

10  Jon Schuppe, "As Violence Spikes in Some Cities, Is 'Ferguson Effect' to Blame?" NBC News, June 2, 2015, http://www.nbcnews.com/news/us-news/violence-spikes-some-cities-ferguson-effect-blame-n368526.

11  Heather Mac Donald, "Trump Is Right About Crime," City Journal, July 22, 2016, http://www.city-journal.org/html/trump-right-about-crime-14659.html.

12  Patrick Worrall, "FactCheck: Do Black Americans Commit More Crime?" Channel 4 News (blog), November 27, 2014, https://www.channel4.com/news/factcheck/factcheck-black-americans-commit-crime.

13  Ibid.

14  Ibid.

15  Hedgeless_horseman, "Blacks Are 13% of US Population 37.6% of Prisoners and 71% of Shooters in Chicago," Zero Hedge, June 23, 2015, http://www.zerohedge.com/news/2015-06-23/blacks-are-13-us-population-376-prisoners-and-71-shooters-chicago.

16  Tim Hains, "Heather MacDonald on Black Lives Matters: Does the Truth Matter?" Real Clear Politics, September 23, 2016, http://www.realclearpolitics.com/video/2016/09/23/heather_macdonald_on_black_lives_matter_does_the_truth_matter.html.

17  Ibid.

18  Heather Mac Donald, "Obama's Tragic Let 'Em Out Fantasy," Wall Street Journal, October 23, 2015, http://www.wsj.com/articles/obamas-tragic-let-em-out-fantasy-1445639113.

19  Sam Frizell, "Hillary Clinton Calls for an End to 'Mass Incarceration,'" Time, April 29, 2015, http://time.com/3839892/hillary-clinton-calls-for-an-end-to-mass-incarceration/.

20  Heather Mac Donald, "Obama's Tragic Let 'Em Out Fantasy," Wall Street Journal, October 23, 2015, http://www.wsj.com/articles/obamas-tragic-let-em-out-fantasy-1445639113.

21  Ibid.

22  Ibid.

23  Scott McConnell, "Heather Mac Donald's Inconvenient Facts," American Conservative, June 10, 2015, http://www.theamericanconservative.com/articles/heather-mac-donalds-inconvenient-facts/.

24  "Criminal Justice Fact Sheet," *NAACP*, 2016, http://www.naacp.org/pages/criminal-justice-fact-sheet.

25  Gary Westphalen, "Sentence Undone: A Life Lost to Drugs and Prison Restored by a President's Clemency," ABC News, October 29, 2015, http://abcnews.go.com/Politics/fullpage/sentence-undone-life-lost-drugs-prison-restored-presidents-34735954.

26  Heather Mac Donald, "Obama's Tragic Let 'Em Out Fantasy," *Wall Street Journal*, October 23, 2015, http://www.wsj.com/articles/obamas-tragic-let-em-out-fantasy-1445639113.

27  Ibid.

28  Nicole Flatow, "The Prison Doors Open and You're Released. You Have No Money or Transportation. Now What?" *Think Progress*, June 21, 2015, https://thinkprogress.org/the-prison-doors-open-and-youre-released-you-have-no-money-or-transportation-now-what-442f6b067dfb.

29  Ibid.

30  Alan Schwarz, "With Clemency from Obama, Drug Offender Embraces Second Chance," *New York Times*, August 14, 2015, http://www.nytimes.com/2015/08/15/us/with-clemency-from-obama-drug-offender-embraces-second-chance.html.

31  Ibid.

32  Ben Casselman, "Finding a Job with a Felony Conviction Is Hard. California May Make It Easier," *FiveThirtyEight.com*, November 3, 2014, http://fivethirtyeight.com/featuresfinding-a-job-with-a-felony-conviction-is-hard-california-may-make-it-easier/.

33  Jamelle Bouie, "Hillary Clinton's Impressive Criminal Justice Speech," *Slate Magazine*, April 30, 2015, http://www.slate.com/articles/news_and_politics/politics/2015/04/hillary_clinton_s_impressive_criminal_justice_speech_the_democratic_front.html.

34  Sari Horwitz, "Justice Department Set to Free 6,000 Prisoners, Largest One-Time Release," *Washington Post*, October 6, 2015, https://www.washingtonpost.com/world/national-security/justice-department-about-to-free-6000-prisoners-largest-one-time-release/2015/10/06/961f4c9a-6ba2-11e5-aa5b-f78a98956699_story.html.

35  Michael D. Shear, "Obama Commutes Sentences for 61 Convicted of Drug Crimes," *New York Times*, March 30, 2016, http://www.nytimes.com/2016/03/31/us/politics/obama-commutes-sentences-for-61-convicted-of-drug-crimes.html.

36  John Whitesides and Amanda Becker, "Clinton Calls for Drug Sentencing Reforms, End to Racial Profiling," Reuters, October 30, 2015, http://www.reuters.com/article/2015/10/30/us-usa-election-clinton-idUSKCN0SO16T20151030.

37  Matt Ford, "The Leader of the Unfree World," *Atlantic*, July 23, 2014, http://www.theatlantic.com/politics/archive/2014/07/the-leader-of-the-unfree-world/374348/.

38  Caitlin Dickson, "America's Recidivism Nightmare," *Daily Beast*, April 22, 2014, http://www.thedailybeast.com/articles/2014/04/22/america-s-recidivism-nightmare.html.

39  "Recidivism," National Institute of Justice, June 17, 2014, http://www.nij.gov/topics/corrections/recidivism/pages/welcome.aspx.

40  Corey Adwar, "Justice Department Report Reveals the Biggest Failure of

America's Prisons," *Business Insider*, April 22, 2014, http://www.businessinsider.com/department-of-justice-report-shows-high-recidivism-rate-2014-4.

41  David Skorton and Glenn Altschuler, "College Behind Bars: How Educating Prisoners Pays Off," *Forbes*, March 25, 2013, http://www.forbes.com/sites/collegeprose/2013/03/25/college-behind-bars-how-educating-prisoners-pays-off/.

42  Lydia DePillis, "Millions of Ex-Cons Still Can't Get Jobs. Here's How the White House Could Help Fix That," *Washington Post*, January 22, 2015, http://www.washingtonpost.com/news/storyline/wp/2015/01/22/millions-of-ex-cons-still-cant-get-jobs-heres-how-the-white-house-could-help-fix-that/.

43  Ibid.

44  Michelle Natividad Rodriguez and Beth Avery, "Ban the Box: U.S. Cities, Counties, and States Adopt Fair Hiring Policies," *National Employment Law Project*, October 2016, http://www.nelp.org/publication/ban-the-box-fair-chance-hiring-state-and-local-guide/.

45  Al Franken, "Juvenile Justice," *Al Franken, U.S. Senator for Minnesota*, https://www.franken.senate.gov/?p=issue&id=169.

46  Lorna Collier, "Incarceration Nation," *American Psychological Association*, October 2014, http://www.apa.org/monitor/2014/10/incarceration.aspx.

47  Ana Swanson, "A Shocking Number of Mentally Ill Americans End Up in Prison Instead of Treatment," *Washington Post*, April 30, 2015, http://www.washingtonpost.com/news/wonkblog/wp/2015/04/30/a-shocking-number-of-mentally-ill-americans-end-up-in-prisons-instead-of-psychiatric-hospitals/.

48  Olga Khazan, "Most Prisoners Are Mentally Ill," *Atlantic*, April 7, 2015, http://www.theatlantic.com/health/archive/2015/04/more-than-half-of-prisoners-are-mentally-ill/389682/.

49  E. Fuller Torrey, Aaron D. Kennard, Don Eslinger, Richard Lamb, and James Pavle, "Study Reveals Severely Mentally Ill Persons More Likely To Be in CA Jails Than Hospitals," *Treatment Advocacy Center*, May 2010, http://www.treatmentadvocacycenter.org/index.php?option=com_content&id=1538&Itemid=68 (page no longer available).

50  Ana Swanson, "A Shocking Number of Mentally Ill Americans End Up in Prison Instead of Treatment," *Washington Post*, April 30, 2015, http://www.washingtonpost.com/news/wonkblog/wp/2015/04/30/a-shocking-number-of-mentally-ill-americans-end-up-in-prisons-instead-of-psychiatric-hospitals/.

51  David Sack, "We Can't Afford to Ignore Drug Addiction in Prison," *Washington Post*, August 14, 2014, https://www.washingtonpost.com/news/to-your-health/wp/2014/08/14/we-cant-afford-to-ignore-drug-addiction-in-prison/.

52  Ibid.

53  Ibid.

54  Juan Williams, "Juan Williams: Retired NYPD Commissioner Bill Bratton Takes a Place Among America's Legendary Lawmen," Fox News, September 16, 2016, http://www.foxnews.com/opinion/2016/09/16/juan-williams-retired-nypd-commissioner-bill-bratton-takes-place-among-americas-legendary-lawmen.html.

55  Ibid.

56  William J. Bratton, "William J. Bratton: How to Reform Policing from Within," *New York Times*, September 16, 2016, http://www.nytimes.com/2016/09/16/opinion/william-j-bratton-how-to-reform-policing-from-within.html.

57 Ibid.

58 Chandra Bozelko, "My Prison Job Wasn't About the Money," *Wall Street Journal*, October 11, 2015, http://www.wsj.com/articles/my-prison-job-wasnt-about-the-money-1444600577.

59 "Education and Vocational Training in Prisons Reduced Recidivism, Improves Job Outlook," Rand Corporation, August 22, 2013, http://www.rand.org/news/press/2013/08/22.html.

60 Ibid.

61 Lois Davis, "To Stop Prisons' Revolving Door," *Los Angeles Times*, September 16, 2013, http://articles.latimes.com/2013/sep/16/opinion/la-oe-davis-prison-education-20130916.

62 John J. Lennon, "Let Prisoners Take College Courses," *New York Times*, April 4, 2015, http://www.nytimes.com/2015/04/05/opinion/sunday/put-schools-back-in-prison.html.

63 The Editorial Board, "How to Get Around a Criminal Record," *New York Times*, October 19, 2015, http://www.nytimes.com/2015/10/19/opinion/how-to-get-around-a-criminal-record.html.

64 Rina Pelta, "LA County Supervisor Wants to Give Companies Incentives to Hire Ex-Cons," 89.3 KPCC, May 11, 2015, http://www.scpr.org/news/2015/05/11/51566/supervisor-wants-to-incentivize-hiring-ex-cons/.

65 Bourree Lam, "Obama's Plan to Help Former Inmates Find Homes and Jobs," *Atlantic*, November 2, 2015, http://www.theatlantic.com/business/archive/2015/11/obama-criminal-record-housing-job/413695/.

66 Ibid.

67 Elaisha Stokes, "For Ex-Cons, Finding Housing May Become Less Difficult in the Big Easy," *Al Jazeera America*, August 14, 2014, http://america.aljazeera.com/articles/2014/8/14/ex-felons-find-shelterinnola.html.

68 Ed O'Keefe, "Cory Booker, Rand Paul Team Up on Sentencing Reform Bill," *Washington Post*, July 8, 2014, http://www.washingtonpost.com/news/post-politics/wp/2014/07/08/cory-booker-rand-paul-team-up-on-sentencing-reform-bill/.

69 Ibid.

70 Newt Gingrich, "A Second Chance for Young Offenders," *Huffington Post*, April 13, 2015, http://www.huffingtonpost.com/newt-gingrich/a-second-chance-for-young-offenders_b_7055246.html.

71 "Who, What, Where and Why," *Economist*, March 13, 2014, http://www.economist.com/blogs/democracyinamerica/2014/03/americas-prison-population.

## CHAPTER 7

1 Joel Klein, "The Failure of American Schools," *Atlantic*, June 2011, http://www.theatlantic.com/magazine/archive/2011/06/the-failure-of-american-schools/308497/.

2 Donald Devine, "Hope for American Schools?" *American Conservative*, July 16, 2015, http://www.theamericanconservative.com/articles/hope-for-american-schools/.

3 Sophie Hollander, "Canada to Resign from Harlem Children's Zone," *Wall Street Journal*, February 10, 2014, http://www.wsj.com/articles/SB10001424052702304104504579374683579192314.

4  Ibid.

5  Danielle Hanson, "Assessing the Harlem Children's Zone," Heritage
   Foundation, March 6, 2013, http://www.heritage.org/research/reports/2013/03/
   assessing-the-harlem-childrens-zone.

6  Geoffrey Canada, "Geoffrey Canada: America's Promise to a New Generation,"
   *NY Daily News*, July 5, 2015, http://www.nydailynews.com/opinion/
   geoffrey-canada-america-promise-new-generation-article-1.2279197.

7  Roland G. Fryer Jr., "Learning from the Successes and Failures of Charter
   Schools," *Hamilton Project*, September 2012, http://scholar.harvard.edu/files/
   fryer/files/hamilton_project_paper_2012.pdf.

8  Dan Lips, Shanea Watkins, and John Fleming, "Does Spending More on
   Education Improve Academic Achievement?" Heritage Foundation,
   September 8, 2008, http://www.heritage.org/research/reports/2008/09/
   does-spending-more-on-education-improve-academic-achievement.

9  Laurence Steinberg, "What's Holding Back American Teenagers?" *Slate
   Magazine*, February 11, 2014, http://www.slate.com/articles/life/education/
   2014/02/high_school_in_america_a_complete_disaster.html.

10 Tom Loveless, "Measuring Effects of the Common Core," Brookings, March 24,
   2015, http://www.brookings.edu/research/reports/2015/03/24-common-
   core-loveless.

11 Jane L. David, "Research Says...High-Stakes Testing Narrows the Curriculum,"
   *Educational Leadership*, March 2011, http://www.ascd.org/publications/
   educational_leadership/mar11/vol68/num06/High-Stakes_Testing_Narrows_
   the_Curriculum.aspx.

12 Sol Stern, "Can New York Clean Up the Testing Mess?" *City Journal*, Spring
   2010, http://www.city-journal.org/2010/20_2_ny-education-testing.html.

13 "Pisa Tests: Top 40 for Maths and Reading," *BBC News*, October 14, 2015, http://
   www.bbc.com/news/business-26249042.

14 "Viewing the United States School System Through the Prism of PISA," OECD,
   2013, http://www.oecd.org/pisa/keyfindings/PISA2012-US-CHAP2.pdf.

15 Ibid.

16 Allie Bidwell, "American Students Fall in International Academic Tests,
   Chinese Lead the Pack," *U.S. News*, December 3, 2013, http://www.usnews.
   com/news/articles/2013/12/03/american-students-fall-in-international-
   academic-tests-chinese-lead-the-pack.

17 Ibid.

18 Ibid.

19 Laurence Steinberg, "What's Holding Back American Teenagers?"
   *Slate Magazine*, February 11, 2014, http://www.slate.com/articles/life/
   education/2014/02/high_school_in_america_a_complete_disaster.html.

20 "U.S. High School Graduation Rate Hits New Record High," U.S. Department
   of Education, February 12, 2015, http://www.ed.gov/news/press-releases/
   us-high-school-graduation-rate-hits-new-record-high.

21 Niraj Chokshi, "For the First Time, the U.S. High School Graduation Rate
   Tops 80 Percent, Report Finds," *Washington Post*, April 28, 2014, http://www.
   washingtonpost.com/blogs/govbeat/wp/2014/04/28/for-the-first-time-the-u-s-
   high-school-graduation-rate-tops-80-percent-report-finds/.

22 Kyla Calvert Mason, "High School Graduation Rates Rise but U.S. Still Lags
   Other Developed Countries," *PBS News*, February 12, 2015, http://

www.pbs.org/newshour/rundown/high-school-graduation-rates-tick-u-s-still-lags-developed-countries/.

23 Lyndsey Layton, "National High School Graduation Rates at Historic High, but Disparities Still Exist," *Washington Post*, April 28, 2014, http://www.washingtonpost.com/local/education/high-school-graduation-rates-at-historic-high/2014/04/28/84eb0122-cee0-11e3-937f-d3026234b51c_story.html.

24 Ibid.

25 Byron G. Auguste, Bryan Hancock, and Martha Laboissiere, "The Economic Cost of the U.S. Education Gap," McKinsey & Company, June 2009, http://www.mckinsey.com/industries/social-sector/our-insights/the-economic-cost-of-the-us-education-gap.

26 Lyndsey Layton, "National High School Graduation Rates at Historic High, but Disparities Still Exist," *Washington Post*, April 28, 2014, http://www.washingtonpost.com/local/education/high-school-graduation-rates-at-historic-high/2014/04/28/84eb0122-cee0-11e3-937f-d3026234b51c_story.html.

27 Laurence Steinberg, "What's Holding Back American Teenagers?" *Slate Magazine*, February 11, 2014, http://www.slate.com/articles/life/education/2014/02/high_school_in_america_a_complete_disaster.html.

28 "Beyond the Rhetoric," National Center for Public Policy and Higher Education, 2010, http://www.highereducation.org/reports/college_readiness/readiness_gap.shtml.

29 "Fast Facts," National Center for Education Statistics, 2016, http://nces.ed.gov/fastfacts/display.asp?id=372.

30 "College Enrollment and Work Activity of 2015 High School Graduates," Bureau of Labor and Statistics, April 28, 2016, http://www.bls.gov/news.release/hsgec.nr0.htm.

31 "Beyond the Rhetoric," National Center for Public Policy and Higher Education, 2010, http://www.highereducation.org/reports/college_readiness/readiness_gap.shtml.

32 "ACT Profile Report—National," *The ACT*, 2014, http://www.act.org/content/dam/act/unsecured/documents/Natl-Scores-2014-National2014.pdf.

33 Allie Bidwell, "U.S. College Readiness Lags in Math, Science," *U.S. News*, August 20, 2014, http://www.usnews.com/news/articles/2014/08/20/act-college-preparedness-remains-flat-for-high-school-graduates.

34 Allie Bidwell, "High School Graduates Still Struggle with College Readiness," *U.S. News*, August 21, 2013, http://www.usnews.com/news/articles/2013/08/21/high-school-graduates-still-struggle-with-college-readiness.

35 Ibid.

36 Tamar Lewin, "Most College Students Don't Earn a Degree in 4 Years, Study Finds," *New York Times*, December 1, 2014, http://www.nytimes.com/2014/12/02/education/most-college-students-dont-earn-degree-in-4-years-study-finds.html.

37 Laurence Steinberg, "What's Holding Back American Teenagers?" *Slate Magazine*, February 11, 2014, http://www.slate.com/articles/life/education/2014/02/high_school_in_america_a_complete_disaster.html.

38 Tamar Lewin, "Most College Students Don't Earn a Degree in 4 Years, Study Finds," *New York Times*, December 1, 2014, http://www.nytimes.com/2014/12/02/education/most-college-students-dont-earn-degree-in-4-years-study-finds.html.

39 Ibid.

40 Ibid.

41 Ibid.

42 Anthony Carnevale, Nicole Smith, and Jeff Strohl, "Projections of Jobs and Education Requirements Through 2018," Georgetown University Center on Education and the Workforce, June 2010, https://cew.georgetown.edu/wp-content/uploads/2014/12/HelpWanted.ExecutiveSummary.pdf.

43 Judith Scott-Clayton and Thomas Bailey, "The Problem with Obama's 'Free Community College' Proposal," *Time Money*, January 20, 2015, http://time.com/money/3674033/obama-free-college-plan-problems/.

44 Tamar Lewin, "Most College Students Don't Earn a Degree in 4 Years, Study Finds," *New York Times*, December 1, 2014, http://www.nytimes.com/2014/12/02/education/most-college-students-dont-earn-degree-in-4-years-study-finds.html.

45 "Are They Really Ready to Work?" *Partnership for 21st Century Learning*, September 29, 2006, http://www.p21.org/storage/documents/FINAL_REPORT_PDF09-29-06.pdf.

46 Victor Luckerson, "The Myth of the Four-Year College Degree," *Time*, January 10, 2013, http://business.time.com/2013/01/10/the-myth-of-the-4-year-college-degree/.

47 "Cost of College Degree in U.S. Has Increased 1,120 Percent in 30 Years, Report Says," *Huffington Post*, August 15, 2012, http://www.huffingtonpost.com/2012/08/15/cost-of-college-degree-increase-12-fold-1120-percent-bloomberg_n_1783700.html.

48 Judah Bellin, "Slimming the College-Tuition Beast," *City Journal*, Summer 2014, http://www.city-journal.org/2014/24_3_college-tuition.html.

49 "Cost of College Degree in U.S. Has Increased 1,120 Percent in 30 Years, Report Says," *Huffington Post*, August 15, 2012, http://www.huffingtonpost.com/2012/08/15/cost-of-college-degree-increase-12-fold-1120-percent-bloomberg_n_1783700.html.

50 Phil Izzo, "Congratulations to Class of 2014, Most Indebted Ever," *Wall Street Journal*, May 16, 2014, http://blogs.wsj.com/numbers/congatulations-to-class-of-2014-the-most-indebted-ever-1368/.

51 Libby Kane, "Student Loan Debt in the U.S. Has Topped $1.3 Trillion," *Business Insider*, January 12, 2016, http://www.businessinsider.com/student-loan-debt-state-of-the-union-2016-1.

52 Scott Gerber, "Here's the Real Problem with America's Educational System," *Time*, June 2, 2014, http://time.com/2806663/american-education/.

53 "Education and Child Policy," CATO Institute, https://www.cato.org/research//ccs/index.html.

54 Lindsey M. Burke, "The Value of Parental Choice in Education: A Look at the Research," Heritage Foundation, March 18, 2014, http://thf_media.s3.amazonaws.com/2014/pdf/IB4173.pdf.

55 Ibid.

56 Ibid.

57 Ibid.

58 "The Way Forward: Scholarship Tax Credits or Vouchers?" CATO Institute, accessed March 27, 2017, http://www.cato.org/education-wiki/scholarship-tax-credits-vouchers.

59  Ibid.

60  Jason Bedrick, "The Year of Educational Choice: An Update," CATO Institute, April 24, 2015, http://www.cato.org/blog/year-educational-choice-update.

61  Jason Bedrick and Lindsey M. Burke, "On Designing K-12 Education Savings Accounts," EducationNext, January 26, 2015, http://educationnext.org/designing-k-12-education-savings-accounts/.

62  Ibid.

63  Ibid.

64  "The Way Forward: Scholarship Tax Credits or Vouchers?" CATO Institute, http://www.cato.org/education-wiki/scholarship-tax-credits-vouchers.

65  Steven Brill, Margaret Spellings, Dean Kamen, Michele Cahill, and Louis V. Gerstner Jr., "How to Fix the Education Crisis," *Bloomberg*, October 13, 2011, http://www.bloomberg.com/bw/magazine/how-to-fix-the-education-crisis-10132011.html.

66  Jared Meyer and Diana Furchtgott-Roth, "Education Reform That Works," *City Journal*, May 12, 2015, http://www.city-journal.org/2015/eon0512dfjm.html.

67  Ibid.

68  Roland G. Fryer Jr., "Learning from the Successes and Failures of Charter Schools," *Hamilton Project*, September 2012, http://scholar.harvard.edu/files/fryer/files/hamilton_project_paper_2012.pdf.

69  Pete Wilmoth, "What Do We Know About Charter Schools? Moving Beyond the Talking Points," *Rand Blog*, April 4, 2013, http://www.rand.org/blog/2013/04/what-do-we-know-about-charter-schools-moving-beyond.html.

70  Jared Meyer and Diana Furchtgott-Roth, "Education Reform That Works," *City Journal*, May 12, 2015, http://www.city-journal.org/2015/eon0512dfjm.html.

71  Katie Ash, "KIPP Schools Boost Academic Performance, Study Finds," KIPP Foundation, February 27, 2013, http://www.kipp.org/news/education-week-kipp-schools-boost-academic-performance-study-finds/.

72  The Editorial Board, "Charter School Experiment a Success: Our View," *USA Today*, April 1, 2013, http://www.usatoday.com/story/opinion/2013/04/01/kipp-charter-schools-editorials-debates/2044375/.

73  Jared Meyer and Diana Furchtgott-Roth, "Education Reform That Works," *City Journal*, May 12, 2015, http://www.city-journal.org/2015/eon0512dfjm.html.

74  Adam Ozimek, "The Unappreciated Success of Charter Schools," *Forbes*, January 11, 2015, http://www.forbes.com/sites/modeledbehavior/2015/01/11/charter-success/.

75  "School Indicators for New York City Charter Schools 2013–2014 School Year," New York City Independent Budget Office, July 2015, http://www.ibo.nyc.ny.us/iboreports/school-indicators-for-new-york-city-charter-schools-2013-2014-school-year-july-2015.pdf.

76  Jared Meyer and Diana Furchtgott-Roth, "Education Reform That Works," *City Journal*, May 12, 2015, http://www.city-journal.org/2015/eon0512dfjm.html.

77  Leslie Brody, "New York City Charter Schools Get Record Number of Applicants," *Wall Street Journal*, April 30, 2014, http://www.wsj.com/articles/SB10001424052702303678404579534173294324490.

78  Nora Kern and Wentana Gebru, "Waiting Lists to Attend Charter Schools Top 1 Million Names," National Alliance for Public Charter Schools, May 2014, http://www.publiccharters.org/wp-content/uploads/2014/05/NAPCS-2014-Wait-List-Report.pdf.

79  The Editorial Board, "Charter School Experiment a Success: Our View," *USA Today*, April 1, 2013, http://www.usatoday.com/story/opinion/2013/04/01/kipp-charter-schools-editorials-debates/2044375/.

80  Donald Devine, "Hope for American Schools?" *American Conservative*, July 16, 2015, http://www.theamericanconservative.com/articles/hope-for-american-schools/.

81  Joel Klein, "The Failure of American Schools," *Atlantic*, June 2011, http://www.theatlantic.com/magazine/archive/2011/06/the-failure-of-american-schools/308497/.

82  Daniel DiSalvo, "Cuomo's Gambit: Thinking Big to Fix Schools," Manhattan Institute, March 25, 2010, http://www.manhattan-institute.org/html/cuomos-gambit-thinking-big-fix-schools-5408.html.

83  Andrew M. Cuomo, "A Response to LI's Protesting Educators," *Newsday*, March 8, 2015, http://www.newsday.com/opinion/oped/ed-fix-clouded-by-the-fog-of-protest-andrew-cuomo-1.10027408.

84  Michael Martinez, "U.S. Schools Chief Calls California Ruling 'a Mandate' to Fix Tenure, Firing Laws," CNN News, June 11, 2014, http://www.cnn.com/2014/06/10/justice/california-teacher-tenure-lawsuit/.

85  Jared Meyer and Diana Furchtgott-Roth, "Education Reform That Works," *City Journal*, May 12, 2015, http://www.city-journal.org/2015/eon0512dfjm.html.

86  Ibid.

87  Devin Leonard, "New Haven Shows How to Fix Public Schools," *Bloomberg*, May 10, 2013, http://www.bloomberg.com/bw/articles/2013-05-09/new-haven-shows-how-you-fix-public-schools.

88  "Impact Evaluation of Moving High-Performing Teachers to Low-Performing Schools," National Center for Education Evaluation and Regional Assistance, April 2012, https://ies.ed.gov/ncee/projects/evaluation/tq_recruitment.asp.

89  "Standards in Your State," Common Core Standards, accessed July 8, 2015, http://www.corestandards.org/standards-in-your-state/.

90  Judah Bellin, "Slimming the College-Tuition Beast," *City Journal*, Summer 2014, http://www.city-journal.org/2014/24_3_college-tuition.html.

91  Michelle Singletary, "It's Time Higher Education Leaders Figured Out How to Bring Down College Costs," *Boston*, September 11, 2011, http://archive.boston.com/business/personalfinance/articles/2011/09/11/its_time_higher_education_leaders_figured_out_how_to_bring_down_college_costs/.

92  Judah Bellin, "Slimming the College-Tuition Beast," *City Journal*, Summer 2014, http://www.city-journal.org/2014/24_3_college-tuition.html.

## CHAPTER 8

1  Richard Fry and Rakesh Kochnar, "America's Wealth Gap Between Middle-Income and Upper-Income Families Is Widest on Record," Pew Research Center, December 17, 2014, http://www.pewresearch.org/fact-tank/2014/12/17/wealth-gap-upper-middle-income/.

2  Jim Tankersley, "Economic Mobility Hasn't Changed in a Half-Century in America, Economists Declare," *Washington Post*, January 23, 2014, http://www.washingtonpost.com/business/economy/economic-mobility-hasnt-changed-in-a-half-century-in-america-economists-declare/2014/01/22/e845db4a-83a2-11e3-8099-9181471f7aaf_story.html.

3  Robert Doar, "The Big but Hidden U.S. Jobs Problem," *Wall Street Journal*,

January 11, 2016, http://www.wsj.com/articles/the-big-but-hidden-u-s-jobs-problem-1452555802.

4 Seth Freed Wessler, "Middle-Class Betrayal? Why Working Hard Is No Longer Enough in America," NBC News, March 16, 2015, http://www.nbcnews.com/feature/in-plain-sight/middle-class-betrayal-why-working-hard-no-longer-enough-america-n291741.

5 Daniel Henninger, "The Clinton Pivot Begins," *Wall Street Journal*, April 28, 2016, http://www.wsj.com/articles/the-clinton-pivot-begins-1461799244.

6 Andrew Ross Sorkin, "President Obama Weighs His Economic Legacy," *New York Times*, April 28, 2016, http://www.nytimes.com/2016/05/01/magazine/president-obama-weighs-his-economic-legacy.html.

7 Ibid.

8 Ibid.

9 "NASDAQ Composite," Google Finance, https://www.google.com/finance/historical?cid=13756934&startdate=Jan%2020%2C%202009&enddate=Dec%2031%2C%202016&num=30&ei=j1CjV8jMMorneriSs-AP; "Dow Jones INDU Average Index," CNN Money, http://money.cnn.com/data/markets/dow/.

10 Josh Zumbrun, "Have Most Economic Indicators Improved Under Obama?" *Wall Street Journal*, August 4, 2014.

11 Joana Taborda, "U.S. New Home Sales Up to 8-Year High," *Trading Economics*, May 24, 2016, http://www.tradingeconomics.com/articles/05242016151600.htm.

12 Barack Obama, "Remarks of President Barack Obama—State of the Union Address as Delivered," White House, January 13, 2016, https://www.whitehouse.gov/the-press-office/2016/01/12/remarks-president-barack-obama-%E2%80%93-prepared-delivery-state-union-address.

13 Nicole Faraguna, "Forward Thinking: Income Inequality Rages On in America," *Daily Item*, April 20, 2015, http://www.dailyitem.com/opinion/forward-thinking-income-inequality-rages-on-in-america/article_506cf6e2-e7a0-11e4-9a9b-6b38825171dd.html.

14 Joel Griffith and Stephen Moore, "Our Dismal GDP Numbers: Under Obama US Stuck in Slow Growth Rut," Fox News, April 29, 2015, http://www.foxnews.com/opinion/2015/04/29/our-dismal-gdp-numbers-under-obama-us-stuck-in-slow-growth-rut.html.

15 "National Income and Product Accounts," Bureau of Economic Analysis, March 25, 2016, http://www.bea.gov/newsreleases/national/gdp/2016/gdp4q15_3rd.htm; "GDP Increases in Second Quarter," Bureau of Economic Analysis, September 29, 2016, https://www.bea.gov/newsreleases/national/gdp/gdphighlights.pdf.

16 "National Income and Product Accounts," Bureau of Economic Analysis, January 30, 2015, http://www.bea.gov/newsreleases/national/gdp/2015/gdp4q14_adv.htm.

17 Tracy Miller, "The Obama Economic Record: The Worst Five Years Since World War II," *Daily Caller*, August 11, 2014, http://dailycaller.com/2014/08/11/the-obama-economic-record-the-worst-five-years-since-world-war-ii/.

18 Joel Griffith and Stephen Moore, "Our Dismal GDP Numbers: Under Obama US Stuck in Slow Growth Rut," Fox News, April 29, 2015, http://www.foxnews.com/opinion/2015/04/29/our-dismal-gdp-numbers-under-obama-us-stuck-in-slow-growth-rut.html.

19 Ibid.

20 Kevin Warsh and Stanley Druckenmiller, "The Asset-Rich, Income-Poor Economy," *Wall Street Journal*, June 19, 2014, http://www.wsj.com/articles/warsh-and-druckenmiller-the-asset-rich-income-poor-economy-1403220446.

21 Howard Schneider and Jason Lange, "Fed Raises Interest Rates, Citing Ongoing U.S. Recovery," Reuters, December 17, 2015, http://www.reuters.com/article/us-usa-fed-idUSKBN0TY2EX20151218.

22 Andrew Soergel, "Where Are All the Workers?" *U.S. News*, July 16, 2015, http://www.usnews.com/news/the-report/articles/2015/07/16/unemployment-is-low-but-more-workers-are-leaving-the-workforce.

23 Stephen Moore, "Under Obama: One Million More Americans Have Dropped Out of Work Force Than Have Found a Job," Heritage Foundation, October 7, 2014, http://www.heritage.org/research/commentary/2014/10/employment-under-obama.

24 "Current Employment Statistics Highlights," U.S. Bureau of Labor Statistics, October 7, 2016, http://www.bls.gov/web/empsit/ceshighlights.pdf.

25 Gary Burtless, "Robust Job Gains and a Continued Rebound in Labor Force Participation," Brookings, March 4, 2016, http://www.brookings.edu/blogs/jobs/posts/2016/03/04-robust-job-gains-continued-rebound-labor-force-participation-burtless.

26 Stephen Moore, "Under Obama: One Million More Americans Have Dropped Out of Work Force Than Have Found a Job," Heritage Foundation, October 7, 2014, http://www.heritage.org/research/commentary/2014/10/employment-under-obama; Tracy Miller, "The Obama Economic Record: The Worst Five Years Since World War II," *Daily Caller*, August 11, 2014, http://dailycaller.com/2014/08/11/the-obama-economic-record-the-worst-five-years-since-world-war-ii/.

27 Tracy Miller, "The Obama Economic Record: The Worst Five Years Since World War II," *Daily Caller*, August 11, 2014, http://dailycaller.com/2014/08/11/the-obama-economic-record-the-worst-five-years-since-world-war-ii/.

28 Ibid.

29 William A. Galston, "The Middle-Class Litmus Test for the Economy," *Wall Street Journal*, September 30, 2014, http://www.wsj.com/articles/william-a-galston-the-middle-class-litmus-test-for-the-economy-1412119100.

30 Katie Johnston, "Most Jobs Added in Boston Since Recession Called Low-Paying," *Boston Globe*, September 22, 2015, https://www.bostonglobe.com/business/2015/09/21/boston-low-wage-jobs-make-majority-jobs-added-since-recession/TZmK7p7izwICWX1YtptTeK/story.html.

31 Dan Kedmey, "47% of Unemployed Americans Have Just Stopped Looking for Work," *Time*, May 22, 2014.

32 Stephen Moore, "Under Obama: One Million More Americans Have Dropped Out of Work Force Than Have Found a Job," Heritage Foundation, October 7, 2014, http://www.heritage.org/research/commentary/2014/10/employment-under-obama.

33 Mark Peters and Ben Leubsdorf, "Case of the Vanishing Worker," *Wall Street Journal*, May 10, 2015, http://www.wsj.com/articles/case-of-the-vanishing-worker-1431299722.

34 Dionne Searcey and Robert Gebeloff, "Middle Class Shrinks Further as More Fall Out Instead of Climbing Up," *New York Times*, January 25, 2015.

35 Jeffrey Scott Shapiro, "Broken Promise? Obama's America Better for Wall

Street than Main Street, Stats Show," *Washington Times*, January 4, 2015, http://
www.washingtontimes.com/news/2015/jan/4/obama-economy-welfare-
dependency-peaks-as-rich-get/.

36  William A. Galston, "The Middle-Class Litmus Test for the Economy," *Wall
Street Journal*, September 30, 2014, http://www.wsj.com/articles/william-a-
galston-the-middle-class-litmus-test-for-the-economy-1412119100.

37  Ibid.

38  Chris Metinko, "Americans Are Still Struggling Paycheck to Paycheck, Lack
Emergency Savings," *Main Street*, February 27, 2015, https://www.mainstreet.
com/article/americans-are-still-struggling-paycheck-to-paycheck-lack-
emergency-savings.

39  Ariel Edwards-Levy, "This Is What Barely Making Ends Meet in America
Sounds Like," *Huffington Post*, June 11, 2014, http://www.huffingtonpost.
com/2014/06/11/poverty-stories_n_5481017.html.

40  Annie Lowrey, "Recovery Has Created Far More Low-Wage Jobs Than
Better-Paid Ones," *New York Times*, April 27, 2014, http://www.nytimes.
com/2014/04/28/business/economy/recovery-has-created-far-more-low-wage-
jobs-than-better-paid-ones.html.

41  Ibid.

42  Dionne Searcey and Robert Gebeloff, "Middle Class Shrinks Further as More
Fall Out Instead of Climbing Up," *New York Times*, January 25, 2015.

43  Ibid.

44  Ibid.

45  Dave Jamieson, "More Than 1 in 10 Americans Who Work Full Time Are
Still Poor," *Huffington Post*, January 23, 2014, http://www.huffingtonpost.
com/2013/12/17/working-poor_n_4463606.html.

46  Joanna Campione, "Nobel Prize-Winner Stiglitz: Three Steps to Solve
Income Inequality," *Yahoo Finance*, April 23, 2015, http://finance.yahoo.
com/news/nobel-prize-winner-stiglitz---three-steps-to-solving-income-
inequality-153834471.html.

47  Drew Desilver, "America's Middle Class Is Shrinking. So Who's Leaving It?"
Pew Research Center, December 14, 2015, http://www.pewresearch.org/
fact-tank/2015/12/14/americas-middle-class-is-shrinking-so-whos-leaving-it/.

48  Sean Gorman, and Tom Kertscher, "Bernie Sanders Says Top 0.1% in U.S.
Have Almost as Much Wealth as Bottom 90%," *PolitiFact*, September 21,
2015, http://www.politifact.com/virginia/statements/2015/sep/21/bernie-s/
bernie-sanders-says-top-01-us-have-almost-much-wea/.

49  William A. Galston, "How to Stoke the Middle-Class Comeback," *Wall
Street Journal*, October 7, 2014, http://www.wsj.com/articles/william-
galston-how-to-stoke-the-middle-class-comeback-1412721445.

50  "America's Wealth Gap Between Middle-Income and Upper-Income Families
Is Widest on Record," Pew Research Center, December 17, 2014, http://www.
pewresearch.org/fact-tank/2014/12/17/wealth-gap-upper-middle-income/.

51  Ibid.

52  Frank Newport, "In U.S., 60% Satisfied with Ability to Get Ahead," *Gallup*,
January 30, 2015, http://www.gallup.com/poll/181340/satisfied-ability-ahead.
aspx.

53  Noam Schieber and Dalia Sussman, "Inequality Troubles Americans Across
Party Lines, Times/CBS Poll Finds," *New York Times*, June 3, 2015, http://www.

nytimes.com/2015/06/04/business/inequality-a-major-issue-for-americans-times-cbs-poll-finds.html.

54  "Americans' Views on Income Inequality and Workers' Rights," *New York Times*, June 3, 2015, http://www.nytimes.com/interactive/2015/06/03/business/income-inequality-workers-rights-international-trade-poll.html.

55  Aimee Picchi, "Is the American Dream Dying?" CBS News, February 26, 2015, http://www.cbsnews.com/news/pew-study-the-american-dream-is-dying/.

56  Ibid.

57  Joseph E. Stiglitz, *The Price of Inequality: How Today's Divided Society Endangers Our Future* (New York: W.W. Norton, 2013), 177.

58  Joseph Stiglitz, "America Is No Longer the Land of Opportunity," *Financial Times*, June 26, 2012.

59  Aimee Picchi, "Nobel Winner Stiglitz: 'American Dream Is a Myth,'" CBS News, April 23, 2015, http://www.cbsnews.com/news/nobel-prize-winner-joseph-stiglitz-american-dream-is-a-myth/.

60  Erin Currier, "The Numbers Show Rags-to-Riches Happens Only in Movies," *New York Times*, January 1, 2015, http://www.nytimes.com/roomfordebate/2015/01/01/is-the-modern-american-dream-attainable/the-numbers-show-rags-to-riches-happens-only-in-movies.

61  Aimee Picchi, "Is the American Dream Dying?" CBS News, February 26, 2015, http://www.cbsnews.com/news/pew-study-the-american-dream-is-dying/.

62  David Harsanyi, "5 Ways to Get America Working Again," *Human Events*, July 23, 2012, http://humanevents.com/2012/07/23/david-harsanyi-5-ways-to-get-america-working-again/.

63  Chris Christie, "My Plan to Raise Growth and Incomes," *Wall Street Journal*, May 11, 2015, http://www.wsj.com/articles/my-plan-to-raise-growth-and-incomes-1431387102.

64  Ibid.

65  Reihan Salam, "Taxation Without Exasperation," *Wall Street Journal*, April 8, 2016, http://www.wsj.com/articles/taxation-without-exasperation-1460129434.

66  Chris Christie, "My Plan to Raise Growth and Incomes," *Wall Street Journal*, May 11, 2015, http://www.wsj.com/articles/my-plan-to-raise-growth-and-incomes-1431387102.

67  Brigitte Dusseau, "New York Protesters Demand $15 Minimum Wage," Yahoo News, April 15, 2015, http://news.yahoo.com/york-protesters-demand-15-minimum-wage-210827173.html.

68  Dave Jamieson, "More Than 1 in 10 Americans Who Work Full Time Are Still Poor," *Huffington Post*, December 18, 2013, http://www.huffingtonpost.com/2013/12/17/working-poor_n_4463606.html.

69  "Support for a Federal Minimum Wage of $12.50 or Above," Hart Research Associates, January 14, 2015, http://www.nelp.org/content/uploads/2015/03/Minimum-Wage-Poll-Memo-Jan-2015.pdf.

70  Annie Lowrey, "Recovery Has Created Far More Low-Wage Jobs Than Better-Paid Ones," *New York Times*, April 27, 2014, http://www.nytimes.com/2014/04/28/business/economy/recovery-has-created-far-more-low-wage-jobs-than-better-paid-ones.html.

71  Jillian Berman, "600 Economists Now Back a $10.10 Minimum Wage," *Huffington Post*, January 27, 2014, http://www.huffingtonpost.com/2014/01/27/economists-minimum-wage_n_4675290.html.

72  Ibid.

73  "Small Business Owners Favor Raising Federal Minimum Wage," American Sustainable Business Council and Business for a Fair Minimum Wage, July 2014, https://www.businessforafairminimumwage.org/sites/default/files/ BFMW_ASBC_Minimum_Wage_Business_Poll_Report_July_2014.pdf.

74  Margaret Collins and Noah Buhayar, "Buffett Says Minimum Wage Increase Isn't Answer to Income Gulf," *Bloomberg*, May 2, 2015, http://www.bloomberg. com/news/articles/2015-05-02/buffett-says-minimum-wage-increase-isn-t- answer-to-income-gulf.

75  Ibid.

76  "New Study: Differences in Childhood Environment Affect Gender Gaps in Adulthood," Equality of Opportunity Project, January 2016, http://www. equality-of-opportunity.org/.

77  Rand Paul, "Economic Freedom Zones," Rand Paul, United States Senator for Kentucky, http://www.paul.senate.gov/files/documents/ EconomicFreedomZones.pdf.

78  Melanie Hunter, "Bloomberg: Make Immigrants Live in Detroit; If They 'Survive 7 Years,' Make Them Citizens," CNS News, August 20, 2012, http:// cnsnews.com/news/article/bloomberg-make-immigrants-live-detroit-if-they- survive-7-years-make-them-citizens.

79  Steve Contorno, "Barack Obama Says United States Only Developed Country Without Paid Maternity Leave," *PolitiFact*, January 21, 2015, http:// www.politifact.com/truth-o-meter/statements/2015/jan/21/barack-obama/ barack-obama-says-united-states-only-developed-cou/.

80  W. Bradford Wilcox, "Pro-Family Policies to Strengthen Marriage and Give Kids a Better Shot at the American Dream," *Conservative Reform*, 2014, http:// conservativereform.com/wp-content/uploads/2014/05/Chapter-12-The- Agenda-Family.pdf.

81  "Expenditures on Children by Families, 2012," United States Department of Agriculture, August 2013, http://www.cnpp.usda.gov/sites/default/files/ expenditures_on_children_by_families/crc2012.pdf.

82  Mike Lee and Marco Rubio, "Pro-Growth, Pro-Family Tax Reform," *Wall Street Journal*, March 3, 2015, http://www.wsj.com/articles/mike-lee-and-marco- rubio-pro-growth-pro-family-tax-reform-1425426777.

83  John H. Cochrane, "Ending America's Slow-Growth Tailspin," *Wall Street Journal*, May 2, 2016, http://www.wsj.com/articles/ending-americas-slow- growth-tailspin-1462230818.

84  Neil Irwin, "Why American Workers Without Much Education Are Being Hammered," *New York Times*, April 21, 2015, http://mobile.nytimes.com/ 2015/04/22/upshot/why-workers-without-much-education-are-being- hammered.html.

## CHAPTER 9

1  "Washington's Hidden Tax: $1.9 Trillion," *Wall Street Journal*, May 11, 2015, http://www.wsj.com/articles/washingtons-hidden-tax-1-9-trillion-1431385233.

2  Matthew J. Belvedere, "Corporate Tax Reform Would Restore Economic Growth: FedEx CEO," CNBC, February 2, 2013, http://www.cnbc.com/ id/100424136.

3  Bob Adelmann, "New York's Fracking Ban Hurts Upstate New Yorkers," New

American, May 11, 2015, http://www.thenewamerican.com/economy/sectors/item/20853-new-yorks-fracking-ban-hurting-upstate-new-yorkers.

4   Eric Jaffe, "America's Infrastructure Crisis Is Really a Maintenance Crisis," *CityLab*, February 12, 2015, http://www.citylab.com/cityfixer/2015/02/americas-infrastructure-crisis-is-really-a-maintenance-crisis/385452/.

5   Hiroko Tabuchi, "Chinese Textile Mills Are Now Hiring in Place Where Cotton Was King," *New York Times*, August 2, 2015, http://www.nytimes.com/2015/08/03/business/chinese-textile-mills-are-now-hiring-in-places-where-cotton-was-king.html.

6   Michael E. Porter and Jan W. Rivkin, "The Looming Challenge to U.S. Competitiveness," *Harvard Business Review*, March 2012, https://hbr.org/2012/03/the-looming-challenge-to-us-competitiveness.

7   Ibid.

8   "2013 Global Manufacturing Competitiveness Index," Deloitte, 2012, https://www2.deloitte.com/content/dam/Deloitte/global/Documents/Manufacturing/gx_2013%20Global%20Manufacturing%20Competitiveness%20Index_11_15_12.pdf.

9   Ibid.

10   Ben Steverman, "How Much Americans Really Pay in Taxes," *Bloomberg*, April 10, 2015, http://www.bloomberg.com/news/articles/2015-04-10/how-much-americans-really-pay-in-taxes.

11   Clyde Wayne Crews, "Ten Thousand Commandments 2016," Competitive Enterprise Institute, May 3, 2016, https://cei.org/10KC2016.

12   "Washington's Hidden Tax: $1.9 Trillion," *Wall Street Journal*, May 11, 2015, http://www.wsj.com/articles/washingtons-hidden-tax-1-9-trillion-1431385233.

13   "Remarks of the President in State of the Union Address," White House, January 25, 2011, https://www.whitehouse.gov/the-press-office/2011/01/25/remarks-president-state-union-address.

14   Richard Williams, "How Obama Is Keeping Small Businesses Down," *U.S. News & World Report*, March 25, 2014, http://www.usnews.com/opinion/economic-intelligence/2014/03/24/obamas-slams-small-businesses-with-excessive-regulations.

15   "Washington's Hidden Tax: $1.9 Trillion," *Wall Street Journal*, May 11, 2015, http://www.wsj.com/articles/washingtons-hidden-tax-1-9-trillion-1431385233.

16   Ibid.

17   "Department of Interior and USFWS Say 'No' to Road Between King Cove and Cold Bay," *Alaska Native News*, February 5, 2013, http://alaska-native-news.com/department-of-interior-and-usfws-say-no-to-road-between-king-cove-and-cold-bay-7235.

18   "Victims of Government: The Case of Steve Lathrop," Victims of Government, March 26, 2013, http://www.ronjohnson.senate.gov/public/index.cfm/victims-of-government-blog?ID=0bd046f4-f7cd-40e5-8589-20cb129faee5.

19   Ibid.

20   Lydia Wheeler, "Study: 2015 Was Record Year for Federal Regulation," *The Hill*, December 30, 2015, http://thehill.com/regulation/administration/264456-2015-was-record-year-for-federal-regulation-group-says.

21   "Regulatory Watch," Small Business Committee, 2016, http://smallbusiness.house.gov/resources/regulatory-watch.htm.

22   Clyde Wayne Crews, "Cost of Complying with U.S. Regulations Higher Than

Canada's GDP," Competitive Enterprise Institute, May 22, 2013, https://cei.org/citations/cost-complying-us-regulations-higher-canadas-gdp.

23  Ibid.

24  "A Government-Made Regulatory Crunch," U.S. Chamber of Commerce, accessed June 27, 2015, https://www.uschamber.com/sites/default/files/legacy/regulations/files/Case3b_regulations.pdf.

25  Jens Laurson and George Pieler, "Dodd-Frank Is Much More Than Regulatory Overreach," *Forbes*, July 23, 2013, http://www.forbes.com/sites/laursonpieler/2013/07/23/dodd-frank-is-much-more-than-regulatory-overreach/.

26  Ibid.

27  Diane Katz, "Dodd-Frank at Year Three: Onerous and Costly," Heritage Foundation, July 19, 2013, http://www.heritage.org/government-regulation/report/dodd-frank-year-three-onerous-and-costly.

28  Abby McCloskey, "Dodd-Frank's Costs Will Be Paid For by Low-Income Bank Customers," *Forbes*, September 26, 2013, http://www.forbes.com/sites/realspin/2013/09/26/dodd-franks-costs-will-be-paid-for-by-low-income-bank-customers/.

29  Elaine He, Roger Kenny, James Sterngold, and Victoria McGrane, "Dodd Frank: How It Changed Banking," *Wall Street Journal*, July 19, 2015, http://graphics.wsj.com/dodd-frank-anniversary/.

30  "A Government-Made Regulatory Crunch," U.S. Chamber of Commerce, https://www.uschamber.com/sites/default/files/legacy/regulations/files/Case3b_regulations.pdf.

31  James L. Gattuso and Diane Katz, "Red Tape Rising: Five Years of Regulatory Expansion," Heritage Foundation, March 26, 2014, http://www.heritage.org/research/reports/2014/03/red-tape-rising-five-years-of-regulatory-expansion.

32  "Regulatory Studies," CATO Institute, http://www.cato.org/research/regulatory-studies.

33  "Population," *Wikipedia*, accessed April 3, 2017, https://en.wikipedia.org/wiki/North_Dakota#Population.

34  Valerie Richardson, "Jerry Brown Turns on Liberal Environmentalists, Rejects California Fracking Ban," *Washington Post*, June 2, 2015, http://www.washingtontimes.com/news/2015/jun/2/jerry-brown-rejects-california-fracking-ban-risks-/.

35  E.J. McMahon, "If Not Fracking, What?" Empire Center for Public Policy, December 17, 2014, http://www.empirecenter.org/publications/if-not-fracking-what/.

36  Bob Adelmann, "New York's Fracking Ban Hurts Upstate New Yorkers," New American, May 11, 2015, http://www.thenewamerican.com/economy/sectors/item/20853-new-yorks-fracking-ban-hurting-upstate-new-yorkers.

37  E.J. McMahon, "If Not Fracking, What?" Empire Center for Public Policy, December 17, 2014, http://www.empirecenter.org/publications/if-not-fracking-what/.

38  Zoë Schlanger, "15 New York Towns, Desperate to Frack, Ponder Secession," *Newsweek*, February 22, 2015, http://www.newsweek.com/15-new-york-towns-desperate-frack-ponder-seceding-pennsylvania-308523.

39  Diana Furchtgott-Roth, "Pipelines Are Safest for Transportation of Oil and Gas," Manhattan Institute, June 23, 2013, http://www.manhattan-institute.org/html/ib_23.htm.

40  "Final Supplemental Environmental Impact Statement for the Keystone XL Project, Executive Summary," U.S. Department of State, Bureau of Oceans and International Environmental and Scientific Affairs, January 2014, http://keystonepipeline-xl.state.gov/documents/organization/221135.pdf.

41  Joe Nocera, "How to Extract Gas Responsibly," New York Times, February 27, 2012, http://www.nytimes.com/2012/02/28/opinion/nocera-how-to-frack-responsibly.html.

42  "Shale Revolution: Opportunity to Jump-Start Economic Growth," Forbes, November 19, 2014, http://www.forbes.com/sites/realspin/2014/11/19/the-shale-revolution-is-an-opportunity-to-jump-start-economic-growth-in-u-s/.

43  Ibid.

44  Mike Orcutt, "Where Is the Global Shale Gas Revolution?" Technology Review, July 20, 2015, http://www.technologyreview.com/news/539366/where-is-the-global-shale-gas-revolution/.

45  Edward Morse, "Welcome to the Revolution," Foreign Affairs, May/June 2014, https://www.foreignaffairs.com/articles/2014-04-17/welcome-revolution.

46  David Harsanyi, "5 Ways to Get America Working Again," Human Events, July 23, 2012, http://humanevents.com/2012/07/23/david-harsanyi-5-ways-to-get-america-working-again/.

47  Bobby Magill and Climate Central, "Nuclear Power Needs to Double to Curb Global Warming," Scientific American, January 30, 2015, http://www.scientificamerican.com/article/nuclear-power-needs-to-double-to-curb-global-warming/.

48  Eric McFarland, "Rethinking the U.S. Surrender on Nuclear Power," Wall Street Journal, April 27, 2015, http://www.wsj.com/articles/rethinking-the-u-s-surrender-on-nuclear-power-1430176276.

49  Jack Spencer, "Competitive Nuclear Energy Investment: Avoiding Past Policy Mistakes," Heritage Foundation, November 15, 2007, http://www.heritage.org/environment/report/competitive-nuclear-energy-investment-avoiding-past-policy-mistakes.

50  Eric McFarland, "Rethinking the U.S. Surrender on Nuclear Power," Wall Street Journal, April 27, 2015, http://www.wsj.com/articles/rethinking-the-u-s-surrender-on-nuclear-power-1430176276.

51  "2013 Global Manufacturing Competitiveness Index," Deloitte, 2012, https://www2.deloitte.com/content/dam/Deloitte/global/Documents/Manufacturing/gx_2013%20Global%20Manufacturing%20Competitiveness%20Index_11_15_12.pdf.

52  Lynne Varner, "Better STEM Education, Training Needed for Mismatched Workers," Seattle Times, November 14, 2013, http://www.seattletimes.com/opinion/better-stem-education-training-needed-for-mismatched-workers/.

53  Ibid.

54  "STEM Crisis or STEM Surplus? Yes and Yes," Bureau of Labor Statistics, May 2015, http://www.bls.gov/opub/mlr/2015/article/stem-crisis-or-stem-surplus-yes-and-yes.htm.

55  Linda Rosen, "The Truth Hurts: The STEM Crisis Is Not a Myth," Huffington Post, November 11, 2013, http://www.huffingtonpost.com/linda-rosen/the-truth-hurts-the-stem-_b_3900575.html.

56  Miriam Jordan, "Demand for Skilled-Worker Visas Exceeds Annual Supply," Wall Street Journal, April 7, 2015, http://www.wsj.com/

articles/u-s-demand-for-skilled-worker-visas-exceeds-annual-supply-1428431798.

57  Tim Henderson, "States, Cities Call For Expanding H-1B Visa Program for Skilled Foreign Workers," *Providence Journal*, June 21, 2015, http://www.providencejournal.com/article/20150621/NEWS/150629986/.

58  Sterling Wong, "Expanding the H1B Foreign Work Visa Quota Would Help Small Businesses Most," *Minyanville*, June 12, 2013, http://www.minyanville.com/business-news/politics-and-regulation/articles/Expanding-the-H1B-Foreign-Work-Visa/6/12/2013/id/50294.

59  Ron Hira, "New Data Show How Firms Like Infosys and Tata Abuse the H-1B Program," Economic Policy Institute, February 19, 2015, http://www.epi.org/blog/new-data-infosys-tata-abuse-h-1b-program/.

60  Jacob Pramuk, "H1-B Visa Program Needs an Overhaul: Experts," MSNBC, April 9, 2015, http://www.cnbc.com/2015/04/09/h-1b-visa-program-needs-an-overhaul-experts.html.

61  Danielle Kurtzleben, "Community Colleges a Key Ingredient to STEM Success," *U.S. News & World Report*, June 29, 2012, http://www.usnews.com/news/blogs/stem-education/2012/06/29/community-colleges-a-key-ingredient-to-stem-success.

62  James Fallows, "High School in Southern Georgia: What 'Career Technical' Education Looks Like," March 27, 2014, *Atlantic*, http://www.theatlantic.com/education/archive/2014/03/high-school-in-southern-georgia-what-career-technical-education-looks-like/359725/.

63  James Fallows, "Building for the Future, in California's Famously Failed City," *Atlantic*, June 14, 2015, http://www.theatlantic.com/education/archive/2015/06/future-in-failed-city/395825/.

64  Stephen Coan, "STEM Is the Key to Stronger Education," *Huffington Post*, December 20, 2012, http://www.huffingtonpost.com/stephen-m-coan/stem-is-the-key-to-strong_b_2338156.html.

65  Ashley Halsey III, "U.S. Infrastructure Gets D+ in Annual Report," *Washington Post*, March 19, 2013, http://www.washingtonpost.com/local/trafficandcommuting/us-infrastructure-gets-d-in-annual-report/2013/03/19/c48cb010-900b-11e2-9cfd-36d6c9b5d7ad_story.html.

66  Emma G. Fitzsimmons and David W. Chen, "Aging Infrastructure Plagues Nation's Busiest Rail Corridor," *New York Times*, July 26, 2015, http://www.nytimes.com/2015/07/27/nyregion/aging-infrastructure-plagues-nations-busiest-rail-corridor.html.

67  Ibid.

68  Ibid.

69  Andrew Rice, "Falling Down," *New York Magazine*, January 27, 2013, http://nymag.com/news/features/tappan-zee-bridge-2013-2/.

70  Laura J. Nelson, "Road Conditions in L.A. Region Judged Worst in Country," *Los Angeles Times*, October 3, 2013, http://www.latimes.com/local/lanow/la-me-ln-worst-roads-20131003-story.html.

71  Scott Thomasson, "Encouraging U.S. Infrastructure Investment," Council on Foreign Relations, April 2012, http://www.cfr.org/infrastructure/encouraging-us-infrastructure-investment/p27771.

72  Angie Schmitt, "More Money Won't Fix U.S. Infrastructure If We Don't Change How It's Spent," Streetsblog USA, February 5, 2015, http://usa.streetsblog.org/

2015/02/05/more-money-wont-fix-u-s-infrastructure-if-we-dont-change-how-its-spent/.

73  Ibid.

74  Angie Schmitt, "More Money Won't Fix U.S. Infrastructure If We Don't Change How It's Spent," Streetsblog USA, February 5, 2015, http://usa.streetsblog.org/2015/02/05/more-money-wont-fix-u-s-infrastructure-if-we-dont-change-how-its-spent/.

75  Randal O'Toole, "Hype for New Infrastructure Is Overrated," Cato Institute, June 19, 2015, http://www.cato.org/publications/commentary/hype-new-infrastructure-overrated.

76  Ibid.

77  Ibid.

78  Andrew Deye, "US Infrastructure Public-Private Partnerships: Ready for Takeoff?" *Harvard Kennedy School Review*, June 16, 2015, http://harvardkennedyschoolreview.com/us-infrastructure-public-private-partnerships-ready-for-takeoff/.

79  Steven Malanda, "The New Privatization," *City Journal*, Summer 2007, http://www.city-journal.org/html/17_3_privatization.html.

80  Eric Jaffe, "America's Infrastructure Crisis Is Really a Maintenance Crisis," *CityLab*, February 12, 2015, http://www.citylab.com/cityfixer/2015/02/americas-infrastructure-crisis-is-really-a-maintenance-crisis/385452/.

81  Kyle Pomerlau and Andrew Lundeen, "2014 International Tax Competitiveness Index," Tax Foundation, September 15, 2014, http://taxfoundation.org/article/2014-international-tax-competitiveness-index.

82  Andrew Lundeen, "The U.S. Has the Highest Corporate Income Tax Rate in the OECD," Tax Foundation, January 27, 2014, http://taxfoundation.org/blog/us-has-highest-corporate-income-tax-rate-oecd.

83  Andrew Sorkin, "Tax Burden in U.S. Not as Heavy as It Looks, Report Says," *New York Times*, August 18, 2014, http://dealbook.nytimes.com/2014/08/18/tax-burden-in-u-s-not-as-heavy-as-it-looks-study-finds/.

84  John Lechleiter, "To Guarantee the U.S.'s Economic Future, We Need Tax Reform Now," *Forbes*, January 15, 2014, http://www.forbes.com/sites/johnlechleiter/2014/01/15/to-guarantee-the-u-s-s-economic-future-we-need-tax-reform-now/.

85  James Politi, "Apple Chief Tim Cook Defends Tax Practices and Denies Avoidance," *Financial Times*, http://www.ft.com/cms/s/0/c1a2383a-c228-11e2-ab66-00144feab7de.html (subscription required).

86  Michelle Hanlon, "The Lose-Lose Tax Policy Driving Away U.S. Business," *Wall Street Journal*, June 11, 2014, http://www.wsj.com/articles/the-lose-lose-tax-policy-driving-away-u-s-business-1402527307.

87  "The Sorry State of Corporate Taxes," Citizens for Tax Justice, February 2014, http://www.ctj.org/corporatetaxdodgers/sorrystateofcorptaxes.php.

88  Ibid.

89  Ibid.

## CHAPTER 10

1  Ezekiel Emanuel and Topher Spiro, "The Coming Shock in Health-Care Cost Increases," *Wall Street Journal*, July 7, 2015, http://www.wsj.com/articles/SB11301772451238044816904581084584272004382.

2  Scott W. Atlas, "Repairing the Obamacare Wreckage," *Wall Street Journal*, June 28, 2015, http://www.wsj.com/articles/repairing-the-obamacare-wreckage-1435507564.

3  Kevin D. Williamson, "Obamacare Is Dead," *National Review*, November 4, 2015, http://www.nationalreview.com/node/426550/print.

4  Sheryl Gay Stolberg and Robert Pear, "Obama Signs Health Care Overhaul Bill, with a Flourish," *New York Times*, March 23, 2010, http://www.nytimes.com/2010/03/24/health/policy/24health.html.

5  Ibid.

6  "Updated Estimates of the Effects of the Insurance Coverage Provisions of the Affordable Care Act, April 2014," Congressional Budget Office, April 2014, https://cbo.gov/sites/default/files/cbofiles/attachments/45231-ACA_Estimates.pdf.

7  Bennie G.P. Lindeque, "American Health Care System Disaster," *Healio Orthopedics*, August 1, 2009, http://www.healio.com/orthopedics/journals/ortho/2009-8-32-8/%7Ba99703e1-261d-431d-83f0-9f194bea3ae7%7D/american-health-care-system-disaster.

8  "Fiscal Year 2016 Budget of the U.S. Government," Office of Management and Budget, 2016, https://www.gpo.gov/fdsys/pkg/BUDGET-2016-BUD/pdf/BUDGET-2016-BUD.pdf.

9  Ibid.

10  Phillip Bump, "How Do Americans Feel About Single-payer Health Care? It's Complicated," *Washington Post*, March 27, 2017, https://www.washingtonpost.com/news/politics/wp/2017/03/27/how-do-americans-feel-about-single-payer-health-care-its-complicated/.

11  Thomas Kaplan and Robert Pear, "Health Bill Would Add 24 Million Uninsured but Save $337 Billion, Report Says," *New York Times*, March 13, 2017, https://www.nytimes.com/2017/03/13/us/politics/affordable-care-act-health-congressional-budget-office.html.

12  Madeline Conway, "Ryan: 'Obamacare Is the Law of the Land' for Foreseeable Future," *Politico Magazine*, March 24, 2017, http://www.politico.com/story/2017/03/obamacare-repeal-failed-paul-ryan-reaction-236478.

13  "Will Obamacare Cut Costs?" *Economist*, March 5, 2015, http://www.economist.com/news/united-states/21645855-growth-americas-health-care-spending-slowing-will-obamacare-cut-costs.

14  "Why Is Health Spending in the United States So High?" OECD, http://www.oecd.org/unitedstates/49084355.pdf.

15  Laura Lorenzetti, "Here's Why You'll Likely Pay More for Your Employer-Sponsored Health Insurance," *Fortune*, June 21, 2016, http://fortune.com/2016/06/21/health-care-rising-costs/.

16  "Medical Cost Trend: Behind the Numbers 2017," PricewaterhouseCoopers, June 2016, http://pwchealth.com/cgi-local/hregister.cgi/reg/pwc-hri-medical-cost-trend-2017.pdf.

17  Richard McGrath, "Why Do Healthcare Costs Keep Rising," McGrath Insurance Group, January 9, 2010, http://mcgrathinsurance.com/2010/01/09/why-do-healthcare-costs-keep-rising/.

18  "Deficit-Reducing Health Care Reform," White House, https://www.whitehouse.gov/economy/reform/deficit-reducing-health-care-reform (page no longer available).

19 "Guaranteed Issue," Healthcare.gov, https://www.healthcare.gov/glossary/guaranteed-issue/.

20 "Essential Health Benefits," Healthcare.gov, https://www.healthcare.gov/glossary/essential-health-benefits/.

21 "Health Insurance for Children Under 26," Healthcare.gov, https://www.healthcare.gov/young-adults/children-under-26/.

22 "Cracking Down on Frivolous Cancellations," Healthcare.gov, https://www.healthcare.gov/health-care-law-protections/cancellations/.

23 "ObamaCare Pre-Existing Conditions," ObamaCare Facts, http://obamacarefacts.com/pre-existing-conditions/.

24 "The Fee You Pay If You Don't Have Health Coverage," Healthcare.gov, https://www.healthcare.gov/fees-exemptions/fee-for-not-being-covered/.

25 "Health Insurance Marketplace Basics," Healthcare.gov, https://www.healthcare.gov/quick-guide/.

26 "Explaining Health Care Reform: Questions About Health Insurance Subsidies," Kaiser Family Foundation, http://kff.org/health-costs/issue-brief/explaining-health-care-reform-questions-about-health/.

27 "Obamacare Medicaid Expansion," Obamacare Facts, http://obamacarefacts.com/obamacares-medicaid-expansion/.

28 "Will Obamacare Cut Costs?" *Economist*, March 5, 2015, http://www.economist.com/news/united-states/21645855-growth-americas-health-care-spending-slowing-will-obamacare-cut-costs.

29 Dan Mangan, "Obamacare Enrollment at 11.1M, as Some Drop Off After Premium Bills Come Due," CNBC News, July 1, 2016, http://www.cnbc.com/2016/07/01/obamacare-enrollment-drops-after--some-miss-premium-payments.html.

30 Rich Lowry, "ObamaCare's Death Spiral, Stage One: Denial," *New York Post*, November 2, 2015, http://nypost.com/2015/11/02/obamacares-death-spiral-stage-one-denial/.

31 "The Decline of ObamaCare," *Wall Street Journal*, October 25, 2015, http://www.wsj.com/articles/the-decline-of-obamacare-1445807092.

32 Megan McArdle, "Cost of Cheapest Obamacare Plan Is Soaring," *Bloomberg View*, November 3, 2015, http://www.bloombergview.com/articles/2015-11-03/cost-of-cheapest-obamacare-plans-is-soaring.

33 Ibid.

34 Ibid.

35 Andy Puzder, "The Slow-Motion Implosion of ObamaCare," *Wall Street Journal*, November 1, 2015, http://www.wsj.com/articles/the-slow-motion-implosion-of-obamacare-1446417104.

36 Adrian Smith, "ObamaCare's Cascading Co-Op Failures," *Wall Street Journal*, November 2, 2015, http://www.wsj.com/articles/obamacares-cascading-co-op-failures-1446509803.

37 Ibid.

38 Stephen T. Parente, "ObamaCare's Prices Will Keep Surging," *Wall Street Journal*, July 16, 2015, http://www.wsj.com/articles/obamacares-prices-will-keep-surging-1437087242.

39 Richard Eisenberg, "For Many, Obamacare Is Becoming the Unaffordable Care Act," *Forbes*, July 5, 2015, http://www.forbes.com/sites/nextavenue/2015/07/05/for-many-obamacare-is-becoming-the-unaffordable-care-act/.

40  Ibid.

41  Ibid.

42  "ObamaCare Isn't Working: More Privately Insured Americans Are Putting Off Medical Care," FreedomWorks, accessed February 18, 2015, http://www.freedomworks.org/content/obamacare-isnt-working-more-privately-insured-americans-are-putting-medical-care.

43  "Obamacare Subscribers: Beware of High Deductibles," Center for Public Integrity, March 17, 2014, http://www.publicintegrity.org/2014/03/17/14425/obamacare-subscribers-beware-high-deductibles.

44  "Dilemma over Deductibles: Costs Crippling Middle Class," *USA Today*, accessed February 18, 2015, http://www.usatoday.com/story/news/nation/2015/01/01/middle-class-workers-struggle-to-pay-for-care-despite-insurance/19841235/.

45  John Ydstie, "Obamacare 'Glitch' Puts Subsidies Out of Reach for Many Families," NPR, accessed February 18, 2015, http://www.npr.org/blogs/health/2014/12/02/367837115/obamacare-glitch-puts-subsidies-out-of-reach-for-many-families.

46  James C. Capretta and Robert E. Moffit, "How to Replace Obamacare," *National Affairs*, Spring 2012, http://www.nationalaffairs.com/doclib/20120321_CaprettaMoffit_Indiv.pdf.

47  Scott W. Atlas, "Repairing the ObamaCare Wreckage," *Wall Street Journal*, June 28, 2015, http://www.wsj.com/articles/repairing-the-obamacare-wreckage-1435507564.

48  Ibid.

49  Ibid.

50  Ibid.

51  John Graham, "Reforming Obamacare: How Congress, and the President, Can Win After King v. Burwell," National Center for Policy Analysis, http://www.ncpa.org/pub/reforming-obamacare-how-congress-and-the-president-can-win-after-king-v-burwell.

52  David Frum, "Republicans Should Reform Obamacare, Not Repeal It," *Atlantic*, June 29, 2015, http://www.theatlantic.com/politics/archive/2015/06/republicans-obamacare-mandate-part-time-work/397199/.

53  Michael Shedlock, "Greenspan: Worried About Inflation, Says 'Entitlements Crowding Out Investment, Productivity Is Dead,'" *MishTalk.com*, March 21, 2016, https://mishtalk.com/2016/03/21/greenspan-worried-about-inflation-says-entitlements-crowding-out-investment-productivity-is-dead/.

54  Nick Timiraos, "Social Security, Medicare Face Insolvency over 20 Years, Trustees Report," *Wall Street Journal*, June 22, 2016, http://www.wsj.com/articles/social-security-medicare-trust-funds-face-insolvency-over-20-years-trustees-report-1466605893.

55  Ibid.

56  Ibid.

57  "Social Security and Medicare," Hillary Clinton, https://www.hillaryclinton.com/issues/social-security-and-medicare/.

58  Aaron Blake, "Donald Trump's Promises Are Taking a Beating in the GOP's Obamacare Replacement," *Washington Post*, March 10, 2017, https://www.washingtonpost.com/news/the-fix/wp/2017/03/10/the-gops-obamacare-replacement-is-looking-like-a-bunch-of-broken-trump-promises/; "Why

Donald Trump Won't Touch Your Entitlements," Donald J. Trump, May 21, 2015, https://www.youtube.com/watch?v=sbiX1asmio4.

59 Susan Jaffe, "Fewer Medicare-Subsidized Drug Plans Means Less Choice for Low-Income Seniors," *Kaiser Health News*, November 23, 2015, http://khn.org/news/fewer-medicare-subsidized-drug-plans-means-less-choice-for-low-income-seniors/.

60 David N. Bass, "The Millennial Perspective," *American Spectator*, April 26, 2012, http://spectator.org/35653_millennial-perspective/.

61 Zachary A. Goldfarb, "Obama Meets with Simpson, Bowles on Deficit Plan," *Washington Post*, April 14, 2011, https://www.washingtonpost.com/blogs/political-economy/post/obama-meets-with-simpson-bowles-on-deficit-plan/2011/04/14/AF9gIGdD_blog.html.

62 Doug Schoen, "The Compromise That Americans Want to Break the Budget Deadlock," *Forbes*, April 2, 2013, http://www.forbes.com/sites/dougschoen/2013/04/02/the-compromising-way-forward.

63 Ezra Klein, "11 Shocking, True Facts About Simpson-Bowles," *Washington Post*, December 4, 2012, https://www.washingtonpost.com/news/wonk/wp/2012/12/04/11-shocking-true-facts-about-simpson-bowles/.

64 Ezra Klein, "Why Republicans Like Simpson-Bowles," *Washington Post*, November 22, 2011, https://www.washingtonpost.com/blogs/ezra-klein/post/why-republicans-like-simpson-bowles/2011/08/25/gIQAx3IClN_blog.html.

65 Doug Schoen, "The Compromise That Americans Want to Break the Budget Deadlock," *Forbes*, April 2, 2013, http://www.forbes.com/sites/dougschoen/2013/04/02/the-compromising-way-forward.

66 Ibid.

67 Kevin D. Williamson, "Obamacare Is Dead," *National Review*, November 4, 2015, http://www.nationalreview.com/node/426550/print.

68 "What It Covers: Social Security," Saving the American Dream, http://savingthedream.org/what-it-covers/social-security/.

CHAPTER 11

1 Ryan Lizza, "Leading from Behind," *New Yorker*, April 26, 2011, http://www.newyorker.com/news/news-desk/leading-from-behind.

2 Richard N. Haass, "The Isolationist Temptation," *Wall Street Journal*, August 5, 2016, http://www.wsj.com/articles/the-isolationist-temptation-1470411481.

3 Charles Krauthammer, "Hangzhou Incident Just Latest of U.S. Slights," *Lowell Sun*, September 10, 2016, http://www.lowellsun.com/opinion/ci_30348590/charles-krauthammer-hangzhou-incident-just-latest-u-s.

4 "2015 Index of U.S. Military Strength," Heritage Foundation, 2015, ims-2015.s3.amazonaws.com/2015_Index_of_US_Military_Strength_FINAL.pdf.

5 Gordon G. Chang, "RIMPAC 2014: It's Smart to Invite China to Participate in World's Largest Maritime Exercises," Fox News, June 26, 2014, http://www.foxnews.com/opinion/2014/06/26/rimpac-2014-it-smart-to-invite-china-to-participate-in-world-largest-maritime.html.

6 Eva Dou and James Hookway, "China Lashes Out over U.S. Plan on South China Sea," *Wall Street Journal*, May 13, 2015, www.wsj.com/articles/china-lashes-out-over-u-s-plan-on-south-china-sea-1431508182.

7 "China Set to Overtake U.S. as Biggest Economy in PPP Measure," *Bloomberg*, April 30, 2014, http://www.bloomberg.com/news/articles/2014-04-30/china-set-to-overtake-u-s-as-biggest-economy-using-ppp-measure.

8   Ian Talley, "U.S. Looks to Work with China-Led Infrastructure Fund," *Wall Street Journal*, March 22, 2015, http://www.wsj.com/articles/u-s-to-seek-collaboration-with-china-led-asian-infrastructure-investment-bank-1427057486.

9   John Train, "Lt. Gen: 'Putin Has Knocked the Pieces Off the Board,'" *American Spectator*, June 27, 2014, http://spectator.org/articles/59756/lt-gen-putin-has-knocked-pieces-board.

10  Ibid.

11  Ryan W. Miller, "Kerry to Meet with Counterparts over North Korea's Nuke Test," *USA Today*, September 16, 2016, http://www.usatoday.com/story/news/world/2016/09/16/north-korea-nuclear-weapons-japan-us-south-korea-un-meeting/90504172/.

12  Kirk Spitzer, "North Korea Conducts Apparent Nuclear Weapons Test," *USA Today*, September 9, 2016, http://www.usatoday.com/story/news/2016/09/08/north-korea-conducts-apparent-nuclear-weapons-test/90101066/.

13  J.J. Green, "North Korean Nuclear Weapons Threaten U.S. West Coast," WTOP, June 1, 2015, http://wtop.com/national-security/2015/06/north-korean-nuclear-weapons-threaten-u-s-west-coast/.

14  Elisabeth Bumiller and Thom Shanker, "Panetta Warns of Dire Threat of Cyberattack on U.S.," *New York Times*, October 11, 2012, http://www.nytimes.com/2012/10/12/world/panetta-warns-of-dire-threat-of-cyberattack.html.

15  Richard A. Bitzinger, "China's Double-Digit Defense Growth," *Foreign Affairs*, March 19, 2015, https://www.foreignaffairs.com/articles/china/2015-03-19/chinas-double-digit-defense-growth.

16  "Russian Defense Budget to Hit Record $81 Billion in 2015," *Moscow Times*, October 16, 2014, http://www.themoscowtimes.com/business/article/russian-defense-budget-to-hit-record-81bln-in-2015/509536.html.

17  Ibid.

18  2015 Index of U.S. Military Strength, Heritage Foundation, http://index.heritage.org/military/2015/about/executive-summary/.

19  Jim Tice, "Army Shrinks to Smallest Level Since Before World War II," *ArmyTimes.com*, May 7, 2016, https://www.armytimes.com/story/military/careers/army/2016/05/07/army-shrinks-smallest-level-since-before-world-war-ii/83875962/.

20  "US Army Is Getting Dangerously Small: US Military Commander," *PressTV.com*, March 9, 2016, http://www.presstv.com/Detail/2016/03/09/454635/US-army-getting-dangerously-small-Lloyd-Austin-Joseph-Votel.

21  Ibid.

22  William J. Perry and John P. Abizaid, "Ensuring a Strong U.S. Defense for the Future," United States Institute of Peace, July 31, 2014, http://www.usip.org/sites/default/files/Ensuring-a-Strong-U.S.-Defense-for-the-Future-NDP-Review-of-the-QDR_0.pdf.

23  John Lehman, "Disarming the Navy Through Bureaucratic Bloat," *Wall Street Journal*, December 30, 2015, http://www.wsj.com/articles/disarming-the-navy-through-bureaucratic-bloat-1451516977.

24  Bill Gertz, "Chiefs: Budget Cuts Weaken Force, Increase Risk of Losing Wars," *Washington Free Beacon*, March 18, 2015, http://freebeacon.com/national-security/chiefs-budget-cuts-weaken-force-increase-risk-of-losing-wars/.

25  Sarah Tully, "Obama Hasn't Fulfilled His Promises on Nuclear Weapons

Reduction," *Business Insider*, October 29, 2014, http://www.businessinsider.com/obama-hasnt-fulifilled-his-promises-on-nuclear-reduction-2014-10.

26  John Vinocur, "Putin's Nuclear Plan Is Working," *Wall Street Journal*, June 15, 2015, http://www.wsj.com/articles/putins-nuclear-plan-is-working-1434392929.

27  "Pushback in Shangri-La," *Wall Street Journal*, June 2, 2015, http://www.wsj.com/articles/pushback-in-shangri-la-1433288603.

28  Katie Hunt, "Island Building in South China Sea 'Justified,' Says Chinese Admiral," CNN News, June 1, 2015, http://www.cnn.com/2015/06/01/asia/china-defends-island-building/.

29  "A 'Great Wall of Sand' in the South China Sea," *Washington Post*, April 8, 2015, http://www.washingtonpost.com/opinions/a-great-wall-of-sand/2015/04/08/d23adb3e-dd6a-11e4-be40-566e2653afe5_story.html.

30  Steve Tsang, "China Cares Little for Other Countries' Territorial Claims," *Guardian*, May 30, 2015, http://www.theguardian.com/world/commentisfree/2015/may/30/beijing-policy-south-china-sea.

31  Trefor Moss, "China's Neighbors Bulk Up Militaries," *Wall Street Journal*, February 26, 2015, http://www.wsj.com/articles/chinas-neighbors-build-up-militaries-1424996255.

32  "Pushback in Shangri-La," *Wall Street Journal*, June 2, 2015, http://www.wsj.com/articles/pushback-in-shangri-la-1433288603.

33  Michelle Florcruz, "China's Military Can Beat the US in South China Sea and Diaoyu/Senkaku Island Conflicts: Poll," *International Business Times*, March 13, 2015, http://www.ibtimes.com/chinas-military-can-beat-us-south-china-sea-diaoyusenkaku-island-conflicts-poll-1846248.

34  "'Disciplined Army, Able to Win': China President Xi Jinping States Strategic Military Goal," *RT.com*, July 1, 2016, https://www.rt.com/news/349096-china-army-mordernization-xi/.

35  Simon Denyer, "Chinese Military Sets Course to Expand Global Reach as 'National Interests' Grow," *Washington Post*, May 26, 2015, http://www.washingtonpost.com/world/asia_pacific/chinese-military-sets-course-to-expand-global-reach-as-national-interests-grow/2015/05/26/395fff14-3fb1-4056-aed0-264ffcbbcdb4_story.html.

36  Hugh White, "It's Time We Talked About War with China," *Real Clear World*, March 4, 2016, http://www.realclearworld.com/articles/2016/03/04/its_time_we_talked_about_war_with_china_111741.html.

37  Howard LaFranchi, "Is Ukraine Crisis Proof That Obama's 'Lead from Behind' Policy Failed?" *Christian Science Monitor*, March 3, 2014, http://www.csmonitor.com/World/Security-Watch/2014/0303/Is-Ukraine-crisis-proof-that-Obama-s-lead-from-behind-policy-failed-video.

38  "Transcript: President Obama's Aug. 28 remarks on Ukraine, Syria and the Economy," *Washington Post*, August 28, 2014, http://www.washingtonpost.com/politics/transcriptpresident-obamas-aug-28-remarks-on-ukraine-and-syria/2014/08/28/416f1336-2eec-11e4-bb9b-997ae96fad33_story.html.

39  "Obama Presses Putin to Strike Ukraine Peace Deal," Newsmax, February 10, 2015, http://www.newsmax.com/Newsfront/Ukraine-Russia-crisis-barack-Obama/2015/02/10/id/623954/.

40  Geoff Dyer, "US Foreign Policy: Trouble Abroad," *Financial Times*, May 26, 2014, https://www.ft.com/content/a7b857c8-e299-11e3-ba64-00144feabdc0.

41  Stephen Blank, "An Agenda of Failure," *U.S. News & World Report*, May

13, 2014, http://www.usnews.com/opinion/blogs/world-report/2014/05/13/
obama-is-to-blame-for-his-failures-in-russia-ukraine-and-elsewhere.

42  Rowan Scarborough, "Putin Is Not Pulling Russian Forces out of Syria,
Despite His Pledge: U.S. Military," *Washington Times*, April 1, 2016, http://
www.washingtontimes.com/news/2016/apr/1/putin-not-pulling-russian-
forces-out-syria-despite/.

43  Theodore Schleifer, "Obama Downplays Russia Weapons System Sale to
Iran," CNN News, April 17, 2015, http://www.cnn.com/2015/04/17/politics/
iran-obama-russia-weapons-sale/.

44  Alec Luhn, "Russia to Reopen Spy Base in Cuba as Relations with US Continue
to Sour," *Guardian*, July 16, 2014, http://www.theguardian.com/world/2014/
jul/16/russia-reopening-spy-base-cuba-us-relations-sour.

45  Cristina Silva, "Russia Oil Crisis: Putin, Maduro Discuss Russian, Venezuela
Production, Economies," *International Business Times*, January 15, 2015, http://
www.ibtimes.com/russia-oil-crisis-putin-maduro-discuss-russian-venezuela-
production-economies-1784504.

46  Ewen MacAskill, "West and Russia on Course for War, Says Ex-Nato Deputy
Commander," *Guardian*, May 18, 2016, https://www.theguardian.com/
world/2016/may/18/west-russia-on-course-for-war-nato-ex-deputy-
commander.

47  Ibid.

48  Franklin Foer, "Putin's Puppet," *Slate Magazine*, July 21, 2016, http://www.slate.
com/articles/news_and_politics/cover_story/2016/07/vladimir_putin_has_a_
plan_for_destroying_the_west_and_it_looks_a_lot_like.html.

49  "Ukrainian Presidential Spokesperson: 100,000 Russian Troops Are Stationed
Near Ukraine's Borders," *Ukraine Today*, August 31, 2016, http://uawire.
org/news/ukrainian-presidential-spokesman-100-000-russian-troops-are-
stationed-near-ukraine-s-borders.

50  Stephen Collinson, "From Russia Without Love? DNC Hack Roils Philly
Convention," CNN News, July 26, 2016, http://www.cnn.com/2016/07/25/
politics/democratic-convention-russia-hack/.

51  Evan Perez and Shimon Prokupecz, "Sources: State Dept. Hack the 'Worst
Ever,'" CNN News, March 10, 2015, http://www.cnn.com/2015/03/10/politics/
state-department-hack-worst-ever/index.html.

52  Franz-Stefan Gady, "Russia Tops China as Principal Cyber Threat to US,"
*Diplomat*, March 3, 2015, http://thediplomat.com/2015/03/russia-tops-china-
as-principal-cyber-threat-to-us/.

53  John Markoff, "Before the Gunfire, Cyberattacks," *New York Times*, August 12,
2008, http://www.nytimes.com/2008/08/13/technology/13cyber.html.

54  Franz-Stefan Gady, "Russia Tops China as Principal Cyber Threat to US,"
*Diplomat*, March 3, 2015, http://thediplomat.com/2015/03/russia-tops-china-as-
principal-cyber-threat-to-us/.

55  James R. Clapper, "Worldwide Threat Assessment of the US Intelligence
Community," *Senate Armed Services Committee*, February 26, 2015, http://cdn.
arstechnica.net/wp-content/uploads/2015/02/Clapper_02-26-15.pdf.

56  Cory Bennett, "Russia's Cyberattacks Grow More
Brazen," *The Hill*, April 12, 2015, http://thehill.com/policy/
cybersecurity/238518-russias-cyberattacks-grow-more-brazen.

57  Ibid.

58  Ben Plesser, "Skilled, Cheap Russian Hackers Power American Cybercrime," NBC News, February 5, 2014, http://www.nbcnews.com/news/world/skilled-cheap-russian-hackers-power-american-cybercrime-n22371.

59  Riley Waters, "Cyber Attacks on U.S. Companies in 2014," Heritage Foundation, October 27, 2014, http://www.heritage.org/research/reports/2014/10/cyber-attacks-on-us-companies-in-2014.

60  Ibid.

61  Bill Gertz, "Congress: U.S. Military Highly Vulnerable to Cyber Attacks," *Washington Free Beacon*, June 1, 2015, http://freebeacon.com/national-security/congress-u-s-military-highly-vulnerable-to-cyber-attacks/.

62  William Wan, "Chinese President Xi Jinping Takes Charge of New Cyber Effort," *Washington Post*, February 27, 2014, http://www.washingtonpost.com/world/chinese-president-takes-charge-of-new-cyber-effort/2014/02/27/a4bffaac-9fc9-11e3-b8d8-94577ff66b28_story.html.

63  Amelia Smith, "China Could Shut Down U.S. Power Grid with Cyber Attack, Says NSA Chief," *Newsweek*, November 21, 2014, http://europe.newsweek.com/china-could-shut-down-us-power-grid-cyber-attack-says-nsa-chief-286119.

64  Bill Gertz, "China Sharply Boosts Cyber Warfare Funding," *Washington Free Beacon*, April 1, 2015, http://freebeacon.com/national-security/china-sharply-boosts-cyber-warfare-funding/.

65  "President Obama Upbraids China over Cyber Attacks," BBC News, March 13, 2013, http://www.bbc.com/news/world-us-canada-21772596.

66  "U.S. Targets Overseas Cyber Attackers with Sanctions Program," Reuters, accessed May 13, 2015, http://www.nytimes.com/reuters/2015/04/02/business/02reuters-usa-cybersecurity.html (no longer available).

67  David E. Sanger, "U.S. Tries Candor to Assure China on Cyberattacks," *New York Times*, April 6, 2014, http://www.nytimes.com/2014/04/07/world/us-tries-candor-to-assure-china-on-cyberattacks.html.

68  Ibid.

69  Michael Riley and Adam Satariano, "Malware Attack on Apple Said to Come from Eastern Europe," *Bloomberg Technology*, February 19, 2013, http://www.bloomberg.com/news/articles/2013-02-19/apple-says-a-small-number-of-mac-computers-infected-by-malware.

70  Devlin Barrett, "Report: Eastern European Hackers More Sophisticated Than Asian Counterparts," *Wall Street Journal*, September 18, 2012, http://blogs.wsj.com/digits/2012/09/18/report-eastern-european-hackers-more-sophisticated-than-asian-counterparts/.

71  Evan Perez and Shimon Prokupecz, "U.S. Charges Iranians for Cyberattacks on Banks, Dam," CNN News, March 24, 2016, http://www.cnn.com/2016/03/23/politics/iran-hackers-cyber-new-york-dam/.

72  Nicole Perlroth, "Report Says Cyberattacks Originated from Iran," *New York Times*, December 2, 2014, http://www.nytimes.com/2014/12/03/world/middleeast/report-says-cyberattacks-originated-inside-iran.html.

73  Shane Harris, "Report: Iranian Hackers Eye U.S. Grid," *Daily Beast*, April 16, 2015, http://www.thedailybeast.com/articles/2015/04/16/report-iranian-hackers-eye-u-s-grid.html.

74  Kevin Liptak, "Obama: No 'Complete Strategy' Yet on Training Iraqis," CNN News, June 9, 2015, http://www.cnn.com/2015/06/08/politics/obama-abadi-iraq-germany-g7/.

75  Ibid.

76  Kyle Wingfield, "Panetta Puts the Onus for Iraq Withdrawal, ISIS's Rise Squarely on Obama," *MyAJC.com*, October 2, 2014, http://kylewingfield.blog. ajc.com/2014/10/02/panetta-puts-the-onus-for-iraq-withdrawal-ISISs-rise-squarely-on-obama/.

77  Tim Arango and Eric Schmitt, "U.S. Actions in Iraq Fueled Rise of a Rebel," *New York Times*, August 10, 2014, http://www.nytimes.com/2014/08/11/world/middleeast/us-actions-in-iraq-fueled-rise-of-a-rebel.html.

78  Liz Sly, "Petraeus: The Islamic State Isn't Our Biggest Problem in Iraq," *Washington Post*, March 20, 2015, http://www.washingtonpost.com/blogs/worldviews/wp/2015/03/20/petraeus-the-islamic-state-isnt-our-biggest-problem-in-iraq/.

79  Ibid.

80  Kristina Wong, "Obama to Send More Troops to Iraq," *The Hill*, April 18, 2016, http://thehill.com/policy/defense/276652-obama-to-send-more-troops-bring-them-closer-to-front-lines-in-iraq.

81  Paul D. Shinkman, "McCain: Obama's ISIS Strategy Based on 'Incrementalism,'" *U.S. News*, April 18, 2016, http://www.usnews.com/news/articles/2016-04-18/mccain-blasts-obamas-anti-isis-troop-increase-as-grudging-incrementalism.

82  Pamela Engel, "ISIS Is Losing More Territory in the Middle East," *Business Insider*, May 16, 2016, http://www.businessinsider.com/isis-losing-territory-2016-5.

83  Eric Schmitt and Anne Barnard, "Senior ISIS Strategist and Spokesman Is Reported Killed in Syria," *New York Times*, August 30, 2016, http://www.nytimes.com/2016/08/31/world/middleeast/al-adnani-islamic-state-isis-syria.html.

84  Carol Morello and Karen DeYoung, "Saudi Arabia's King Salman Skipping Camp David Summit," *Washington Post*, May 10, 2015, http://www.washingtonpost.com/world/national-security/saudi-arabias-king-salman-skipping-camp-david-summit/2015/05/10/2b6cad27-55df-47e1-a6c6-11a04020c788_story.html.

85  Geoff Earle, "Obama Says Iran Sponsors Terrorism," *New York Post*, May 13, 2015, http://nypost.com/2015/05/13/obama-says-iran-sponsors-terrorism/.

86  Reuters, "Vietnam in Talks to Buy Fighter Jets to Counter China," *New York Post*, June 5, 2015, http://nypost.com/2015/06/05/vietnam-in-talks-to-buy-fighter-jets-to-counter-china/.

87  Jacqueline Klimas, "U.S., India Join Forces to Counter Beijing Aggression in South China Sea," *Washington Times*, June 4, 2015, http://www.washingtontimes.com/news/2015/jun/4/us-india-join-forces-to-counter-beijing-aggression/.

88  Noah Barkin and Jeff Mason, "Obama Says Putin on Doomed Drive to Recreate Soviet Glories," Reuters, June 8, 2015, http://www.reuters.com/article/2015/06/08/us-g7-summit-ukraine-obama-idUSKBN0OO1P920150608.

89  Rob Portman, "The U.S. Needs to Rethink Its Failing Ukraine Strategy," *Wall Street Journal*, June 3, 2015, http://www.wsj.com/articles/the-u-s-needs-to-rethink-its-failing-ukraine-strategy-1433274250.

90  John E. Herbst, "Imposing Costs on Putin Will Deter War," *Atlantic Council*, May 13, 2015, http://www.atlanticcouncil.org/blogs/ukrainealert/imposing-costs-on-putin-will-deter-war.

91  Noah Barkin and Jeff Mason, "Obama Says Putin on Doomed Drive to Recreate Soviet Glories," *Reuters*, June 8, 2015, http://www.reuters.com/article/2015/06/08/us-g7-summit-ukraine-obama-idUSKBN0OO1P920150608.

92  Evan Moore, "Commit to Victory," *U.S. News*, June 8, 2015, http://www.usnews.com/opinion/blogs/world-report/2015/06/08/obama-needs-a-real-plan-for-defeating-the-islamic-state-group.

93  Richard N. Haass, "The Isolationist Temptation," *Wall Street Journal*, August 5, 2016, http://www.wsj.com/articles/the-isolationist-temptation-1470411481.

## CHAPTER 12

1   Dennis Prager, "The Scariest Reason Trump Won," *National Review*, May 10, 2016, http://www.nationalreview.com/article/435195/donald-trump-won-because-many-republicans-arent-conservative.

2   Joshua Keating, "Why Does Ruth Bader Ginsburg Like the South African Constitution So Much?" *Foreign Policy*, February 6, 2012, http://foreignpolicy.com/2012/02/06/why-does-ruth-bader-ginsburg-like-the-south-african-constitution-so-much/.

3   "Study: Americans Don't Know Much About History," NBC News, July 17, 2009, http://www.nbclosangeles.com/news/local/Study-Americans-Dont-Know-About-Much-About-History.html.

4   Ibid.

5   Dennis Prager, "The Scariest Reason Trump Won," National Review, May 10, 2016, http://www.nationalreview.com/article/435195/donald-trump-won-because-many-republicans-arent-conservative.

6   Daniel Nussbaum, "UC Irvine Student Gov. Bans American Flag from 'Inclusive' Space," *Breitbart*, March 6, 2015, http://www.breitbart.com/california/2015/03/06/uc-irvine-student-gov-bans-american-flag-from-inclusive-space/.

7   Dennis Prager, "Why US Students Voted to Remove American Flag," *Real Clear Politics*, March 17, 2015, http://www.realclearpolitics.com/articles/2015/03/17/why_uc_students_voted_to_remove_american_flag_125948.html.

8   "The Case Against Woodrow Wilson at Princeton," *New York Times*, November 24, 2015, http://www.nytimes.com/2015/11/25/opinion/the-case-against-woodrow-wilson-at-princeton.html.

9   Nick Anderson, "Princeton Will Keep Woodrow Wilson's Name on Buildings, but Also Expand Diversity Efforts," *Washington Post*, April 4, 2016, https://www.washingtonpost.com/news/grade-point/wp/2016/04/04/princeton-will-keep-woodrow-wilsons-name-on-buildings-but-it-will-take-steps-to-expand-diversity-and-inclusion/.

10  Meg P. Bernhard, "House Masters 'Unanimously' Agree to Change Title," *Harvard Crimson*, December 2, 2015, http://www.thecrimson.com/article/2015/12/2/house-masters-change-title/.

11  Kenneth R. Rosen, "University of Texas at Austin Moves Confederate Statue," *New York Times*, August 30, 2015, http://www.nytimes.com/2015/08/31/us/texas-university-moves-confederate-statue.html.

12  Jess Bidgood, "Amherst College Drops 'Lord Jeff' as Mascot," *New York Times*, January 26, 2016, http://www.nytimes.com/2016/01/27/us/amherst-college-drops-lord-jeff-as-mascot.html.

13  Peter Holley, "More Cities Celebrating 'Indigenous Peoples Day' Amid

Effort to Abolish Columbus Day," *Washington Post*, October 12, 2015, https://www.washingtonpost.com/news/morning-mix/wp/2015/10/11/more-cities-celebrating-indigenous-peoples-day-as-effort-to-abolish-columbus-day-grows/.

14  Andrew M. Duehren and Daphne C. Thompson, "In Debate over Names, History and Race Relations Collide," *Harvard Crimson*, January 19, 2016, http://www.thecrimson.com/article/2016/1/19/faust-name-title-changes-/.

15  Eric Bledsoe, "Confronting the Hard Truths of America's Civic Illiteracy," *Washington Examiner*, February 1, 2016, http://www.washingtonexaminer.com/confronting-the-hard-truths-of-americas-civic-illiteracy/article/2581929.

16  "New Report Exposes the Crisis in Civic Education Among College Students," American Council of Trustees and Alumni, January 13, 2016, http://www.goacta.org/news/New_Report_Exposes_the_Crisis_in_Civic_Education_among_College_Students.

17  "Civics 2010," *The Nation's Report Card*, 2010, http://www.nationsreportcard.gov/#civics/.

18  Ellen Condliffe Lagemann and Harry Lewis, "Renewing Civic Education," *Harvard Magazine*, March–April 2012, http://harvardmagazine.com/2012/03/renewing-civic-education.

19  William Kristol, "Ayaan Hirsi Ali Speaks," *Weekly Standard*, April 9, 2014, http://www.weeklystandard.com/ayaan-hirsi-ali-speaks/article/786719.

20  Jason L. Riley, "I Was Disinvited on Campus," *Wall Street Journal*, May 3, 2016, http://www.wsj.com/articles/i-was-disinvited-on-campus-1462313788.

21  Derek Draplin, "Conservative Columnist George Will Disinvited to Speak at Women's College," *College Fix*, October 7, 2014, http://www.thecollegefix.com/post/19630/.

22  Jason L. Riley, "I Was Disinvited on Campus," *Wall Street Journal*, May 3, 2016, http://www.wsj.com/articles/i-was-disinvited-on-campus-1462313788.

23  "Watch: Bloomberg Booed for Criticizing Campus 'Safe Spaces,'" Fox News, May 2, 2016, http://insider.foxnews.com/2016/05/02/michael-bloomberg-booed-criticizing-campus-safe-spaces-university-michigan.

24  Heather Mac Donald, "Racial Hysteria Triumphs on Campus," *City Journal*, November 9, 2015, http://www.city-journal.org/html/racial-hysteria-triumphs-campus-11698.html.

25  Austin Huguelet and Daniel Victor, "'I Need Some Muscle': Missouri Activists Block Journalists," *New York Times*, November 9, 2015, http://www.nytimes.com/2015/11/10/us/university-missouri-protesters-block-journalists-press-freedom.html.

26  Ibid.

27  Trent Baker, "Dershowitz Rips Safe Spaces, Microaggression, Political Correctness on College Campuses," *Breitbart*, January 3, 2016, http://www.breitbart.com/video/2016/01/03/dershowitz-rips-safe-spaces-microaggression-political-correctness-on-college-campuses/.

28  Jonathan Chait, "Can We Start Taking Political Correctness Seriously Now?" *New York Magazine*, November 10, 2015, http://nymag.com/daily/intelligencer/2015/11/can-we-take-political-correctness-seriously-now.html.

29  Taylor Maycan, "Study: Nearly Half of Millennials Not on Board with Free Speech," *USA Today*, November 25, 2015, http://college.usatoday.com/2015/11/25/millennials-free-speech-pew-survey/.

30  Ibid.

31  Gabriel Sherman, "The Strongest Candidate Is the Strongest Candidate," *New York Magazine*, January 27, 2016, http://nymag.com/daily/intelligencer/2016/01/iowa-new-hampshire-gop-voters-poll.html.

32  Katie Pavlich, "Neighbor Didn't Report Suspicious Activity of San Bernardino Killers for Fear of Being Called Racist," *Townhall.com*, December 3, 2015, http://townhall.com/tipsheet/katiepavlich/2015/12/03/neighbor-didnt-report-suspicious-activity-of-san-bernardino-killers-for-fear-of-being-called-racist-n2088543.

33  Roberto Foa and Yascha Mounk, "Are Americans Losing Faith in Democracy?" Vox, December 18, 2015, http://www.vox.com/polyarchy/2015/12/18/9360663/is-democracy-in-trouble.

34  "Little Change in Public's Response to 'Capitalism,' 'Socialism,'" Pew Research Center, December 28, 2011, http://www.people-press.org/2011/12/28/little-change-in-publics-response-to-capitalism-socialism/.

35  "Millennials: A Portrait of Generation Next," Pew Research Center, February 2010, http://www.pewsocialtrends.org/files/2010/10/millennials-confident-connected-open-to-change.pdf.

36  "Sharp Drop in American Enthusiasm for Free Market, Poll Shows," World Public Opinion.org, April 6, 2011, http://www.commondreams.org/news/2011/04/06/sharp-drop-american-enthusiasm-free-market-poll-shows.

37  Peter Beinart, "The End of American Exceptionalism," *Atlantic*, February 3, 2014, http://www.theatlantic.com/politics/archive/2014/02/the-end-of-american-exceptionalism/283540.

38  Joshua Keating, "Why Does Ruth Bader Ginsburg Like the South African Constitution So Much?" *Foreign Policy*, February 6, 2012, http://foreignpolicy.com/2012/02/06/why-does-ruth-bader-ginsburg-like-the-south-african-constitution-so-much/.

39  Michael Barone, "American Exceptionalism: How Has It Fared in the Obama Years?" *Townhall.com*, January 15, 2016, http://townhall.com/columnists/michaelbarone/2016/01/15/american-exceptionalism-how-has-it-fared-in-the-obama-years-n2104685.

40  Greg Jaffe, "Obama's New Patriotism," *Washington Post*, June 3, 2015, http://www.washingtonpost.com/sf/national/2015/06/03/obama-and-american-exceptionalism/.

41  Barack Obama, "Remarks by the President at the United States Military Academy Commencement Ceremony," White House, May 28, 2014, https://www.whitehouse.gov/the-press-office/2014/05/28/remarks-president-united-states-military-academy-commencement-ceremony.

42  Greg Jaffe, "Obama's New Patriotism," *Washington Post*, June 3, 2015, http://www.washingtonpost.com/sf/national/2015/06/03/obama-and-american-exceptionalism/.

43  Peter Beinart, "The End of American Exceptionalism," *National Journal*, February 3, 2014, https://www.nationaljournal.com/s/627873/end-american-exceptionalism.

44  Greg Jaffe, "Obama's New Patriotism," *Washington Post*, June 3, 2015, http://www.washingtonpost.com/sf/national/2015/06/03/obama-and-american-exceptionalism/.

45  Ibid.

46  Robert Kagan, "Is Democracy in Decline? The Weight of Geopolitics," Brookings, January 26, 2015, http://www.brookings.edu/research/articles/2015/01/democracy-in-decline-weight-of-geopolitics-kagan.

47  Henry Kissinger, "The Long Shadow of Vietnam," *Newsweek*, April 30, 2000, http://www.newsweek.com/long-shadow-vietnam-157483.

48  Peter Beinart, "The End of American Exceptionalism," *National Journal*, February 3, 2014, https://www.nationaljournal.com/s/627873/end-american-exceptionalism.

49  Dennis Prager, "The Scariest Reason Trump Won," *National Review*, May 10, 2016, http://www.nationalreview.com/article/435195/donald-trump-won-because-many-republicans-arent-conservative.

# INDEX